Antique Trader™
METALWARES
P R I C E   G U I D E

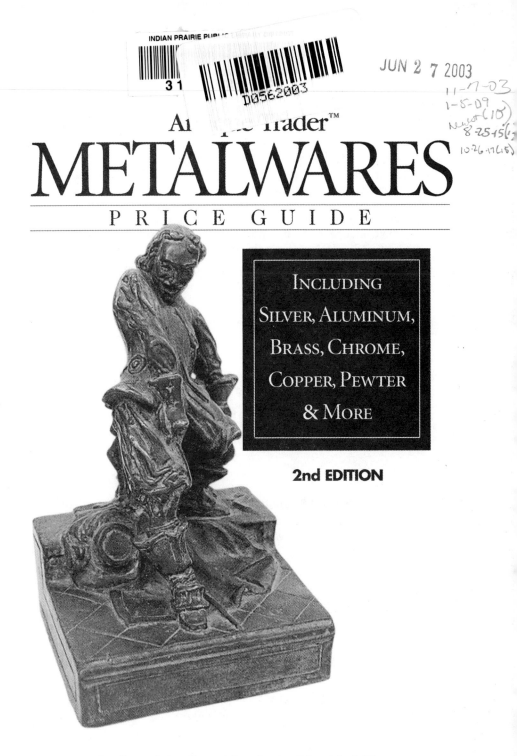

> INCLUDING
> SILVER, ALUMINUM,
> BRASS, CHROME,
> COPPER, PEWTER
> & MORE

2nd EDITION

Edited by **Kyle Husfloen** I Contributing Editor **Mark Moran**

Published by

krause publications
An F&W Publications Company

700 East State Street • Iola, WI 54990-0001
715-445-2214 • 888-457-2873
www.krause.com

Please call or write for our free catalog of publications.
Our toll-free number to place an order or obtain a free catalog is 800-258-0929
or please use our regular business telephone 715-445-2214.

Library of Congress Catalog Number: 2002105759
ISBN: 0-87349-449-0

Printed in the United States of America

TABLE OF CONTENTS

INTRODUCTION

In 1995, Antique Trader Books published the first price guide specifically designed to provide current market information on all the major types of metalwares, from Copper through Tin & Tole. We're pleased to bring you here a completely new and expanded edition of that popular reference.

Since nearly every American household still makes use of some decorative or utilitarian items made of metal, we're certain that having this guide to both collectible (not quite antique) and antique metalwares will prove invaluable. Included are some very early pieces, such as 18th century ironware, silver and pewter, as well as early 20th century objects made of aluminum, chrome, copper and spelter. With more than 4,000 individual entries, we're sure to list a metal piece you're likely to have around the house, from kitchen utensils and doorstops to lighting devices and silver flatware.

The contents of our guide are arranged alphabetically by the name of the metal and within each section by the name of the object. As with all Antique Trader price guides, we took great pride in providing detailed and accurate descriptions of each item so you'll have the clearest idea of what it looks like and what makes it unique. In addition, you'll appreciate the 1,000 black and white photographs that highlight these listings. As another special bonus we are providing a special 16-page full-color supplement to show off some great metal objects at their very best.

We had the help of a number of shops, collectors, auction houses, and dealers in preparing this new guide. First, special thanks to Dannie Woodard, the leading authority in 20th century hammered aluminum. Dannie had prepared the special feature and extensive listing on Aluminum for our first *Metalwares Price Guide* and we were so pleased she agreed to update and expand the material in that category for this edition. Also, we received a wonderful selection of Silver Plate Flatware from Bill and Mary Pohl of Angel Lady Antiques, South Windsor, Connecticut, and our Sterling Silver Flatware section was updated with the help of Rhona Nabi of Silver Lady Antiques, Foxboro, Massachusetts. Of course, Contributing Editor Mark Moran did a tremendous amount of work in locating collectors and dealers willing to share their collections and expertise, and he provided a majority of the photographs included here. My sincerest thanks go to all of you for your tremendous efforts in helping to produce this unique and useful reference.

In conclusion, I just wish to remind our readers that they should use this book only as a guide to pricing since regional market demand and condition can lead to variations in pricing from one part of the country to another. We have done our very best to prepare accurate descriptions, which have been carefully proofed and reviewed. Please note however, neither the compilers, editors nor publisher can assume responsibility for any losses that might be incurred as a result of consulting this guide, or of errors, typographical or otherwise.

As editor, I hope you'll find this an invaluable guide in evaluating treasures you may own or pieces you are searching for. I'm sure this comprehensive overview of a very large collecting field will prove indispensable to collectors, dealers and appraisers across the country. I'll look forward to hearing from you, and your comments and suggestions are always welcome. Meanwhile, good luck and happy collecting.

Kyle Husfloen, Editor

Antique Trader Metalwares Price Guide – 2nd Edition:
SPECIAL CONTRIBUTORS

Aluminum:
1310 S. Bowie Dr.
Weatherford, TX 76080
e-mail: al1310@aol.com

Silver Plate Flatware:
Bill & Mary Pohl
Angel Lady Antiques
P.O. Box 418
South Windsor, CT 06074
(860) 644-5912
Fax: (860) 644-2627
Web site: www.silverplatepatterns.com/

Sterling Silver Flatware:
Rhona Nabi
The Silver Lady Antiques
P.O. Box 27
Foxboro, MA 02035
(781) 784-9184
e-mail: silant@aol.com

PHOTOGRAPHY CREDITS

Photographers who have contributed to this volume include: Joe Hallahan, Dubuque, Iowa, and Mark Moran, Rochester, Minnesota.

For other photographs, artwork, data or permission to photograph in their shops, we express sincere appreciation to the following auctioneers, galleries, museums, individuals and shops:

Alderfers, Hatfield, Pennsylvania; Auction Team Koln, Cologne, Germany; Jim and Dorothy Bernatz, Rochester, Minnesota; Carol Bohn, Mifflinburg, Pennsylvania; Ruth Capper, Dellroy, Ohio; Charlton Hall Galleries, Columbia, South Carolina; Craftsman Auctions, Pittsfield, Massachusetts; Wm. Doyle Galleries, New York, New York; DuMouchelles, Detroit, Michigan; Dr. Robert Elsner, Boynton Beach, Florida; Garth's Auctions, Delaware, Ohio; Marion Grammer, Boynton Beach, Florida; Green Valley Auctions, Mt. Crawford, Virginia; Henry/Peirce Auctions, Homewood, Illinois; Jackson's Auctioneers & Appraisers, Cedar Falls, Iowa; G. and V. Kranz, Rochester, Minnesota; John Kruesel, Rochester, Minnesota; Mom's Antique Mall, Oronoco, Minnesota; David Rago Arts & Crafts, Lambertville, New Jersey; Skinner, Inc., Bolton, Massachusetts; Paul Smith, Harlan, Iowa; Sotheby's, New York, New York; Judy and George Swan, Dubuque, Iowa; Temple's Antiques, Eden Prairie, Minnesota; R. and K. Townsend, Rochester, Minnesota; Mike White, Fraser, Colorado; and C. Williams, Rochester, Minnesota.

Special Report

Aluminum

By Dannie Woodard,

author of Hammered Aluminum Hand Wrought Collectibles, Books I & II

Once an object in great demand, the aluminum giftware of the 1930s and '40s faded into obscurity and lay dormant for forty years before it began to attract the attention of collectors. Both the appearance of the metal and its low price boosted its popularity, but today some collectors pay hundreds of dollars for a choice item.

Aluminum giftware and accessories have been made by numerous processes. The predecessors of some of the popular collectibles of today were small items such as memo pad covers, combs, eyeglass holders and even large hairpins. Many of these pieces were decorated with delicate bright-cut designs of flowers or monograms.

In the late 1920s, the Wendell August Forge, a manufacturer of decorative wrought iron, became interested in adapting aluminum to hand-wrought architectural use and to the production of giftwares. This production continued, interrupted only by World War II. The popularity of these items spurred the formation of numerous other companies, but most were short-lived.

There were probably several hundred makers of hammered aluminum, but very few of them continued production after World War II. The wartime use of aluminum in defense products stopped its use for gift items, and post-war mass production affected its desirability. Only the companies using start-to-finish hand-production methods survived. The forges of Wendell August, Arthur Armour, and DePoncea were survivors, and their products are choice collectibles today.

The firms of Palmer-Smith, Continental, Rodney Kent, Cellini Craft, and Everlast were other producers of some of today's most popular aluminum wares. Quality pieces made by other companies are being discovered, and many of these are gaining in popularity.

The enduring beauty of the hand-wrought decorative articles was created by a meticulous process involving skilled and talented artisans. Each design was cut by hand by die cutters who, working on steel with small chisels, produced finely detailed designs ranging from the very simple to the extremely intricate.

To make the desired articles, the draftsman started with a piece of aluminum cut to the approximate size and shape that was needed. The material was then positioned onto the selected die and hammered to produce the repousseé design that is so attractive on hand-forged articles. Further shaping and working was done on a wooden form and, for some designs, smoke or carbon blackening was used to create the pattern's dark patina.

In addition to the popular repousseé style, several other techniques were employed. One, an incised or carved design known as intaglio, is found on several lines of aluminum ware. This method was not as widely used as that of repousseé.

Other giftware took on a wide variety of appearances. Brightly polished pieces, spun items, machine-embossed patterns, and anodized aluminum were, for a brief time, popular accessories for the home. Cast aluminum has also become popular with many collectors. Items marked "Bruce Fox" or "Bruce Cox" account for most of this type. In addition, pieces of furniture such as chairs have become very popular with some collectors.

Usually a company's chosen design was used on an entire line of accessories, with a variation of a leaf or flower featured on the pieces. In addition, the techniques used to produce the finished appearance, whether brightly polished or lustrously hand-rubbed, became an integral part of the look and feel of each company's product. Even the appearance of the hammer marks is distinctive.

Today's unstable prices should encourage collectors to be as knowledgeable and careful as possible when considering their purchases. Many things affect the value of an item: pitting and scratches, loose handles or missing glassware should be considered in determining the value. Often lids and inserts are mismatched and even made by different companies. Some aluminum giftware was made by using a simulated hammered look and featured machine embossing. Lightweight polished aluminum was also used in some products. These pieces do not have the value of the items made of thicker aluminum, hand-hammered and with repousseé or intaglio patterns.

Although aluminum giftware was probably never produced as abundantly as Depression or carnival glass, it is becoming apparent that its styles and patterns are almost as numerous. At present, prices vary from region to region and even from shop to shop, although collectors are complaining that there is very little to be found in the shops. The largest displays of aluminum are found on the Internet at auction sites, mainly eBay. There the collector may become very confused by contradictory prices. Many nice pieces will receive no bids, while others reach astronomical heights. An item identical to one day's high seller may receive no bids on a following day. The lesson to be learned here is that one item's high selling price does not mean all aluminum is extremely valuable, not does it mean that no bids mean aluminum is worthless. As in all marketing, the buyer and the seller need to reach each other at the right time and place for a sale to take place.

NOTE: Ms. Woodard's books are available from Aluminum Collector's Books, P.O. Box 1346, Weatherford, TX 76086. Book One is $20; Book Two is $24.95, plus $1.50 postage for the two.

Price Listings:

Cast Aluminum Art Deco Ashtray

Ashtray, cast, figural, an Art Deco design w/an angular terrier seated at the edge of a fanned angular tray, 3 1/4 x 5 1/8", 4 3/8" h. (ILLUS.) ....$ 65

Ashtray, hammered, large center flower, wrap-around platform base forms cigarette rests, Buenilum, 4 1/2" d. 25

Ashtray, hammered, bittersweet decoration, Wendell August #60, 5 1/2" d. 15

Ashtray, cast, horsehead decoration, Bruce Fox, 5 1/2 x 5 1/2" 25

Basket, bread, hammered, oval w/twisted handle, duck on pond decoration, Cromwell 12

Basket with Wheat Design

Basket, flat round form w/upturned fluted rim, double handle w/twist design, wheat decoration, Milcraft, 14" d. (ILLUS.) **14**

Basket, hammered aluminum frame w/flower clusters, Paden City glass insert, looped handle, fluted edge, Cromwell, 14" d. **35**

Basket, hammered, china plate insert, morning glories on frame, square w/rolled sides, looped diagonally-placed handle, Wrought Farberware, 12" w. **38**

Basket, hammered, double-style, handle w/square knot, fern & flowers decoration, Canterbury Arts, 9" w. **12**

Basket, hammered, twisted handle, sailing ship decoration, Hand Forged #29, 10" d. **8**

Basket, oval w/turn-in sides joined by a double twist handle, orange design, Arthur Armour, rare, 14 x 18" (ILLUS.) **295-350**

Basket, polished aluminum frame w/stamped rose design, fluted, etched glass insert, double aluminum strand handle, twisted in center, Farber & Shlevin, 9 1/2" d. **20**

Basket, polished aluminum, frame w/stamped rose pattern, twisted handle, pottery insert, Farber & Shlevin, 7" d. **18**

Basket, polished w/stamped flowers, unmarked, 7" d. **5**

Aluminum Beverage Server & Stand

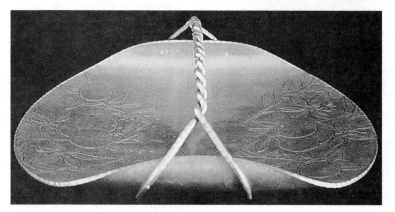

Rare Orange Pattern Basket

Beverage server, cover & stand, tapering cylindrical body w/wide upturned loop side handle & spigot near the base, low domed cover w/large loop handle, on a separate ring base w/twisted strap angled legs curving in to support a center burner, Buenilum, overall 20" h. (ILLUS. on previous page) 95

Book ends, hammered, applied horseshoe, Everlast, pr. 95

Book ends, hammered, chopped corners, daisy decoration, Wendell August, pr. 150

Bowl, cov., hammered, cast aluminum "baker man" on cover, Cellini Craft 85

Bowl, hammered, petal design w/grape cluster in center, Wendell August #807 85

Bowl, polished, repoussé flower design in center, butterfly handles, Hand Forged 12

Bowl, hammered, blackbird & fledglings decoration, De Ponceau, 5 3/4" d. 30

Bowl, machine-embossed pattern, Wrought Aluminum, 7" d. 5

Aluminum Bowl with Pottery Insert

Bowl, lightly scalloped cupped rim w/hammered design, small yellow & tan pottery insert in center decorated w/a crowing rooster, Modern Hand Made #147, 7 1/2" d. (ILLUS.) $35-50

Bowl, hammered, Big Horn sheep decoration, Hand Forged #2, 8 3/4" d. $5

Bowl, hammered, intaglio band of stylized daisy, Everlast, 9" d. $5

Bowl, hammered, Bromeliad-like flowers, Buenilum, 9 1/4" d. $15

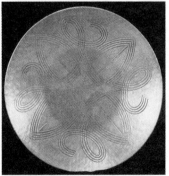

Shallow Aluminum Bowl

Bowl, wide shallow form w/engraved four-petal & line loop decoration, Canterbury Arts, 11" d. (ILLUS.) 12

Bowl, hammered, footed, flat, scalloped edge w/tiny berries between scallops, Cellini Craft, 11 1/2" d. 33

Bowl, hammered, fruits decoration, Everlast, 12 1/2" d. 12

Bowl, hammered, scalloped edge, oak leaves & acorns decoration, Everlast, 13" d. 12

Bowl, hammered, hunter scene, LA Handwrought (bell symbol), 15" d. 95

Box, cov., cigarette, hammered, applied leaves & rosette on cover, World 40

Box, cov., cigarette, hammered, pine decoration, Wendell August 95

Wendell August Pine Motif Box

Box, cov., flattened square form, pine bough design on the cover, opens to three compartments, Wendell August (ILLUS.) 125

Box, cov., hammered square w/sturdy hinged cover, schooner decoration, Arthur Armour 125

Bread tray, hammered, anchor decoration, Everlast 12

Bread tray, hammered, chrysanthemum decoration, applied leaves, Continental 14

Bread tray, hammered, grape clusters, handles w/leaves, World 10

Bread tray, hammered, scalloped edges, tulip decoration, Rodney Kent 15

Bread tray, hammered, wild rose decoration, Continental 9

Bread tray, machine-embossed, pansy decoration, National Silver Co. 5

Bread tray, polished, stamped wild rose decoration, unmarked 5

Butter dish, cov., deep glass dish in crisscross design, aluminum undertray & cover w/tulip finial, Rodney Kent 20

Butter dish, cov., machine-embossed chrysanthemum on aluminum cover, floret finial, pressed glass base, Forman Family 18

Butter dish, cov., polished, glass insert for 1/4 lb., looped finial, Buenilum 18-20

Butter dish, cov., polished, round w/glass insert, looped finial on domed cover, undertray w/beaded edge, Buenilum, 6 1/2" d. 18-20

Butter dish, cov., polished, stamped Bali Bamboo patt., crisscross patterned glass insert for 1/4 lb., Everlast #B55 25

Candelabra, hammered, holds three candles on a thick bar w/large center loop, Buenilum, 14" w., 6" h., pr. 125

Candelabra, hammered, two-light, rectangular base w/scrolled band, Wendell August #840, pr. **150**

Buenilum Three-light Candelabrum

Candelabrum, three-light, each cylindrical socket w/a flat round drip tray, on two looped arms & a tall twisted strand stem on a slightly domed round foot, Buenilum, 13 1/2" h. (ILLUS.).................................. **85-125**
Candleholder, applied leaves on stem, Continental, 4 1/2" h.............................. **30**
Candleholder, hammered, scalloped base, Everlast, 4" w., 3 1/2" h. **20**
Candleholders, anodized (polished), crystal ball, Kensington, pr. **35**
Candleholders, hammered, deep saucer base, twisted stem, Wendell August, 6" w., 8" h., pr.................................... **125**
Candleholders, hammered, double platform base, three cupped lotus leaves, holds one candle, Wendell August, pr......... **225**
Candleholders, hammered, flower sprigs, Findley, 5" w., 3 1/2" h., pr. **35-40**
Candleholders, simulated hammer marks, the tall socket flanked by pairs of upright leaves w/an applied floret on each, on a wide flat base w/inwardly scrolled feet, World Handforged, pr. (ILLUS. below) **25**
Candy dish, cov., hammered aluminum cover, fruits decoration, pear finial, thick glass base dish, unmarked Everlast........... **35-45**
Candy dish, cov., hammered, aluminum cover w/chrysanthemum & floret, footed pressed glass base dish, Continental, 6" d.. **35**

Candy dish, cov., hammered aluminum cover w/flower sprigs & "spoon handle" curl, footed etched glass base dish, Buenilum, 6" d..................................... **35-45**
Candy dish, cov., hammered aluminum holder & cover w/applied ribbon decoration, tulip finial, ribbon & flower decorative handles extending into feet, divided glass insert dish, Rodney Kent, 6" d. **35**
Casserole, cov., hammered, Bali Bamboo patt., baking dish insert, stylized bamboo cover finial, Everlast, 7" d. **15**
Casserole, cov., hammered, butterfly & dogwood decoration & ring handle on cover, baking dish insert, grooved handles, Arthur Armour, 9" d.......................... **95-125**

Aluminum Covered Casserole

Casserole, cov., hammered, footed ring-style caddy, vegetables & wheat decoration, ridged fan-shaped handles & cover finial, Pyrex glass insert, Crown, 8 1/2" d. (ILLUS.).. **25**
Casserole, cov., hammered, intaglio design of stylized leaves & flowers, flattened cover knob, side handles, baking dish insert, Everlast, 9 1/4" d. **10**
Casserole, cov., hammered, leafy vine & open pea pod cover finial, baking dish insert, Everlast #1038, 7"d....................... **12**
Casserole, cover & undertray, hammered, Bittersweet patt., twisted bar handle on cover, baking dish insert, Wendell August #735, 9 x 13 1/2" undertray, 3 pcs................. **125**
Chafing dish, cov., hammered, black handle & knob finial on cover, Spain **12**

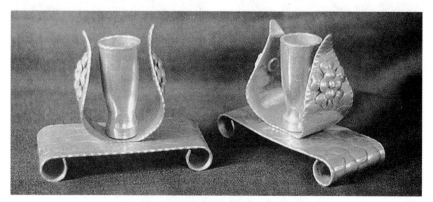

World Handforged Candleholders

Chafing dish, cov., hammered, grape cluster design around cover w/beaded knob surrounded w/leaves, baking dish insert, Everlast, 10" d. 25

Chafing dish, cov., hammered, tulip decoration, decorative ribbon & flower handles & legs, baking dish insert, Rodney Kent. 30

Coaster, hammered, tropical fish decoration, Wendell August w/old mark 15

Hammered Aluminum Coaster Set

Coaster set, hammered, four coasters w/stamped bamboo motif, the rectangular holder w/four short feet, fluted rim & indents for coasters, Everlast, 4 x 6 3/4", the set (ILLUS.) 13

Coasters, embossed, chrysanthemum pattern, in caddy w/decorative leaves, Continental, set of 8 25

Coasters, embossed tulip motif, in caddy w/decorative ribbon & flower design handle, Rodney Kent, the set 30

Coasters, hammered, rose decoration, in caddy w/curled handle, Everlast, set of 6 .. 16-20

Coasters, hammered, spiral design, Everlast, set of 6 16

Coasters, polished, beaded edge, in caddy w/double looped handle, Buenilum, set of 8 25

Aluminum Cocktail Shaker

Cocktail shaker, cov., chrysanthemum decoration, pouring spout on shoulder, handle w/decorative leaf, Continental #530, 12" h. (ILLUS.) 50-75

Cocktail shaker, cov., double looped finial on cover, Buenilum, 9 1/2" h. 85-95

Condiment server, hammered, apple blossom design on undertray & slotted cover on glass jar, Wendell August #592, the set 35-50

Condiment server, hammered, Ferris-wheel style, three "baskets" holding dishes, Continental. 55

Condiment server, hammered, revolving-type, cruets & covered jars in apple design, twisted center handle, Continental 45

Condiment server: oval handled tray & two cov. glass containers; the hammered tray w/an arched & pierced central handle w/a ribbon & flower design, lids on containers w/spoon slots & bud finials, Rodney Kent, the set (ILLUS. below) 50

Rodney Kent Condiment Server

Cast Aluminum Turtle Corkscrew

Corkscrew, cast, model of a turtle w/a cork screw tail, original worn paint, 2 1/4 x 4 1/4" (ILLUS.) **95**

Crumber set: brush & rectangular tray; the tray w/a rolled handle w/applied blossoms & leaf spring & an engraved tulip cluster in tray, the brush w/a wooden handle applied w/a blossom & leaf sprig, Rodney Kent 3444, tray 3 1/4 x 8 1/2", 2 pcs... **25-35**

Crumber set: scraper & tray; hammered, scalloped edges, grape decoration on each piece, Everlast, the set............................. **35**

Crumber set: tray & brush; hammered, looped handles, Buenilum, the set.............. **35-40**

Crumber Set with Wild Rose Design

Crumber set: tray & scoop; the two pieces forming a disc, the larger tray section w/a tight curl handle, stamped wild rose sprig decoration, the scoop w/a long curved bar handle, Continental #725, 2 pcs. (ILLUS.).... **18-25**

Crumber Set with Fruit Designs

Crumber set: tray & scraper; hand-forged, tray w/angular handle, both w/fruit designs, Everlast (ILLUS.)............................... **27-35**

Crumber set: tray & scraper; long tray w/serpentine edges, half-round scraper w/flat end handle, rose decoration, Everlast, 2 pcs. (ILLUS. below) **27-35**

Small Fish-shaped Dish

Dish, rounded flattened model of a fish, old circular Everlast mark, small (ILLUS.)....... **25-40**

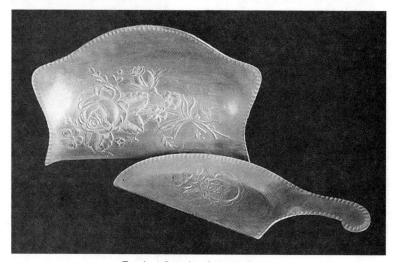

Everlast Crumber Set with Roses

Small Dish with Flamingo Decoration

Dish, shallow round sides w/upturned rim, a figural cast aluminum flamingo in center, Palmer-Smith #71, dish 6 1/4" d., flamingo 4" h. (ILLUS.) **70**

Doorstop, galleon, cast, three-masted ship under full sail w/long banners atop each mast, raised star & cross on center sail, original painted surface, by O.B. Campbell, St. Johns, Michigan, 11 3/4 x 13" **30**

Dresser set: two covered glass dishes on a tray; hammered, covers w/tulip finials, ribbon & flower design caddy handles extend to form feet, Rodney Kent #403, tray 6 x 12", the set **45**

Drink mixer, hammered, one-piece construction, large hole for long-handled stirring spoon, Everlast, 7" h. **50-60**

Gravy boat on attached undertray, hammered, w/ladle, looped handles, Buenilum **35**

Gravy boat on attached undertray, hammered, wrapped handle w/decorative leaf, w/aluminum ladle, chrysanthemum decoration, Continental #610 .... **35-45**

Ice bucket, cov., hammered, handled, cover w/applied leaves under knob, Everlast Ice Cooler (with polar bear) #5008 .... **20**

Ice bucket, cov., hammered, side handles, roses decoration, hammered ball cover knob, Everlast, 9 1/2" h. **25-35**

Ice bucket, cov., hammered, thin aluminum, handled, Nassco **6**

Ice bucket, cov., hammered, tulip cover finial, ribbon & flower handles, Rodney Kent **35**

Ice bucket, cov., polished, footed, large looped cover finial, Knight Kraft **18**

Covered Ice Bucket

Ice bucket, cov., wide slightly tapering cylindrical body w/decorative raised band around the rim, loop handles at sides, low domed cover w/wide ring finial, Keystone #115 (ILLUS.) **25-35**

Open Ice Bucket with Willow Design

Ice bucket, open, cylindrical body w/curved rim tabs supporting a ring, embossed bands of willow leaves down the sides, Wendell August Forge, 7" d. (ILLUS.) **300-400**

Ice tongs, aluminum & brass, Kensington Ware **12-15**

Jewelry, bracelet, hammered, zinnia link design, Wendell August **55**

Jewelry, bracelet, stamped w/Western motif on each section, unmarked **25-30**

Jewelry, brooch, hammered, pine design, Wendell August, 1 1/2 x 2" **45**

Jewelry, cuff bracelet, hammered, flowers & leaves, unmarked **25**

Two Everlast Pendants

Jewelry, pendant, domed round form w/flat fluted rim enclosing center w/raised embossed floral design, w/chain, unmarked Everlast (ILLUS. left) **45**

Jewelry, pendant, flattened oval shape w/embossed leafy design, w/chain, unmarked Everlast (ILLUS. right) **45**

Lamp, table, hammered, walnut decoration, aluminum shade, Wendell August ... **1,700-1,900**

Lamp, table, hammered, zinnia design, silk shade, Wendell August...................... **1,000-1,200**

Lamp-bank, Pine patt., holder for desk supplies & writing pen & calendar, unmarked but attributed to Wendell August Forge **1,252**

Magazine rack, hammered, thick aluminum, world map decoration, Arthur Armour.. **350**

Match box cover, hammered, "penny box" size, Wendell August... **35**

Match box cover, polished, kitchen-size, stylized fish & water design, Palmer-Smith... **55**

Match folder cover, polished, ducks decoration, unmarked... **5**

Meat server, hammered, well & tree-type, curved band supports each end, floret & leaves decoration, Continental #544, 11 x 15 1/2"... **35-50**

Napkin holder, hammered, decorative ribbon & flower band forms feet, Rodney Kent... **27**

Napkin holder, hammered, trefoil shape, roses decoration, Everlast............................. **25**

Napkin holder, polished, cactus decoration, Farber & Shlevin **12**

Napkin holder, polished, machine-embossed roses, World **15**

Nut bowl & picks, hammered, fruits & flowers decoration, looped handles, pedestal base, Cromwell, 10" d., the set................... **15-20**

Nut bowl & picks, wide flat-bottomed bowl w/low, incurved sides raised on a flaring domed pedestal foot, center post for nut picks, looped side handles, overall stamped fruit & flower decoration on bowl, Hand Finished Aluminum, the set (ILLUS.)... **17-27**

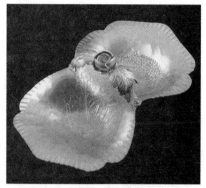

Nut Dish with Chrysanthemum Design

Nut dish, oblong two-section type w/tapering scalloped & fluted rim, stamped large chrysanthemum decoration, center arched leaf handle w/blossom finial, Continental #754, 5 1/2 x 8" (ILLUS.).................... **15**

Nut Set with Fruit & Flower Design

Unique Round Nut Dish

Everlast Patio Cart

Nut dish, shallow round bowl w/a tiny floret in the center & a unique stamped tab side handle, Florence Kimbell (ILLUS. on previous page) **30-40**
Patio cart, hammered, intaglio leaves decoration, complete w/serving pieces, wheels & push handle, Everlast (ILLUS. on previous page) **650**

Cast Aluminum Pencil Sharpener

Pencil sharpener, cast, figure of colonial woman holding tray, marked on reverse Baker Chocolate Girl - reg. U.S. patent office, w/original red, white & blue paint, 1/2 x 1", 1 7/8" h. (ILLUS.) **135**

Aluminum Milk Bottle Pencil Sharpener

Pencil sharpener, cast, in the form of a milk bottle, 5/8 x 1 1/4" (ILLUS.) **40**

Bullet-shaped Pencil Sharpener

Pencil sharpener, cast, in the shape of a bullet, 5/8 x 1 3/8" (ILLUS.) **45**
Pie server, round w/stepped flared sides & flanged rim w/embossed stylized leaf & fruit decoration, geometric beaded handles, glass pie plate fits inside, Everlast (ILLUS. below) **18**
Pitcher, hammered, applied floret & leaves on body, World **25-30**
Pitcher, hammered, flared at top, Everlast **15**
Pitcher, hammered, grooved bulbous form, berry & leaf decoration on handle, Cellini Craft **75**
Pitcher, hammered, looped & twisted handle, Buenilum **25**
Pitcher, hammered, mums decoration, handle w/leaf decoration, Continental **35**
Pitcher, hammered, thin aluminum, grooved band around center, Italy **10**

Pitcher with Signed Floral Decor

Everlast Aluminum Pie Server

Pitcher, oval cylindrical body w/embossed flower & leaf design up the sides, angled handle, artist-signed within decoration, Canterbury Arts (ILLUS. on previous page)........ 75
Pitcher, polished, straight sides, twisted handle, Buenilum... 15
Pitcher, w/ice guard spout, hammered, Bali Bamboo patt., Everlast 65
Pitcher, w/ice guard spout, hammered, pine decoration, Wendell August #760 85
Pitcher, w/ice guard spout, hammered, tulip decoration, tiny tulips on ice guard, ribbon-styled handle, Rodney Kent............... 35-45
Pitcher, hammered, intaglio band of stylized daisies, double twisted handle of large rods, Everlast, 6" h. 35-45

Pitcher with Leaves on Handle

Pitcher, plain baluster-form body w/angled shoulder tapering to a flaring rim w/curled strap ice guard at the spout, flaring domed foot, strap handle w/applied leaf at top & base, Cromwell, 8 1/2" h (ILLUS.)............... 15-25

Aluminum Advertising Postage Scale

Postage scale, Art Deco style w/"De Bourgh Mfg. Co. - Minneapolis, Minn." & phone number printed in gold on black Bakelite base, top unscrews to reveal graded spring-loaded column, 2 5/8 x 3", 4 1/8" h. (ILLUS.) 95
Punch bowl & ladle, hammered, grapes decoration, Wendell August, 2 pcs............... 350

Wendell August Punch Bowl & Ladle

Punch bowl, tray & ladle, deep rounded bowl on footring, stamped bar band around the rim, fleur-de-lis decoration in center of bowl & tray, Wendell August #517, bowl 14 1/4" d., tray 18" d., 3 pcs. (ILLUS.).................. 425
Punch bowl, tray & ladle, hammered w/blue crock liner, ring handles, Keystone, the set.. 125
Punch bowl, undertray & ladle, a deep flaring bowl w/geometric Art Deco designs on a wide round matching undertray, Laird, underplate 20" d., bowl 14" d., the set (ILLUS. below) 450-475
Punch set: bowl, cups, tray & bottle opener; spun aluminum, bamboo rail on tray, Russel Wright design, bowl 11 1/2" d., 6 1/4" h., the set... 1,250
Punch set: bowl, ladle & glass cups; hammered, pedestal base, hammered cup hooks, Everlast, the set 175-225

Relish Server with Glass Insert

Art Deco Aluminum Punch Bowl

Relish server, round w/the wide dimpled outer rim embossed w/fruit & flowers, the center shallow well w/further fruits & flowers &
fitted w/a three-part clear glass insert,
Cromwell (ILLUS. on previous page) **27-32**

Two-part Relish Server

Relish server, two-part, shallow rectangular trays w/serrated flaring edges, each
fitted w/a two-part fluted glass insert,
trays joined by a wide arched flower-
stamped pierced strap handle, unmarked
Rodney Kent (ILLUS.).................................. **30-35**

Server with Baskets

Server, carousel-type w/four baskets suspended on chains, disc foot, original
came w/four 10 oz. Fire King glass inserts w/scalloped edges, Everlast,
13 1/2 w., 10 1/2 h. (ILLUS.) **45-55**

Covered Server with Acorn Design

Server, cov., shallow base w/wide, flattened
petal-form rim, domed cover w/arched
handle flanked by leaves & a stamped
design of bands of leaves & acorn clus-
ter, Continental #512, 11" d. (ILLUS.) **35-45**

Server, shallow rectangular tray w/forked
overhead handle from end to end, fitted
w/six squared pressed glass dishes w/a
fruit design in the bottom, Keystone #606,
10 x 14 1/2", the set (ILLUS. below)................. **35**

Serving set: tray & utensils; the wide flattened rectangular tray w/curved edges &
fluted corners centered by a rectangular
blue pottery insert, tray decorated w/a pine
decoration, w/a matching spatula utensil &
salad serving fork, Wendell August #525,
tray 14 x 24", the set (ILLUS. top next
page).. **150-195**

Serving utensil, gravy ladle, polished, double looped handle, unmarked Buenilum.......... **15**

Serving utensil, pie or cake server, hammered, twisted double looped handle,
unmarked Buenilum... **35**

Serving utensil, punch ladle, polished,
twisted double looped handle, unmarked
Buenilum... **35-45**

Serving utensils, salad fork & spoon, hammered, twisted handles, unmarked Wen-
dell August, pr... **65**

Serving utensils, salad fork & spoon,
wooden w/bamboo design section at
each end, unmarked, pr. **25**

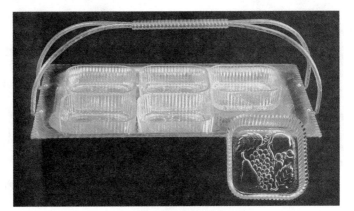

Long Server with Glass Inserts

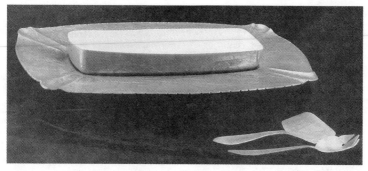

Server with Utensils

Serving utensils, salad fork & spoon, wooden w/decorative aluminum inset on handle in an Everlast pattern, unmarked, pr.............. **15**

Silent butler, hammered, cattails decoration, unmarked, 5 x 6".................................... **15**

Everlast Silent Butler with Flowers

Silent butler, oblong dish w/scalloped edge & slightly domed hinged cover embossed w/stylized lilies & leaves, flat hammered handle, Everlast (ILLUS.) **25**

Silent butler, oval, hammered, flower cluster decoration, Henry & Miller, 4 1/2 x 6"........ **15**

Silent butler, oval, hammered, fruits decoration, Everlast, 7 x 9"................................ **20**

Fern & Berry Decor on Silent Butler

Silent butler, round dish w/embossed Fern & Berry pattern on the hinged lid, flat hammered handle, Canterbury Arts (ILLUS.)......................... **27-35**

Silent butler, round, hammered, apple blossoms decoration, thick handle, notched edge, Wendell August #95, 7" d... **45-55**

Silent butler, round, hammered, bird on twig decoration, N.S. Co., 6" d................. **12-15**

Silent butler, round, hammered, floral bouquet w/roses decoration, Canterbury Arts, 6" d.. **20**

Silent butler, round, hammered, rose decoration, Everlast, 6" d............................ **12**

Silent butler, round, hammered, tulip decoration, Rodney Kent, 7 1/2" d. **18-20**

Silent butler, round, hammered, wooden handle, Corduroy patt., Continental #1505, 8" d....................................... **20**

Silent butler, round, polished, intaglio design of roses, World, 6 1/4" d. **10**

Silent Butler with Wild Rose Design

Silent butler, squared dish w/rounded corners, low domed hinged cover w/stamped wild rose decoration & curved thumb rest, strap side handle w/curled end, Crown Aluminum, 3 1/4" sq. plus handle (ILLUS.)........ **18-22**

Smoking set: hammered undertray, ashtrays & cov. cigarette box; blue pottery box, bittersweet decoration on metal, Wendell August #75, the set........................... **195**

Smoking stand, hammered, ducks pattern on ashtray, "bubble" protrusions on domed base, twisted stand & ring around top, Wendell August #926, 22 1/4" h....................... **275**

Sugar, creamer & tray, hammered, Bali Bamboo patt. on each piece, Everlast #B21 on tray, 3 pcs. 35

Sugar, creamer & tray, hammered, chrysanthemum decoration on sugar & creamer, plain tray w/scalloped edges, Continental #515, 3 pcs. 25-35

Sugar, creamer & tray, hammered, plain sugar & creamer, grape decoration on tray, Everlast, 3 pcs. 20-25

Sugar, creamer & tray, plain, World, 3 pcs. 20

Rare Wendell August Forge Table

Table, round removable tray top w/pine bough decoration, fitted in a twisted ring frame on square legs w/twisted sections joined by a cross-stretcher, Wendell August Forge #925 (ILLUS.) 650

Tidbit tray, hammered, tiered w/three trays, grape decoration, center standing w/ring handle, Everlast, 14" h. 22

Tidbit tray, machine-embossed, tiered, unmarked 10

Tidbit tray, polished, floral decoration, side handle, Hammercraft. 7

Toast rack, hammered, wheat decoration, Wendell August #709 65

Toast rack, w/two each covered butter & jam jars, hammered, center toast rack, Rodney Kent 55

Tray, hammered, rope pattern, ring handles w/small balls, Palmer-Smith #18, 10" d. 95

Tray, hammered, intaglio design of stylized daisies, ribbed tab handles, Everlast, 9 x 11" 12

Tray, hammered, square, rose bouquet decoration, Everlast, 12" w. 15

Tray, machine-embossed flowers, Wright Aluminum, 12" d. 10

Square Tray with Siesta Scene

Tray, square w/rounded corners, stamped scene of Mexican peasant asleep under a palm tree, wide border w/curved paneling, Everlast, 12" w. (ILLUS.) 20-30

Tray, oval, smooth, stamped wild roses decoration, fluted, unmarked, 12 1/4" l. 8

Tray, hammered, grooved bar handles, scenic design of horseback riders & lake, Arthur Armour, 9 x 13" 125

Tray, hammered, twisted handles, Wild Rose patt., fluted edge, Continental #703, 13 1/2" d. 15

Hammered Aluminum Tray

Tray, hammered, w/rolled handle, serrated rim, stamped wild rose decoration, style 1071, Continental Silver Co., 6 1/4 x 13 1/2" (ILLUS.) 12

Tray, hammered, tab handles, heron & marsh scene, Leroy DeLoss, 8 x 13 1/2" 100-150

Tray with Celtic Knot Design

Tray, rectangular w/tab end handles, intaglio curvilinear or Celtic Knot design, Canterbury Arts, 9 1/2 x 13 1/2" (ILLUS.) .. 14-16

Tray, hammered, tab handles, oak leaves decoration, Wrought Farberware, 10 1/2 x 13 1/2" 10

Tray with Water Lilies

Tray, oval, incised looping band of stylized water lilies around the rim, Palmer-Smith #82L, 10 1/2 x 13 1/2" (ILLUS.) 65-75

Tray, hammered, daisies or sunflowers decoration, DePonceau, 14" d. 35-45

Tray, hammered, handled, tulip decoration,
Rodney Kent, 14" d. 25

Tray with Bowl of Fruit Design

Tray, round w/looped side handles w/leaf
terminals, center w/embossed fruit
wreath framing a bowl of fruit, Cromwell,
14" d. (ILLUS.) 20-25
Tray, hammered, handled, nautical motif,
Lehman, 9 x 14" 35
Tray, hammered, tab handles, tropical fish
decoration, Everlast, 9 x 14" 45
Tray, hammered, tab handles, Bittersweet
patt., Wendell August, 9 1/2 x 14" 55
Tray, spun, raffia-wrapped handle grips,
Russel Wright design, 14 1/2" d. 65
Tray, rectangular w/rounded corners &
grooved end handles w/leaf ends, shal-
low heavily hammered interior w/scene of
stag & doe, Continental Silver Co. #523,
10 1/2 x 14 1/2" (ILLUS. below) 45-55

Tray, hammered, looped handles, lake
scene w/dock, fluted edge, Cromwell,
12 1/2 x 14 1/2" 18-20
Tray, anodized highly polished compass de-
sign in brass, Kensington, 15" d. 20-25

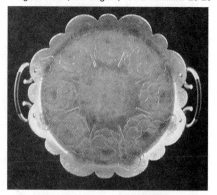

Tray with Ring of Pansies

Tray, wrapped handles, hammered, scalloped edge, ring of large pansies, Conti-
nental #852, 15" l. (ILLUS.) 65
Tray, hammered, looped handle w/leaf dec-
oration, fruits decoration, Cromwell,
15 1/2" d. 20-25
Tray, hammered, loop handles, apple blos-
soms decoration, fluted sides, Federal
Silver Co., 11 1/2 x 15 1/2" 20
Tray, hammered, handled, gold anodized,
chessmen decoration, Arthur Armour,
10 x 16" 45-55
Tray, hammered, handled, bird & flowers
decoration, N.S. Co., 11 x 16" 27

Handled Tray with Scene of Deer

Tray with Ornate Landscape Scene

Tray, double handles curved to side w/flower decoration, hammered frame w/berry stems, American Limoges plate insert, Wrought Farberware, 16 1/2" d. **35-45**

Tray, machine-embossed, handles, hunt scene, crimped edges, Beautyline Designed Aluminum, 11 1/2 x 16 1/2" **10**

Tray, hammered, bar handles, hunt scene, Keystone, 13 x 17" **35-45**

Tray, hammered, handled, oak leaf & acorn decoration, Continental #520, 17 1/2" l. **30**

Tray, hammered, coach & four decoration, Clayton Sheasley, 7 1/2 x 17 1/2" **65-75**

Tray, hammered, floral decoration, Clayton Sheasley, 7 1/2 x 17 1/2" **40-60**

Tray with Poppy Decoration

Tray, flattened bullet-form w/slightly curved rim, notched at one end, embossed w/a large poppy blossom, Wendell August Forge #523, 8 1/2 x 18" (ILLUS.) **75-85**

Tray, ribbed fanned end handles, rectangular w/cut corners, ornate detailed landscape scene w/mountains, a lake, trees & flying birds, Continental #555, 12 1/2 x 18 1/4" (ILLUS. above) **50-65**

Tray, hammered, small hand-stamped flowers, Palmer-Smith #33, 9 1/2 x 20" **125**

Tray, flat handles w/flowers, simulated hammer marks, machine-embossed roses, World, 14 x 20" **15-18**

Tray, hammered, handled, Bali Bamboo patt., Everlast, 14 1/2 x 20 1/2" **45**

Tray, hammered, tab handles, saguaro cactus decoration, Wendell August, 13 1/4 x 21" **150-175**

Tray, hammered, grooved bar handles, hunt scene, Arthur Armour, 14 1/2 x 21 1/2" . **150-195**

Tray, hammered, handled, chrysanthemum decoration, handles w/decorative leaves, Continental #524, 11 x 22" **45**

Tray, loop end handles, oval w/upturned scalloped rim, large stamped oval wreath of leafy branches, fern leaves, berries & blossoms, signed "C.C. Pflanz," Canterbury Arts, 17 x 22" (ILLUS. top next page) **50-75**

Tray, polo players decoration w/trophy inscribed with winners' names, dated "4-23-39," Wendell August, 8 x 23" **95**

Trivet, hammered, oval, cork pads, leaves decoration, Everlast, 5 1/2 x 7" **10**

Trivet, hammered, cork pads, wildflowers decoration, Everlast, 10" d. **12**

Trivet, hammered, cork pads, ivy decoration, Everlast, 8 x 11" **12**

Trivet, hammered, cork pads, Tapestry patt., Arthur Armour, 8 1/2 x 11" **20-30**

Tumbler, hammered, applied floret & leaves, World, 20 oz. **10**

Tumbler, hammered, bamboo joint design, Everlast **10**

Tumbler, hammered, beaded base, Buenilum **6**

Tumbler, hammered, footed, chrysanthemum decoration, Continental **18-25**

Tumbler, hammered, plain, Buenilum **5**

Large Tray with Leaf & Berry Wreath

Tumbler, hammered, plain, Everlast...................... 5
Tumbler, hammered, plain, Leumas...................... 4
Tumbler, hammered, stemmed base, light-
weight, unmarked 6
Tumbler, spun, wheat decoration, West
Bend... 4

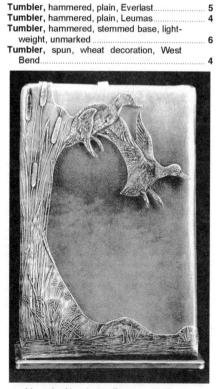

Vase in Aluminum Frame with Ducks

Vase, hammered, blue pottery in aluminum
holder w/flying ducks & marsh scene,
Wendell August #840 (ILLUS.)..................... **450**
Vase, hammered, fluted top, World, 8" h............. **45**

Continental #630 Vase

Vase, hammered, flared foot & slightly flar-
ing cylindrical body w/incurved rim, chry-
santhemum decoration, Continental #30,
10" h. (ILLUS.) **55**
Vase, hammered, hollyhock decoration,
Wendell August #858, 12" h. **300**
Vase, hammered, urn-shaped w/handles,
World #207, 12" h... **125**

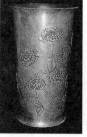

Large Wendell August Vase

Vase, wide slightly flaring cylindrical form
w/rolled rim, zinnia decoration, Wendell
August, 12" h. (ILLUS.)............................. **275-300**

Wastebasket, hammered, fluted top, apple blossoms decoration, Wendell August #900 95

Wastebasket, hammered, lightweight, water lilies stamped design, West Bend 10

Wastebasket with Bittersweet Design

Wastebasket, hammered, oval, Bittersweet patt., folded grooved top rim, Wendell August Forge (ILLUS.) 125

Wastebasket Signed in the Design

Wastebasket, hammered, oval cylindrical form, embossed detailed floral bouquet design, signed in the pattern "CC Pflanz," Canterbury Arts (ILLUS.) 195

Wastebasket, hammered, oval, dogwood & butterfly decoration, Arthur Armour.............. 115

Wastebasket, hammered, oval, floral bouquet decoration, Canterbury Arts 150-195

Everlast Apple Wastebasket

Wastebasket, hammered, oval w/ruffled rim, embossed Apple (hawthorn) patt., Everlast (ILLUS.) 75

Wastebasket, hammered, wildflowers decoration, Everlast.................................... 65

Wine Cooler & Stand

Wine cooler & stand, a tapering cylindrical container w/flared & ruffled rim, angled side handles, fitted in a ring support on a tall standard above a disc over four outswept supports on a ring foot, applied panels of grapes under the handles, sometimes marked "Everlast Ice Cooler," Everlast #5005, cooler 8 1/2 d., 9 1/2 h., overall 34" h., 2 pcs. (ILLUS.) 150

Brass

In olden days brass was referred to as a factitious or artificial metal, meaning it was an alloy, not an element. Brass is an alloy of copper and zinc; each must be mined and refined before the alloy can be produced. Prior to 1871, brass was made by combining copper with calamine, which is the ore of zinc, as metallurgists did not know how to extract the zinc from the ore. The refining process was patented in England in 1871. This discovery did much to aid in the production of brass as we know it. Braziers and brass founders were important members of the community as they were responsible for creating many of the utilitarian and decorative items used in daily living. Brassware was made of sheet metal or it was cast in a mold. Early brass ingots were hammered into sheets; however, with the inception of rolling mills in America in the eighteenth century, the work was made much simpler. The work of the brass founder was done on a small scale, perhaps in a smelting hut, which suggests a rather unsubstantial set-up. It would probably consist of a furnace with a chimney to carry off the smoke, a pair of bellows and a hearth where the fire was made. It is this hearth that distinguishes the furnace from a forge. In the middle of the hearth was a small cavity about ten to twelve inches wide. It was divided in two by an iron grate; the upper part held the crucible and fuel, the lower portion received the ashes. Dry wood was used as the fuel, and when the maximum temperature was reached, the crucible full of metal was placed in the middle covered by an earthen lid. When the metal reached the molten state it would be poured into a mold. After the article was removed from the mold it needed finishing, such as the removal of rough edges. The final step would be the polishing. Some items were signed by the maker but, as a rule, they are unsigned. Some items that were made in brass are andirons, fireplace tongs and shovels, pots, pans and kettles, various types of tools, bells, buttons and buckles, furniture hardware, door knockers, bed and foot warmers, candlesticks, candle sconces, teakettles and many, many other useful and ornamental items.

Andirons, cast, figural, cast in the half-round as a profile of a hound seated at attention w/rear legs & tail tucked underneath hind quarters, late 19th - early 20th c., 13 1/4" h., facing pair........................... **$3,220**

Fine Decorated Federal Andirons

Andirons, Federal style, a large belted ball top w/a tall turned finial resting on a high square plinth engraved w/flowers & a bow-knotted wreath surrounding a monogram "B," a stylized flower on two flanking sides, on arched spurred front legs w/ball feet, attributed to R. Wittingham, New York, early 19th c., surface scratches, grime, 19 3/4" h., pr. (ILLUS.) **4,313**

Trench Art Ashtray

Ashtray, Trench art-type, round base of a 105mm shell casing w/the central pierced stem, World War I era, 4" d. (ILLUS.)............. **15**

Cast Brass Operative Badge

Badge, cast, circle stamped w/"American Protective League" at outer rim, surrounding inner rim stamped w/"Auxiliary to U.S. Dept of Justice," which surrounds the number "106" in the middle, all topped by banner stamped "Operative" topped by spread-winged eagle, 1 3/8 x 2 3/8" (ILLUS.) **145**

Plated Brass Peace Officers Badge

Badge, plated, star shape printed w/"Peace Officer" that sits inside ring printed w/ "Minnesota Public Safety Commission," 2 1/4" d. (ILLUS.).. **185**

Seth Thomas Brass Barometer

Barometer, aneroid-type, model of a ship's wheel, Seth Thomas, American (ILLUS.)..... **150**

Bonschur & Holmes Barometer

Plated Brass Souvenir Bookmark

Barometer, aneroid-type, round frame w/silvered metal dial, 5" d. beveled glass cover w/mercury half-round thermometer, by Bonschur & Holmes, Philadelphia, Pennsylvania (ILLUS.) **225**

Bookmark, plated, teardrop-shape souvenir of the Empire State Building w/image of building in oval above page clip, 1 1/2 x 3 3/4" (ILLUS.) **35**

Box, hand-forged, book-shaped, the covers engraved overall w/biblical scenes, Europe, ca. 1750, 2 1/2 x 4 3/4", 1" h. (ILLUS. below) **1,500**

Early European Brass Basin

Brass Cachepot

Basin on pedestal, the deep rounded bowl w/a wide flattened rim & flanged base raised on a funnel-form ringed & tiered pedestal base, Europe, 18th c., 10 1/4" d., 7 3/4" h. (ILLUS.) **489**

Cachepot, rounded tapering paneled shape w/ring handles attached to four lion head decorations, short scroll feet, late 19th c., 11 3/4" d., 10 h. (ILLUS.) **448**

Early Engraved Book-shaped Box

Candelabra, brass & crystal, six-light, a pyramid prism finial supporting a crystal beadwork stem, decorated w/scrolling arms, prism garlands & beads, brass base supporting six scrolling arms ending w/candleholders, 19th c., 13" d., 29" h., pr. (some decoration missing) 728

Candleholder, brass, Arts & Crafts style, three-light w/a tiered design, three square candle sockets w/square rims raised on a C-form squared upright & spaced along an angled flat bar w/an angular curled tall upper foot & a squared small curl at the lower end, impressed "Hand Wrought L.C. Shellbarger," early 20th c., 12" l., 6" h. 330

Candleholders, brass, ship's gimbal spring-loaded holders, traces of original nickel finish, 19th c., 11" h., pr...................... 316

Brass Gorham Candleholders

Candleholders, round wide foot w/gadrooned band tapering to a tulip-form socket w/a gadrooned band, marked "Gorham Giftware L17," 3 3/4" h., pr. (ILLUS.) 40

Candlestick, brass, a dished saucer base centering a short spiral-twist standard supporting a cylindrical socket, polished, early, 6 1/4" h. (minor dents, old solder on threads of base) 220

Candlestick, brass, a flaring paneled & stepped base below the slender trumpet-form standard w/base & top rings below the cylindrical ringed socket, copper-colored patina w/traces of silver plating, 19th c., 9 1/2" h... 220

Candlestick, brass, a round dished base centered by a domed support for the columnar shaft w/flared rim & side push-up knob, England, late 18th - early 19th c., 6 3/4" h... 385

Candlestick, brass, a round ringed & domed foot below the solid knob- and ring-turned shaft w/a wide center drip pan, tall cylindrical socket, late 18th - early 19th c., 7 3/8" h. (minor dents) 1,100

Candlestick, brass, a square platform base raised on small peg feet, a conical lower shaft tapering to a flaring ring-turned upper shaft supporting the tall ring-turned candle socket, single-piece shaft, early, 9" h............. 248

English Candlestick with Bell

Candlestick, brass, a wide flat-bottomed dished base w/low upright sides centering a tall slender ring-turned shaft w/an open yoke suspending a bell below the tall knobbed cylindrical socket w/flared rim, England, 12 1/2" h. (ILLUS.) 495

Candlestick, brass, capstan-form, a wide flared cylindrical base supporting a wide flat disk centered by the turned & shaped cylindrical socket w/pick hole at the side, probably 18th c., 5 1/4" h. (repair to top flange) 495

Candlestick, brass, domed base & baluster stem w/mid-drip pan, early Dutch, 12 3/8" h.. 3,520

Candlestick, brass, hand-hammered, a flared rim on an egg-shaped candlecup, slender shaft ending in a bulbed cone on a disk base, incised mark of Jarvie, Chicago, early 20th c., 11" h. (spotting).............. 431

Candlestick, brass, Queen Anne-style, a round slightly domed scalloped foot centering a very slender shaft topped by a compressed knob below the cylindrical socket w/flared rim, w/push-up, England, 18th c., 9 3/8" h. (repair to rim) 275

Candlestick, brass, Queen Anne-style, scalloped domed foot below the knob-turned slender shaft below a tapering flange & the tall cylindrical socket w/scalloped socket rim, England, 18th c., 7 7/8" h. (minor casting flaws)........................ 660

Candlestick, brass, ring-turned & stepped domed base w/a ring-turned & tapering columnar shaft below the tall cylindrical socket, polished, 19th c., 8 1/2" h.................. 248

Candlestick, brass, round domed base w/flat top centered by a baluster-turned stem & tall cylindrical socket, Spain, probably 18th c., 8 3/4" h............................... 550

Candlestick, brass, round flat-topped domed foot centered by a rod- and ring-turned shaft w/a ring-turned tall cylindrical socket, shaft screws into base, early, 7 1/2" h.. 440

Candlestick, brass, wide round shallow dished base centered by a shaft w/an urn-form section below a spiraled section below the ringed cylindrical candle socket, standard screws into the base, early, 6 3/4" h.. 303

Early Dutch Brass Candlesticks

Candlesticks, brass, a domed, stepped round base below the ring- and knob-turned standard centered by a wide disk-form drip tray, tall ring-turned cylindrical shaft, Holland, 18th - 19th c., minor battering, 7 1/2" h., pr. (ILLUS.)........................... 385

Early English Brass Candlesticks

Candlesticks, brass, a flaring petal-form rounded base supporting a ringed graduated shaft w/a side candle ejector knob & a tall cylindrical socket w/flared rim, one ejector knob missing, minor dents, England, mid-18th c., 8 1/4" h., pr. (ILLUS.) .. **1,380**

Candlesticks, brass, a stepped domed round foot below a small double-knop stem supporting a tall cylindrical shaft bulbed at the bottom & w/a flared rim, w/push-ups, 19th c., 8" h., pr. **220**

Candlesticks, brass, a tall open double spiral-twist standard w/a tall slender ringed socket w/flattened rim, on a wide round dished foot w/flared sides, Europe, late 19th c., 18 1/4" h., pr. **460**

Candlesticks, brass, flaring domed & stepped octagonal base below the tapering knob-turned standard & waisted cylindrical socket, early, 9" h., pr. **660**

Candlesticks, brass, "King of Diamonds" patt., a squared foot w/beveled corners supporting a tall knob- and ring-turned shaft w/a bulbous diamond pattern central knob, tall cylindrical socket w/flattened rim, w/push-ups, England, late 19th c., 12 1/2" h., pr. **495**

Candlesticks, brass, Neo-classical w/push-ups, 5 1/2" h., pr. **105**

Candlesticks, brass, octagonal base w/turned standard, w/push-ups, Victorian, 12" h., pr. **121**

Early Pricket Candlestick

Candlesticks, brass, pricket-type, a dished top centered by a tall tapering candle spike above a baluster-, ring- and knob-turned stem above a lower disk on a flaring cylindrical base raised on ball feet, ecclesiastical markings, early, 15" h., pr. (ILLUS. of one) **3,300**

Brass Pricket-type Candlestick

Candlesticks, brass, pricket-type spike above ring & turned column over wide drip pan above ring & turned baluster stem on domed circular ringed foot, Europe, late 17th to early 18th c., dents & repairs, 15" h., pr. (ILLUS. of one) **805**

Candlesticks, brass, "Prince of Diamonds" patt., a squared domed foot below the tall shaft w/ringed sections above & below the central bulbous diamond patterned section, a tall cylindrical socket w/flared rim, w/push-ups, marked "The Diamond Prince," England, 19th c., 11 7/8" h., pr........ **448**

Candlesticks, brass, "Princess of Diamonds" patt., a squared domed foot below the tall shaft w/ringed sections above & below the central bulbous diamond patterned section, a tall cylindrical socket w/flared rim, w/push-ups, marked "The Diamond Princess," England, 19th c., pr. **448**

Candlesticks, brass, Queen Anne-style, a round scalloped base below the slender ring-turned shaft w/a tall cylindrical socket w/flattened rim, England, 18th c., 7 1/2" h., pr. **1,870**

Candlesticks, brass, Queen Anne-style, scalloped base & baluster stem w/seam, 6 3/4" h., pr. (one has old repair) **990**

Candlesticks, brass, Queen Anne-style, square base w/invected corners, detailed stem w/scalloped lip, 8" h., pr..................... **1,045**

Candlesticks, brass, "Queen of Diamonds" patt., a squared domed foot below the tall shaft w/ringed sections above & below the central bulbous diamond patterned section, a tall cylindrical socket w/flared rim, w/push-ups, marked "The Queen of Diamonds," England, 19th c., 11 1/4" h., pr. **644**

Candlesticks, brass, round tapering foot below a baluster- and ring-turned shaft w/a tall cylindrical socket w/flattened rim, original push-ups, 19th c., 12" h., pr.............. 275

Candlesticks, brass, rounded stepped & domed foot w/scalloped edge tapering to a tall slender paneled & ring-turned shaft below the tall ring socket w/a removable scalloped bobêche, France, late 18th - early 19th c., 9 5/8" h., pr............................ 1,650

Candlesticks, brass, square base, knob-turned column w/flaring socket, late 19th to early 20th c., 10 1/2" h., pr................ 110

Candlesticks, brass, square bobêche over baluster-shaped stem & square base, ca. 1800, 9 1/2" h., pr............................ 280

Candlesticks, brass, tapering baluster-form fluted shaft, domed paneled square base w/dentil borders, 19th c., 9 5/8" h., pr. (small base loss, wear) 403

Early Brass Candlesticks

Candlesticks, brass, trumpet-form base tapering to wide drip pan below cylindrical sausage-turned column, England, late 17th c., 7 9/16" h., pr. (ILLUS.)................ 13,800

Candlesticks, brass, Victorian w/push-ups, diamond & beehive detail, 10 3/4" h., pr...... 110

Candlesticks, brass w/push-ups, baluster-shaped stem resting on chamfered base, early 19th c., 10 1/2" h., pr........................... 308

Candlesticks, brass, wide domed base w/turned baluster stem, mid-drip plate, not seamed, one w/casting hole filled w/solder, 11 1/4" h., pr.................................. 495

Chamberstick, brass, a shallow round dished base w/upright finger loop handle at the side, a cylindrical shaft w/candle ejector knob & a flared flattened socket rim, 19th c., 4 3/4" h. 275

Chandelier, Rococo-style, cast, six-light, long triple leafy scrolled drop arms above a central inverted dome issuing six arms ending in sockets, each ornately cast w/acanthus leaves w/further pendent trumpet-form blossoms & leaves, cast-in label w/"Made in Spain," mid-20th c., 24" d., 20" h. (braised repairs on two flowers).. 330

Chandelier, six-light, the six boldly scrolled brass arms hung w/cut glass chains, each arm ending in a gas socket w/an etched glass shade & blue stained-glass decorative sockets & bobêches, American-made, late 19th c., 38" h...................... 863

Brass Chandelier w/Steuben Shades

Chandelier, w/five Steuben art glass shades, domed brass ceiling mount terminating w/a hook, chain drop supporting fixture w/raised leaf decorations & five shade mounts & bell-form gold lustre glass shades w/gold hearts & threading & gold Aurene interiors, silver fleur-de-lis acid stamp, Corning, New York, drop 39 1/2", 19" d., chips to some top rims (ILLUS.).. 1,265

Steuben Glass & Brass Chandelier

Chandelier, w/six Steuben art glass shades, circular domed ceiling mount w/three chain drops, supporting round domed fixture w/etched curvilinear & floral motifs & extensions suspending six bell-form glass shades w/ruffled rims, creamy white lustre & pulled gold Aurene striations on rims, gold Aurene interiors, shape No. 2282, silver fleur-de-lis acid stamp, drop 23", 20 1/2" d., dents on shade mounts (ILLUS.) 6,325

Chandelier, Dutch Baroque-style, eight-light, a wrought-iron chain suspending a ring-turned slender standard, the medial collar issuing eight spurred scrolling candlearms centering star designs & terminating in drip pans & cylindrical candle sockets, a large ball-shaped lower drop w/a pendent finial, late 19th - early 20th c., 24" d., 18" h. 1,035

Chandelier, six-light, a long ring- and knob-turned standard w/ornate S-scrolls attached to the sides above the six downswept S-scroll candlearms ending in drip pans & tall cylindrical candle cups, a large ball drop at the bottom w/a baluster-turned drop finial, Holland, 18th c., 17" d., 19" h. 1,495

Chandelier, Queen Anne-style, six-light, a slender ring- and urn-turned top section suspended from a heavy hanging ring, a large spherical ball base suspending a small ring, six S-scroll long arms issuing from the top section & ending in wide-dished drip pans centered by tall tapering cylindrical candle sockets, 18th c., 27 1/2" d., 21" h. plus hanging chain (chain not old) 3,080

Elaborate Brass Cigarette Dispenser

Cigarette dispenser, two concentric circles form base, w/a shaft connected to a globe that holds cigarettes, top part of globe pulls open & retracts to close, cigarettes pop out when globe is opened, when open 4 1/4 x 6 1/2", 11 1/4" h. (ILLUS.) 150

Coal scuttle, tapered form w/two hinged lids, bail handle, decorated w/repoussé work w/masks & scrolled foliage, 19th c., 20" h. 259

Plated Brass Corkscrew

Corkscrew, plated, retractable, in the shape of a beer bottle w/Anheuser Busch label, when open measures 5/8 x 2 1/2 x 2 3/4" (ILLUS.) 75

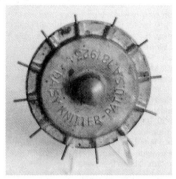

Stamped Brass Daisy Knitter

Daisy knitter, stamped, w/retractable spokes, patent number stamped in circle around center knob, 5/8 x 1 7/8" (ILLUS.) 25

Door knocker, cast, urn & acorn form w/original fastenings, America or England, late 19th - early 20th c., 4 1/4 x 7 3/4" 115

Doorknocker, figural, model of a grotesque sea creature, late 19th c., 12" h. 863

Drink Heating Set

Drink heating set, Arts & Crafts style, a Colonial Revival design w/a tall square brass lidded tankard w/strap handle & a long-handled heating rod w/egg-shaped tip, on a square iron base marked "Cape Cod Trademark" & w/an embossed image of a fish, probably for mulling wine, early 20th c., 12" h., the set (ILLUS.) 295

Ewers, a wide round stepped base below a very slender stem supporting a slender tapering ovoid body engraved around the middle w/a palmette band w/an applied mask mount at the front, a very tall slender ringed neck ending in a high upright curved spout, a long slender arched & scrolled handle from the top rim to the shoulder, late 19th c., 16 3/4" h., pr. (one handle loose) 248

Early Fireplace Fender

Fireplace fender, brass & wire, long slender upper & lower brass rails curving at the ends to form fender & enclosing a decorative latticework wire band above a fine wire lower vertical band interwoven w/wire scrolls, upper rail set w/three ball finials, America or England, late 18th - early 19th c., minor dents, 18 x 43 1/2", 12 1/4" h. (ILLUS.) **2,070**

Fireplace fender, brass & wire, long slender upper & lower brass rails curving at the ends to form fender & enclosing a decorative latticework wire band above a fine wire lower vertical band interwoven w/wire scrolls, America or England, late 18th - early 19th c., 15 x 49 1/2", 10" h. **2,875**

Masonic Emblem Picture Frame

Frame, cast, table model, in the form of the Masonic emblem w/a picture opening in the center, swing-out wire back support, gilt finish, patent-dated in October 1899, 7" w., 9 5/8" h. (ILLUS.) **145**

Floral-decorated Brass Frame

Frame, stamped, table model, delicate pierced designs of flowers, leaves & branches across the top & base, late 19th c., 5 x 8 1/4" (ILLUS.) **58**

Frame, stamped, table model, horizontal oval form supported by ornate pierced scrolls at the sides, late 19th c., 6 1/4 x 10 1/4" (ILLUS. below) **65**

Hall lanterns, brass, four-light, Georgian-style, round w/glazed panels between the brass uprights, one panel a hinged door, the upper rim w/beaded swags suspended from ribbons, undulating braces from the top rim to the center shaft which drops down into the center & curves up to end in candle sockets, England, 12 1/2" d., 14 3/4" h., pr. (electrified) **4,025**

Hat rack, wall-type, Arts & Crafts style, square form w/embossed oak leaves & acorns on a textured ground, three iron double hooks, fitted w/a mirror, early 20th c., 20 1/2" w. **316**

Rare English Brass Honor Box

Oval Victorian Frame with Scrolls

Honor box, cov., deep rectangular sides, raised on four tiny bun feet, the top w/a T-shaped coin slot & flip-up cover, top w/engraved design & inscription "A sixpence put into the till, when the lid opens you may fill, when you have fill'd with out delay, shut down the lid or a shilling pay - William Shanlike," England, 18th c., w/key, 5 3/4" l. (ILLUS. on previous page) **4,620**

Cast Brass Incense Burner

Incense burner, cast, classical urn shape w/pagoda form lid, raised on three slender legs joined by stretchers, early 20th c., 2 1/4" d., 4 3/4" h. (ILLUS.) **40**

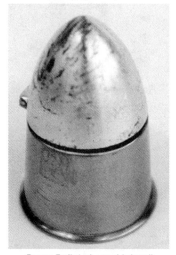

Brass Bullet-shaped Inkwell

Inkwell, bullet-shaped w/ring foot, hinged plated top, English, 2 1/4" d., 3 1/4" h. (ILLUS.) **175**

Roycroft Hammered Brass Inkwell

Inkwell, cov., hammered, round on spreading foot, w/glass insert, cover w/rounded finial, maker's mark on bottom, Roycroft, 3 1/4" d., 3 1/4" h. (ILLUS.) **950**

Brass Jewelry Box with Jewels

Jewelry box, cov., rectangular, flat-topped domed cover w/Art Nouveau-style cast scrolls & inset amethyst-colored glass jewels, the low base cast w/fern leaves & beading, marked "Latauska - Patented July 28, 1924," 4 3/4 x 6 1/2", 2" h. (ILLUS.) **129**

Early Signed Kerosene Lantern

Kerosene lantern, brass & glass, a tall clear cylindrical glass globe topped by a pierced cylindrical brass cap w/pierced air holes & a domed top w/a swing strap handle, the base w/a short cylindrical font & burner on a round foot, bottom labeled "N.E. Glass Co. Patented Oct. 24, 1854," split in foot, top dented, 16 1/2" h. plus handle (ILLUS.) **330**

Kettle, cylindrical spun form w/wrought-iron
bail handle, marked "Haydens Patent,"
19th c., 24 1/2" d., 18" h. 193
Kettle, spun, cylindrical w/wrought-iron bail
handle, marked "The American Brass
Kettle," 13 3/4" h. (minor splits) 165
Kettle, round spun-type w/iron bail handle,
14" d. (dents) 61

Early Brass Kettle Stand

Kettle stand, a rectangular scroll-pierced
top above a deep pierced apron w/scroll-
cut edges & upturned end handles,
raised on two bulbous cabriole brass
front legs & cast iron back legs & apron,
probably　England,　19th　c.,
11 1/2 x 14 3/4", 13 1/4" h. (ILLUS.) 440

Early French Microscope

Microscope, brass & iron, single adjustable
lens on pedestal base w/"U"-form foot,
marked "E. Hartnack & A. Prasmowski,
Paris," France, ca. 1870 (ILLUS.) 171

Early Viennese Microscope

Microscope, brass & iron, single adjustable
lens on pedestal base w/"U"-form foot,
marked "C. Reichart, Wien," Vienna,
Austria, ca. 1880 (ILLUS.) 246
Microscope, brass & steel, w/an 8x eye-
piece & single-power lens, Spencer Lens
Company, w/mahogany case, 14 1/4" h. 105

Brass Microscope from 1780

Microscope, by "J. Simons, London," on
wood base w/shallow drawer for attach-
ments, English, 1780 (ILLUS.) 2,875
Microscope, small size w/two brass sec-
tions w/a mirror, includes four fittings
w/different magnifications, three slides
included w/botanical specimens & early
handwritten note w/details about the
slides, 19th c., 3 x 7 3/4", 2 1/8" h., cased
set 165

Mirror in Fancy Cast Frame

Mirror, cast, table model, the upright oblong frame cast at each side w/a putto, leaves, grape cluster & roses across the top & scrolls & a basket of flowers across the bottom, goldtone finish, late 19th - early 20th c., 8 x 12 1/4" (ILLUS.) **165**

Mirror, table model, hand-hammered, a curved, stepped rectangular frame w/an attached hinged stand, impressed mark of Rorag Wien, Vienna, Austria, early 20th c., 12" h. (minor discoloration) **259**

Brass Rococo Design Mirror Frame

Mirror frame, hanging-type, an ornate rectangular rococo design composed of pierced scrolls & a tall scroll finial, early 20th c., 11 1/2 x 16 1/2" (ILLUS.) **145**

Small Model of an Airedale

Model of a dog, stylized Art Deco seated Airedale on oval base, 2" h. (ILLUS.) **50**

Brass Mortar & Pestle

Mortar & pestle, footed short bell-form mortar w/flaring rim, matching ring-turned pestle, mortar 5" d., 3 1/2" h. (ILLUS.) **110**

Unusual Duck Head Paper Clamp

Paper clamp, cast, hanging-type, figural, model of a mallard duck head, painted w/red glass eyes, spring-loaded, late 19th - early 20th c., 5" l. (ILLUS.) **125**

Figural Fox Paperweight

Paperweight, cast, figural, a walking fox atop a thin rectangular plaque raised on scrolls over a round base, 2 1/4 x 5 3/4", 4 3/4" h. (ILLUS.) **45**

Brass Art Deco Perfumer

Perfumer, footed, tapering cone shape w/raised Art Deco design, wide flaring stopper, black glass insert, marked on bottom "Apollo 3197," 5 1/2" h. (ILLUS. previous page) **100**

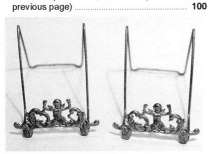

Miniature Picture Easels

Picture easels, miniature, cast-brass & iron, gold-tone finish, decorated w/cherubs & C-scrolls, one marked on back "Howell" & one marked "H," 3 3/4 x 4 x 5 3/4", the pr. (ILLUS.) **100**

Pitcher, cov., Art Nouveau style, floral decorated cone-shaped body w/a simple scrolling handle, rounded molded base, cover w/spade-shaped finial, ca. 1890, 14" h. **146**

Planter, table top type, oval w/deep upright sides raised on four short scroll-cast feet, molded top & bottom edges & decorated around the sides w/continuous wide band of classical urns & leaf clusters, France, ca. 1865, 7 x 9 1/2", 6 1/4" h. **380**

Samovar, footed bulbous urn-form w/flaring neck, including chimney & underliner, Russia, late 19th c., 20 1/2" h. **230**

Brass Spring-loaded Scale

Scale, spring-loaded, w/ring handle and stamped w/company name and weight measures, Frary, 1 x 1 3/4", 10" h. (ILLUS.) **15**

Old Brass School Bell

School bell, hand-held type, simple turned-wood handle, 8" h. (ILLUS.) **69**

Brass Sewing Clip

Sewing clip, marked "Webster's patented Feb. 3, 1874," 5/8 x 2 1/2" (ILLUS.) **75**

Skimmer, round pierced brass bowl w/a long wrought-iron handle, 19th c., 18 1/2" l. **99**

Brass Smoking Accessories

Smoking set, three pieces w/raised square design on rims, set includes 11 1/4" d. tray, match holder & 11 1/4" h. cigarette holder, Bradley & Hubbard, the set (ILLUS.) **350**

Spectroscope, brass tubes on a base, signed "James Queen, Philadelphia," 9 1/4" h. (some areas of corrosion on tubes) **220**

Cast Brass Advertising Spoon

Spoon, cast, in stylized Arabic motif, w/long handle w/crescent-shaped end stamped "Monarch," advertising Monarch Ranges of Keewaskum, Wisconsin, in bowl w/picture of range in diamond within border, 1 1/4 x 6 3/8" (ILLUS.) **125**

Surveyor's level, brass & enameled brass, engine-turned rings for the sighting tube, w/a mahogany case, Bausch, Lomb & Saegmuller, case 8 3/8 x 21" (some wear) **303**

Surveyor's level, lacquered brass, marked "C.L. Berger & Sons, Boston Mass - 31217" on base, in fitted wood case, ca. 1920 .... **840**

Surveyor's level, W. & L.E. Gurley, w/original carrying case & tripod, case 6 3/8 x 11 1/4", the set (some case wear) **303**

Surveyors transit, the silver dial labeled "Herm Pfister, Maker, Cincinnati," complete w/a mahogany case w/paper label "Wm. H. Pfister, successor to Herm Pfister," w/tripod & transit, Ohio, 12" h. transit .. **1,320**

English Brass Telescope on Tripod

Telescope, on adjustable oak tripod stand, long brass case w/various adjusting mechanisms, w/original fitted mahogany case, made by J.H. Steward Ltd. of London, ca. 1900, 46" l. (ILLUS.) **1,792**

Brass Telescope on Tripod

Telescope, on expandable tripod base, made by Thomas J. Evans, English, ca. 1900, 24 1/2" h. (ILLUS.) **560**

Trivet, long slender spade form w/hearts & diamond cut-outs, 10" l. **110**

Trivet, slender spade-form w/a heart-shaped handle w/heart opening above a diamond opening & a large central heart opening, on three peg feet, 9 5/8" l. **138**

Urns, Art Deco style, flattened baluster form w/a flared base & wide flared neck, designed by Josef Hoffmann, marked "Wiener Werkstatte - Made in Austria," ca. 1925, 6 1/4" h., pr. (small unobtrusive dents to rim corners) **1,380**

Roycroft Brass Bud Vase

Vase, bud-type, trapezoid base holding curved arm ending in open circle that holds glass vial-like vase, maker's mark on bottom, Roycroft, 7 1/4" h. (ILLUS.) **395**

Hammered Brass Trench Art Vase

Vase, Trench art-type, hammered, domed foot below swelled cylindrical body w/flaring ruffled rim, overall hand-hammered background w/embossed bow & roses, ca. 1917, 4 1/2" d., 11 1/2" h. (ILLUS.) **135**

Vase, hand-hammered Arts & Crafts style, shell casing-type w/a slightly tapering cylindrical lower section w/a widely flaring upper section w/a deeply ruffled rim, Dirk Van Erp, early 20th c., impressed "U.M.C. Co.," 6" d., 9 3/4" h. (light wear to patina) **1,430**

Wall sconce, a cast fixture w/scrolled arms, candle cup & drip dish fitted into a stepped circular bracket, 19th c., 11 3/8" l. **374**

Wall sconces, each w/oval reflector plate decorated w/pair of winged putti flanked by stylized foliage & fruit, centers a convex reserve w/C-scroll embossed surrounds, two removable serpentine projecting candle-arms below, cylindrical candle cups w/dished drip plates, 12 1/2" w., 16" h., pr.. **13,800**

Whale oil lamps, ring-turned inverted acorn-form fonts w/burners on a baluster- and knob-turned standard on a domed round foot, 8 1/2" h., pr. **715**

Brass Whale Oil Lantern

Whale oil lantern, a squared metal font base below the upright square framework enclosing four beveled clear glass panels, one forming a hinged door, a domed metal top w/mushroom-form vent cap, wire bail handle w/turned wood grip, fitted w/unusual whale oil burner, damage & splits to vent cap, 9 1/4" h. plus handle (ILLUS.) **110**

Wick Trimmer & Stand

Wick trimmer & stand, a ringed & slightly flaring cylindrical cup atop a knopped stem on a stepped, squared foot, ring handle w/thumb rest at side of rim, holds scissor-form trimmer, handle soldered, England, probably 19th c., 4" h. (ILLUS.) **330**

Dutch Brass Wine Cooler

Wine cooler, deep ovoid form w/wide ga-drooned band below the flaring ribbed neck, lion mask & ring end handles, raised on four paw feet, Holland, early 19th c., 8 1/4 x 12", 6 1/4" h. (ILLUS.) **715**

Bronze

The era known as the Bronze Age occurred between the Neolithic Period, which was a phase of the Stone Age, and the Iron Age. The Bronze Age was a stage of cultural development when bronze, an alloy of copper and tin, was utilized in the production of many forms of tools, weapons and other articles. Bronze is basically an alloy of copper and tin, but it can also contain small amounts of zinc and phosphorus. Alloys with up to eight percent tin are used mainly for cold-worked products such as sheets, wire and coins. Gears, bearings and marine hardware utilize the alloy with eight to twelve percent tin. The principal product of the twenty to twenty-five percent alloy is bells, as this alloy is very hard and extremely brittle. From an engineering standpoint, the alloy containing less than twenty percent tin is the most useful. In modern usage some alloys containing no tin are considered bronze. These alloys consist of mixtures of copper and aluminum, silicon or beryllium. As one of the oldest artificially produced alloys, bronze articles have been found in archaeological digs and have been instrumental in giving us some insight into life as it existed in early times. There are, of course, many bronze items, both decorative and utilitarian, that are easily found today. Some of these articles include vases, chalices, jardinieres, lamps, marine hardware, urns and, although not included in this survey, statuary. The early wares are rarely signed, but the more recent pieces from the 17th century onward are sometimes marked by their maker.

Tiffany Floor Model Ashtray

Ashtray, floor model, an elaborate platform base w/ribbed tripartite shaft w/knob ends flaring to support a shallow dished tray & bowl-form holder w/mesh ash receiver, impressed "Tiffany Studios New York 1658," 24 1/2" h. (ILLUS. on previous page)......... **$1,265**

Tiffany Studios Bronze Ashtray

Ashtray, floor model, gold finish, flared base supporting long shaft holding bowl-shaped tray w/hinged top & match holder, marked on base "Tiffany Studios, New York, No. 1649," 9 x 28" (ILLUS.)............. **2,995**

Ashtray, floor model, bright gold patina w/etched surface on an elaborate artichoke pattern on a platform base & shaft, supporting a hinged conforming gilt-metal ash receiver, base impressed "Tiffany Studios New York 1651," 25 1/2" h. **1,035**

Bronzed Baby Shoes

Baby shoes, high-button, worn-looking, 2 1/2 x 4", 6 1/2" l., the pr. (ILLUS.)................ **35**

Cast Bronze Book End

Book ends, cast, copper finish, flat base merging into upright embossed w/heads of Abraham Lincoln & George Washington in profile, 4" h., the pr. (ILLUS. of one)...... **195**

Knight Book End

Book ends, cast, silver finish, stepped base, arched open Moorish-style upright w/figure of knight in armor holding a shield standing between pillars w/background of embossed vining leaves, marked on reverse "Travelers Convention, Palm Beach, Florida, 1931 - patent pending," 3 x 4 1/2", 8" h., the pr. (ILLUS. of one)............................ **250**

Bronze Racehorse Book Ends

Book ends, gold finish, marbled onyx bases hold models of racehorses, 3 x 9 1/4", 8" h., the pr. (ILLUS.)...................................... **475**

European Bronze Sack-form Bowl

Bowl, sack-form, ovoid w/flattened front & back, two handles projecting from each side, the lower half w/a naturalistic texture & green patina, the upper section cast overall w/scrolls & dots, Gustave Gurschner, impressed "Gurschner - 157," Europe, ca. 1900, 6" h. (ILLUS. on previous page) 1,610

Bowl, wide shallow dished form w/flattened etched rim, gold doré finish, signed "Tiffany Studios - New York - #1707," 9" d. 275

Box, cov., Art Deco style, rectangular w/deep sides, the cover cast in relief w/a scene of a child w/two geese, light patina, attributed to Alice M. Wright, initialed "AMW," 4" l. 201

Box, cov., Arts & Crafts style, rectangular w/a hinged lid decorated w/an etched central six-sided oval reserve flanked by scroll designs & geometric outlining, mottled texture on recessed areas, wood-lined interior, impressed marks of Silver Crest, early 20th c., 3 5/8 x 6 1/4", 1 1/2" h...................... 40

Box, cov., hand-hammered, Arts & Crafts style, rectangular w/flat overhanging cover centered by a figural antelope, original patina, probably Europe, early 20th c., 3 x 4"...... 143

Cachepot, patinated & parcel gilt in Japanese taste, of deep lobed circular-form, tapering to a ring foot, body applied w/gilt birds in flight or perched on blossoming branches, rim & base also in gilding, 11" d. (some wear) 862

Candelabra, gilt-decorated, five-light, Empire-Style, modeled as a winged classical female figure on a floral-cast columnar pedestal, supporting above her head a floral corona topped by swan-form candlearms, Europe, late 19th c., 26 1/2" h., pr. 3,737

Egyptian Revival Candleholder

Candleholder, Egyptian Revival style, trapezoidal footed base w/two rectangular inserts of turquoise or enamel chips, angled shaft supports candle socket w/bobêche, all decorated w/Egyptian symbols & designs, 4 1/2" h. (ILLUS.).......... 250

Candlesticks, Arts & Crafts style, hand-hammered, short baluster-form on stepped round base, unmarked, early 20th c., 2 3/4" h., pr....................... 230

Candlesticks, w/candle cup supported by three arms raised on a slender rod standard above a circular foot, impressed "Tiffany Studios New York D882," brown patina, ca. 1900, 17 3/4" h......................... 6,900

Bronze & Glass Ceiling Lantern

Ceiling lanterns, patinated bronze & engraved glass, cylindrical-form, surmounted by crown of five foliate scroll supports w/a mark terminal above a curved clear glass pane engraved w/central star within a stylized floral border, vertical supports cast w/pendant husks, golden brown patina, 28 1/2" h., pr. (ILLUS. of one)............ 3,162

Fine Chinese Bronze Censer

Censer, cov., wide ovoid body tapering to a flared neck w/serrated rim & w/large scrolling zoomorphic head handles, raised on a waisted pedestal base cast w/a finely detailed dragon, the round stepped & vented cover topped by a large Foo dog finial, rich dark brown patina, China, Ching Dynasty, 24 1/2" h. (ILLUS. on previous page) **575**

Art Deco Glass & Bronze Chandelier

Chandelier, Art Deco style, a cast-bronze paneled ceiling mount & lower shade mount cast w/a border of angular designs, the center w/a frosted glass bowl-form shade w/molded stylized flowers & geometric designs, four angled & pointed arms each suspending a conical frosted glass shade w/a molded geometric floral design, ca. 1930, 30" d., overall 26 1/2" h. (ILLUS.) **2,300**

Chandelier, Art Deco style, a domed metal ribbed ceiling plate suspending a heavy chain composed of alternating ringed alabaster knobs & oblong ribbed metal segments supporting the light fixture modeled as a stylized long-billed & long-tailed bronze bird w/the wide spread wings composed of alabaster panels, inscribed Albert Cheuret, France, ca. 1925, 24" h **94,000**

Patinated Bronze Chandelier

Chandelier, eight-light, French ormolu, the scrolled acanthus corona above a pierced barrel upright mounted w/a pair of satyrs supporting flambeaux & grotesque beast branches, w/a further pair of dragon branches each terminating in two lights, the lower section cast w/a coiled dragon, w/cut & frosted glass shades, possibly by Ferdinand Barbedienne, Paris, ca. 1880, 43 1/2" h. (ILLUS.) **18,000**

Chandelier, Empire-style, gilt- and patinated bronze, twelve-light, a large round central patinated bronze disk w/a conical top & a slightly round bottom centered by a pineapple drop, the edge band mounted w/four large figural spread-winged gilt-bronze swans each supporting three candle sockets, suspended from four chains composed of metal disks, rods & classical masks hung from the upper small round support ring w/gilt acanthus finials, Europe, 19th c., 36" h. **7,200**

Chandelier, Louis XV-Style, gilt-bronze, 18-light, of scrolling leafage basket-form, supporting six arms, each cresting in three foliate bobêches & urn-form candle sockets, Europe, 19th c., 35" d., 40" h. **4,312**

Louis XV-Style Chandelier with Putto

Chandelier, Louis XV-Style, nine-light, gilt-bronze, a scroll-cast ceiling plate suspending a long central rod flanked by three long scrolled supports each issuing three short scrolled arms ending in light sockets, a figure of a putto at the center above leafy swags, early 20th c., 36" h. (ILLUS.) **10,800**

Louis XVI Gilt-Bronze Chandelier

Chandelier, Louis XVI, gilt-bronze, twelve-light, the leaf-tip-cast central standard supporting foliate-scrolled candle branches, the upper section fitted w/a gilt-bronze & marble urn within a tri-form cage hung w/tasseled drapery, France, 18th c., 56" h., overall 86" h. (ILLUS.)...... **18,400**

Napoleon III Bronze Chandelier

Chandelier, Napoleon III, twelve-light, gilt- and patinated bronze, a central circular tier supporting S-scrolled candlearms modeled w/anthemion & foliage, suspended from flattened oval link chains, France, mid-19th c., 28" d. (ILLUS.).. **4,600**

Louis XVI-Style 15-light Chandelier

Chandelier, Louis XVI-Style, fifteen-light, gilt-bronze & glass, the top section w/five C-scrolled glass-trimmed arms supporting five long glass-trimmed arms, each arm ending w/one upturned socket & one exterior downturned socket w/beaded trim, a lower metal basket-form framework densely trimmed w/prisms & enclosing five additional sockets, a scroll-decorated base w/a pineapple drop, Europe, early 20th c., 54" h. (ILLUS.) **5,100**

Neoclassical-style Chandelier

Chandelier, Neoclassical-style, eight-light, the trumpet-form fluted central standard topped by flat leaves, flaring outward to the eight fluted cornucopia-shaped candlearms w/squat ovoid fluted nozzles, the standard ending in a similar ovoid form, finishing in an inverted pineapple finial, electrified, late 19th c., 28" w., 28" h. (ILLUS.) **3,450**

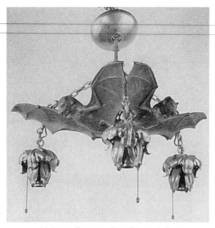

Unique Bronze Bat Chandelier

Chandelier, three-light, figural, composed of three large full-bodied spread-winged bats in a triangular formation suspended from bronze chains & a metal ceiling mount, suspending three brass foliate light fixtures, rich brown patina, early 20th c., 21 1/2" h. (ILLUS.) **7,188**

Dish, shallow round form w/a foliate border, textured surface, stamped "Tiffany Studios New York 1677," early 20th c., 6 1/2" d. (minor spotting) **144**

Small French Art Nouveau Ewer

Ewer, Art Nouveau style, ovoid melon-lobed body tapering to a narrow neck w/long pointed rim spout, high arched & looped vine handle w/leaf terminal, signed "P. Loiseau-Rousseau," light gilt patina, France, ca. 1900, small (ILLUS.) **144**

Ewers, hammered body cast & applied w/an animal-form spout & foliate handle, Dutch, 18th c., 16" h., pr. **1,955**

Rare Victorian Bronze Doorknob

Doorknob, round w/a boldly cast Victorian Aesthetic design of an Oriental style flying crane among flowering branches w/stylized borders, marked on reverse "Russel & Erwin Mfg. Co. New Britain Ct. USA," made as part of a series, early 1880s (ILLUS.) **660**

Louis XV-Style Hall Lantern

Hall lantern, Louis XV-Style, gilt-bronze, four-light, a rounded cylindrical gilt-bronze frame enclosing three clear glass curved panels, the frame decorated w/a top foliate-scrolled band & hung w/floral festoons topped by four tall arched & leaf-scrolled supports, a pierced metal gallery band around the bottom, France, 19th c., 34" h. (ILLUS.) **8,625**

William IV-style Hall Lantern

Hall lantern, William IV-style, gilt-bronze & glass, hexagonal w/each arched clear glass panel cut w/a central starburst, the ornate reeded framework w/scroll-cast arched panel tops & base scrolls at each corner, six upper scroll arms join at the top of the central reeded shaft, England, 19th c., 18" w., 30" h. (ILLUS.) **2,875**

Oriental-style Bronze Heater

Heater, cov., Oriental-style, high tripod base w/raised lizards, incised water buffalo, bats, trees, double-ring handles in mythical trunks on the hexagonal bowl, pierced detail on the lid w/raised birds & foo dog finial, chocolate brown patina (ILLUS.) **330**

Humidor, cov., Renaissance-style, the cover & sides w/panels of figures & foliage, E.F. Caldwell & Co., New York, early 20th c., 6" l. **431**

Early Meiji Bronze Incense Burner

Incense burner, in the form of a seated shishi w/ball, Japanese, early Meiji period, 9 1/4" h. (ILLUS.) **448**

Bronze Incense Burner on Base

Incense burner on base, cov., Oriental style w/finely detailed casting, stump base w/character signature (foundry mark?), old painted signature inside domed lid reads "Gruschwitz," footed pot w/relief turtle & dragon medallions, patina, 14 1/2" h. (ILLUS.) **495**

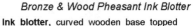

Bronze & Wood Pheasant Ink Blotter

Ink blotter, curved wooden base topped w/polychrome image of a pheasant on irregular surface, 3 x 5, 4" h. (ILLUS.) **695**

Rare Art Nouveau Bronze Jardiniere

Jardiniere, Art Nouveau style, figural, "Sommeil," a long low oval bowl w/incurved sides cast w/blossoms & leaves & mounted at each end w/a sleepy nude Art Nouveau maiden, raised on a low oblong floral-cast base w/blossoms, end handles, inscribed "Vital Cornu - Susse Fres. edt. Paris," France, ca. 1900, 29" l. (ILLUS.).. **21,850**

Fine French Bronze Jardiniere

Jardiniere, Louis XVI-Style, gilt-decorated, tall cylindrical form, the body w/a continuous cast bacchanal scene, the base band w/a Greek key border & fitted w/satyr masks & hung w/fruiting swags, raised on a shaped central pedestal & four tall slender C-scroll supports on the crossform base, the wide ringed rim case w/delicate leaf bands & large acanthus leaf mounts & side mounts for ring handles, signed "F. Barbedienne," France, late 19th c., overall 33" h. (ILLUS.)......... **20,700**

Elaborate Bronze Lamp

Lamp, electric, cold-painted, base a thin sheet representing a carpet, holds figure of Arab holding writing tablet & sitting next to small round table w/Arabic-style coffee urn, background of bamboo branches, decorated w/round shield & crossed sword & rifle, holds rectangular Moorish-style lighting unit w/domed roof, notched upper & lower rims and crescent moons dangling from corners and sitting atop dome, red & green glass inserts, bottom marked w/"B" in a vase and "Namgreb," made in Austria, 19 x 19 1/2" (ILLUS.)... **2,950**

Bronze Satyr Lamp Base

Lamp base, figural, a kneeling, leering satyr holding out in each hand an urn-form torch w/pedestal & knob w/three-light electric socket, black marble base, probably American, patinated, early 20th c., abrasions, 29" h. (ILLUS.).......................... **1,725**

Art Deco Advertising Letter Opener

Letter opener, gold finish, overall Art Deco design, advertising Howell projectors, indistinct mark on reverse, 9 1/4" l. (ILLUS.).. **55**

Bronze Commemorative Letter Opener

Letter opener, oval head embossed "100 Years - American Dental Association - 1859-1959," reverse marked "With compliments of Ritter & Co., Rochester NY," feathered wings grip envelope slicer, 6 5/8" l. (ILLUS.) **18**

Letter rack, upright backplate w/serpentine rim above three narrow letter pockets on a narrow rectangular base, Zodiac patt., original patina, impressed Tiffany Studios - New York - #1090, 12 1/2" l., 8 1/2" h. **660**

Aquamarine Luminiere

Luminiere, aquamarine, silvered, gilt & cold-painted bronze, three fish, seaweed & shells on green onyx base, Marcel-André Bouraine, French, 21" l. (ILLUS.) **23,000**

Magazine rack, bronze, upright circular sides w/an openwork design of a greyhound in stride, scrolling leaf border, American-made, ca.1930, 4 1/2 x 11 7/8", 12" h. **374**

Bronze Bausch & Lomb Medal

Medal, rectangular w/rounded corners, embossed "Bausch & Lomb Honorary Science Award" below embossed classical-style figure of woman holding lens in one hand & garland in other, 1 3/4 x 2 1/4" (ILLUS.) **35**

Cast Bronze Commemorative Medallion

Medallion, cast, commemorative, bordered rectangle w/"Massachusetts Bay Tercentenary in New England - 1630-1930" on one side and detailed scenes depicting Native Americans, Pilgrims, a flying witch, a plane, Priscilla & John Alden, etc., on reverse, all in relief, 2 5/8 x 3 1/2" (ILLUS.) **145**

Bronze Aviation Medallion

Medallion, commemorative, bordered rectangle w/embossed decoration of plane flying over beacon and "The Spirit of Aviation - 1928" on front, marked on reverse "Chicago Central Aerial Beacon, Roanoke Tower, LaSalle and Madison Streets, erected and maintained by Greenebaum & Sons Investment Co., founded 1855," 1 1/4 x 1 3/4" (ILLUS.) **45**

Medallion Honoring Labor

Medallion, commemorative, honoring labor, rectangular, w/embossed scene of classically garbed woman w/arm around boy & pointing to distant industrial scene and the word "Labor" radiating from it, 2 x 2 1/4" (ILLUS.) **75**

James J. Hill Memorial Medallion

Medallion, commemorative, in honor of James J. Hill, front shows embossed bust of Hill under Memorial w/his name underneath, reverse marked "Sept. 16, 1838 to May 29, 1916 - One of the world's greatest builders," 3 1/8" d. (ILLUS.) **65**

Bronze Commemorative Medallion

Medallion, commemorative, round, heavily embossed stylized Eastern cross on right, writing at left, to honor the 1985 national gathering in Washington, D.C. of the survivors of the Armenian genocide by the Ottoman Empire in 1915, 2 3/8" w. (ILLUS.) **65**

Dental Congress Medallion

Medallion, commemorative, round, in honor of 4th International Dental Congress held in St. Louis in 1904, front features eagle perched on scroll holding olive branch, reverse shows figure of woman holding olive branch, 2 1/4" d. (ILLUS.) **125**

Pittsburgh Bicentennial Medallion

Medallion, commemorative, round, in honor of bicentennial of Pittsburgh, front embossed w/image of city spread out under the words "Pittsburgh Bicentennial - 1758-1958," reverse features image of Fort Pitt, 3" d. (ILLUS.) **75**

Benjamin Franklin Medallion

Medallion, commemorative, round, w/embossed bust of Benjamin Franklin in profile encircled by his name and birth date, 1 7/8" d. (ILLUS. on previous page) **55**

Union Medallion

Medallion, commemorative, round, w/embossed likenesses of George Meany & William Schnitzler above "George Meany - President," "Wm. Schnitzler, Secretary & Treas." and "Amalgamated Meat Cutters & Butcher Workmen of North America, A. F. of L.," 3" d. (ILLUS.) **55**

Columbian Exposition Medallion

Medallion, commemorative, round w/raised rim, "World's Columbian Exposition - 1892-93" in banner across front & decorated w/embossed images of a spread-winged eagle, Christopher Columbus, George Washington & the signing of the Declaration of Independence, 2 1/4" d. (ILLUS.) **125**

U.S.S. Enterprise Medallion

Medallion, commemorative, silver finish, embossed w/image of U.S.S. Enterprise aircraft carrier surrounded by "U.S.S. Enterprise - Worlds Largest Ship - First Nuclear Powered Aircraft Carrier," commemorates its launching on Sept. 14, 1960 at Newport News, Va., 2 1/2" d. (ILLUS.) **45**

Chester A. Arthur Medallion

Medallion, commemorative, w/embossed profile of 21st president of United States in center surrounded by "Chester A. Arthur," dated Sept. 20, 1881, 3" d. (ILLUS.) **135**

Graf Ferdinand Zeppelin Medallion

Medallion, memorial for Graf Ferdinand Zeppelin, w/embossed profile of him on front surrounded by "Graf Ferdinand V. Zeppelin [star] 8 Juli 1838 - 8 Marz 1917" around rim, reverse shows figure of Mercury holding zeppelin, 2 5/8" d. (ILLUS.) **35**

Bronze Medallion with Bust

Medallion, round w/relief-cast bust of a Classical goddess, 5 3/4" d. (ILLUS.)............ **350**

Small Bronze Airedale Model

Model of a dog, stylized walking Airedale on a thick rectangular base, 1 1/2 x 4", 2 7/8" h. (ILLUS.).. **90**

Decorative Cast Bronze Owl

Model of owl, cast, hollow, some engraved design, Oriental lettering on back, 4 3/4" h. (ILLUS.)... **300**

Mortar & pestle, the cylindrical mortar cast w/masks & shaped dividers, Europe, late 19th c., 6" d., 2 pcs. **144**

Bronze Fairy Paperweight

Paperweight, circular base printed w/"The Good Fairy," holds figure of girl w/long hair & outstretched arms dressed in short dress that appears to be blowing in the wind, 2 x 3", 6" h. (ILLUS.) **145**

Milk Bone Elephant Paperweight

Paperweight, model of an elephant w/a large Milk Bone Dog Biscuit in its trunk, used as an advertising premium, 20th c., 4 1/4 x 5" (ILLUS.).. **250**

Bronze MGM Lion Paperweight

Paperweight, tapered rectangular base embossed "Metro Goldwyn Mayer Lion - The Greatest Star on the Screen," holds model of roaring MGM lion, 2 3/8 x 3 1/8", 5" l. (ILLUS.) **285**

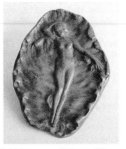

Art Nouveau Bronze Plaque

Plaque, Art Nouveau design, shallow oblong form cast w/a relief figure of a female nude standing in billowing surf, back marked "Extra" w/indistinct mark, 5 x 7" (ILLUS.)... **300**

Plate, gilt finish, dished form w/wide flat Greek key & shell border w/green enamel ovals in the center of the shells, marked "Louis Tiffany Furnaces, Inc. 309," 8 1/4" d. (minor wear)................................... **165**

Posnet (footed cooking pot), three short canted legs support the wide slightly flaring cylindrical pot w/a long straight handle extending from the rim, marked by Taylor of Richmond, Virginia, early 19th c., overall 20" l., 6" h. **4,200**

Sun dial, cast, round, mounted on a clay chimney pot, 33" h. **220**

Table lamp, Art Deco style, ring-turned ovoid standard supported on the back of four stylized lions seated on a reeded-edge square base & four low square feet, brown patina, signed on base "Oscar B. Bach," ca. 1925, 14" h. **3,450**

Art Deco Bronze Tea Cart

Tea cart, Art Deco style, a two-tier rectangular frame w/four corner uprights & legs on casters, the top ends w/a wide scroll-arched frame enclosing gilded loop & diamond scrolls, greenish patina on frame, designed by Edgar Brandt, ca. 1930, glass shelves missing, 18 x 29", 32" h. (ILLUS.).. **4,600**

Twine holder, Bookmark patt., hexagonal form w/hinged lid, gilded w/a reddish patina in the lower recesses of the decoration, impressed "Tiffany Studios New York 905," early 20th c., 3" h. (minor spotting) **1,035**

Umbrella stand, Classical style, a foliate standard surmounted by a crouching elf, the arms formed from snakes, raised on turtle feet, 19th c., 35 1/2" h. **1,092**

Fine Japanese Bronze Urn

Urn, cov., wide ovoid body w/an overall basketweave design, a low cylindrical foot below the wide round body cast in relief w/a mantis & grapevine, the wide angled shoulder also w/grapevine, a short cylindrical neck supporting a domed cover w/figural squirrel finial, the sides of the shoulder w/upright looped vine handles, set on a separate stand in the form of clusters of bamboo joined by narrow bamboo vines, stamped "Kosai tsuku-ru," Japan, Meiji Period, 12 1/4" h. (ILLUS.)................................ **6,325**

Gilt-Bronze Urn

Urn, gilt-bronze, ovoid-shape tapering to smaller flared neck, w/two handles, ornately decorated w/flowers & a bee, signed "Leon Lambert," impressed "Siot - Paris - U327," ca. 1900, original liner, 14 1/2" h. (ILLUS. on previous page) **6,325**

Fine Neoclassical Bronze Urn

Urns, campana-form, a bulbous base below the high cylindrical sides below the wide rolled rim, the sides cast in high relief w/a continuous scene of nude classical figures, lappet-cast rim & leafy scroll-cast bottom w/ribbed loop handles, raised on a ringed & reeded flaring pedestal w/square foot, Europe, 19th c., 13 1/2" h., pr. (ILLUS. of one) **5,175**

French Classical Bronze Urn

Urns, Classical Revival style, tall bullet-form body w/waisted flaring neck & upright scrolled shoulder handles, raised on three animal legs headed by cherub masks, the body cast w/a scene of Pegasus & Bellerophon, on a tripartite marble base, France, early 20th c., 18" h., pr. (ILLUS. of one) **2,185**

Urns, cov., Louis XVI-Style, gilt-decorated, tall slender ovoid body raised on a short ringed & flaring round pedestal on a square back w/blocked corners, the lower body cast w/an upright band of leafy bullrushes, leafy vine bands running up the sides & forming handles & continuing around the tapered neck w/flared rim supporting the domed leaf-cast cover, France, late 19th c., overall 18" h., pr. **2,875**

European Neoclassical Bronze Urn

Urns, cov., Neoclassical style, ovoid body tapering to a wide cylindrical neck, raised on a ringed pedestal & square foot, the body w/leaf-cast handles & overall bands of flowers, grapes, scrolls & gadrooning, the low domed cover w/cast foliage & an acorn finial, Europe, 19th c., 50" h., pr. (ILLUS. of one) **4,025**

Gilded French Bronze Urns

Urns, gilt-decorated, tall ovoid body raised on a short flaring round pedestal & square plinth, tapering to a short waisted neck flanked by arched entwined loop handles ending in a carp's mask, the body w/lappet bands around the shoulder & base & cast around the middle w/a wide continuous classical figural band, signed F. Barbedienne, Paris, France, late 19th c., 16" h., pr. (ILLUS. on previous page) **2,875**

Vase, club form w/two handles on neck, melon ribbed body, 19th c., Japanese, 8 1/4" h. (ILLUS. right, w/poppy & foliage vase) **138**

Vase, cylindrical w/raised rim & base w/relief designs & good patina, mark for Shoyeido, Japan, ca. 1800, 12 1/2" h. **165**

Vase, footed slender ovoid form tapering to a short neck w/flat rim, etched overall, the textured surface decorated around the shoulder w/drooping polished slender stylized vines, impressed mark of Silver Crest, early 20th c., 7" h. (some discoloration) **230**

Vase, tall cylindrical oval form cast around the sides w/relief figures of men on horseback, four small figures form the feet, cast signature on the base, removable tin liner, China, 19th c., 15" h. **385**

Japanese Bronze Vases

Vase, w/poppy & foliage design in relief, signature chop on base, patina w/red, Japanese, 8 1/2" h. (ILLUS. left) **275**

Vase, ovoid body tapering to a squared base on pointed tab feet, the rounded shoulder tapering to a short rolled neck issuing whiplash scrolls down the sides w/arching foliate designs around the rim & upper portion & incised w/ground cover about the lower half, brown patina, by Hector Guimard, inscribed "HG," impressed "RC" twice & "309," France, ca. 1900, 5 1/2" h. **17,250**

Vase, figural, wide bulbous body tapering to a wide cylindrical short neck w/molded rim, the lower body cast in bold relief w/the large faces of various Art Nouveau women peering out from among leafy clusters which continue up the shoulder & neck, Antonin Larroux, France, brown patination, ca. 1900, 11 1/2" h. **4,312**

Vase, the baluster-form body w/oversized faceted rim, modeled w/section of paneling resembling a swollen bamboo stalk, brownish red patina, inscribed "Lucian Bonvallet - Paris" w/monogram, ca. 1900, 15 3/8" h. **8,050**

Japanese Seascape Bronze Vase

Vase, baluster-form, cast w/a petal-form mouth & short neck, the sides w/high-relief designs of eagles, fleeing plovers, rockwork & crashing waves, Japan, Meiji Period, 19th c., 29" h. (ILLUS.) **3,162**

Japanese Bronze Vase

Vases, tall ovoid body w/a flattened rim, the sides cast in high-relief w/a scene of herons & weeping willow trees w/open branch handles, raised on matching pierced round stands, signed, Japan, late 19th c., 17" h., pr. (ILLUS. of one) **920**

Neoclassical Bronze Vases

Vases, Barbedienne-style, tall slender ovoid body tapering to a flaring mouth, raised on four hoof feet resting on a quatrefoil base, Neoclassical relief designs of bacchantes picking grapes & a classical bust, late 19th c., 17 1/2" h., pr. (ILLUS.) .. **3,105**

Wall sconce, gilt-decorated, four-light, the backplate cast w/a central shield fitted w/a winged male term issuing four foliatescrolled candle branches, Europe, ca. 1900, electrified, 38" h. **2,875**

Chrome

The only ore mineral of chromium is the mineral chromite, a chromium and iron oxide in the spinel group of minerals. The chromium element is relatively new, having been discovered by N.L. Vauguelin in 1798. Chromium metal is prepared by reducing the ore in a blast furnace with carbon or silicon to form an alloy of chromium and iron called ferrochrome. Chromium is difficult to work in its pure metal form as it is brittle at low temperatures and its high melting point makes it difficult to cast. The most important use of chromium is in chrome plating, because it forms a hard, wear-resistant and attractive surface. One of the major companies in the United States to utilize chrome plating in the manufacture of household items began as the Waterbury Manufacturing Company, which later evolved into the Chase Brass and Copper Company. This Waterbury, Connecticut, firm began setting sales records in the 1930s. Although the country was in the midst of an economic depression, people still had a desire for the low-priced but expensive-looking household items. Special departments known as Chase Shops, featuring a plethora of exciting Art Deco pieces, sprang up in stores across the country. Hostesses who could not afford to use expensive silver were delighted by the lovely chrome serving pieces. Even Emily Post, the foremost authority on etiquette at the time, endorsed the use of chrome articles when entertaining. Because of the war effort, the Chase Company discontinued its line of decorative housewares during World War II. By the time the war ended, the Art Deco chrome, formerly so popular, had lost its favor with consumers. Many other companies produced chrome items at the same time and suffered similar losses. Today the Art Deco craze has made the chrome

items popular again. Almost anything for entertaining and decoration can be found in chrome from book ends to candleholders, electric casseroles and coffee makers to cocktail sets and ice crushers to serving bowls.

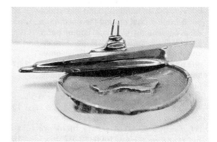

Chrome-plated Ashtray

Ashtray, ridged round base w/indents for cigarettes, w/image of Australia embossed in center, topped w/streamlined model of submarine, 5 1/2 x 7 3/4", 2 3/4" h. (ILLUS.) **$50**

Art Deco Chrome Ashtray Set

Ashtray set, a flat square chrome base w/rolled-under edges & an upright center handle holds a stack of three clear glass rectangular ashtrays, a cast-metal bronzed figure of an Art Deco nude at the back, 5" sq., 6 3/4" h., the set (ILLUS.) **85**

Glass & Chrome Basket

Basket, shallow round purple glass bowl fitted in a pierced & arched chrome frame w/a rounded footring, arched & pointed chrome swing bail handle, Farber Bros. mark on base, 5 3/8 " d., 2" h. plus handle (ILLUS.) **30-40**

Manning-Bowman Chrome Set

Beverage set: cov. pitcher, six glasses & tray; Art Deco style, footed conical-form bodies, the pitcher w/a short capped rim spout, stepped & domed cover & angular Bakelite handle, the oval tray w/marble-ized green & yellow Bakelite handles & surface, Manning-Bowman Co., ca. 1930, minor corrosion, tray 9 x 18 1/4", pitcher 13 1/4" h., the set (ILLUS.) **575**

Cow Bottle Opener/Corkscrew

Bottle opener-corkscrew, figural, model of a stylized cow w/bottle opener on head & the tail a corkscrew, overall 5 1/4" l. (ILLUS.) **75**

Boudoir lamp, cylindrical base w/an upright cylindrical metal shade depicting the styl-ized head of a woman, impressed linear facial features, American, ca. 1930, 10 1/4" h. (light pitting & spotting) **230**

Box w/hinged cover, shallow rectangular form w/the flat cover decorated w/a low-relief figure of a walking putto carrying bunches of grapes flanked by small leap-ing goats, designed by Rockwell Kent, impressed mark "R.K. - Chase - U.S.A.," 5 1/4 x 6 1/2", 1 1/2" h. **690**

Glass & Chrome Candlesticks

Candlesticks, thick clear glass candle socket w/flattened, flaring rim fitted in a pierced lacy chrome stem w/flaring ringed foot, "Krome Kraft - Farber Bros." mark on base, 4 3/4" h., pr. (ILLUS.) **80-90**

Glass & Chrome Cocktail Glass

Cocktail, rounded purple insert in pierced chrome stem by Farber Brothers, 5 3/8" h. (ILLUS.) **30**

Art Deco Chrome Cocktail Shaker

Cocktail shaker, cov., Art Deco style, ta-pering ovoid rocket-form, standing up-right on small fin feet, complete w/all at-tachments, Baltman & Co., ca. 1930, minute pitting, 3 1/2" d., 12" h. (ILLUS.) **1,610**

Compote on Chrome Nude Lady Base

Compote, open, chrome Farberware Nude
Lady stem w/amethyst bowl insert
(ILLUS.)... **125-150**
Decanter w/stopper, tapering teardrop-
form purple glass body set in a pierced
lacy chrome frame w/flaring foot, clear
glass tall pointed stopper, Farber Bros.
mark on chrome, 12" h. **60-70**

Chrome Hood Ornament

Hood ornament, stylized figure of nude
woman w/flowing hair and arms clasped
at sides, w/blue translucent plastic wings,
style number 511, 4 1/2 x 8 1/4 x 9 1/2"
(ILLUS.).. **135**

Glass & Chrome Ice Bucket

Ice bucket, high swing bail handle, deep
round cylindrical emerald green glass
bowl set in a pierced & arched chrome
base, Farber Bros. mark on base,
4 1/2" d., 6" h. plus handle (ILLUS.)........ **75-100**

Chrome-plated Iron

Iron, w/wooden handle, made by Diamond
Iron Lamp Manufacturing Co., 1936,
6 1/4" l. (ILLUS.) **50**
Lamp, desk-type, Art Deco style, composed
of a horizontal tubular shade pivoting on
an angular arm mounted on a rectangular
base, ca. 1930, 15" h................................. **1,035**

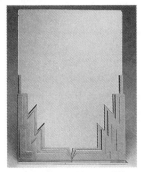

Rare Art Deco Chrome Mirror

Mirror frame, Art Deco style, squared outer
border w/inner border of stepped & zigzag cast design, supporting a large rectangular mirror, impressed "Hagenauer -
Wien - Made in Austria - Handmade," ca.
1925, 17" h. (ILLUS.) **4,025**

Chrome-plated Decorative Mouse

Model of mouse, streamlined design w/tail straight out behind, ears upright, 3 1/4" l. (ILLUS.)... **22**

Glass & Chrome Salt & Peppers

Salt & pepper shakers, bulbous green glass body tapering to a short neck w/applied green shoulder handle, chrome cap & pierced & arched chrome frame, Farber Bros. mark, 3 1/2" h., pr. (ILLUS.)........ **20-25**

Green Glass & Chrome Server

Server, cov., ovoid green glass body w/paneled sides & applied green glass handle, chrome collar w/spout & hinged cover w/pointed finial, 5" d., 10" h. (ILLUS.)... **125-150**

Serving piece, electric, three metal-lidded glass canisters in a circular electric base, signed by Chase, 15" d., 5" h........... **115**

Silent butler, shallow round purple glass bowl fitted in a pierced & arched chrome frame w/thick round foot, hinged low domed chrome cover w/engraved sunburst & thumbrest, turned wood handle, Farber Bros. mark, 5 1/4" d. w/4 3/4" l. handle, 2 3/4" h. (ILLUS. below)... **85-95**

Store display, figural, tubular metal outline of a woman's head & elongated neck curving down to spiral base, 20th c., 19 1/2" h. (minor chrome loss)............... **230**

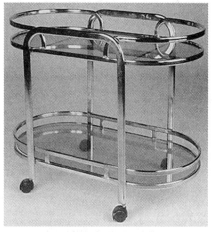

Chrome & Glass Art Deco Tea Cart

Tea cart, Art Deco style, oval metal curvilinear framework w/oblong smoky glass top & lower shelf, on casters, ca. 1930, 18 1/2 x 31 1/2", 25 3/4" l. (ILLUS.)............... **805**

Chrome & Glass Silent Butler

Copper

Copper was the first metal used by man and it is second only to iron in its utility. In Roman times, much of the copper was mined on the island of Cyprus. In the 1700s, copper was found in large quantities in four sites in the United States: the Great Lakes region now known as Michigan; an area in Connecticut; Belleville, New Jersey; and a large mining site in Maryland. Today copper is mined in many parts of the world, and the largest producer is Chile, followed by the United States, Canada and the former Soviet Union. Also known for their production of copper are Zaire, Zambia and Peru. The coppersmith, as well as the brazier or brass founder, was a very necessary member of early American communities, and his products varied depending on where he was located. The coppersmith made the items needed for day-to-day living, such as pots, pans, kettles, coffeepots, chocolate pots, ladles, teakettles and skimmers. A smith who plied his trade in an inland city made the utilitarian items as well as kettles for hatters, dyers, brewers and others. The smiths working in or near a seaport concentrated on making special items for use on ships. Copper has also been used by artisans in creating decorative pieces for the home. Many impressive copper items became especially popular during the Arts & Crafts period of the early 20th century. Especially popular and collectible are vases, candle sconces, candleholders, desk sets, humidors, clock cases, ashtrays, boxes and trays. Because of the malleability of copper, some of these articles are enhanced by hammered or tooled decoration. Although copper was the first metal used by man, it still ranks high in popularity today.

Covered Elephant Box

Box, cov., plated, stylized figure of tusked trumpeting elephant, top heavily hand-decorated, made in India, 3 x 3 3/4", 6 3/4" l. (ILLUS.)... $145

Candle lantern, sheet copper, Arts & Crafts style, an upright square form w/one side forming a hinged door, each side pierced through w/banded designs w/three starbursts in vertical alignment, each centered by a colored glass jewel, a low pointed four-sided top, original dark patina, Bradley & Hubbard, early 20th c., stamped mark, 7" sq., 12" h........................... 385

Hammered-copper Candleholder

Candleholder, hammered, Arts & Crafts style, footed domed base w/short standard holding bowl-shaped socket w/slightly curved bobêche, applied hammered-brass strap handle, 4 1/2" h. (ILLUS.).. 295

Gustav Stickley Copper Coal Scuttle

Coal scuttle, flared base, rolled rim, strap swivel handle, Gustav Stickley, 24" h. (ILLUS.)... **10,925**

Copper & White Metal Coffeepot

Coffeepot, cov., footed cylindrical body w/a wide shoulder to the short neck & hinged domed cover w/urn finial, cast white metal scroll handle, spout & shoulder band, late 19th - early 20th c., 10" h. (ILLUS.) 45

Fireplace fender, Arts & Crafts style, straight-edged w/rectangular repoussé panels decorated w/an oval & foliate design, accented w/oval & heart-shaped turquoise blue stone insets, England, early 20th c., 53" l., 3 1/2" h........................... 259

Hammered-copper Mold

Food mold, hand-hammered, tin-lined, decorated w/design of fruit & leaves, ring for hanging, 4 1/4 x 7 1/2" (ILLUS. on previous page) **85**

Unusual Copper Funnel

Funnel, deep rounded, ringed bowl w/slender tapering spout, riveted strap side handle w/spring-loaded thumb control, marked on handle "Patent Allowed," overall 8" w., 7 3/4" l. (ILLUS.) **85**

Stickley Bros. Copper Jardiniere

Jardiniere, Arts & Crafts style, hand-hammered, deep slightly tapering rounded form w/closed rim, heavily embossed around the sides w/stylized grape clusters, fine original patina, Stickley Brothers, early 20th c., stamped "302," few small dents, 13" d., 8" h. (ILLUS.) **2,420**

Dirk Van Erp Jardiniere

Jardiniere, hammered, Arts & Crafts style, bulbous shape, Dirk Van Erp, early 20th c. (ILLUS.) **7,475**

Hammered Copper Jardiniere

Jardiniere, hammered, Arts & Crafts style, squat bulbous shape w/red blush patina, Dirk Van Erp, early 20th c. (ILLUS.) **37,375**

Copper Dirk Van Erp Table Lamp

Lamp, hammered, Arts & Crafts style, table model, bulbous base w/conical shade held by four metal supports ending in metal squat round finial, early Dirk Van Erp, early 20th c. (ILLUS.) **48,875**

Minnow bucket, cov., deep oval form w/iron end rim handles, w/a matching oval lift-out insert pierced overall w/small holes & w/a hinged flat lid, brass overlaid initials on the outer top rim, signed "R.W.J. Davison," England, late 19th-early 20th c., 8 1/2 x 15", 9 1/2" h. **275**

Teakettle, cov., dovetailed construction, wide flat bottom & swelled cylindrical sides below a flat shoulder centered by a short cylindrical neck w/a fitted domed cover w/acorn finial, long angled gooseneck spout, high swing bail & wood handle, signed inside lid Maurice Cohen & Co. London, 12" h. (dents) **165**

Copper Teakettle

Teakettle, cov., marked "Britton" on applied strap swivel handle, knob handle on cover, old solder repairs to handle, spout & base, 9 1/2 x 12 3/4", 12" h. (ILLUS.)........... **225**

Revere Ware Copper Teakettle

Teakettle, cov., Revere Ware, w/applied black Bakelite handle and bird whistle spout, marked on bottom "Revere Solid Copper - Rome, N.Y.," 7 1/4 x 7 1/2" (ILLUS.).. **100**

Copper Strap-on Water Bottle

Water bottle, strap-on type, wide, oval, shallow, gently arched shape w/small brass spout & screw-on cap, one strap guide missing, 8 x 12", 3" h. (ILLUS.)............... **79**

Iron

One of the most common elemental metals found in nature, raw iron has been used by man since the dawn of history. Scientists believe early man may have extracted iron from meteorites, pounding it to form primitive tools and weapons. Eventually man learned to smelt the raw metal and by 1200 B.C., the beginning of the Iron Age, it was being widely used in many cultures. Iron is utilized by two different methods. One is the casting of the molten ore in a mold to form the desired item. The other is the hand-wrought or forged method where the metal is heated to the red hot stage and formed by hammering the piece into the desired form. Cast iron has been used for a multitude of purposes including the manufacture of many types of kitchenware, such as kettles, pots, muffin pans, griddles, skillets and teakettles. It has also been utilized in everything from childrens banks to parlor stoves, building fronts to firebacks and fountains to doorstops.

Hand-wrought iron was used for many utilitarian and decorative articles including ornamental hardware, fireplace andirons and fireplace tools, kitchen tools and the decorative racks to hold the tools. Many farm implements were also made of hand-wrought iron such as plows, pitchforks, shovels and, of course, horse shoes. Because of its inherent strength and durability, iron work is commonly found at antiques shops and auctions and can form the nucleus of a very interesting collection. In recent years, reproductions of both cast and wrought iron have flooded the market, so care is needed when buying. Newer cast pieces tend to be coarser and cruder than their original counterparts, and items such as banks and toys often have ill-fitting joints and rough edges. New iron wares also tend to rust much more quickly than early examples, so be suspicious if a piece has a thin, even, rust red surface.

Aebleskiver pan, cast, Griswold #32 .... **$50**
Andirons, cast, figural Scottie dogs, molded in the half-round as a dog seated on its hind legs begging, well detailed hair, eyes & nose, each facing right, stamped "JM 68," early 20th c., 16 1/4" h., pr.......... **4,600**
Andirons, cast, figural, standing facing baseball players in the half-round, a pitcher facing a batter, wearing white uniforms w/blue socks, belts & caps, black shoes, stamped "R.B.S.- 09," early 20th c., 19 3/8" h., pr. **9,775**
Andirons, cast, figural swords, each cast in the round as a large sword standing on the tip of the blade, red-painted hilt & black blade, early 20th c., 23 3/4" h., pr.... **1,380**
Apple peeler, cast, "F.W. Hudsons Improved Apple Parer Leominster, Mass Pat Dec. 2, 1862" **175**
Apple peeler, cast, Goodell, 1898 .... **55**
Apple peeler, cast, "Lockey & Howland, Pat Dec 5, 1856" **65**
Apple peeler, cast, Manfu'd by Goodell Co, Antrim, H. Pat Mar 18, 1884, vertical arc shape... **200**
Apple peeler, cast, "Patd Oct. 5, 1880," unmarked Peck, Stow & Wilcox **275**
Apple peeler, "Nonpareil Parer, Patented May 6, 1858 J.L. Haven & Co. Cin. O" .... **1,000+**
Apple segmenter, cast, "R. Buchi Chicago Patd Aug 28, 1923" **100**
Apple segmenter, cast, "Tollman Mfg Co, Mt. Joy, Pa Pat Apld Apple Cutter" **20**

Star-shaped Architectural Brace

Architectural brace, cast, in form of five-pointed star w/hole in center, repainted, 9 1/4 x 9 3/4" (ILLUS.) **65**

Griswold #770 Ashtray

Ashtray, Griswold #770, square, has matchbook holder on end, 3 3/8 x 6 1/2" (ILLUS.)... **15**
Ashtray, Wagner #1050E, round, 6 1/4" d....... **8-10**
Bean pot, cast, Blue Valley Co., Kansas City, Mo. **100**

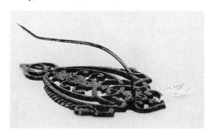

Cast-iron Bill Hook

Bill hook, cast, pointed shield form w/pierced leaf & scroll design, 3 1/2 x 6" (ILLUS.)... **11**

Airedale & Scottie Book End

Book ends, cast, a model of an Airedale & Scottie dog standing on a mound w/brushes & tree roots, bronzed finish, 4 1/2 x 5 1/4", pr. (ILLUS. of one) **130**

Cast-iron Bison Book End

Book ends, cast, antiqued bronze finish, model of bison on rock, marked "COPR 1930 American Bison - 924," 5 1/2 x 5 3/4", pr. (ILLUS. of one).. **115**

Cast-iron Book End with Chariot Race

Book ends, cast, antiqued copper finish, high-relief design of Roman chariot race, marked "695," 5 1/4 x 6 1/4", pr. (ILLUS. of one) **115**

Cast-iron The Thinker Book End

Book ends, cast, bronze finish, image of Rodins "The Thinker," marked w/style number 582, 2 x 4 1/4", 4 1/4" h., the pr. (ILLUS. of one) **85**

Cowboy & Bucking Bronco Book End

Book ends, cast, copper finish, flat rectangular base supporting upright featuring cowboy on bucking bronco, marked on front "OFW" and on reverse "Copyright A&C, 136," 2 x 4 1/4", 6" h., the pr. (ILLUS. of one) **195**

Cast-iron Book End with Galleon

Book ends, cast, gently arched square upright, cast in high-relief w/a galleon under full sail on a rolling sea, painted in blues, white, black, yellow & green, 5 x 5 1/2", pr. (ILLUS. of one) **55**

Cast-iron Owl Book End

Book ends, cast, gothic arch upright w/large relief cast spread-winged owl, original ivory paint w/wear, marked on back "Design Patented - 1155," 4 x 6 1/2", pr. (ILLUS. of one) **69**

Crouching Lion Book Ends

Book ends, cast, model of crouching lion on large rock, original gold paint, marked "COPR 1930 - Crouching Lion - 916" & "C" in triangle within circle, 5 1/2 x 6", pr. (ILLUS.) **195**

Polychrome Cast-iron Book End

Book ends, cast, polychrome three-dimensional design of peasant girl at water fountain, w/leaf swags twining around edges of upright, 2 x 4", 5 1/2" h., the pr. (ILLUS. of one on previous page) **145**

Cast-iron Laughing Cat Book End

Book ends, cast, rounded square upright centered by cast model of laughing cat, overall shaded brown paint, marked "DAL," 1925, pr. (ILLUS. of one) **115**

Cast-iron Washington Book End

Book ends, cast, squared upright w/arched top, high-relief scene of George Washington on horseback w/troops, antiqued bronze finish, 5 1/2" h., pr. (ILLUS. of one) **115**

Book End with Longfellow Portrait

Book ends, flat gently arched back w/low-relief bust of Longfellow w/quill pen & inkwell, light rust on gold-painted finish, 3 5/8 x 4 1/2", pr. (ILLUS. of one) **60**

Cast-iron Parrot Bottle Opener

Bottle opener, cast, model of a stylized parrot on perch, original paint, 5" h. (ILLUS.) **95**

Rare Cast-iron Dove-shaped Box

Box, cov., cast, in shape of a sitting dove, ca. 1840, rare, 3 x 7", 4" h. (ILLUS.) **1,200**
Bread pan, cast, Griswold #2, two loaf **600**
Bread stick pan, cast, Griswold #6, pattern #23 .... **85**
Brownie pan, cast, Griswold #9, pattern #947, 7 x 10 3/8 x 1" deep **145**
Bundt pan, cast, Griswold #965 .... **950-1000**
Cake mold, cast, Griswold #866, model of lamb **90-100**
Cake mold, cast, Griswold, model of rabbit **750**
Can opener, cast, Blue Streak, clamp-on **85**
Can opener, cast, "Duket Mfg. Co. Toledo, Ohio, Patd. 8-11-25," 6 1/4" **20**
Can opener, cast, Worlds Best, Dillsburg, Pa. **40**

Hand-forged Candle Lantern

Candle lantern, hand-forged, flat front, half-round back, punched vents in conical top, w/applied carrying handle, ca. 1850, 6 x 7 1/2", 14 1/4" h. (ILLUS. on previous page) 350

Candle Lantern with Fluted Reflector

Candle lantern, hand-forged, w/fluted reflector & pitcher handle, ca. 1820, 5 x 7", 9 1/4" h. (ILLUS.) 250-350

Eighteenth Century Candle Lantern

Candle lantern, hand-forged, w/tapered vents in conical top, applied strap handle, shaved horn panes instead of glass, French or English, ca. 1750, 7 x 9", 16" h. (ILLUS.)... 700

Iron Candle Lantern

Candle lantern, hand-forged, w/three glass panels, circular vents in conical top, ring-shaped strap handle, ca. 1820, 6 x 6 3/4", 13" h. (ILLUS.) 300-500

Candle or Whale Oil Lantern

Candle or whale oil lantern, hand-forged, w/tapering vents & pierced top, wire ring handle, bull's-eye glass panes, French, ca. 1710, 8 1/2 x 8 1/2", 13 1/2" h. (ILLUS.)... 500-600

Cast-iron Double Candleholder

Candleholder, cast, domed swag, ribbon & medallion decorated base, straight Greek-style shaft ending in flame decoration & supporting two curved candle branches w/swag designs, ribbons and medallions, ending in ribbed sockets w/flared rims atop drip pans, central support bisecting shaft and upcurving to meet each candle branch at midpoint, overall simulated verdigris patina, 15 1/2" h. (ILLUS.)..................................... 175

Candleholder, wrought, domed wooden base & handle w/old red paint, 5" h.............. 275

Candleholder, wrought, table model, an arched low tripod base w/penny feet supporting a very slender upright pointed rod fitted w/an adjustable flat cross-arm w/square brackets & fitted at each tip w/a candle socket w/drip tray, 22 1/4" h. 770

Candleholder, wrought, trammel-style, a thin bar w/a slender sawtooth trammel bar ending w/a short arm supporting a small oval pan w/two cylindrical candle sockets & a rushlight holder, sockets w/push-ups, 27" l. **495**

Candlestand, wrought, a rounded arch tripod base w/penny feet centering a tall tapering turned & pointed bar mounted w/an adjustable double arm w/a candle socket at each end, squared iron brackets w/hooks below the arms, 19th c., 23 1/4" h. **1,815**

Candlesticks, wrought, wedding ring hogscraper-type, round base & cylindrical shaft w/brass ring, mid-19th c., 13 1/4" h., pr. (corrosion) **4,025**

Cast-iron Candy Hammer

Candy hammer, cast, ball-peen, 3 3/4" l. (ILLUS.) **22**

Cats Card Tray

Card tray, in the form of three grey & white cats, marked on back "B&H" and style number 1640, made by Bradley & Hubbard, 5 1/2 x 7" (ILLUS.) **295**

Ornate Victorian Cast-iron Chandelier

Chandelier, cast, four-light, a tall central bar shaft flanked by four long tapering scroll-pierced flanges tapering down to upturned flat arms ending in pierced cup sockets for supporting clear pressed-glass kerosene lamp fonts, complete w/fonts, burners & chimneys, ca. 1875-85 (ILLUS.) **1,100**

Chandelier, wrought, eight-light, a central shaft w/hook at each end w/eight curved arms which extend to form candle sockets, American, early 19th c., 23" d., drop 25" **2,875**

Chandelier, wrought iron & molded glass, Art Deco style, the inverted wide conical pale pink glass shade molded w/a border of roses centering a star, suspended from four candlearms connected at the center to three iron bars applied w/stylized circle & tassel decoration, France, ca. 1925, 48" h. **1,265**

Chandelier, wrought, six-light, a wide central ring w/six incurved scrolled iron drops & six S-scroll iron bar arms around the top each ending in a candle socket, three shaped short iron bars for the three hanging chains, blacksmith-made, probably 19th c., 22 1/2" d., overall 38" h. **770**

Cherry pitter, cast, "Enterprise Cherry Stoner Pat Appl d For No 12," 13" **125**

Cherry pitter, cast, "The Boss Raisin Seeder, Pat. Pdg.," 11 3/4" **150**

Cherry seeder, cast, Enterprise, 1903 .... **70-75**

Cherry seeder, cast, "Family Cherrystoner" **40**

Sheet Iron Christmas Light

Christmas light, soldered sheet iron, star-shaped, w/opaque white glass inserts (one missing) & hole in hinged back for bulb, ca. 1930, 4 1/2 x 12 1/4 x 12 1/2" (ILLUS.) **150-200**

Gilt-finish Cast-iron Travel Clock

Clock, cast, gilt finish, travel size, Art Nouveau w/rococo influence, swirling leafy openwork decoration, on four ornate flared feet, 2 x 3 3/4", 5 1/4" h. (ILLUS. on previous page)... 395

Coffee mill, cast, upright, counter-type, two-wheel, cast-iron drawer at bottom on a wooden base, worn original black paint w/red & gold trim & decals, marked Land, 12" h.. 660

Elgin National No. 10 Coffee Mill

Coffee mill, cast, upright, Elgin National No. 10 floor model w/double 28" wheels & nickel-plated copper hopper, made by C.H. Woodruff & Co., complete & very good original condition (ILLUS.)................. 1,800

Double Grinding Upright Mill

Coffee mill, cast, upright, iron cup could be used to catch the ground coffee or as a hopper cover to protect coffee beans when not in use, "Clawson & Clark's Double Grinding Mill, Pat. Sept. 28," 86 embossed on 6" wheel (ILLUS.)...................... 1,050

Enterprise No. 14 Coffee Mill

Coffee mill, cast, upright, Enterprise No. 14 large countertop mill w/nickel-plated brass hopper & tin catch can, double 25" wheels, original paint & flower decals, iron nameplate on front marked No. 14 (ILLUS.).. 1,600

Lane Brothers No. 13 Swift Mill

Coffee mill, cast, upright, No. 13 Swift Mill, double 11 1/2" wheels w/spiderweb spoke design, pivoting hopper cover, rectangular tin catch can, faded red paint w/decals & gold striping, complete & original, Lane Brothers (ILLUS.)............................ 850

Peugeot Freres 2A Coffee Mill

Coffee mill, cast, upright, single 13" wheel
mill w/gears, raised iron hopper w/tin
dome, wooden drawer inside iron box,
original green paint w/gold trim, Peugeot
Freres 2A (ILLUS.) **550**

No. 20 Crown Coffee Mill

Coffee mill, cast, upright, two 8 3/4"
wheels, pivoting cover on cast iron hopper, original black paint & decals,
Landers, Frary & Clark No. 20 Crown,
very good condition (ILLUS.) **1,000**

1898 Enterprise Coffee Mill

Coffee mill, cast, upright, two 8 3/4"
wheels, pivoting cover on hopper, original red paint, decals & pin striping, 1898
patent date marked on grinding burrs,
very good condition (ILLUS.) **1,150**

Enterprise #7 Coffee Grinder

Coffee mill, cast, upright, w/17" wheels, pivoting cover on hopper, original red paint,
decals & pin striping, 1898 patent date
marked on grinding burrs, Enterprise #7
(ILLUS.).. **1,400**

Enterprise No. 4 Coffee Mill

Coffee mill, cast, upright, w/nickel-plated
brass hopper, 10 3/4" wheels, Enterprise
No. 4 (ILLUS.) **1,500**

Enterprise No. 650 Coffee/Corn Mill

Coffee mill, cast, wall-mounted, corn & coffee mill, 19" wheel, black w/gold trim & lettering, Enterprise No. 650, excellent original condition (ILLUS.)................................ **325**

Iron Steamship Coffee Mill

Coffee mill, cast, wall-mounted, steamship mill, crank in front w/gear arrangement, grind adjusting screw below, about 6" h. (ILLUS.) **150**

Old 74 Cast-iron Coffee Mill

Coffee mill, cast, wall-mounted, Old 74 made by Edward Cornwall of Connecticut in the 1830s (ILLUS.) **300**

Enterprise No. 00 Coffee Mill

Coffee mill, cast, wall-mounted, w/open hopper & hanging iron cup, original black paint & decals, Enterprise No. 00, 9" h. (ILLUS.).. **350**

Iron Post-mounted Coffee Mill

Coffee mill, post-mounted, blacksmiths-type, 6" hopper, forged crank on right side, cylindrical drum grinding arrangement, late 1700s (ILLUS.) **450**

Arcade Favorite No. 17 Coffee Mill

Coffee mill, side-mount type, all iron w/wood back, hopper & lid, Arcade Favorite No. 17, 4" w. (ILLUS.) **110**

Dr. Edwards Coffee Mill

Coffee mill, side-mount type, cast iron w/wood back, hopper embossed w/Dr. Edwards name & 1859 patent date (ILLUS.) **300**

ELMA Coffee Mill

Coffee mill, upright, cast iron w/crank & gears (no wheels), raised hopper w/tin dome, wood drawer, original red paint, made by ELMA, Spain, about 13" h. (ILLUS.) **225**

Crown Coffee Mill

Coffee mill, upright, Landers, Frary & Clark No. 11 Crown Coffee Mill, approx. 12" h. (ILLUS.) **325**

Peckham Iron Coffee Mill

Coffee mill, wall or post-mounted, 4" wide hopper & grind adjusting knob at bottom, Peckham (ILLUS.) **350**

Wrought-iron Cowbell

Cowbell, wrought, w/leather collar, strap
handle, 2 x 4", 9" h. (ILLUS.)............................. **25**

Spong No. 2 Coffee Mill

Coffee mill, wall or shelf-type, w/open hopper, black w/gold trim, decal & embossed
lettering, cylindrical metal catch cup,
Spong No. 2, England, new condition
(ILLUS.)... **100**
Corn bread pan, cast, Griswold, Model F,
pattern #955, 7 1/2 x 14" **75**
Corn sheller, cast, hand-held, tri-fold sec-
tions, marked "C.M. O' Hara"............................ **210**
Corn sheller, cast-iron w/wood handle,
hand-held, marked "The Bird Pat July 6
1869, Springfield Ohio" **585**

Dark Lantern Used by James Garfield

Dark lantern, hand-forged, w/red glass
panes, burned whale oil, 1835, carried by
future President James A. Garfield at the
age of 16 on an Erie Canal tow boat,
2 3/4 x 3 1/2", 5 3/4" h. (ILLUS.) **1,200**

Crispy Corn Stick Pan

Corn stick pan, cast, "Crispy Corn Stick,"
Griswold #273, 5 3/4 x 12 1/2" (ILLUS.) **25-35**
Corn stick pan, cast, Griswold #262,
8 1/2 x 4 1/2 x 3/4"... **85**
Corn stick pan, cast, Griswold #280, seven
alternating ears **500**
Corn stick pan, cast, Wagner, "Junior
Krusty Korn Kobs," #1319, July 6, 1920 .... **18-20**
Corn stick pan, cast, Wagner, "Krusty Korn
Kobs," #1318, July 6, 1920, 15" **25-28**

Cast-iron Advertising Dish/Ashtray

Dish/ashtray, cast, advertising-type, almond-shaped w/scalloped flanged rim,
the back embossed "Enduro Enamel -
Wincroft Stoveworks - Middletown, PA,"
interior coated in blue enamel, late 19th -
early 20th c., 3 x 4" (ILLUS. of back) **145**

Figural Woodpecker Door Knocker

Door knocker, cast, figural, model of a red-bellied woodpecker hinged on a tree trunk, original worn paint, 2 1/2 x 3 3/4" (ILLUS.) **165**

Cast-iron Door Knocker

Door knocker, cast, in the form of a basket of flowers w/ribbon garland, original worn paint, 2 3/4 x 4" (ILLUS.) **65**

Door knocker, cast, large tall grotesque face w/tall pointed scroll top ears & crest & scalloped leaves below the chin, large ring knocker fitted in the mouth, old cream paint over earlier green, late 19th-early 20th c., 8 1/2" w., 21" h. **633**

Doorstop, Aunt Jemima, full-figured black Mammy w/hands on hips, wearing white kerchief, large dark blue crossed shawl over a red blouse, wide white apron over long red dress, 8 x 13 1/4" **264**

Basket of Flowers Doorstop

Doorstop, Basket of Flowers, large creamy yellow lily blossoms & thick green leaves in a creamy yellow basket w/a criss-cross design & upright arched handle, slight paint wear (ILLUS.) **138**

Flat-backed Boston Terrier

Doorstop, Boston Terrier, flat-backed style, black & white dog facing legs, standing on an oblong grassy base painted black, 9 5/8 x 11 3/4" (ILLUS.) **396**

Cast-iron Vase of Flowers Doorstop

Doorstop, cast, black triangular stepped base holding white handled vase of flowers in polychrome decoration of yellow, white, green, peach & black, 10" h. (ILLUS.) **145**

Cast-iron Carriage Doorstop

Doorstop, cast, image of enclosed coach pulled by two horses, w/driver in front and trumpeter standing at back, English, 3 1/2 x 13", 7 1/2" h. (ILLUS. on previous page).. 350

Cast-iron Ship Doorstop

Doorstop, cast, in the form of a polychrome three-masted ship w/billowing sails, on two feet, style number 205, 3 x 11", 11" h. (ILLUS.).. 150

Cast-iron Elephant Doorstop

Doorstop, cast, long narrow base holding figure of trumpeting elephant, style number indistinct, 2 1/4 by 11 1/4", 8 1/2" h. (ILLUS.).. 250

Figural Airedale Doorstop

Doorstop, cast, model of a standing Airedale facing viewer, traces of original paint, 8 5/8" l., 8" h. (ILLUS.)........................... 300

Cast-iron Covered Wagon Doorstop

Doorstop, cast, pioneer couple driving covered wagon pulled by pair of oxen, worn original beige paint, marked w/style number 64,© and "LVL" (?), 2 x 10", 6 1/2" h. (ILLUS.)... 145

Doorstop, Colonial Lawyer, standing man in front of square pedestal, white wig, red long coat w/black trim, black kneebreeches, holding a gold-trimmed black tricorn hat in one hand, rounded base, marked "Trade (triangle - WS) Mark," 9 5/8" h. (some wear).. 176

Doorstop, Court lady w/open fan, elegantly dressed 18th c. lady in a low-cut, wide tiered deep red gown w/gold swag trim, white bouffant hair w/red bow, gold necklace, large open yellow fan in one hand........ 154

Doorstop, Daisy Bowl, high mound of bright Shasta daisies, dark blue mums & small yellow blossoms in a white ribbed rounded bowl w/a flaring ringed base, Hubley No. 452, 5 1/8 x 7 1/2" (slight wear).............. 171

Daisy Bowl & Flower Basket Doorstops

Doorstop, Daisy Bowl, large, high bouquet of dark yellow black-eyed Susans in a squatty bulbous footed black bowl, Hubley, 6 x 7" (ILLUS. right)................................. 198

Doorstop, Drum Major, standing figure carrying long yellow baton, tall plumed red hat, red jacket & white pants, on small pale green square base, 13 1/2" h. (slight wear).. 264

Doorstop, Duck w/Top Hat, walking comical bird in green & yellow wearing dark red hat & pants, rectangular black base, 7 1/2" h. (some paint wear)........................... 176

Doorstop, Flower Basket, low wide dark green latticework basket w/short pointed & ringed center handle, filled w/a wide, low bouquet of mixed flowers in shades of dark blue, lavender & purple, 10 7/8 x 11".................................. 149

Doorstop, Flower Basket, small wicker basket w/wide flaring rim & wide arched handle centered by a blue ribbon above mixed roses & flowers in red, yellow & blue, black beveled base, 8 1/4" h. (light paint wear)...................................... 143

Doorstop, Flower Basket, tall, widely flaring tan wicker basket w/a narrow center handle tied w/a large yellow ribbon above a mixed bouquet of yellow blossoms & green leaves, stepped pale green & black base, some paint wear (ILLUS. on previous page left with Daisy Bowl)...................... 242

Flowerpot Doorstop

Doorstop, Flowerpot, on semi-circular base in brown paint, filled w/yellow & orange/red flowers & green leaves, marked on the back "Hubley 330," 7 1/4" h. (ILLUS.)................................... 55

Doorstop, French Basket, tall yellow wicker basket w/high arched handle w/ribbon, pink, blue, yellow & purple flowers, Hubley No. 69, 11" h. (some light paint wear)..... 232

Doorstop, Fruit Basket, tall wicker basket w/high rounded rim & arched entwined handle, filled w/a low mound of mixed fruits including grapes, banana & oranges, on a black rectangular base (some paint wear)...................................... 149

Doorstop, Geisha, Japanese lady kneeling on rectangular base & playing stringed instrument, pale yellow floral-painted kimono, deep red base, Hubley, 6 x 7" (slight wear)...................................... 231

Doorstop, German Shepherd, flat-backed style, raised on a narrow trestle bar-style base (worn brown paint)........................ 132

Girl Holding Flowers Doorstop

Doorstop, Girl Holding Flowers, full-figured mid-Victorian girl wearing a blue & white bonnet, white shawl & long, full, blue dress, holding a bouquet of colored flowers in her hands, some paint wear, pot metal, 7 1/2" h. (ILLUS.)............. 220

Doorstop, Gladiolus, yellow flowers in a white urn-form vase, Hubley, 10" h. 160

Doorstop, Greyhound, tall slender dog in white w/black spots standing on a narrow oblong green base (some paint wear) 198

Cast-iron Horse Doorstop

Doorstop, Horse, in the form of a prancing circus horse in dappled bronze color, w/long black tail & mane, red & white striped band around horse's mid-section, on painted wooden stand, original painted surface, base probably an old replacement, 4 3/4 x 9 1/4 x 11" (ILLUS.).. 200

Doorstop, Minuteman, standing man in colonial dress resting his hands on a standing rifle at front, black tricorn hat & long coat, white & yellow kneebreeches, square black base (some paint wear)........... **209**

Doorstop, Parrot in Ring (small), round gold ring w/a small perched green, red & yellow parrot, on a dark green rectangular base, 7 x 8" (some paint wear) **127**

Doorstop, Parrot, large full-bodied yellow & green parrot w/topknot perched on a dark brown stump base, Albany Foundry, 12 1/2" h. (some paint wear) **165**

Doorstop, Petunias & Asters, yellow & blue flowers in a short wicker basket, Hubley No. 470, 9 1/2" h. (some paint wear) **154**

Doorstop, Rose Basket, yellow roses & blue, pink & red blossoms in a yellow wicker basket, Hubley No. 121, 11" h........... **132**

Doorstop, Rose Vase, pink roses & green leaves in a white cornucopia-form vase on rectangular base, Hubley, 10 1/8" h. **165**

Doorstop, Scottie dogs, two Scotties w/perked ears sit on base, original black paint, 8 1/2" l. **100**

Doorstop, Squirrel, figure of squirrel sitting on a log & holding nut to mouth w/front paws, oval-shaped base, old black paint, unmarked Bradley and Hubbard, 10 3/4" h.. **495**

Doorstop, Squirrel, figure of squirrel sitting on hind legs & holding nut to mouth w/front paws, half-round base, 6 3/4" h. **330**

Doorstop, Squirrel, figure of squirrel sitting on log eating a nut w/front paws, on oval-shaped base, old white, brown & green paint, unmarked Bradley & Hubbard, 11 1/8" h. (minor wear) **550**

Doorstop, Terrier, free-standing full-bodied dog w/head turned toward viewer, short tail erect, white w/brown patches (slight wear)... **83**

Doorstop, Whippet, standing black dog w/white spots, on thin rectangular base, 6 3/4 x 7 1/2" (slight paint wear) **160**

Doorstop, Woman Holding Flower Basket, standing lady in Colonial dress & bonnet, her arms at her sides w/each hand holding a basket of flowers, blue dress w/blue band, cJo No. 1270, 8" h. (some paint wear)... **220**

Lil Red Riding Hood Doorstop

Doorstop, Lil Red Riding Hood, short, stocky girl in red hood & cape w/green bow at neck, holding basket of goodies in one arm, on oblong worn green mound base, Hubley No. 95, 9 1/2" h. (ILLUS.)........ **396**

Doorstop, Maid, curtsying, white cap & long apron over long black dress, green base, cJo No. 1242, 8 7/8" h. (slight wear) **253**

Marigolds in Ringed Vase

Doorstop, Marigolds, large yellow marigolds w/smaller dark blue, red & pale blue flowers in a ringed inverted beehive-form vase on a black rectangular base, Hubley No. 315, some paint wear, 7 1/2 x 8" (ILLUS.) **154**

Early Cast-iron Drawer Pull

Drawer pull, cast, long flat bar centered by an embossed face of a spaniel-type dog, worn black paint, late 19th - early 20th c., 4" l. (ILLUS.)... **20**

Dutch Oven

Dutch oven, cast, Griswold #8, "Tite-Top,"
6-quart capacity, w/lid, handle, trivet
(ILLUS.)... **50-75**
Dutch oven, cast, Wagner, #1268E **50**
Egg beater, cast, "Cyclone Pat. 6-25-1901
Reissue 8-26-1902," 11 1/2"............................ **85**
Egg beater, cast, "Dover Egg Beater
U.S.A.," 10 3/4"... **40**
Egg beater, cast, "Holt's Patented Flared
Dasher Egg Beater N.Y. U.S.A., 10 1/2"......... **45**
Egg beater, cast, "Perfection Pat'd Feb. 22,
1898 Albany N.Y.," 10 1/4"............................ **350**

R.P. Scott & Co. Eggbeater

Egg beater, cast, "R.P. Scott & Co. Newark
N.J. Patented," 10 1/2" (ILLUS.)................. **1,250**

Cast-iron Spiral Envelope Holder

Envelope holder, cast, spiral holder w/two
feet at each end, marked "K Diamond,"
3 x 3 1/2", 3" h. (ILLUS.) **48**
Fireplace grill, cast, Horace Greeley-type,
fan-shaped grill w/grease reservoir,
raised on three legs, Campbell Foundry
Co., Harrison, New Jersey, 19th c.,
16 3/4 x 25", 3 1/4" h. **230**

Cast-iron Flag Stand

Flag stand, cast, base w/four ball-and-claw
feet, embossed w/stars and "Loyalty,"
"Fraternity," "Charity" and "WRC,"
3 1/2 x 6 1/4" (ILLUS.) **35**

Cast-iron Two-piece Fluter

Fluter iron, cast, two-piece, rectangular
footed base w/fluting grooves & hand-
held roller, painted & plated, marked
"American Machine Co. Philadelphia,
Pa.," late 19th - early 20th c., base 3 3/4",
the set (ILLUS.)................................. **165**

*Patented Cast-iron & Steel
Chopper*

Food chopper, cast, iron loop handle
w/four-section bell-shaped steel blade,
handle marked "NRS & Co., Groton, NY -
Patented May 2, 93 - No. 40," 5 1/2" l.
(ILLUS.) **25**
Food chopper, iron & wood, the wide flat
blade w/rounded shoulders flanking a
large inverted heart cut-out below the
pointed baluster-turned wood handle w/a
brass ferule, 19th c., 10 3/4" l. **275**
Food press, cast, Sensible, 2-quart **135**

Old Wrought-iron Fork
Fork, wrought, two prongs, 19" (ILLUS.) **18-22**

Unique Fraternal Order Emblem

Fraternal order emblem, cast, wall-type,
for the Modern Woodmen of America, a
large crossed ax & hammer joined by a
ribbon & w/a center banner reading "MW
of A," original red, white, gold & green
paint, 7 3/4 x 12 1/4" (ILLUS.) **400**

Miniature Souvenir Frying Pan

Frying pan, cast, miniature, w/polychrome
painted image of Statue of Liberty and
sailing ships, souvenir of Galesville, Wisconsin, made by John Wright of Wrights-
ville, Pennsylvania, w/original box, pan
measures 3 1/4 x 4 3/4" (ILLUS.) **25**
Griddle, cast, Griswold #7, rectangular,
7 x 16 1/2" **40**
Griddle, cast, Griswold #9, rectangular,
9 1/2 x 21" **40-45**
Griddle, cast, Wagner #9 (1109E) **45-55**
Grill, cast, Wagner #8, utility grill **60**

Old Painted Harness Hook

Harness hook, cast, a long top hook w/up-
turned tip above a short curved hook, old
flaking white paint, late 19th - early 20th
c., 7 1/2" l. (ILLUS.) **20**
Hearth toaster, wrought, rotating-type,
twisted double-arch rack bars & three
twisted & stylized tree designs, American, early 19th c., 14 x 15", 6 3/4" h. (cor-
rosion) **920**
Hearth trivet, wrought, three tall slender
legs supporting a horseshoe-shaped trivet top w/spade & scroll openwork designs, carved wooden handle extending
from top, American, early 19th c.,
14 1/2" l., 7 5/8" h. (corrosion, holes) **316**
Ice shaver, cast, "The Griswold Mfg Co
Classic Ice Shredder No 2 Erie PA USA" **300**

Beehive-form Inkwell

Inkwell, cast, base w/flared scalloped rim holds beehive form w/stylized leaf decoration & hinged lid, marked "patent applied for," 2 1/2 x 4 1/4" (ILLUS.)..................... **245**

Elaborate Cast-iron Double Inkwell

Inkwell, cast, elaborate double inkwell & pen rest decorated w/cherubs & pierced floral & scroll design, black finish may be repaint, 3 x 11 1/2 x 12 1/2" (ILLUS.) **265**

Jar lid reformer, cast, "The Eakin Mfg Co. Salem, Ohio," 7"... **40**

Jar opener, cast, "Mfd by Hoffman Hinge & Fdry Co. Cleveland, O," 8" **30**

Kettle, cast, Griswold #8, flat bottom, 7-quart... **40-50**

Knife sharpener, cast, "Dazey Sharpit, Dazey Churn & Mfg. Co. St. Louis, Mo.," 5 1/2"... **25**

Two-lip Ladle

Ladle, cast, two pouring "lips," 22" (ILLUS.) **20**

Cast-iron Lawn Sprinkler

Lawn sprinkler w/copper tubing, cast, Rain King model D, various patent numbers, Sunbeam Corp., Chicago, 4 1/2 x 7 1/2", 9 1/2" h. (ILLUS.)... **55**

Lemon squeezer, cast, hinged, two handles, 7 1/2"... **40**

Lemon squeezer, cast-iron w/decorated porcelain insert, marked "The Arcade No 2 Lemon Squeezer" **30**

English Mailbox on Base

Mailbox on base, cast, oblong base has shaped corners & holes for mounting to floor, round column w/leaf designs & urn-shaped detail below octagonal box w/relief designs of horns on either end & a man on horseback w/horn, peaked roof w/scale designs, crown finial, late white enameling, areas of rust, English, 11 1/2 x 16 1/2", 46" h. (ILLUS.).................... **358**

Cast-iron Match Holder

Match holder, cast, hanging, flat rectangular back, top features openwork design w/middle peak flanked by two pillars, holder in form of leering face, 2 x 3 1/2", 7 1/4" h. (ILLUS.) **125**

Cast-iron Elephant Match Holder

Match holder, cast, in the form of a walking elephant carrying box for matches on its back, folds of elephant's neck used for striking, black paint, 3 x 8", 5" h. (ILLUS.) **75**

Victorian Shoe-form Match Holder

Match holder, cast, model of a high-topped Victorian lady's shoe raised on a rectangular base, worn original paint, late 19th c., 3 1/4 x 4 5/8", 5 1/2" h. (ILLUS.) **75**

Iron Crescent Stove Match Holder

Match holder, w/pierced silver-plate emblem w/"Crescent Stove - 1901," circular rimmed base, 2 x 3 1/4" (ILLUS.) **145**

Single-edge Meat Tenderizer

Meat tenderizer, cast, single edge & square grid for tenderizing, 7 1/2" (ILLUS.) **10**

Iron Miner's Candlestick

Miner's candlestick, a.k.a. "sticking tommy," hand-forged, cylindrical holder for candle, w/two sharp prongs, one straight, one hooked, for fixing holder in mine wall, timber, hat, etc., ca. 1840, 1 3/4 x 2 3/4 x 7 1/2" (ILLUS.) **300**

Ornate Cast-iron Mirror Frame

Mirror frame, cast, table model, a large oval frame w/scrolls at the top swiveling between a wide U-form harp supported by the seated semi-nude woman, old gold finish, late 19th - early 20th c., marked w/style number 372, 14" h. (ILLUS. on previous page) **250**

Cast-iron Hand

Model of hand, cast, life-size form of human hand hinged at wrist, marked twice on reverse w/style numbers Y1657 & Y1658, exact use unknown but may be a lodge piece or door knocker, 1 1/2 x 4 3/8", 7" l. (ILLUS.).. **850**

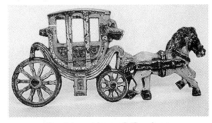

Cast-iron Horse & Carriage

Model of horse & carriage, cast, flat design w/wire support, polychrome painted finish in white, black & red, early 20th c., 11 1/4" l., 5" h. (ILLUS.) **69**
Mold, cast, curved fish design **145**
Mold, cast, Turk's head-style, Griswold #140 ..... **200**

Unmarked Mortar & Pestle

Mortar & pestle, cast, unmarked, 19th c., 8" h. mortar (ILLUS.) **35-40**
Muffin pan, cast, Griswold #10 .... **20**
Muffin pan, cast, Griswold #17 .... **75**

Iron Perfection Nut Cracker

Nutcracker, cast, clamp-style for attaching to table edge, clamp-form cracker, marked "Perfection Nut Cracker - Made in Waco, Texas - Patented 1914," 6 x 6 1/2" (ILLUS.) **69**

Eagle Head Nutcracker

Nutcracker, cast, eagle head, four-legged base (ILLUS.) **75-85**

Home Nut Cracker

Nutcracker, cast, handle embossed w/ "Home Nut Cracker," patented 1915, 4 x 11 1/2" (ILLUS.) **69**

The Gem Nutmeg Grater

Nutmeg grater, cast iron, tin & wood, "The Gem" (ILLUS.) **85**

Rare Francis Nutmeg Grater

Nutmeg grater, cast, marked "Francis Grater
Patd," rare (ILLUS.) .... **1,000+**

Figural Cast-iron Paper Clamp

Paper clamp, cast, hanging-type, bold-re-
lief bust of a smiling black man, old worn
gold finish, marked on back w/style num-
ber 5247, 2 1/2 x 4" (ILLUS.) **125**

Cast-iron Scottie Paperweight

Paperweight, cast, figural, model of a seated Scottie dog, worn original paint, ca.
1930s, 3 1/4" h. (ILLUS.) **75**

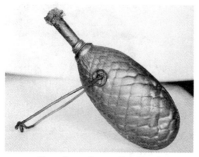

Parade or Campaign Torch

Parade or campaign torch, wrought, in the
form of a pineapple, w/wick protruding
from tube in top, wire handle, old gold
painted surface, burned kerosene or
whale oil, c. 1880, 3 x 3 1/4", fully ex-
tended 9 3/4" l. (ILLUS.) **350**
Patty mold, cast, Griswold #72 .... **50**
Pea sheller, cast, clamp-on type, marked
"Gem Pea Sheller Pat'd July 1866" **335**

Rollman Peach Stoner

Peach stoner, cast, "Rollman Mfg. Co. Pat
Pend Mount Joy PA U.S.A.," 8 3/4"
(ILLUS.) **250**

Two-arm Plant Holder

Plant holder, cast, Victorian, decorated
w/tendrils & scrolls & stylized leaf motif,
two pierced circular holders, ca. 1880,
5 1/2 x 10 x 15" (ILLUS.) **300-400**

Cast-iron Plant Holder

Plant holder, cast, Victorian, four-arm holder w/pierced base & circular arms w/C-
scrolls, ca. 1880, 17 x 18", 6 1/2" h.
(ILLUS.) **300-500**

Cast-iron Plant Holder or Lamp Arm

Plant holder or lamp arm, cast, Victorian, decorated w/tendrils & scrolls & stylized leaf motif, ca. 1880, 5 3/4 x 7 1/2 x 10 1/2" (ILLUS.)... **150-200**

Cast-iron World War I Soldier Plaque

Plaque, cast, round w/relief cast scene of World War I soldier carrying German helmets & motto "And they thought we couldn't fight," 9" d. (ILLUS.)........................... **195**
Popover pan, cast, Griswold #10, 7 5/8 x 11".. **35-40**
Raisin seeder, cast, clamp-on type, long goose neck, marked "The Crown, Pat. Applied For," 6" h. **85**

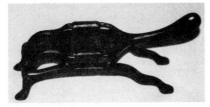

Patented Raisin Seeder

Raisin seeder, cast, four leg base, "Patd May 7, 95," 6" (ILLUS.) **500**
Raisin seeder, cast iron w/tin tray, "EZY Raisin Seeder, Pat May 21, 1895" **250**
Roaster, cast, Griswold #5, oval........................ **120**
Roaster, cast, Wagner #3, oval........................ **185**
Roll pan, cast, Griswold #11 .... **45**
Sad iron, cast, "Geneva Fluting Iron," two pieces, bottom 2 1/2 x 5" **45-50**
Sad iron, cast, Ober #6, 5 3/4" l............................ **25**

Miniature Cast-iron Sad Iron

Sad iron, miniature, double-pointed base marked "Dover USA," iron uprights w/turned wood handle, 1 1/2 x 3 1/4", 2 1/8" h. (ILLUS.) **69**

Toy Cast-iron Iron & Trivet

Sad iron & trivet, cast, toy size, pointed iron w/upright handle on pierced three-footed trivet w/end handle, 3 3/4" l., pr. (ILLUS.).. **32**

Miniature Sausage Grinder

Sausage grinder, cast, miniature, marked "J.P. Co., NYC," 2 1/2 x 3 3/4" (ILLUS.) **35**

Cast-iron Shackles

Shackles, cast, original connecting chain, no key, 3 1/2" w., overall 16" l., pr. (ILLUS.).. **185**

Old Iron Sheep Shears

Sheep shears, wrought, one-piece construction w/loop strap handle & long pointed blades, worn surface, 10 1/4" l. (ILLUS.) **20**

Cast-iron Shoe Last Top

Shoe last top, cast, w/original red paint, 1 3/4 x 5" (ILLUS.) **14**

Large Cast-iron Shoe Last Form

Shoe last top, cast, w/original red paint, size number 3, 2 1/2 x 8" (ILLUS.) **12**
Skillet, cast, Eagle Stove Works #12 .... **300**

Griswold #3 Skillet

Skillet, cast, Griswold #3, 6 1/2" (ILLUS.) **10-15**
Skillet, cast, Griswold #8, "Odorless," pat. Oct. 17, 1898, 14" d. **35-40**
Skillet, cast, Griswold, square egg skillet, 4 3/4" sq. **45**

Cast-iron Griswold Skillet

Skillet, cast, Griswold trademark & "Model 0 - No. 562 - Made in Erie, Pa.," 5" w., 6 3/4" l. (ILLUS.) **85**
Skillet, cast, large emblem, no heat ring, Griswold #2 .... **350**
Skillet, cast, large emblem w/smoke ring, Griswold #14 .... **200**
Skillet, cast, Wagner #3, 6" d. **10-12.50**
Skillet, cast, Wagner #6, 9" d. **20-25**
Stove lid lifter, cast, "Jewel," ca. 1890 .... **15**

Thayer's Household Combination Tool

Stove tool, cast, "Thayer's Household Combination, #83," used for stove, pot or lid lifter, meat tenderizer, trivet, pat. 1881 (ILLUS.) **35**
Sugar nippers, cast, scissors-shaped, 9 1/2" **150**

Cast-Iron Sugar Nippers

Sugar nippers, cast, stamped leaf designs at rivet, handle stamped "B. Smith," minor edge damage to one end and short split in spring, 9 1/2" l. (ILLUS.) **275**

Iron & Glass Claw & Ball Feet

Table or stool feet, cast, a large iron talon grasping a clear glass ball, original black paint, light rust, late 19th - early 20th c., 5" h., set of 4 (ILLUS.) **70**

Teakettle, cov., cast, deep squared body w/side flanges & a paneled spout, bail handle & a tin cover, marked "Troy, NY," old black repaint, 19th c., 9" l., 5 1/4" h. plus handle **83**

Cast-iron Toy Coupe

Toy, cast, 1920s-era model coupe w/fold-out rumble seat, vulcanized rubber wheels, original worn blue paint, 2 1/4 x 2 1/2", 6 1/2" l. (ILLUS.)... **495**

Toy, cast, beer wagon w/driver & a black & a white horse, green wagon w/red wheels, possibly by Kenton Hardware Co., 15 1/4" l. (ILLUS. below, bottom)...................... **595**

Toy Harley-Davidson Motorcycle

Toy, cast, Harley-Davidson motorcycle racer w/turning head, cycle gas tank marked "H.D.," original blue & black paint, vulcanized rubber wheels, made by Arcade, 2 1/4 x 4" (ILLUS.).. **1,395**

Toy, cast, ice wagon, green covered wagon w/worn yellow wheels pulled by a black horse, 8 1/4" l. (ILLUS. below, top)................ **395**

Toy Cast-iron Ice Wagon

Early Cast-iron Toy Beer Wagon

Cast-iron Surrey with Fringe Toy

Hubley Cast-iron Toy Race Car

Toy, cast, race car w/removable driver, original worn red paint, numbered 271091, Hubley, 2 x 2", 5 1/8" l. (ILLUS.) **225**

Cast-iron Toy Stock Truck

Toy, cast, stock truck w/plank-sided bed, in original red paint, possibly by Williams, 1 3/4 x 4 3/4", 2 3/8" h. (ILLUS.) **225**

Toy, cast, surrey w/fringe on top, surrey w/driver & passenger pulled by two black horses, original paint, Stanley Toys, overall 11 3/4" l. (ILLUS. top of page) **295**

Cast-iron Toy Touring Car

Toy, cast, touring car w/original orange paint, possibly made by A.C. Williams, 1 3/4 x 4 1/8, 2" h. (ILLUS.) **245**

Cast-iron Motor Express Truck

Toy, cast, toy truck w/Art Deco-influenced streamlined design, "Motor Express" in red paint on side of silver trailer, red & silver cab, vulcanized rubber wheels, marked "Made in USA" and style number 2387, original paint, 2 x 7 1/2", 2 1/8" h. (ILLUS.) **595**

Trivet, cast, designed w/a four-pointed star in center & four Duchy hearts in between points, 6 1/4" d. **235**

Strause Gas Iron Company Trivet

Trivet, cast, for gas iron, almond-shaped w/pierced center w/the design of an early iron, top edge reads "Double Point'l Want U' Comfort Iron - Strause Gas Iron Co.," unpainted, early 20th c., 7 1/2" l. (ILLUS.) **50**

Enterprise Sad Iron Trivet

Trivet, cast, for sad iron, pierced script "E" in the center, edges read "Enterprise M'f'g Co. Phil'a. U.S.A.," old black paint, 6 1/8" l. (ILLUS.) **25**

W.H. Howell Sad Iron Trivet

Trivet, cast, for sad iron, pointed w/cast "H" in center, reads around edges "W.H. Howell Co. - Geneva, Ill.," old black paint, 6" l. (ILLUS.) **25**

Cleveland Foundry Company Trivet

Trivet, cast, for sad iron, pointed w/center pierced w/a star & sunburst, reads around the edge "The Cleveland Foundry Co.," old black paint, 6" l. (ILLUS.) **25**

Wrought-iron Hanging Utensil Rack

Utensil rack, wrought, hanging style, stepped crest w/scrolled rods & center rod w/twisted detail, five hooks on rod w/diamond-shaped ends, 21 1/4" l., 13" h. (ILLUS.) **495**

Waffle iron, cast, Griswold #8, 1901, black iron w/wooden handles **20**

Waffle iron, cast, Wagner #9 .... **75**

Rare Cast-Iron Washboard

Washboard, cast, rectangular flattened form w/narrow molded edges & flat bracket legs w/round cut-outs below the corrugated washing surface below a smooth top band pierced w/a heart, original surface, Pennsylvania, 19th c., 12 1/2 x 22 1/2" (ILLUS.) **2,415**

Mid-century Rooster Weathervane

Weathervane, stamped sheet iron, a rooster w/a fancy tail atop a long arrow over scrolls, plastic mount & egg-shaped sleeve above directionals, adjustable base, ca. 1950, 22 3/4" l., 26 3/4" h. (ILLUS.) **400**

Old Iron Wick Trimmer

Wick trimmer, cast, scissors w/design in handle, attached "box" to hold trimmed wicks, 6" (ILLUS.) **25**

Early Iron Windmill Weight

Windmill weight, cast, model of a rooster w/arched grooved tail, worn original white paint & red comb & wattle, ca. 1900, size without stand 18" w., 17" h. (ILLUS.)......... **2,400**

Lead

One of the oldest metals known to man, this heavy bluish-grey element has been used for thousands of years as a building material, to produce decorative objects and as a base for a glaze on inexpensive pottery. It has been known for centuries that lead is toxic to humans, so few household objects were made using the raw metal. It could be combined with other metals, such as tin and antimony, to form more durable pieces, but contrary to popular myth, very little or no lead was used in the best antique pewter. The English, in particular, had stringent regulations controlling the quality of pewterwares, and pewterers in the American colonies followed those standards. Since lead alloys are easily worked and produce objects that resist water corrosion, many pieces of garden statuary and ornaments have been made using lead. Early works can bring high prices in today's antiques market.

Birdbath, lead & stone, figural, lead figure of a cherub supporting shell, raised on a stone pedestal, 47" h. **$1,610**

Little Boy & Umbrella Lead Fountain

Fountain, cast lead, figural, a little boy standing atop a rocky base & looking up while opening an umbrella, plumbed for water, 16" h. (ILLUS.) **2,875**

Cast-lead Paperweight

Paperweight, cast, figure of sleeping child curled up w/head resting on sleeping dog, made by Golden Novelty Manufacturing Co., 4 1/2" l. (ILLUS.).............................. **45**

Paperweights, cast, round, one cast w/a baseball cap, the other w/a baseball glove, worn black paint, ca. 1950, 3" d., pr. (ILLUS. below) **80**

Baseball Cap & Glove Paperweights

Miniature Cast Lead Statue

Statue, cast, miniature figure of a seated nude boy checking the bottom of one foot, 4 3/4" h. (ILLUS.) **35**

Charging Toy Soldier

Toy soldier, figure on flat base, holding rifle as though charging w/fixed bayonet, muzzle broken off, worn paint, 3" h. (ILLUS.) **20**

Lead Marching Toy Soldier

Toy soldier, figure on flat base, marching, w/rifle over shoulder, green helmet, marked "Made in USA," w/"M" in circle and style number "4578," 3 1/2" h. (ILLUS.) **24**

Lead Toy Soldier

Toy soldier, figure on flat base, standing at attention w/rifle at side, WWI-style helmet, worn paint, marked "Made in USA - 707," 3" h. (ILLUS.) **19**

Toy Soldier in Poncho

Toy soldier, flat base, marching figure wearing poncho & green helmet, rifle slung over shoulder, marked "USA - 523 - M," 2 3/4" h. (ILLUS.) **45**

Pewter

Pewter is a silver-grey alloy of tin with various amounts of antimony, copper and lead. Early pewter used bismuth rather than antimony, but this produced a lowered melting point and made the metal brittle. The proportions of each metal were, to a large measure, based on what was available, the purpose for which the metal would be used and the preference of the worker. Incidentally, brittania metal utilizes the same ingredients but never contains lead. It was produced from earlier formulas in the early 19th century. Pewter goes back to the Bronze Age. Examples of pewter wares have been found in various parts of the Roman Empire and there have been excavations of pewter in Britain. Pewtering was a well-established craft in England by the mid-1300s as indicated by the presence of the Craft of Pewterers, which regulated quality and workmanship. The manufacture of pewter items in America began in Colonial times. The English, trying to control the American production of pewter, imposed stiff regulations and taxes on tin. After the Revolutionary War, Americans were free to trade with whomever they chose. Early pieces were made by the casting technique using molds; articles requiring multiple castings were soldered or fused. About 1827 the stamping technique was adopted in America. Stamping consisted of shaping a flat sheet of metal between a male and a female die. In 1834 another technique was introduced in America. This was a spinning process that produced the various sections of the article, which were then soldered in the same fashion as the cast pieces. After all of the above processes, the pieces were skimmed, which entailed holding a sharp steel tool on a wooden handle against the article as it rotated on a lathe. This removed small amounts of metal in a spiral pattern. After this the piece was burnished while it was still on the lathe. This was done with a tool that had a polished stone or steel face that smoothed out small areas of roughness. Next the piece was buffed using a disk made of pieces of hide or cloth treated with a ground abrasive polishing powder. All varieties of housewares were made of pewter, including candlesticks, basins, plates, goblets, porringers, coffeepots, teapots, chocolate pots, cruet sets and creamers and sugar bowls. Also included in the pewter production were church-related items such as flagons, chalices, beakers, church cups and baptismal basins. It is interesting to note that, while most pewter articles are marked in some way, ecclesiastical pewter pieces are rarely found with a maker's mark. Many examples that were listed in early inventories are now very rare. It is thought that as they became obsolete, they were melted down. Some such items are nursing bottles, buttons, buckles, picture frames, various types of boxes and chamber pots.

By the mid-19th century, pewter was out of style as an everyday houseware product and was superseded by inexpensive silver plated wares, which often used pewter (or brittania) as the base metal to be highlighted with the silver plating. It was not until the revival of interest in early American antiques in the 1920s that pewter once again attracted the public's fancy. During this revival period many pewter objects were made that closely resembled their 18th and 19th century ancestors. Fortunately for today's collectors, these later copies often carry a manufacturer's marking and the words "Genuine Pewter," a phrase never used on antique originals.

Baptismal bowl, round domed foot tapering to a pedestal supporting a deep wide round bowl w/flattened flaring rim, Roswell Gleason, Dorchester, Massachusetts, 1822-71, 8 1/8" d., 5" h............ **$1,265**

Basin, eagle touch of Samuel Pierce, Greenfield, Massachusetts, 1792-1830, 13 1/4" d. (edge damage, wear w/dents & pitting) 220

Basin, round, eagle touch of Samuel Danforth, Hartford, Connecticut, 1795-1816, 8" d., 1 7/8" h. (wear, pitting, split in rim) 165

Basin, round, faint eagle touch, possibly Gershom Jones, Providence, Rhode Island, late 18th - early 19th c., 7 3/4" d. **275**

Nathaniel Austin Pewter Basin

Basin, round w/deep sides w/flared rim, eagle touch of Nathaniel Austin, Charlestown, Massachusetts, 1763-1807, wear, corroding, 8" d. (ILLUS.) 193

Basin, round w/deep slightly flared sides, eagle touch of Thomas Danforth III, Philadelphia,   Pennsylvania,   1807-13, 7 7/8" d. 990

Basin, round w/deep slightly flaring sides & wide flat bottom, eagle touch of Thomas Danforth III, Stepney, Connecticut & Philadelphia, 1777-1818, 12" d. (light pitting).. **1,155**

Basin, round w/flanged rim, touch marks of Townsend & Compton, England, late 18th - early 19th c., 9 1/8" d. (wear, pitting) 165

Basin, round w/upright sides & narrow flanged rim, Richard Lee (senior or junior), New England, late 18th - early 19th c., 8 3/4" d., 2" h. (polished) 578

Basin, round w/upright sides, Thomas D. Boardman, Hartford, Connecticut, 1805-50, 9 1/4" d. (minor pitting, scratches) 489

Basin, round w/wide flanged rim, eagle touch of Ashbil Griswold, Meriden, Connecticut,   1807-15,   13 1/8" d.   (wear, scratches) 495

Shallow Pewter Basin

Basin, shallow, partial Love touch mark & faint "London" (Jacobs #207, in or near Philadelphia, last half of the 18th c. or early 19th c.), American (ILLUS.) 350

Basin, w/flanged rim, partial eagle touch of Samuel Kilbourne, Baltimore, Maryland, 1814-39, 12" d. (dents) **468**

Basin, round w/deep upright sides, touch of Samuel Hamlin, Hartford, Connecticut, & Providence, Rhode Island, 1767-1801, 5 3/4" d., 2" h. (wear, repair) **523**

Basin, round deep sides w/molded rim, faint eagle touch, possibly Gersham Jones, Providence, Rhode Island, 1774-1809, 7 3/4" d. **275**

Basin, round w/flanged rim, touch mark of Samuel Hamlin, Hartford & Middletown, Connecticut, 1767-73, 7 3/4" d. **193**

Basin by Nathaniel Austin

Basin, deep wide rounded sides w/narrow flattened rim, eagle touch of Nathaniel Austin, Charlestown, Massachusetts, 1763-1800, wear & dents, 8" d. (ILLUS.) **550**

Basin, deep wide rounded sides w/narrow flattened rim, partial eagle touch of Thomas Danforth Boardman et al., Hartford, Connecticut, 1805-50, 8" d. (minor wear) **385**

Basin, round deep sides w/molded rim, touch marks of Townsend & Compton, England, late 18th - early 19th c., 9 1/8" d. (wear, pitting) **165**

Basin, wide flattened bottom, low sides w/molded rim, hammered bouge, partial London touch mark, 13" d., 3 1/4" h. (areas of pitting) **248**

Basin, wide w/rounded sides & narrow flattened rim, touch mark of Compton, Fenchurch Street, London, England, dark patina, 14" d., 3 1/2" h. **424**

Basket, Art Nouveau floral relief design, Kayserzinn, Germany, early 20th c., 11 1/2" w., 9" h. **259**

Bowl, shallow round form w/flanged rim, eagle touch of Blakeslee Barn(e)s, Philadelphia, 1812-17, 11 1/8" d. (wear, scratches) **358**

Bowl, wide shallow rounded form w/wide flanged rim, eagle touch of Ashbil Griswold, Meriden, Connecticut, 1802-42, wear & knife scratches, 11" d. (ILLUS. back w/mug page 89) **468**

Candlestick, round domed foot w/a ring- and knob-turned shaft below the cylindrical socket w/flattened rim, mark of Rufus Dunham, Westbrook, Maine, 1837-61, 6" h. (edges a bit battered) **165**

Candlestick, round stepped foot below the baluster- and ring-turned standard & tall cylindrical socket w/flattened wide rim, unmarked, 19th c., 9 7/8" h. **165**

Candlestick, domed foot below tall flaring & ringed cylindrical standard below the corseted candle socket w/flattened rim, touch of Henry Hopper, New York City, 1842-47, 9 1/2" **237**

Candlesticks, round foot tapering up to a ringed, tall waisted stem supporting a tall inverted bell-form socket w/wide rim, beaded detail, w/push-ups, probably American, 19th c., 10" h., pr. **385**

Candlesticks, wide round low domed foot below the ringed & flared cylindrical shaft below the tall corseted socket w/fitted bobéche, touch mark of Henry Hopper, New York, 1842-47, 10" h., pr. **660**

Candlesticks, low domed foot below the tall ringed & flaring cylindrical shaft supporting the corseted socket w/rolled rim, reeded bands around foot, top of shaft & on the rim, unmarked, 19th c., 10 1/4" h., pr. **248**

Chalices, round foot & ringed stem below the tall slightly flaring bell-form cylindrical cup, Leonard, Reed & Barton, Taunton, Massachusetts, 1835-40, 7" h., pr. (polished) **385**

Chamber lamp, lemon-shaped font on a short stem & dished round base w/side loop handle, touch mark of Roswell Gleason, Dorchester, Massachusetts, 1821-71, 4 3/4" h. (original whale oil burner w/one loose tube) **198**

Chandelier, six-light, the central baluster- and knob-turned standard suspending a large round ball w/acorn drop finial, the top of the ball issuing six long S-scroll arms ending in candle sockets w/drip trays, Europe, probably 19th c., 24" d. (several arms sagging from metal fatigue) **550**

Large Pewter Charger

Charger, faint touch marks on back, front rim also has touch marks of rooster-like bird and "Ø" repeated four times, hanger added, 20 1/4" d. (ILLUS.) **110**

Charger, flanged rim, touch mark "B.L.," 13 1/4" d. (wear, pitting) **193**

Charger, "London" mark w/sailing ship touch w/"United States of America, Flourish, Maxwell," Scottish, made for American trade, 16 5/8" d. **495**

Charger, "Love" touch mark w/double "London" marks, late 18th or early 19th c., 13" d..... **440**

Charger, round w/flanged rim, Frederick Bassett, New York & Hartford, 1761-99, 16" d............. **7,800**

Charger, round w/flanged slightly rolled rim w/tooled line, partial angel touch mark & "G.N.K.," 15 3/8" d......................... **330**

Charger, round w/wide flanged rim, crowned rose touch mark, rim stamped w/initials, England, late 18th c., 12 1/4" d. (some wear)................. **275**

Charger, round w/wide flanged rim, crowned rose touch marks & "London," England, late 18th c., 15" d. (wear, battering)................. **330**

Charger, round w/wide flanged rim, John Danforth, Norwich, Connecticut, 1773-95, 12 1/8" d. (knife scratches & minor dents) .. **1,265**

Charger, round, wide flanged rim, "Love" touch, Pennsylvania, ca. 1750-93, 13 1/2" d. (some wear, minor battering)....... **880**

Pewter Charger

Charger, Scottish, made for the American trade w/sailing ship touch mark & "Success to the United States," also partial Graham & Wardrop touch mark (Glasgow, 1776-1806, Cotterell #1943), 16 1/2" d. (ILLUS.)................. **440**

Charger, shallow round form w/flanged rim, unmarked, England, late 18th - early 19th c., 16 1/4" d. (wear, pitting) **275**

Charger, wide flanged rim, round, eagle touch of Thomas Danforth of Hartford, Connecticut w/"Boardman - Warranted," ca. 1820-30, 13 1/2" d. (minor wear & scratches) **825**

Charger, wide flanged rim, touch of David Melville, Newport, Rhode Island, 1776-93, 12 1/4" d. (wear, scratches)................. **605**

Charger, round w/flanged rim, "London" touch marks, England, 10 7/8" d. (polished, scratches) **303**

Charger, round dished center w/wide flanged rim, "Love" touch, late 18th c., 12" d. (wear, pitting, scratches)................. **440**

Charger, round dished form w/wide gently upcurved reeded rim w/stamped initials, crown & rose touch marks, Europe, 12 1/4" d. (wear) **193**

Charger, round w/wide flanged rim, engraved coat-of-arms on the rim, marked "Nicholson" & partial eagle touch "Robert...," England, 13 1/2" d................. **303**

Charger, round w/wide flanged & reeded rim, English crowned rose touch mark, 14 1/4" d. (some wear) **220**

Very Large European Pewter Charger

Charger, very wide round dished center w/a very wide flanged rim w/beaded edge, Europe, wear, pitting & small repair, 24" d. (ILLUS.)................. **2,750**

Chocolate mold, cast, hinged, incised design of a diesel train engine & tender, marked "E & Co. NY 1225," closed 7" l. (ILLUS. open, below)................. **110**

Chocolate set: cov. pot, six small cylindrical tumblers & a tray; Art Nouveau style, the tall pot in the form of a stylized duck w/slender handle down the back, on a slightly dished oval tray, marked "Kayserzinn," Germany, early 20th c., pot 8" h., the set................. **275**

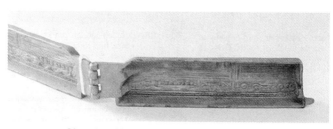

Chocolate Mold with Image of Diesel Engine

Coffee & tea service: cov. coffeepot, cov. teapot, cov. sugar bowl, creamer & shaped oval tray; Art Nouveau style, the footed ovoid hollowware pieces w/angular handles & raised oblong panels of stylized flowers & leaves, an engraved initial on each piece, raised or impressed marks for Kayserzinn, Germany, late 19th - early 20th c., tray 20" l., coffeepot 10" h., the set 345

Tall Pewter Coffeepot

Coffeepot, cov., bulbous body w/tooled lines & stepped domed lid w/wooden wafer finial, black paint on finial & handle, touch mark "F. Porter Westbrook No. 1" (Freeman Porter, Westbrook, Maine, ca. 1835-1860), 11 1/4" h. (ILLUS.) 358

Coffeepot, cov., tall lighthouse-form, hinged domed cover w/knopped finial, tapering body w/multiple encircling rings, molded S-shaped handle, William Calder, Providence, Rhode Island, 1817-56, 11 1/4" h. 1,150

Coffeepot, cov., tall lighthouse-form, hinged domed cover w/wafer finial, tapering body, stepped base, paneled spout, scrolled ear handle, touch mark for Sellow & Co. Cincinnati, 11" h. (minor wear & finial bent) 413

Communion flagon, cov., flared round base w/tall cylindrical gently tapering body w/a medial band, stepped domed hinged cover w/thumbrest, simple C-scroll handle, rim spout, Reed & Barton, mid-19th c., 11 1/4" h................. 220

Cookie board, cast, rectangular, divided into twelve segments representing varied topics including berries, birds, flowers, animals & people, wooden backing, 4 1/2 x 7 1/2" 165

Cookie board, cast, rectangular, w/twelve square segments each w/a different scene representing a human occupation, wooden back, 4 3/4 x 8" (attachment damage to top corners)................... 193

Creamer, short pedestal base below the wide baluster-form body w/a peaked center band, ornate C-scroll handle & wide integral rim spout, touch mark of Boardman & Hart, New York, 1828-53, 6 1/2" h. (dents, handle crooked)................... 110

Dish, deep dished center w/wide flanged rim, Samuel Hamlin, Sr. or Jr., Providence, Rhode Island, late 18th - early 19th c., 13 3/4" d................... 2,280

Dish, deep dished round center w/flanged rim, Peter Young, New York or Albany, 1775-95, 13 3/4" d.................... 480

Dish, round shallow form w/wide flanged rim, eagle touch of James Porter, Connecticut Valley, 1795-1803 & Baltimore, Maryland, 1803, 13" d. (areas of pitting) 330

Dish, round shallow form w/wide flanged rim, Samuel Danforth, Hartford, Connecticut, 1795-1816, 13 1/8" d. (pitting) 413

Sheldon and Feltman Flagon

Flagon, cov., flaring stepped round base, tall cylindrical body w/double rings around the center, flared rim w/hinged stepped, domed cover, short curved rim spout, long C-scroll handle, Smith, Sheldon & James Feltman, Jr., New York, 1847-48, area of pitting on base, dents, 10 5/8" h. (ILLUS.)............................ 385

Flagon, cov., ringed base & slightly tapering cylindrical body w/a stepped dome cover w/thumbrest, S-scroll handle, arched rim spout, eagle touch of Boardman & Co., New York, New York, 1825-27, 7 3/4" h. .. 2,860

Flagon, cov., tall slightly tapering cylindrical body w/a flaring ringed base, hinged pointed pagoda cover w/pointed finial, wide rim spout, C-form handle, lion touch of Thomas D. Boardman, Hartford, Connecticut, 1830+, 11 1/2" h. (base slightly battered)................................ 440

Flagon, cov., tall slightly tapering cylindrical body w/a flaring ringed base & rings below the flaring rim, domed cover w/knob finial, S-scroll handle w/thumbrest, wide rim spout, Israel Trask, Beverly, Massachusetts, 1807-56, 12 1/4" h. 1,100

Flagon, cov., tall tapering cylindrical body w/flared ringed base & mid-body ring, flared rim w/arched rim spout, hinged domed cover w/thumbrest, long S-scroll handle w/flat terminal, Reed and Barton, mid-19th c., 9 5/8" h. (minor pitting on handle)................................ 440

Flagon, cov., tall tapering cylindrical sides on a flaring domed round base, stepped domed hinged cover w/beehive finial, double scroll handle, Samuel Danforth, Hartford, Connecticut, 1795-1816, 6 1/4" d., 13 1/2" h.................... 14,400

Flagon, tall cylindrical form decorated w/stylized wheat stalks & hops in low-relief, impressed Kayserzinn mark & "4289," Germany, early 20th c., 15 7/8" h. 201

Lamp, a dished tray base w/loop edge handle, centered by an acorn-form font w/whale oil burner, Henry Hopper, New York City, 1842-47, 5" h. (polished) 193

Lamp, fluid-burning, a domed round foot & ringed stem supporting a slightly flaring cylindrical font w/domed top fitted w/a camphene burner, mark of Eben Smith, Beverly, Massachusetts, 1813-56, 6 7/8" h. (no snuffer) 413

Pewter Lamp

Lamp, round base, acorn font w/burning fluid burners & snuffer caps, touch mark for "Capen & Molineux, NY" (1848-1854), 9 1/4" h. (ILLUS.) 413

Lamp, whale oil, cylindrical font w/burner raised on a ring-turned & knopped stem on a stepped round foot, 19th c., 6" h. plus burner 165

Lamp, whale oil, upright disk-form font w/whale oil burner flanked on each side by an upright framed bull's-eye focusing lens, raised on a ring-turned pedestal & stepped disk foot, unmarked, 19th c., 9" h. (repair, burner not a good fit) 385

Lamp, low domed round foot tapering to a slender stem supporting the acorn-form font w/old whale oil burner, touch mark of Eben Smith, Beverly, Massachusetts, 1814-1856, 5 5/8" h. (corroded) 193

Lamp, round dished foot supporting a slender turned shaft supporting the inverted acorn-form font w/camphene burners, mark of Capen & Molineux, New York City, 1848-54, polished, 7 5/8" h. 303

Lamps, whale oil, ovoid-shaped font w/double burner raised on a tall conical pedestal base w/tooled rings, unsigned, 8" h., pr. (minor dents in base) 248

Measure, ovoid body w/a wide slightly flaring short neck, C-form strap handle, attributed to Boardman, 19th c., quart, 6 5/8" h. (dents, wear & repair) 523

Measure, tankard-form w/tapering cylindrical sides & S-scroll handle, attributed to Parks Boyd, Philadelphia, unmarked, late 18th - early 19th c., quart, 5 1/2" h. (repair) 550

Measures, cylindrical w/molded base & rim, a long angled side handle, France, late 19th - early 20th c., 1 3/4" to 7" h., graduated set of 7 121

Pewter Three-rabbit Chocolate Mold

Mold, chocolate, in the form of three upright rabbits, hinged at feet, closed measures 3 x 13", 8 1/2" h. (ILLUS.) 395

Four-egg Pewter Chocolate Mold

Mold, chocolate, in the shape of four Easter eggs decorated w/lambs, rabbits & chicks, hinged down middle of mold, closed measures 3 x 8 1/4", 10 1/2" h. (ILLUS.) 395

Pewter Masonic Ice Cream Mold

Mold, ice cream, in the form of Masonic symbol, marked "948 1/2 E&G Co. NY," closed measures 1 x 4 1/2 x 5 1/2" (ILLUS.) 70

Pewter Owl Ice Cream Mold

Mold, ice cream, in the shape of an owl, hinged at side, marked "175," closed measures 2 x 3 3/8", 4 1/4" h. (ILLUS. on previous page) 145

Mug, straight-sided w/low fillet-molded foot, ball terminal & C-scroll handle, Samuel Hamlin, Providence, Rhode Island, 1801-56, quart, 4 7/8" d., 6" h. 5,700

Mug, straight-sided w/molded foot & ball terminal C-scroll handle, William Will, Philadelphia, 1764-98, quart, 4 5/8" d., 5 1/2" h. 9,000

Mug, tapering cylindrical form w/heavy C-form handle, Jacob Whitmore, Middletown, Connecticut, 1758-90, 4 1/2" h. (polished, wear, small scratches, handle w/possible repair at top) 4,015

Mug, tapering cylindrical form w/flared base & ring around lower body, cast C-scroll handle, indistinct interior touch, American (wear & dents) 578

Group of American Pewter Pieces

Mug, tapering cylindrical form w/flared base & ring around lower body, cast C-scroll handle, eagle touch of Thomas Danforth Boardman et al., Hartford, Connecticut, 1805-42, somewhat battered, handle re-soldered, small split in base, 4 1/2" h. (ILLUS. front left) 935

Pitcher, cov., tankard-type, slightly tapering cylindrical body w/flared foot, hinged stepped & domed cover, deep rim spout, C-scroll handle, eagle touch of Boardman & Co., New York, New York, 1825-27, 7 5/8" h. (bottom edge damage, spout battered) 660

Pitcher, long flaring neck on a bulbous base w/raised oak leaves & acorns, raised mark for Kayserzinn, Germany, early 20th c., 11" h. (wear) 316

Pitcher, water, bulbous ovoid body w/flat rim & rim spout, angled handle, faint touch of Rufus Dunham, Westbrook, Maine, 1837-60, 6 3/4" h. (repair, corrosion, battering) 193

Pitcher, water, wide baluster-form body w/a rim spout & simple C-scroll handle, faint touch of Rufus Dunham, Westbrook, Maine, 1837-60, 6 1/2" h. (small handle split, repairs) 220

Pitcher, water, wide baluster-form body w/angled & pointed handle & wide integral rim spout, touch mark of Freeman Porter, Westbrook, Maine, 1835-60, 7" h. (wear, dents) 303

Pitcher, water, bulbous baluster-form body w/wide rim spout & cast C-scroll handle, medial band, touch mark of Sellew & Co., Cincinnati, Ohio, 1832-60, 9" h. (dented ring below belly rib) 358

Plaque, Art Nouveau style, oval, decorated in relief w/maidens, stamped WMF marks, Germany, ca. 1900, 23" l. 1,840

Plate, flanged rim, crowned rose touch of Jacob Whitmore, Middletown, Connecticut, 1758-90, 8" d. (wear, scratches) 220

Plate, flanged rim, eagle touch of Samuel Danforth, Hartford, Connecticut, 1795-1816, 7 7/8" d. 385

Thomas D. Boardman Plate

Plate, flanged rim, eagle touch of Thomas Danforth Boardman, Hartford, Connecticut, early 19th c., wear & pitting, 10 3/4" h. (ILLUS.) 330

Plate, flanged rim, eagle touch of Thomas Danforth III, Philadelphia, 1807-13, 7 3/4" d. (wear, pitting, small rim split) 193

Plate, flanged rim & hammered bouge, William Will, Philadelphia, 1764-1798, 8" d. 1,200

Plate, flanged rim, "Love" touch, Pennsylvania, ca. 1750-93, back w/scratch-engraved initials & "1856," 8 1/2" d. 275

Plate, flanged rim, "Made in Newp...." touch of David Melville, Newport, Rhode Island, 1776-93, 8" d. (wear) 358

Plate, flanged rim, partial eagle touch, probably Parks Boyd, Philadelphia, 1795-1819, 8" d. (worn, battered) 220

Plate, flanged rim, partial rampant lion touch, probably Thomas Danforth II, Middletown, Connecticut, 1755-82, 8" d. (worn, battered) 193

Plate, flanged rim, touch mark of Frederick Basset, New York, New York, late 18th c., rare, 8 3/8" d. (very worn, battered) 275

Plate, flanged rim, touch of David Melville, Newport, Rhode Island, 1776-93, 8 1/4" d. (wear, light pitting) 193

Plate, flanged rim, touch of Nathaniel Austin, Charlestown, Massachusetts, 1763-1807, stamped initials in rim, 8 5/8" d. (wear, pitting) 330

Plate, round, partial touch marks for Thomas Danford (Taunton, Massachusetts, & Norwich, Connecticut, 1727-1773), 9" d. 248

Plate, round w/deep center well & flanged rim, William Calder, Providence, Rhode Island, 1817-56, 11 3/8" d. (light overall pitting) 358

Plate, round w/flanged rim, Boardman & Co., New York, New York, 1805-50, 9 3/8" d. (scratches, some battering) 215

Plate, round w/flanged rim, eagle touch of Thomas Danforth III, Stepney or Rocky Hill, Connecticut & Philadelphia, 1777-1818, 7 7/8" d. (minor wear & battering) 385

Plate, round w/flanged rim, Joseph Danforth, Middletown, Connecticut, 1780-88, 7 7/8" d. (some wear & pitting) 440

Plate, round w/flanged rim, "London" touch of John Skinner, Boston, Massachusetts, 1760-90, 8 1/2" d. 303

Plate, round w/flanged rim, Roswell Gleason, Dorchester, Massachusetts, 1822-71, 9 1/4" d. (some wear & dents) 275

Plate, wide flanged rim, eagle & rectangular touches of Blakeslee Barnes, Philadelphia, 1812-17, 11 1/4" d. (wear, scratches, edge damage) 303

Plate, wide flanged rim, "Love" touch, Pennsylvania, ca. 1750-93, 8 7/8" d. 231

Plate, wide flanged rim, touch mark of Jacob Whitmore, Middletown, Connecticut, 1758-90, 8" d. (battering, wear) 138

Plate, wide flanged rim, touch of Benjamin Harbeson, Philadelphia, ca. 1800, 7 7/8" d. (wear, corroded area) 248

Plate, wide flanged rim, touch of John Danforth, Norwich, Connecticut, 1773-93, 9 3/8" d. (wear, scratches) 248

Plate, wide flanged rim, touch of Roswell Gleason, Dorchester, Massachusetts, 1821-71, 9 1/4" d. 165

Plate, flanged rim, double touch w/eagle & initials of Blakslee Barns, Philadelphia, Pennsylvania, 1812-17, 7 3/4" d. (minor rim dents & wear) 385

Plate, flanged rim, eagle touch of Samuel Kilbourn, Baltimore, Maryland, 1814-39, 7 3/4" d. (minor wear) 220

Plate, flanged rim, eagle touch of Samuel Kilbourn, Baltimore, Maryland, 1814-39, 7 3/4" d. (wear, scratches) 358

Plate, flanged rim, eagle touch of Thomas Badger, Boston, Massachusetts, 1787-1815, 7 3/4" d. (minor wear, scratches) 385

Plate, flanged rim, eagle touch of Thomas Danforth III, Philadelphia, 1777-1818, 7 3/4" d. 385

Plate, flanged rim, mark of Samuel Ellis, London, England, late 18th c., scratch-engraved initials on rim "H.L.," 7 3/4" d. (some wear & scratches) 110

Plate, flanged rim, touch of Samuel Kilbourn, Baltimore, Maryland, ca. 1820, 7 3/4" d. (wear, scratches) 275

Plate, round w/flanged rim, "Love" touch, late 18th c., 7 7/8" d. (minor wear) 303

Plate, flanged rim, double touches of Blak(e)slee Barn(e)s, Philadelphia, Pennsylvania, 1812-17, 8" d. 275

Plate, flanged rim, eagle touch of William Danforth, Middletown, Connecticut, 1792-1820, 8" d. (wear, scratches) 275

Plate, round w/wide flanged rim, eagle touch of Robert Palethorp, Jr., Philadelphia, 1817-21, 8 3/8" d. (minor wear) 440

Plate, flanged rim, eagle touch of Thomas Badger, Boston, 1787-1815, 8 1/2" d. (bottom pitted & worn) 248

Plate, flanged rim, touch mark of Nathaniel Austin, Charlestown, Massachusetts, 1763-1807, 8 1/2" d. 248

Plate, flanged rim, touch of David Melville, Newport, Rhode Island, 1776-93, 8 1/2" d. 160

Plate, flanged rim, eagle touch of George Lightner, Baltimore, Maryland, 1806-15, 8 3/4" d. (minor rim dents) 358

Plate, impressed "EF" on rim, touch mark of John Skinner, Boston, Massachusetts, 1760-90, 9 3/16" d. (minor pitting, scratches) 345

Plate, dished center & wide flanged rim, lion touch mark of Thomas D. Boardman, 1830 on, 9 1/2" d. (pitted) 385

Plate, flanged rim, eagle touch & marks of Nathaniel Austin, Charlestown, Massachusetts, 1763-1800, 9 1/2" d. (battered, rim repair) 220

Plate, round w/flanged rim, eagle touch of Boardman & Co., New York, 1825-27, 10 3/4" d. (wear, corrosion, scratches) 275

Plate, deeply dished w/wide flanged rim, touch mark of Parks Boyd, Philadelphia, 1795-1819, 11" d. (wear, scratches) 550

Plate, flanged rim, touch mark of Joseph Danforth, Middletown, Connecticut, 1780-88, 12" d. 358

Plates, set of eight, all have "London" touch marks, some are marked "Superfine," rims stamped "I.H.B.," 9 1/4" d., the set 935

B. Barn(e)s Pewter Plates

Plates, dished w/wide flanged rim, eagle touch mark of Blak(e)slee Barn(e)s, Philadelphia, 1812-17, some battering, wear & scratches, 7 7/8" d., set of 6 (ILLUS. of part) 1,870

Large Pewter Platter

Platter, oval Art Nouveau-style platter decorated w/raised images of a muskie chasing a smaller fish, w/crabs, sea horses, starfish and squid around rim, marked on back "Kayserzinn 4325," 11 1/2 x 23 3/4" (ILLUS.) 170

Porringer, cast pierced floral scroll tab handle, anchor touch of William Billings, Providence, Rhode Island, 1791-1806, 5" d. 880

Porringer, cast pierced floral scroll tab handle, eagle touch of Samuel E. Hamlin, Jr., Providence, Rhode Island, 1801-56, 5 1/2" d. 660

Porringer, cast pierced floral scroll tab handle, eagle touch of William Calder, Providence, Rhode Island, 1817-56, 5" d. (small split in handle) 330

Porringer, cast pierced floral scrolled tab handle, eagle touch of Thomas Danforth Boardman, Hartford, Connecticut, 1804 - after 1860, 5 1/2" d. 495

William Calder Porringer

Porringer, cast pierced foliate scroll handle, eagle touch of William Calder, Providence, Rhode Island, 1817-56, minor dents, 5 1/4" d. (ILLUS.) 660

Dolphin-handled Pewter Porringer

Porringer, pierced double-dolphin & shield cast handle, unmarked American, minor pitting, small rim splits, 19th c., 5 3/4" d. (ILLUS.) 275

Porringer, round w/cast pierced crown handle, unmarked, 5 1/2" d. 193

Porringer, round w/pierced crown & scroll handle, Thomas D. & Sherman Boardman, Hartford, Connecticut, 1810-30, 5" d. (minor pitting & scratches, polished) 440

Porringer, round w/pierced floral scroll handle, Samuel Hamlin, Jr., Providence, Rhode Island, 1801-56, 5 3/8" d. (minor dents) 550

Porringer, round w/pierced floral scroll handle, Thomas D. & Sherman Boardman, Hartford, Connecticut, 1810-30, 5 1/4" d. (dent) 660

Porringer, round w/pierced floral scroll handle, William Billings, Providence, Rhode Island, 1791-1806, 5 1/8" d. (minor pitting & scratches, polished) 550

Porringer, round w/pierced floral scroll handle, William Calder, Providence, Rhode Island, 1817-56, 5" d. 660

Porringer, round w/pierced geometric handle, Samuel E. Hamlin, Jr., Providence, Rhode Island, 1801-56, 4 1/8" d. (minor pitting, polished) 495

Porringer, round w/pierced Old English-style handle, Thomas D. & Sherman Boardman, Hartford, Connecticut, 1810-30, 4" d. 715

Porringer, round w/pierced scroll & crown handle, touch mark "IG," New England, 4 1/4" d. (minor dent) 330

Porringer, round w/plain rounded tab handle w/hanging hole, attributed to Pennsylvania, 5 1/4" d. plus handle, 2" h. (polished, small rim split near handle) 440

Porringer, small round bowl w/scroll-pierced pointed tab handle, Richard Lee (senior or junior), New England, late 18th - early 19th c., 3 3/4" d. (polished) 1,183

Porringer, round w/scroll-pierced tab handle, touch mark of Thomas D. & Sherman Boardman, Hartford, Connecticut, 1810-30, 4 1/2" d. 297

Porringer, cast crown handle, marked "IC," attributed to the Boston area, 4 3/4" d. 193

Porringer, round w/plain rounded tab handle w/hanging hold, scratch-engraved date "1848" on back of handle, 5 1/4" d. (wear) 110

Porringer, round bowl w/pierced Old English style handle, unmarked American, 19th c., bowl 5 1/2" d. 193

Porringer, round w/cast crown handle, marked "S.G." on handle, New England, 5 1/2" d. 303

Soup plate, flanged rim, thistle touch mark, England, rim engraved w/initials, 9 3/4" d. 138

Rare American Pewter Sugar Bowl

Sugar bowl, cov., round slightly domed foot below the stepped tapering rounded body w/a beaded rim band, the stepped, domed cover w/a beaded rim band & urn-form finial, attributed to Parks Boyd, Philadelphia, ca. 1800, finial & bowl slightly bent, 5" d., 4 1/2" h. (ILLUS.) **6,900**

Sugar bowl, cov., thick pedestal base supported w/wide squatty bulbous lower body w/a wide flared upper body, double C-scroll cast handles, inset domed & pointed cover w/incomplete wafer, attributed to Robert Palethorpe, Jr., Philadelphia, 1817-22, 8 1/8" h. (somewhat battered, handles resoldered) **220**

Syrup jug, cov., flared base on tall cylindrical body w/wide flared rim, hinged pointed cover w/button finial, double C-scroll cast handle, integral rim spout, unmarked American, mid-19th c., 6 1/8" h. **193**

Tankard, Art Nouveau style, cylindrical w/C-form handle, decorated w/raised stylized fruiting branch flanking the handle & extending around the body, impressed marks of Liberty & Co., England, early 20th c., 5 3/8" h. (dents, minor pitting & corrosion) **201**

Early Swiss Pewter Tankard

Tankard, cov., cylindrical ringed body w/a wide flaring ringed foot, cupped rim w/spout, flat hinged cover w/forked thumbrest, strap handle, top dated "1605," stamped "Zanon...Antoine," Switzerland, 8 1/4" h. (ILLUS.) **748**

Tankard, cov., cylindrical w/flared ringed base, hinged stepped domed cover, S-scroll handle w/pierced thumbpiece, interior touch of H.A. and Sons, w/letter to Charles Montgomery, 6 7/8" h. (minor dents) **1,705**

Tankard, cov., flared ringed base & gently tapering cylindrical sides, hinged stepped domed cover w/scrolled ram's horn thumbrest, S-scroll handle w/fish tail terminal, Frederick Bassett, New York or Hartford, Connecticut, 1761-99, quart, 5" d., 7" h. **30,650**

Rare American Pewter Tankard

Tankard, cov., slightly tapering body w/banded base & rim, hinged domed cover w/molded thumbrest & overhanging rim, cased S-scroll handle, Peter Young, Albany, New York, ca. 1795, 4 3/4" d., 7" h. (ILLUS.) **16,100**

Rare Early American Pewter Tankard

Tankard, cov., slightly tapering cylindrical
form w/ringed base, the flat-topped
domed cover w/a crenate lip & chair back
thumbpiece, the hollow scroll handle w/a
ball terminal, John Will, New York City,
1752-74, 4 5/8" d., 5 1/2" h. (ILLUS. on
previous page) **38,125**

Tankard, cov., slightly tapering cylindrical
body w/flaring foot & lower body ring,
stepped & domed hinged cover w/thumb-
piece, cast C-scroll handle, faint interior
touch w/"WC," possibly William Charles-
ley, England, 7" h............................ **550**

Tazza, Arts & Crafts style, a wide shallow
rounded bowl w/incurved sides flanked by
pierced gryphon handles, raised on a slender stem w/a flaring round foot, hammered
surface w/a row of small embossed beads
around the top of the bowl & around the
foot, impressed mark "W & Co. English
Pewter - Hand-beaten - Homeland," early
20th c., 11" d., 10" h. (minor surface wear)..... **173**

Teapot, cov., bulbous pear-shaped body tapering to a high domed cover w/pointed
finial w/ivory wafer, swan's-neck paneled
spout, arched C-scroll handle, Thomas
D. & Sherman Boardman, Hartford, Con-
necticut, 1810-30, 8" h. (polished) **880**

Teapot, cov., flared pedestal base below
the squatty bulbous body w/a stepped
shoulder to the short flaring neck, hinged
pointed domed cover, C-scroll handle,
swan's-neck spout, J.D. Locke, New
York City, 1835-60, 9" h. **413**

Teapot, cov., flaring ringed foot below the
spherical body tapering to a flaring neck,
hinged domed cover, D-form scroll handle, swan's-neck spout, George Richardson, Sr., Boston, Massachusetts, 1818-
28, Cranston, Rhode Island, 1828-45,
8" h. (pitting) **330**

Teapot, cov., footed, half-round lower body
w/a short waisted & widely flaring neck,
domed cover w/disk finial, ornate C-scroll
handle & swan's-neck spout, Boardman
& Hart, New York, 1828-53, 7 1/2" h. (minor dents)........................ **358**

Teapot, cov., footed, squatty bulbous body
tapering to a short flared neck, hinged
domed cover w/wooden finial wafer,
swan's-neck spout, pointed arched scroll
handle w/black paint, J.W. Cahill &
Co., ca. 1830s, 7" h. (polished) **358**

Teapot, cov., footed, squatty bulbous body
w/a short flaring neck, hinged pointed
domed cover, swan's-neck spout & ornate
scroll handle, mark of Smith & Co., Boston,
Massachusetts, 1847-49, 6 3/4" h.................. **303**

Teapot, cov., footed, squatty bulbous body
w/wide center band tapering to a low flaring neck, hinged domed cover w/disk finial, pointed scroll black-painted metal
handle, swan's-neck spout, Josiah Danforth, Middletown, Connecticut, 1825-37,
6 3/4" h. (worn handle paint)........................ **385**

Teapot, cov., footed tall baluster-form body
w/a domed hinged lid w/finial, swan's-neck
spout & angled scroll handle, Roswell
Gleason, Dorchester, Massachusetts,
1822-71 (minor pitting, finial incomplete)........ **413**

Allen Porter Pewter Tall Teapot

Teapot, cov., footed tall baluster-form body
w/a high domed cover & disk finial, high C-
scroll black-painted handle, tall swan's-
neck spout, Allen Porter, Westbrook,
Maine, 1830-40, 12 1/4" h. (ILLUS.)................ **413**

Teapot, cov., lighthouse-form, tall tapering
cylindrical body w/raised rings around the
top & base & w/engraved shield-shaped
panels surrounded by flowers on each
side, domed hinged cover w/disk finial,
pointed C-scroll black-painted wooden
handle, swan's-neck spout, Eben Smith,
Beverly,   Massachusetts,   1813-56,
11 3/4" h............................ **468**

Teapot, cov., pear-shaped w/high domed
hinged cover, ornate C-scroll handle &
swan's-neck spout, attributed to Samuel
Pierce,   Greenfield,   Massachusetts,
1807-31, 7" h............................ **743**

Teapot, cov., pedestal base below the gently flaring cylindrical body w/a high waisted neck, domed cover w/wood finial,
painted ornate scroll handle, swan's-
neck spout, George Richardson, Sr.,
Boston, Massachusetts, & Cranston,
Rhode Island, 1818-1828, 9 1/2" h. (han-
dle repaint, minor cover repair)...................... **330**

Teapot, cov., pigeon-breasted body on a
short pedestal base w/flaring foot, flared
rim & inset domed hinged cover w/wood-
en blossom finial, ornate C-scroll handle
& swan's-neck spout, touch of Roswell
Gleason, Dorchester, Massachusetts,
1821-71, 9 1/2" h. (finial repaired)................. **110**

Teapot, cov., Queen Anne-style, squatty
bulbous pear-shaped body w/a pointed
domed hinged lid, shaped spout &
arched C-scroll handle, Israel Trask,
Beverly, Massachusetts, 1807-56 (pit-
ting, wear, old repair)...................... **715**

Teapot, cov., ring-turned round pedestal
foot below a flaring cylindrical lower body
& tall waisted upper body w/flaring rim,
hinged stepped & domed cover w/disk
finial, large pointed scroll black-enam-
eled handle, swan's-neck spout, Rufus
Durham, Westbrook, Maine, 1837-61,
12" h. (minor dent on base)............................ **468**

Teapot, cov., round flaring foot below the
rounded bulbous lower body w/an incurved shoulder band below the tall
waisted upper body w/a flaring rim,
hinged stepped & domed cover w/finial,

swan's-neck spout, ornate scroll metal handle, eagle touch probably of Luther Boardman, South Reading, Massachusetts, 1836-42, 10 3/4" h. **468**

Teapot, cov., round foot & short pedestal below the wide squatty bulbous body w/a wide shoulder tapering to a short flaring neck, hinged domed cover w/disk finial, re-enameled black metal C-scroll handle, swan's-neck spout, Daniel Curtis, Albany, New York, 1822-40, 9" h. **440**

Teapot, cov., round pedestal foot below the tall body w/a slightly flaring cylindrical lower section below a tall stepped & slightly waisted upper body w/flared rim, hinged domed cover w/finial, ornate black-painted C-scroll handle, swan's-neck spout, William Savage, Middletown, Connecticut, late 1830s, 10" h. (light overall pitting)........... **440**

Teapot, cov., round short pedestal foot below the wide squatty bulbous body w/angled shoulders to the short flaring neck, hinged domed cover, paneled spout, angled C-scroll handle, eagle touch of Ashbil Griswold, Meriden, Connecticut, 1802-42, 8 1/4" h. (small hole in handle, repaired hinge, splits in bottom) **248**

Teapot, cov., round stepped foot below the wide squatty bulbous body tapering to a short flaring neck, hinged domed cover w/wooden disk finial, pointed scrolled handle, swan's-neck spout, tooled line trim, Roswell Gleason, Dorchester, Massachusetts, 1822-71, 7 1/2" h. (light pitting) **330**

Teapot, cov., short foot below the bulbous body w/a tall wide waisted neck & hinged domed cover, high C-scroll metal handle & swan's-neck spout, Josiah Danforth, Middletown, Connecticut, 1821-1843, 7" h. (minor dents) **440**

Teapot, cov., short pedestal base below squatty wide swelled cylindrical body tapering to flared neck w/hinged domed cover, ornate C-scroll handle & swan's-neck spout, Sellew & Co., Cincinnati, 1832-60, 7 7/8" h. (repairs) **220**

Teapot, cov., short pedestal base & bulbous ovoid body tapering to a flaring neck, hinged pointed domed cover, swan's-neck spout & C-scroll metal handle, tooled lines around body, probably Joshua B. Graves, Middletown, Connecticut, ca. 1850, 9" h. (minor dents) **292**

Teapot, cov., slightly tapering cylindrical body w/hinged pagoda cover w/finial, ornate C-scroll handle & swan's-neck spout, mark of H.B. Ward & Co., Wallingford, Connecticut, ca. 1850s, 10 1/4" h. (minor dents, soldered repairs) **220**

Teapot, cov., squatty pear shape w/a hinged stepped & pointed domed cover w/wooden disk finial, paneled swan's-neck spout, arched black-painted C-scroll handle, Roswell Gleason, Dorchester, Massachusetts, 1822-71, 6 3/4" h. (split in finial, flake in handle) **825**

Teapot, cov., tall baluster-form body w/tooled ring base & wide raised band around the middle, domed cover w/small wood wafer finial, ornate C-scroll black-painted metal

handle, swan's-neck spout, eagle touch of Ashbil Griswold, Meriden, Connecticut, 1802-42, 10" h. (minor dents & pitting) **578**

Teapot, cov., tall footed form w/slightly flaring cylindrical lower body below a tall waisted neck w/flared rim, hinged domed cover w/finial, C-scroll handle & swan's-neck spout, Josiah Danforth, Middletown, Connecticut, 1821-1843, 10 1/4" h. (some well done soldered repairs, wooden finial reglued) **220**

Teapot, cov., tall footed inverted pear-shaped baluster-form w/flaring rim & inset hinged cover w/blossom finial, swan's-neck spout & angled C-scroll handle, Roswell Gleason, Dorchester, Massachusetts, 1822-71, 10 1/2" h. (ILLUS. front right w/mug, page 89) **220**

Teapot, cov., tall footed pigeon-breasted body w/flared rim & hinged domed cover, ornate C-scroll handle & swan's-neck spout, impressed mark of Leonard, Reed & Barton, Taunton, Massachusetts, 1835-40, 12 1/4" h... **192**

Teapot, cov., tall footed tapering undulating body w/flared rim & domed hinged cover, C-scroll handle & swan's-neck spout, touch of Sellow & Co., Cincinnati, Ohio, 1832-60, 11 1/4" h... **275**

American Lighthouse-form Teapot

Teapot, cov., tall lighthouse form, flared ringed base on the tall gently tapering body w/a flared rim & high domed cover w/finial, swan's-neck spout & ornate C-scroll black-painted metal handle, John Munson, Yalesville, Connecticut, 1846-52, 11" h. (ILLUS.).. **605**

Teapot, cov., tall lighthouse-form, flared base & tall gently tapering body w/domed cover, ornate C-scroll handle & swan's-neck spout, Freeman Porter, Westbrook, Maine, 1835-60s, 10 3/4" h. **468**

Teapot, cov., tall lighthouse-form, flared & ringed base below the tapering cylindrical sides w/a raised center band, pointed domed hinged cover w/finial, ornate C-scroll handle, swan's-neck spout, John H. Whitlock, Troy, New York, 1836-44, 11 1/4" (areas of pitting, well done repair) **330**

Teapot, cov., tall lighthouse-style body w/stepped flared base, hinged domed cover, long C-scroll handle, swan's-neck spout, Sellew & Co., Cincinnati, Ohio, 1832-60, 11 7/8" h. (repair at base, light pitting) 330

Teapot, cov., tall pigeon-breasted form, a paneled domed pedestal base supporting a wide squatty bulbous paneled body tapering to a flaring paneled neck, hinged domed paneled cover & fluted spout, scrolled wooden handle, Roswell Gleason, Dorchester, Massachusetts, 1822-71, 10" h. 303

Teapot, cov., tall ring-footed baluster-form w/hinged domed cover w/button finial, ornate C-scroll black-painted metal handle, swan's-neck spout, eagle touch of Ashbil Griswold, Meriden, Connecticut, 1802-42, 11 1/2" h. (foot restoration) 303

Teapot, cov., tall slightly tapering cylindrical body w/flared foot, hinged domed cover, S-scroll handle, swan's-neck spout, Simpson & Benham, New York, New York, 1845-47, 11" h. (minor soldered repair) 385

Teapot, cov., tapering cylindrical body w/hinged domed cover, ornate C-scroll handle, swan's-neck spout, touch of Morey & Ober, Boston, Massachusetts, 1852-55, 7 1/8" h. 385

Teapot, cov., wide flaring foot below the wide half-round lower body & wide tapering shoulder to a short flaring neck, domed cover w/disk finial, high C-scroll black handle, swan's-neck spout, Sellew & Co., Cincinnati, Ohio, 1830-60, 71/2" h. (small dent, tiny paint flake on handle) 303

Teapot, cov., individual-size, footed small bulbous body tapering to a tall waisted neck w/pointed cover w/button finial, long swan's-neck spout & wooden C-scroll handle, mark of Atkin Brothers, Sheffield, England, 19th c., 6 1/4" h. 138

Teapot, cov., low tapering foot below the squatty bulbous body tapering to a flared neck w/hinged domed cover, swan's-neck spout & angled scrolled handle, touch mark of George Richardson, Cranston, Rhode Island, 1830-45, 7 1/4" h. 248

Teapot, cov., footed spherical body w/a flaring neck & hinged domed cover, swan's-neck spout, metal C-scroll handle w/worn black paint, George Richardson, Cranston, Rhode Island, 1830-45, 7 1/2" h. (wear, dent in handle) 193

Teapot, cov., cylindrical w/flared base & rim, hinged domed cover w/button finial, swan's-neck spout & ornate S-scroll handle in black, touch mark of Morey & Ober, Boston, Massachusetts, 1852-55, 8" h. 303

Teapot, cov., pedestal base below squatty rounded central body flanked by flattened bands below the tall waisted neck & pointed domed cover, simple swan's-neck spout & ornate C-scroll handle in black, marked "Hall, Boardman & Co. - Best Britannia Metal," Philadelphia, 1846-48, 8 1/8" h. 248

Teapot, cov., flared foot below a bulbous lower body w/a stepped band below the very tall waisted neck w/cupped & flared rim, stepped & domed hinged cover w/button finial, swan's-neck spout & ornate C-scroll handle, eagle touch probably of Luther Boardman, South Reading, Massachusetts, 1836-42, 10 3/4" h. 468

Teapot, cov., tall footed pear-shaped body w/hinged domed cover w/cast floral finial, ribbed swan's-neck spout & long C-scroll handle, attributed to Homan & Co., ca. 1850s, 11" h. 110

Teapot, cov., tall baluster-form body w/hinged domed cover w/finial, swan's-neck spout & ornate C-scroll handle, unmarked American, ca. 1850, 11 3/4" h. (minor repairs, finial probably replaced) 193

Pewter Art Nouveau Tray & Cover

Tray, cov., Art Nouveau style, the shallow dished rectangular tray molded w/stylized scrolling lobes, the matching oval high domed cover w/open handle & molded leaves & engraved w/a monogram, Kayserzinn, Germany, ca. 1900, 21 1/2" l. (ILLUS.) 862

Tumblers, footed cylindrical form w/slightly flared rim & a thin raised band around the upper half, maker's mark "W.R. Loftus - 146 Oxford St.," pub name "The Cricketeers," England, 1/2 pt., set of 6 523

Art Deco Pewter Vase

Vase, Art Deco style, hand-hammered, the flaring conical body mounted at the rim w/scroll handles, raised on a small domed foot, impressed "M. Daurat" w/artist's monogram, France, ca. 1930, across handles 13 3/4" w. (ILLUS.) 1,610

Vases, slender trumpet form tapering to a stepped round base, decorated w/raised & stylized vertical branches bearing fruit, impressed Tudric marks of Liberty & Co., England, early 20th c., 11" h., pr. (wear) 230

Sheffield Plate

The term "Sheffield Plate" refers to a very specific variety of silver plated ware produced in England during the 18th and early 19th century. Beginning in the 1740s, manufacturers in the city of Sheffield developed a technique of bonding thin ingots of copper and pure silver using tremendous heat and pressure. These ingots could then be rolled out into very thin sheets of metal that would be used to fashion decorative objects. These pieces appeared identical to sterling silver pieces but could be sold at a fraction of the cost. Any fashionable silver object could be copied in Sheffield plate, including epergnes, coffee- and teapots, candlesticks, serving dishes and trays. For nearly a century, true Sheffield plate was widely popular with the British and American buying public; however, in the mid-1840s, the development of the process of silver plating through electrolysis soon killed off the Sheffield plate trade. The new form of plating was faster, cheaper and required less pure silver to obtain the same effect. True Sheffield plate wares were only produced in England and never in the American colonies or the United States. The earliest English Sheffield was not often marked by the manufacturer because the authorities were afraid such markings might mislead the buying public. By the late 18th century, however, some Sheffield platers were allowed to use simple markings that would not be confused with the strictly controlled sterling silver hallmarks. Because the layer of silver used in Sheffield plate was quite thin, the copper base metal may begin to show through after years of polishing. Serious wear can affect the market value of Sheffield plate pieces, but they should never be replated since this destroys their value as antiques. Also, in the late 19th and early 20th centuries, many silver plating companies began to use the term "Sheffield Plate" as part of their markings. This silver plate ware has no relationship to the original hand-crafted English wares, which were never marked with this phrase.

Basket, a high oval footring w/a narrow band of rectangular piercing, the long boat-form basket w/a similar pierced band near the rim, tapering forked central swing handle, engraved heraldic device in the interior, early 19th c., 13 1/4" l. **$374**

Sheffield Plate Candelabrum

Candelabra, three-branch, a tall slender ring-turned tapering shaft w/cast scroll bands & a domed foot supporting a foliate-cast section issuing three scrolled upswept slender arms ending in a scroll-cast socket & drip pan, the central shaft w/another socket fitted w/a flame-form finial, England, early 19th c., slight rosing, 25 1/2" h., pr. (ILLUS. of one) **3,220**

One of a Set of Sheffield Candlesticks

Candlesticks, on a square weighted base beaded at the top & bottom rim & engraved w/a band of husk drops, columnar standard engraved w/spiraling band of husks, a flat leaf capital w/a square beaded socket rim, 19th c., 11" h., set of 4 (ILLUS. of one) **1,955**

Candlesticks, telescoping-type, baluster-form, flute & rib decoration, early 19th c., 7 3/4" h., set of 4 (rosing) **575**

Candlesticks, flat-rimmed urn-form socket above a ringed neck & slightly tapering cylindrical standard on a ringed, stepped round foot, gadrooned borders, two w/scrolling double-arm three-socket inserts, Matthew Bolton, England, early 19th c., w/arms overall 20" h., set of 4 (light rosing) **2,875**

Cheese warmer, cov., rectangular, w/rounded corners & gadrooned borders, wooden handle, 19th c., 6 1/2" sq. (edge damage on cover, rosing) **115**

Fine Sheffield Coffee Urn

Coffee urn, cov., wide tapering ovoid body raised on a ringed pedestal & flaring ringed domed foot, a short wide rolled neck w/gadrooned rim, stepped domed cover w/pointed acanthus leaf finial, scrolled spigot at base w/scrolled loop handle, chased lion head handles w/rings at the sides, early 19th c., minor dents, 26 1/2" h. (ILLUS. on previous page) 1,760

Cruet stand & bottles, rectangular form stand w/reticulated design & center handle, square cut glass clear square bottles w/polished plaid design, two w/Sheffield hallmarked covers, Gorham silver mustard spoon, early 19th c., overall 8 5/16" h., the set 805

Cup, two-handled, the tall cylindrical body w/a rounded bottom & slightly flared rim, decorated w/a chased & engraved armorial within a large cartouche & partially fluted base, hollow C-form handles, low domed foot, weighted, early 19th c., 6 3/4" h. (solder repairs) 345

Sheffield Silver Dish Cover

Dish cover, high oval domed form w/a wide gadrooned central section around the reeded loop handle, a beaded medial band, engraved armorial whippet, early 19th c., 22" l., 11" h. (ILLUS.) 575

Dish-cross, a deep round fuel well at the center of four flat sliding cross arms each fitted at the top w/a scrolled & shell-tipped dish support & raised on a matching foot, early 19th c., some wear, 12 1/2" l. 517

Entree dishes, shaped oval, each fluted at the ends, mounted w/foliate & reeded rims, engraved on each cover w/an armorial, mounted w/leaf-capped handles, 12 1/4" l., the pair.. 517

Epergne, Classical style, the oval stand w/gadrooned rim, supported by four reeded column legs w/paw feet, the four reeded branches supported by a central boss w/cast lions masks, below a reeded boss topped by a cast acorn finial, w/five cut glass inserts, Matthew Boulton, Birmingham, England, late 18th - early 19th c., 10 7/8" l., 12 1/4" h. (losses) 1,840

Classical Sheffield Hot Water Urn

Hot water urn, cov., classical urn-form, the deep body w/the lower half decorated w/repoussé spiral gadrooning & the flaring upper half w/an everted repoussé foliate gadrooned rim, raised on a ringed pedestal w/band of gadrooning on a square base raised on paw feet, the wide domed cover w/a gadrooned band & reeded foliate finial, first half 19th c., 18" h. (ILLUS.) 1,035

Fine Sheffield Hot Water Urn

Hot water urn, cov., classical urn-form, the round domed base w/beaded rim, the trumpet-form pedestal w/a band of guilloché centered by flowerheads & accented w/husks, the urn-form body w/flat leaf engraving to the bottom w/a wide central band of engraved anthemion, upright angular shoulder handles ending in flat leaves, the tall waisted neck w/a domed cover w/flat-leaf engraving & a foliate baluster finial, w/inner sleeve, Philip Ashberry & Sons, early 19th c., 22 3/4" h. (ILLUS.)... 748

Early Sheffield Plate Hot Water Urn

Hot water urn, cov., the large ovoid body decorated w/wide sawtooth reeded bands around the top & bottom, tapering to a gadrooned neck back & tapering domed cover w/figural pineapple finial, outscrolled loop shoulder handles & shaped spigot w/a leaf-capped turned wood handle, raised on a gadroon banded & reeded tall pedestal w/a shaped square base w/a pierced zigzag design apron & raised on four scroll legs w/shell feet, the body w/a large engraved central monogram, interior fitted w/a liner, few splits, some wear, late 18th - early 19th c., overall 19 1/2" h. (ILLUS. on previous page) **1,380**

Hot water urn, cov., classical-style, caryatid accents, wooden handles, early 19th c., 17 1/2" h. (damaged) **345**

Sheffield Plate Meat Cover

Meat cover, dome-shaped body w/engraved coat of arms and Greek key design at base, beaded base rim, cornucopia & beaded handle at top, made by Henry Wilkinson & Co., England, ca. 1838, 11 x 14 x 18" (ILLUS.) **672**

Plateau, four-part oval, comprising rectangular sections, each w/rounded end, all applied with scrolling acanthus alternating w/leaf-capped shells, fitted w/mirrored plate, on leaf-capped paw feet, each section fitted in a baize-lined wood case, early 19th c., 73" l. **7,187**

Roast cover, oblong domed form w/gadrooned rim, engraved crests, early 19th c., 20 3/8" l. **489**

Serving dish, cov., gadroon borders, acanthus leaf & shell details, lion head handles, paw feet, engraved crests, early 19th c., 9 9/16 x 16 3/4", 10 3/8" h. **1,610**

Soup tureen, cov., ovoid body w/applied gadroon & shell border w/two fluted handles w/leaf terminals, on four scroll & flat leaf feet, the domed cover w/reeded band & leaf-form finial, the body & cover w/let-in engraved heraldic device, fitted w/a drop-in liner, early 19th c., 16" l., 10 3/4" h. (restorations, rosing) **1,725**

Soup tureen, cov., two-handled, mounted w/leaf-capped reeded handles w/lion's mask terminals, gadrooned rims w/acanthus & shells at intervals, on four shell & acanthus-capped claw feet, Matthew Boulton, London, early 19th c., 15 3/4" l. **1,495**

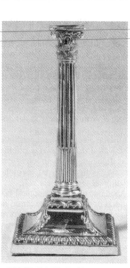

Sheffield Plate Taperstick

Taperstick, Corinthian column form on rectangular gadrooned base, crested, w/pseudo-hallmarks, made by Thomas Law, Sheffield, ca. 1765-70, 6 1/2" h. (ILLUS.) **480**

Tea urn, cov., shaped ovoid form, mounted w/scroll handles & a reeded spigot, the domed cover w/an orb-form finial, early 19th c., 21 1/2" h. **1,495**

Sheffield Classical Style Tea Urn

Tea urn, cov., wide classical urn-form w/a tapering curved shoulder supporting the domed cover w/urn finial, lion mask & ring shoulder handles, engraved band of leafy scrolls around the shoulder, a shaped spigot near the bottom of the body above the tapering pedestal on a square plinth w/ball feet, early 19th c. (ILLUS.) **1,400**

Teakettle, cover & stand, plain inverted pear-form, the rim beaded, the cover w/repoussé engraved leaves & urn finial, w/serpentine spout, resting on a pierced circular stand w/bright-cut & engraved foliates, on three footed scroll legs, Wilkinson & Co., Sheffield, England, last quarter 18th c., stand 14 1/4" l., the set **690**

Teakettle, cover & stand, the bulbous lobed pot w/a domed chased & engraved cover w/cast foliate finial, the body w/repoussé & engraved flowers, on four scroll & shell feet, w/a shaped rectangular stand w/cast scroll sides w/lion & horse terminals, on four foliate feet, Elkington & Co., mid-19th c., 12" h., the set **431**

Vegetable dish, cov., squatty bulbous oval base raised on four knob feet topped by acanthus leaf detail, upturned loop end handles w/acanthus leaf terminals, flared gadrooned rim supporting a stepped & domed cover w/a leaf-cast ring handle, early 19th c., 16" l. (minor wear) **688**

Warming dishes, liners & covers, rectangular, surrounded by gadrooned borders & rims, applied w/reeded foliate handles & knop, raised on scrolled feet headed by foliage, early 19th c., 14 1/4" l., pr. **1,725**

Wine coasters, rounded form w/everted gadrooned rims, wood bases, England, mid-19th c., 6" d., pr. **230**

Wine coolers, campana-form, a knopped stem supporting the urn-form body w/foliate-capped handles & rim, fitted w/a liner & collar, engraved w/a crest, early 19th c., 12" h., pr. **2,530**

Sheffield Plate Wine Cooler

Wine coolers, classical urn-form, fitted w/handles, decorated w/gadroon, shells, floral bands & acanthus leaf designs, 19th c., pr. (ILLUS. of one) **1,904**

Wine coolers, cylindrical footed form, the side engraved w/an armorial & mounted w/a pair of ring handles near the top, fitted w/a liner, collar & pierced gallery, early 19th c., 7" h., pr. **5,175**

Sheffield Handled Wine Coolers

Wine coolers, cylindrical w/a wide gadrooned rim over applied looped foliate-cast handles, embossed cartouche on the front, complete w/liner & collar, overall 10" w., 4 3/4" h., pr. (ILLUS.) **3,450**

Wine coolers, urn-form, leaf-capped reeded handles, engraved w/a crest above a monogram, gadrooned rim, fitted w/collar & liner, early 19th c., 9 1/2" h., pr. **2,587**

Silver

The search for silver was one of the enticements that lured Europeans to the New World. The Spanish Conquistadors, of course, discovered fabulous amounts of silver in Mexico and South America, but the early English settlers along the Eastern Seaboard were frustrated not to find similar riches in that region. As the English colonies grew and prospered, however, there soon was a demand for the services of trained goldsmiths and silversmiths. By the late 17th century, several smiths were working in the New England region. Their custom-made wares mirrored the styles popular in England and the Continent. The various styles consisted of the Renaissance tradition from 1650 to 1690; the Baroque from 1690 to 1720; and the lighter lines of Hogarth from 1720 to 1750. This was followed by the Rococo style from 1750 to 1775, with a return to the Classical style, which received its major thrust from England and the talent of Robert Adam, from 1775 to 1810. The period from 1810 to 1840 was taken over by the heavier forms influenced by Egyptian, Greek and Roman antiquities. The actual mass manufacture of silver objects in America began in the early 1840s. Prior to that time, most items were custom-made. Early American silver pieces had no official stamps or letter dates to identify them, as was common in England and many other countries. Only the maker's name or initials were used to mark objects before the mid-19th century. With the advent of factory-made silver items, many of the wholesalers and retailers started marking the wares they sold.

It should be noted that the word "coin" can be found on silver articles made during the period from about 1830 to 1860. This indicated that the silver used was of the same quality as was used for coinage although, since the silversmith could now buy sheet silver, the objects usually did not contain melted coins as they had previously. Sterling, the English standard, referred to a metal which was .925 or 925/1000 parts silver with 75/1000 parts of an added metal, usually copper, to give it strength and stiffness. This term appeared on Baltimore silver from the 1800 to 1814 period but was not used elsewhere in this country until after about 1860. Connecticut, Pennsylvania, New York and New Jersey became the heart of the silver industry in America, and many well-known companies continue in business today producing fine wares.

American (Sterling & Coin)

After dinner coffee service: cov. coffeepot, creamer, sugar & oval tray; each piece w/paneled sides, worked w/stylized floral designs in the Art Deco style, Wm. B. Durgin Co., coffeepot 11 1/2" h., the set.. **$977**

Sterling Silver Baby Rattle

Baby rattle, w/embossed cat heads on both sides & mother-of-pearl handle also used for teething, marked "Gorham Sterling - N236," engraved "MAS," 3 3/4" l. (ILLUS.) **195**

Sterling Baby's Cup

Baby's cup, model of a rabbit dressed in suit making up the handle, marked "S&B Sterling 719," 2 1/2 x 2 3/4 x 4" (ILLUS.)................. **135**

Bank, figural, a model of smiling egg-shaped Humpty Dumpty seated atop a rectangular high brick wall-form base w/a coin slot on top, 3 3/4" h. **287**

Basket, a wide shallow round bowl w/reeded rim raised on a wide low round flaring base, swing bail handle, the interior acid-etched w/festoons & foliate sprays on a trelliswork ground, Tiffany & Co., New York, early 20th c., 9" d. **632**

Basket, coin, oval boat-shape, the shaped rim & base w/molded scrolling, cast loop end rim handles, the sides embossed overall w/flowers, on four cast acanthus leaf feet, engraved presentation in center, S. Kirk & Son., Baltimore, 1846-61, 6 3/4 x 9 5/8" excluding handles................ **1,610**

Basket, deep flaring sides w/two sides turned up & joined by a swing bail reeded handle, the sides pierced overall w/scrolls, the shaped rim w/a border, engraved w/a monogram, Black, Starr & Frost, ca. 1900, 13 7/8" l............................. **1,380**

Alvin Sterling Flower Basket

Basket, flower-type, a round stepped foot below the tall slender trumpet body w/a wide cupped rim w/four applied floral roundels flanked by engraved floral sprays & linked by husk swags, the foot engraved w/floral sprays & swags & the sides engraved w/floral drops & lappets, the shaped rim centered by a high upright arched handle pierced w/flat leaves & bat's wing fluted roundels, Alvin Silver Co., early 20th c., 22 1/2" h. (ILLUS.) **1,035**

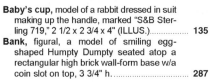

Frank W. Smith Decorative Basket

Basket, oblong form w/two upturned sides, a wide looped reticulated border band w/a fleur-de-lis design above lattice-pierced sides w/central reserves, a high center reeded swing handle, by Frank W. Smith Silver Co. for Bailey, Banks & Biddle, 11 1/2" h. (ILLUS. on previous page)............. **468**

Basket, oval shape w/fixed upright handle, chased medallion & swag design, pierced sides, inscribed w/presentation dates of 1893-1918, a long list of names under the base, Whiting Mfg. Co., 7 1/2" h... **330**

Basket, shallow round form in a basketweave design composed of thin woven silver strips, a high arched & forked strip handle w/a hanging medallion w/initials SA, John O. Bellis, San Francisco, ca. 1910, 14 1/8" d., 9" h. **4,312**

Basket, the pierced basket applied w/floral sprays on the shaped edge, w/tapered upright handle, monogrammed on interior, stepped oval foot, Tiffany & Co., 1902-07, 9" h... **978**

Baskets, two-handled w/ropetwist edging & openwork woven bodies, Howard and Co., New York, New York, ca. 1886, 7" w., 1 1/2" h., pr. **978**

Beaker, coin, cylindrical w/top & base molded rims, engraved, Anthony Rasch, Philadelphia, 1807, 3" d., 3" h. (minor dents) **489**

Beaker, coin, slightly tapering cylindrical form w/a reeded top & base rim, marked by E. & D. Kinsey, Cincinnati, Ohio, 1840-61, 3 1/2" h. **403**

Beaker, coin, tapering cylindrical form w/molded rim, engraved w/a contemporary foliate cipher sprouting flowers, on a rim foot, Myer Myers, New York, ca. 1775, 3 7/8" h... **14,400**

Bookweight, rectangular w/shaped top, the front acid-etched w/a scene of men playing lacrosse, the back at top w/crossed ribbon-tied lacrosse sticks, Tiffany & Co., ca. 1875-91, 2 x 11"............................... **460**

Bouillon cups w/liners, sterling frame w/grotesque mask & floral designs, holding Lenox porcelain cups, Gorham Mfg. Co., Providence, Rhode Island, set of 12.. **977**

Bowl, a rounded eight-lobed bowl w/a wide upward flaring eight-scalloped rim pierced w/a decorative border band & engraved w/designs, anniversary presentation dated "1896-1921," Towle Silversmiths, Newburyport, Massachusetts, 13" d., 3" h. **220**

Bowl, a wide everted rim around the center stamped w/lobing centered by floral sprays, J.E. Caldwell & Co., Philadelphia, early 20th c., 10" d............................... **173**

Bowl, footed w/deep upright sides, overall fine repoussé decoration of roses & leaves, Jacobi & Jenkins, Baltimore, 1894-1908.. **770**

Sterling Oblong Bowl

Bowl, oblong, center engraved "KTV - Oct. 28 - 1879-'04," sides decorated w/deep relief flowers & scrolls, marked "Sterling" w/a sword in a wreath and the number "1148 1/2," 5 5/8 x 7 1/4" (ILLUS.)................. **245**

Hand-hammered Oval Bowl

Bowl, oval, hand-hammered surface, deep, flaring bowl on short base, marked "F.S. Co. - Sterling - Y-3," 3 1/4 x 5 5/8", 3 1/4 h. (ILLUS.) **125**

Hand-hammered Sterling Bowl

Bowl, oval, hand-hammered surface, flaring sides made up of petal sections, paw feet, indistinct maker's mark, 2 x 3 1/2 x 4 3/4" (ILLUS.)................................. **95**

Bowl, oval on a stepped conforming foot, the shallow lobed bowl w/broad border of stylized fruit & flowers & reeded rim, Gorham Mfg. Co., Providence, Rhode Island, ca. 1930, 13 3/4" l. **1,610**

Bowl, ovoid w/reticulated sides, on four scroll & flowerhead feet, the body w/guilloché & scroll piercing, the shaped edge w/applied shells, scrolls & husk drops, scroll handles, monogrammed, Black, Starr & Frost, New York, late 19th c., 12 3/4" l., 5" h. **1,725**

Sterling Bowl with Decorated Rim

Bowl, round, concentric sides, rim decorated w/flowers & scrolls & leaves, marked "Gorham Sterling - 109," 5 1/2" d. (ILLUS.) **75**

Sterling Bowl by Gorham

Bowl, round, flat bottom, flaring rim w/scalloped edge decorated w/stylized scrolls, marked "Gorham Sterling - 739," 6 1/4" d. (ILLUS.) **75**

Round Alvin Silver Bowl

Bowl, round, plain concentric sides, rim w/stylized leaf & scroll designs, marked "Alvin Sterling - 108," 5 5/8" d. (ILLUS.) **65**

Bowl, round, the shaped rim reticulated w/embossed foliates, S-scrolls & husk swags w/six cartouches surrounding embossed bouquets, the interior w/a central monogram, the flared sides w/C-scroll & foliate chasing, on a banded spreading foot, Bailey, Banks & Biddle Co., first quarter 20th c., 10 3/4" d. **546**

Bowl, round w/a ruffled everted rim, embossed gadrooning & raised & engraved band, the sides w/repoussé reeding, Black, Starr & Frost, late 19th - early 20th c., 12" d. **259**

Whiting Sterling Silver Bowl

Bowl, round, w/scalloped edge & raised design of flowers, leaves & scrolls, mark of the Whiting Mfg. Company & "Sterling - 5593," 925/1000 fine, 9" d. (ILLUS.) **395**

Bowl with Beaded Edge

Bowl, simple round, flat-bottomed bowl w/flaring sides w/beaded rim, engraved "WHS," marked on bottom "Sterling - AFRB - 5182," 7 3/4" d. (ILLUS.) **85**

Bowl, small dished round center w/widely flanged & gently upturned rim, hand-hammered w/lightly chased & enameled inside w/a band of turquoise & white grapevine & a matching central patera, by Mary C. Knight, Boston, Massachusetts, 1906, 4 1/2" d. **4,025**

Square Reed & Barton Sterling Bowl

Bowl, square, flaring sides w/reeded design, Reed & Barton mark, style number "X301," 9 1/2" square (ILLUS.) **195**

Bowl, coin, footed paneled octagonal form, Rococo-style feet, engraved decoration & monogram, J. & I. Cox, New York, 1817-35, 5 1/8" w., 3 1/8" h............................ **288**

Bowl, Art Nouveau design w/a round form on a flared foot, the shaped rim & base w/applied floral details, Shiebler, ca. 1900, 9 5/8" d., 6 1/8" h............................... **1,150**

Bowl, shaped border pierced w/shells & scrolls, the rim applied w/scrolls, the base engraved w/a monogram & dated 1905, on four scroll feet, gilt interior, Gorham Mfg. Co., Providence, Rhode Island, 13" l. **862**

Bread basket, oval w/reticulated edge & swing center handle, on four scroll feet, monogrammed, Black, Starr & Frost, late 19th - early 20th c., 10 1/4" l., 8 1/4" h......... **259**

Bread tray, oval w/ornate scalloped & molded scroll rim w/reticulated scrolling, rolled sides w/molded foliate swags, Graff, Washbourne & Dunn, New York, New York, early 20th c., 8 1/4 x 12 3/4" **633**

Child's Sterling Breakfast Set

Breakfast set: child's bowl & underplate; the deep round bowl w/acid-etched acorn branches on the rim & cut cardwork squirrels around the sides w/a lower portion w/engraved stylized cobblestones, the round dished plate w/an identical rim band, Tiffany & Co., early 20th c., bowl 5 1/8" d., plate 7 1/2" d., 2 pcs. (ILLUS.) ... **2,185**

Cake basket, a stepped foot supporting a round body stamped w/scrolls & shells, the edge w/foliate reticulation, upright reticulated handle raised on scrolls, Wm. B. Durgin Co., retailed by Bigelow, Kennard & Co., 20th c., 12 1/2" l., 8 1/4" h. **690**

Cake basket, oval, the wide spreading foot w/low rounded sides chased w/four grape clusters forming four landscape panels, one each of a windmill, boatmen, a bridge & a watermill, a low grapevine-embossed stem below the wide plain oval bowl w/a wide & deeply rolled rim chased w/bunches of fruit, a center diamond-pierced swing handle, S. Kirk & Son Co., Baltimore, ca. 1905, 14 1/4" l..... **6,325**

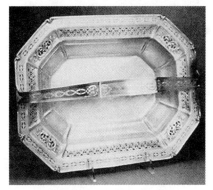

Reed & Barton Cake Basket

Cake basket, rectangular w/angled corners, the stepped & flaring rim reticulated w/loop bands, scrolls & chain bands, angled strap handle from end to end also reticulated w/looping bands, cast foliate feet, Reed & Barton, early 20th c., 9 1/8 x 12", 5 3/8" h. (ILLUS.)........................ **748**

Cake plate, oval w/a low flared foot, Art Nouveau scroll design, monogrammed, Bailey, Banks & Biddle, late 19th c., 9 x 10 3/8", 4" h. **460**

Cake plate, round w/a shaped reticulated rim w/embossed swags & foliate-centered cartouches, the center w/engraved foliage, on a circular molded foot, Shreve, Crump & Low, Boston, early 20th c., 10 1/2" d. **546**

Cake plate, the waved rim w/molded scallop shell decoration, the face w/openwork engraved band, on a reticulated & engraved trumpet-form base, monogrammed in the center, Tiffany & Co., New York, 1907-47, 12 1/2" d., 5 3/4" h. ... **2,185**

Candy dishes, sterling, reticulated rim in a scroll & floral design, on feet, Whiting, late 19th c., 7 3/8" d., 1 3/4" h., pr. **288**

Cann, coin, bulbous form w/molded rim & applied molded circular foot, cast hollow scroll handle w/molded body drop at upper joining, initialed on base "CTL," maker's mark for William Swan, Boston, 1757-74, 5 1/8" h. (dents) 1,840

Cann, coin, footed plain baluster-form body w/a capped double-scroll handle, one side engraved w/a script monogram, the other w/another monogram & "A Gift," Elias Pelletreau, Southampton, New York, ca. 1770, 6 1/8" h. 13,200

Cann, coin, molded foot below the tapering cylindrical body w/slightly everted rim, scroll handle w/acanthus grip, marked by Myer Myers, New York, ca. 1750, 4 1/2" h. 21,850

Ornate Kirk & Son Center Bowl

Center bowl, a low oval pedestal foot supporting a long oval boat-shaped bowl w/high incurved ends topped by large figural butterfly handles, the foot & side ornately decorated w/repoussé designs of leafy fruits & flowers, S. Kirk & Son, late 19th c., 13" l. (ILLUS.) 2,530

Center bowl, in the Rococo taste, w/four reserves each depicting different flower species, S. Kirk & Son, 19th c., 10 1/4" l. 633

Center bowl, oval, the everted rim worked in repoussé w/foliage, Gorham Mfg. Co., Providence, Rhode Island, 21 1/2" l. 3,450

Center bowl, round, w/an undulating rim, the sides worked in repoussé w/floral swags, Black, Starr & Frost, 8 1/2" d. 805

Gorham Sterling Center Bowl

Center bowl, round w/deep rolled rim w/molded scroll edge & embossed & engraved foliate & scroll decoration, on a stepped round base, Gorham Mfg. Co., Providence, Rhode Island, ca. 1910, 14 1/4" d. (ILLUS.) 1,870

Center bowl, round w/everted rim, engraved w/scrolls, bellflowers & floral drops, offset w/four scroll-reticulated cartouches, engraved & dated 1925 in the center, Whiting Mfg. Co., 10" d. 201

Centerpiece, a large hemispherical bowl w/a shaped interior & wide rolled rectangular lappet rim, raised on a base composed of four cast dolphins separated by shells, Black, Starr & Frost, New York, early 20th c., marked & numbered, 12 1/2" d. 3,600

Centerpiece, Art Nouveau style, a fluted hexagonal form resting on the wide everted rim pierced & engraved w/flowers & scrolls, the rim applied w/cast whiplash scrolls, marked by Mauser Mfg. Co., New York City, ca. 1900, 16" d. 2,587

Centerpiece, oval w/a wide interior border engraved w/scrolling foliage, the wide everted rim pierced & applied w/foliage & scrolls, retailed by J.E. Caldwell & Co., late 19th c., 16" l. 1,380

Centerpiece, a circular base on a low foot supporting two concentric tiers, each w/a trumpet-form base, Tiffany & Co., New York, early 20th c., 10" h. 1,092

Centerpiece, a reticulated trumpet-form silver vase on a stepped foot w/a porcelain cream & gold-rimmed Lenox liner, the base w/three arms, each suspending a reticulated silver basket w/Lenox liner, monogrammed, silver by Gorham Mfg. Co., Providence, Rhode Island, retailed by Smith, Patterson Co., 1911, 10" w., 10 3/4" h. 1,150

Charger, Martel line, hammered round form w/shaped & waved rim w/chased lobing, each lobe w/an embossed leaf & buds, embossed monogram in one lobe, on a domed foot, Gorham Mfg. Co., Providence, Rhode Island, ca. 1900, 13" d. 5,463

Child's set: a 5 1/2" d., 2 3/8" h. bowl w/rolled flared rim, the exterior w/a central band of embossed children s toys, the matching plate w/a rolled rim & similar band, Gorham Mfg. Co., Providence, Rhode Island, ca. 1910, 2 pcs. 1,725

Sterling Christmas Ornament

Christmas ornament, in the form of an angel w/hands clamped in front, 3/4 x 1/12", 3 7/8" h. (ILLUS. on previous page)................ **62**

Sterling Christmas Ornaments

Christmas ornaments, in the shape of a dove & an owl, each marked "Copyright RMTRUSH Sterling" & dated 1972 & 1974 respectively, each 1 x 2 3/4", each (ILLUS.)................ **65**

Cigar box, cov., low rectangular form w/cedar lining & humidor fitting, the cover w/applied monogram "FHR," marked on the base by the Kalo Shop, Chicago, Illinois, early 20th c., 13 1/4" l........................ **1,725**

Silver Cigar Case

Cigar case, rectangular hinged three-section style, 2 5/8 x 5 1/2" (ILLUS.) **69**

Cigarette case, rectangular w/engraved diagonal lines on front & back, the gilt interior monogrammed, Tiffany & Co., New York, early 20th c... **144**

Cocktail shaker, cov., tall hand-hammered, slightly ovoid form w/a lift-off top, a diamond-shaped applique on the side, the cylindrical cap w/a pointed spout, stamped w/the Gorham trademark & "Sterling - A10059 - 1," ca. 1920s, 4" d., 10" h. (three minor dents)............................. **220**

Coffee & tea service: cov. coffeepot, cov. teapot, cov. sugar bowl, creamer & waste bowl; each w/a baluster-form body decorated w/scroll & rib details, ivory heat stops, Gorham Mfg. Co., Providence, Rhode Island, 1901, coffeepot 8" h., the set.............. **1,093**

Coffeepot, cov., a rosebud finial on the domed molded hinged cover over a baluster-form body w/a paneled lower portion & applied Greek key banding, elaborately engraved w/Rococo C-scrolls, shells & other foliate devices, the naturalistic C-scroll handle w/rose design, on a circular molded base w/a similar Greek key banding, monogrammed, marked on base by Ball, Black & Co., New York, ca. 1850, 12 3/8" h. (very minor dents) **920**

Coffeepot, cov., Art Nouveau style, of tall slender double-gourd form w/a wide squatty bulbous base raised on a short pedestal w/wide undulating foot, a small domed cap, long slender vine-entwined swan's-neck spout, large scrolled openwork blossom & leaf handle, the body chased & applied w/irises on a ground lightly finished w/tendrils & matting, marked, Reed & Barton, Taunton, Massachusetts, ca. 1905, 11 3/8" h. **3,450**

Coffeepot, cov., coin, classical urn-form, square foot & tapering round pedestal support the wide urn-form body w/beaded rims & a tapering neck supporting the tapering tall cover w/urn finial, swan's-neck spout, leafy scroll-carved double-scroll wood handle, engraved w/contemporary cipher "JLC," base marked "P.GARRETT" in rectangle, Philip Garrett, Philadelphia, ca. 1790-1800, 15 1/2" h................................. **10,350**

Coffeepot, cov., footed tapering cylindrical body w/a stepped domed hinged cover w/berry finial & chased floral & foliate band, the body w/a central reserve depicting a country fishing scene surrounded by C-scrolls, floral & foliate designs, a crab stock handle w/acorns & oak leaves, ribbed swan's-neck spout, monogrammed, Obadiah Rich, Boston, ca. 1830, 10" h. (minor dent) **1,725**

Coffeepot, cov., coin, of large partly fluted, oval vase-form, w/urn finial & swan's-neck spout, engraved w/contemporary foliate ciphers on both sides, conforming pedestal foot, Joel Syre, New York, New York, ca. 1805, 13 1/2" h............................ **5,175**

Rare Early American Coffeepot

Coffeepot, cov., coin, tall inverted pear-form engraved on one side w/later arms in 18th c. style, the domed foot w/embossed beaded border repeated on the rim of the domed cover w/a wrythen urn finial, a shell-decorated swan's-neck spout, the leaf-capped carved wood handle rising from a cast shell upper terminal, double stamped mark of Joseph & Nathaniel Richardson, Philadelphia, ca. 1780, 12 7/8" h. (ILLUS.) **30,650**

Coffeepot, cov., coin, urn-form, round foot on a square thin platform, tapering pedestal to the tall body w/beaded rims & waisted shoulder, hinged domed cover surmounted by an urn-form finial, leaf-capped wood scroll handle & beaded scroll spout, body engraved w/a monogram, marked by Joseph Shoemaker, Philadelphia, ca. 1795, 15 1/2" h. **10,350**

Coffeepot, cov., slightly tapering cylindrical form, chased overall w/various blossoms on a stippled ground, the angular handle cast w/a ram's head, S. Kirk & Son Co., early 20th c., 8 1/2" h. **1,610**

Communion cup, coin, the straight-sided bowl above a rounded foot w/applied disk, the bowl engraved w/a church presentation inscription dated 1802 within a bright-cut swag, Boston, early 19th c., 6 1/4" h. **1,380**

Dominick & Haff Sterling Compote

Compote, La Salle patt., deep round fluted & flaring bowl w/a wide rolled rim decorated w/a pierced border band, knopped stem & paneled domed foot w/pierced border band, monogrammed, Dominick & Haff, ca. 1930, 10" d., 7 1/2" h. (ILLUS.) **400**

Compote, open, a wide shallow bowl w/a flattened, flaring exterior rim cast w/three scenes, one w/two hounds flanking a trophy of game, one of two leopards flanking a swag of grapes & one of two water birds flanking a trophy of fish, raised on a tall slender pedestal chased w/overlapping leaves & berries on a round domed & reeded foot w/a thin ropetwist rim band, William Forbes for Ball, Black & Co., New York, 950 standard, ca. 1865, 11 3/4" d. **1,725**

Compote, open, round w/a molded rim w/embossed beaded foliate band, the body w/engraved band w/central cartouches, cast loop handles, on a trumpet-form base w/embossed band, monogrammed, Gorham Mfg. Co., Providence, Rhode Island, 1874, 8" d., 5 3/4" h. **546**

Compote, open, round w/raised reticulated rim, the center monogrammed w/an engraved foliate border, on a molded round foot, Dominick & Haff, New York, New York, early 20th c., 8" d. **173**

Compote, open, the bowl w/a wide band of floral repoussé, on a trumpet foot w/repoussé, Baltimore Sterling Silver Co., late 19th c., 2 3/4" h. **173**

Compotes, open, lobed round bowl on a molded base, chased scroll & floral decoration, engraved monogram, Black, Starr & Frost, 1876, 7" d., pr. **690**

Compotes, open, round w/molded everted rim w/openwork foliate designs & scrolls, on similarly decorated domed base, monogrammed in the center, one w/engraved date on the base, Graff, Washbourne & Dunn, New York, New York, early 20th c., 10 1/2" d., pr. **1,725**

Shell-shaped Victorian Compote

Compotes, open, shell-shaped, the shell bowl w/a gadrooned border & reticulated edge, w/a cast handle topped w/a caryatid above a design of fish tails, seaweed & shells, on three dolphin feet, Howard & Co., third quarter 19th c., 8 3/4 x 10 1/2", 8 1/2" h., pr. (ILLUS. of one) **6,325**

Cordials, tapered ovoid bowl on a spreading foot, monogrammed, made for Georg Jensen, Inc., 20th c., 2 3/8" h., set of 8 .... **173**

Early Richardson Creamer

Creamer, coin, bulbous ovoid body tapering to a scalloped rim & long pointed spout, ornate scroll handle & three applied cast cabriole legs, the body decorated in Rococo style w/C-scrolls & baskets of flowers, Joseph Richardson, Philadelphia, 1711-84, buffed, dents, minor tear, old repair, 4" h. (ILLUS. on previous page) **1,495**

Creamer, coin, classic urn-form w/high arched spout, tall looped handle down the side & a domed pedestal foot, beading at the girdle & rim, engraved w/a name under the spout, Harding & Co., Boston, mid-19th c., 8 1/4" h. **201**

Creamer, coin, Classical fluted helmet-form, on a slender pedestal w/round base on a square foot, the sides engraved w/tasseled drapery below a band of running leaves & roundels, slender loop handles, foot engraved w/leaftips at the angles & a circle of husks on the raised center, the front of the body engraved w/a contemporary monogram "JR," the foot engraved "J.R. Sept 2, 1791 - J.R. Nov 3, 1798," the base weight later, Paul Revere, Jr., Boston, ca. 1798, unmarked, 7 1/8" h. **17,250**

Creamer, coin, Classical style, a round domed foot w/applied floral edge banding supporting a wide bulbous lobed lower body tapering to an applied floral shoulder band below the short waisted neck & high arched spout, ornate C-scroll handle, monogrammed, Geradus Boyce, New York City, ca. 1830-40, 6 1/2" h. **460**

Creamer, coin, ovoid form w/an applied rim, molded base & strap handle, engraved on the bottom, Joseph Foster, 1760-1839, 4 3/4" h. (minor dents) **489**

Creamer, coin, tall helmet shape, a wide arched spout & high loop handle from rim to base of tapering body, raised on a short pedestal over a square foot, engraved w/a monogram, molded rim around top, marked on the foot rim by Paul Revere, Jr., Boston, ca. 1790, 6 1/2" h. **7,200**

Creamer, cov., coin, a rosebud finial on a domed, molded hinged cover over a baluster-form body w/paneled lower portion & applied Greek key banding, elaborately engraved w/Rococo C-scrolls, shells & other foliate devices, the naturalistic handle w/rose motif, on a circular molded base w/similar Greek key banding, monogrammed, marked on base by Ball, Black & Co., New York, ca. 1850, 9 1/4" h. (minor dents) **460**

Creamer, coin, Classical style, applied reeded bandings & strap handle, monogrammed, Joseph Lownes, Philadelphia, 1758-1820, 4 7/8" h. (minor dents) **460**

Creamer, covered sugar bowl & undertray, Arts & Crafts style w/a hammered surface, impressed mark "Hand Wrought - at the Kalo Shop - 158," Chicago, New York, ca. 1920, undertray 9 3/4" d., creamer 3 3/4" h., 3 pcs. **345**

Japanesque Design Creamer & Sugar

Creamer & open sugar bowl, each w/a tapering ovoid hammered surface also engraved w/a Japanese-style landscape, the sugar bowl w/two cranes, the creamer w/a quail, simple loop handles, Whiting Mfg. Co., late 19th c., creamer 3 3/4" h., pr. (ILLUS.) **1,150**

Creamer, open sugar bowl & undertray, each pear-shaped on a domed foot, serpentine handles & stamped w/a band of C-scrolls & flowerheads at the girdle, oval tray w/matching stamped edge, Gorham Mfg. Co., Providence, Rhode Island, ca. 1951, tray 9 3/4" l., creamer 4" h., the set **173**

Cup, coin, short round foot supporting a tall bell-form body, slender S-scroll handle, engraved cartouche w/"John Laurens Babbidge from N.B. July 1, 1853," w/hallmarks on bottom & "Pure Silver Coin," 3 5/8" h. **220**

Cup, two-handled, baluster-form w/scroll handles, applied leaf decoration, vintage band around base, Tiffany & Co., ca. 1900, 6 5/16" h. **633**

Cup, cov., the wide rounded & low domed foot w/a chased rococo band & short beaded band pedestal supporting the deep cup body w/chased florals flanking a large central scroll cartouche enclosing an engraved crest & motto, the high domed cover chased w/florals & scroll cartouches topped by a seated putto w/bouquet finial, ornate leafy S-scroll handles down the sides, Tiffany & Co., New York, ca. 1894, 13 1/4" h. **2,875**

Demitasse set: cov. pot, open sugar pot & creamer; Dublin patt., ribbed pear-shaped forms, pot w/wooden handle, Tuttle, pot 8" h., the set **431**

Dinner bell, wide domed bell w/a die-rolled band of moresque ornament around the bottom, the handle a realistic figure of a dancing bacchante w/a sistrum, marked & numbered "2500-5239," Tiffany & Co., New York, 1851-69, 6 1/2" h. **2,300**

Dish, cov., coin, footed, bowl ornamented w/applied gadrooning at the rim & applied strawberry handles, a strawberry finial attached to lid, bowl engraved "CPJ," marked by Eoff & Shepherd, New York City, & Ball, Black & Co., New York, 6" d., 6 1/4" h. (very minor dent) **431**

Fine Coin Silver Covered Dish

Dish, cov., coin., wide rounded base raised on four scroll & shell feet, topped w/a flattened scalloped rim supporting a high stepped domed cover w/twisted & pointed finial, the base decorated w/repoussé flowers & scrolls w/a matching design on the cover centered by a scrolled cartouche w/engraved mottoed crest & initials, Ball, Tompkins & Black, New York, New York, 1839-50, 5 1/2" h. (ILLUS.) **489**

Sterling Silver Dish

Dish, flat bowl w/upraised rim consisting of pierced panels decorated w/scrolls & stylized leaves, Simpson, Hall, Miller & Co. mark & "Sterling - 660 - N.P.," 4 5/8" d. (ILLUS.) **50**

Dish, round, a shallow dished center framed by a wide flattened rim ornately chased w/flowers & leaves, monogrammed in the center, S. Kirk & Son, Inc., early 20th c., 10" d., 1 1/4" h. **392**

Dresser box, cov., ovoid, decorated w/bands of acid-etched designs around the body & around the border of the cover, gold-washed interior, Tiffany & Co., early 20th c., 3 7/8" d., 2 3/4" h. **431**

Dresser set: hand mirror, hair brush, two clothes brushes, cov. powder jar, three small silver-stoppered jars, comb, shoe horn, manicure scissors, file & cuticle tool; sterling, each w/a design featuring an Art Nouveau lady's head & vining floral designs, monogrammed, Kerr Sterling, late 19th c., the set (some face wear, mirror needs resilvering) **431**

Dressing case w/silver fittings: comprising a spirits flask, pair of bottles, talcum powder jar, a toothbrush holder, a shaving brush holder, a folding spoon, a brush box, a cigarette tray, a razor box, two pill boxes, a soap box, two jars, a silver-mounted traveling clock, a hairbrush & a clothes brush; all silver pieces engraved w/initials "C.D.," contained in a compartmented leather carrying case w/detachable tray wallets & various loose fittings, silver by Tiffany & Co., ca. 1925, the set (some pieces unmarked, one replacement marked "Cartier") **2,875**

Entree dishes, cov., low oval rounded base w/flattened rim, matching domed cover w/flattened top centered by a detachable finial in the form of a lion holding a shield, the top & base both embossed overall w/flowers in the Kirk style, unmarked, late 19th c., 12 3/4" l., pr. **3,737**

Ewer, coin, classical-form, footed large ovoid body w/a tall waisted neck & wide arched spout, high arched S-scroll plain handle, the body w/a large engraved coat-of-arms, Obadiah Rich, Boston, mid-19th c., 12 1/2" h. **920**

Tall Kirk & Son Sterling Ewer

Ewer, cov., coin, a round disk foot & slender pedestal supporting a tall slender ovoid body tapering to a tall neck w/high arched rim spout & tall squared loop handle, the shaped rim w/molded scrolls, the hinged domed cover w/embossed & engraved acanthus leaves w/grape cluster finial, the handle w/a ram's head mount, the body embossed overall w/foliate designs surrounding architectural scenes on a matte ground, the pedestal w/acanthus leaves & the foot w/embossed foliage, w/an engraved crest, S. Kirk & Son, Baltimore, probably 1846-61, 18 1/4" h., (ILLUS.) **7,475**

Fish knife, the back tipt handle w/a bright-cut border & engraved crest, the blade w/bright-cut foliate designs, Shreve, Crump & Low, Boston, late 19th c., 12 3/8" l. 143

Fish servers, bas-relief dolphin design handle w/an engraved & reticulated blade & fork, Albert Coles, New York, mid-19th c., pr. 863

Flask, ovoid, chased & embossed on each side w/scenes of monks in the wine cellar, hinged lid w/locking collar, engraved on top of lid, R. Wallace & Sons, early 20th c., 5 1/2" l. 690

Flask, ovoid form w/broad shoulders, engraved w/a monogram, Black, Starr & Frost, early 20th c., 8" h. 345

Fruit bowl, Art Nouveau design w/a bas-relief lily rim design, engraved central monogram, Meriden, late 19th c., 11 5/8" d., 2 3/8" h. 345

Fruit bowl, Francis I patt., lobed quadrangular form, the shaped rim everted, w/embossed scrolls & fruit, Reed and Barton, Taunton, Massachusetts, 20th c., 11 1/2" d. 546

Fruit bowl, round w/applied scroll rim & chased roses, engraved monogram, Kirk & Sons, 1896-1925, 9 1/8" d., 4" h. 575

Fruit bowl, round w/shaped flared rim w/foliate engraved band, the body w/overall foliate engraving w/a central cartouche, on a circular molded foot, Gorham Mfg. Co., Providence, Rhode Island, late 19th - early 20th c., 11" d. 345

Goblet, coin, deep bowl w/fluted lower half, on a stem w/flaring round foot, beaded edge molding, mark of Richard Humphries, Philadelphia, ca. 1780, 6" h. .. 10,925

Hip flask, acid-etched Arabesque patt., engraved monogram, 1907-38, 6 1/4" h. 345

Ice cream set: six bowls, six ice cream spoons & a serving spoon; the bowl w/a spherical finial on the hexagonal handle, spoons w/gold-washed engraved bowls, each engraved w/an Old English "T," 1860-70s, the set 489

Ice spoon, pierced & gold-washed bowl w/three-dimensional polar bear, crossed harpoons form handle, Gorham Mfg. Co., Providence, Rhode Island, 1869, 11 1/8" l. 4,313

Jar, cov., cubical, the square cover w/molded scroll rim & embossed foliate top, the body w/embossed foliate designs between molded scroll bands at the shoulder & base, monogrammed on the base, Duhme & Co., Cincinnati, Ohio, late 19th - early 20th c., 3 3/4" h. 690

Julep cup, coin, slightly tapering cylindrical form, tooled rings at rim & base, mark of Edward & David Kensey, Newport, Kentucky & Cincinnati, Ohio, 1836-50, 3 3/8" h. 413

Ladle, Arts & Crafts style, hammered surface w/notched handle & entwined raised "KP" monogram, impressed "Sterling Kalo 8597" on handle, Kalo Shop, Chicago, early 20th c., 8 1/8" l. 259

Ladle, Medallion patt., the handle w/a profile medallion of a classical woman, ovoid

bowl w/regilded interior, Gorham Mfg. Co., Providence, Rhode Island, retailed by Tiffany & Co., New York, late 19th c., 12 1/2" l. 690

Ladle, coin, molded handle w/V-slashed, double molded bowl, marked on handle, monogrammed & dated "1782," Joseph Richardson, Jr. & Nathaniel Richardson, Philadelphia, 1785-91, 13 3/4" l. 863

Loving cup, scallop-molded round domed foot & short pedestal supporting a high ovoid lobed body w/a ruffled flattened rim, molded large scrolls around the lower body & under the rim, w/three angled stag horn handles mounted around the sides, Gorham Mfg. Co., Providence, Rhode Island, early 20th c., 7 3/4" h. 862

Loving cup, three-handled, the bomb vase-form embossed & chased w/grapevine, matching cast base rim & capped handles, Theodore B. Starr, New York, New York, ca. 1910, 11 5/8" h. 6,325

Fine Gorham Loving Cup

Loving cup, wide slightly waisted cylindrical body w/a gently scalloped rim, applied around the top & base w/realistic grapevines which also form three vine feet & three angled vine-covered handles, the side engraved w/a view of a terraced house, Gorham Mfg. Co., Providence, Rhode Island, ca. 1899, 9 1/8" h. (ILLUS.)... 4,888

Martini set: cocktail shaker, eight cups & an oval wood tray w/silver gallery; Tiffany & Co., New York, early 20th c., shaker 9 1/2" h., the set 2,990

Sterling Silver Schnauzer

Model of Schnauzer, standing dog w/mouth open slightly, 2 1/4 x 6 x 7" (ILLUS. on previous page) **375**

Unusual Gorham Montieth

Montieth, the wide gadrooned round foot supporting the deep bowl decorated in the late 17th c. style w/large impressed pairs of V-scrolls w/leaftip ends & a deeply scalloped rim w/putto masks spaced between long horizontal scrolls, bail ring handles at the sides suspended from large grotesque masks, engraved w/the Order of the Thistle, Gorham Mfg. Co., Providence, Rhode Island, late 19th c., 12 1/2" d. (ILLUS.) **4,312**

Miniature Sterling Muffineer

Muffineer, miniature, baluster-form decorated w/stylized floral designs, marked "Sterling" w/indistinct company initials, 1 1/2" h. (ILLUS.) **195**

Mug, child's, coin, octagonal w/a molded rim band & double base bands, C-scroll handle, the body engraved w/a scroll design, inscribed on the front & base, Bailey & Kitchen, Philadelphia, 1832-48, 3 3/8" h. **288**

Mug, coin, baluster-form w/chased overall floral design, S. Kirk & Sons, 1846-61, 4" h. **518**

Early Victorian Coin Silver Mug

Mug, coin, octagonal, each panel chased & embossed w/floral sprays & C-scrolls, a plain central cartouche, reeded rim & base band, angled loop handle, J.E. Caldwell & Co., Philadelphia, mid-19th c., 3 1/2" h. (ILLUS.) **230**

Mug, coin, presentation-type, hexagonal baluster-form w/gently flared top, handle w/foliate decoration above a hexagonal molded flaring base, long inscription dated 1852, Geradus Boyce, New York, New York, 5 1/4" h. (minor dents) **863**

Mug, Colonial Revival style, pear-shaped w/a banded rim & scroll handle, on a molded round base, monogrammed, James Woolley, Boston, early 20th c., 5 1/4" h. **546**

Mug, coin, presentation-type, w/a portrait medallion & a seal, Edward A. Tyler, New Orleans, ca. 1860, 4" h. (minor split in handle, minor dents) **1,610**

Napkin Ring with Elephant Head

Napkin ring, arched band mounted w/the head of a trumpeting elephant, marked "Sterling," 2 1/4" l. (ILLUS.) **55**

Napkin rings, Art Nouveau style, each w/a band of slender entwined flowers, monogrammed, Gorham Mfg. Co., Providence, Rhode Island, late 19th c., 1 1/2" w., pr. **460**

Nutmeg grater, shell-form, engraved "Winslow," 19th c., 2 1/8" d. (minor loss & corrosion to grater) **316**

Pencil sharpener, on a trumpet foot, w/key twisted & ovoid cover, The Merrill Shops, first quarter 20th c., 4 5/8" l., 3 1/2" h. **748**

Pitcher, baluster-form, on four paw feet w/shell & floral cartouche joins, the body chased w/a guilloché band enclosing flowerheads, the scroll handle w/foliate joins, the everted rim w/acanthus scroll band, marked by Tiffany & Co., New York, 1895-1902, 10 1/4" h. **4,025**

Tiffany Chrysanthemum Pitcher

Pitcher, Chrysanthemum patt., bulbous lower body w/a wide swelled cylindrical neck w/a wide rim spout, hollow loop handle, repoussé & engraved flowers & scrolls, Tiffany & Co., ca. 1880, 9 1/4" h. (ILLUS. on previous page) 4,025

Pitcher, coin, classical style w/a round foot w/applied floral banding & a short pedestal supporting the squatty bulbous lobed body flaring to a medial applied floral band below the high arched wide spout & rim w/another applied floral band, large S-scroll handle, monogrammed, Geradus Boyce, New York, New York, 1820-57, 6 1/2" h. 460

Pitcher, coin, classical-style, round domed foot & short pedestal below the wide bulbous body w/a stepped shoulder & high, wide arched spout, large S-scroll handle, original presentation inscription dated 1836, marked by Jones, Lows & Ball of Boston, 10 7/8" h. 853

Pitcher, coin, octagonal baluster-form w/repoussé & chased decoration, applied scroll handle, moldings, shell & scroll feet, a coat-of-arms engraved below spout, marked by William I. Teney, New York City, ca. 1840, 11 1/4" h. 1,150

Pitcher, coin, presentation-type, graceful form w/scrolled handle, round stepped base, inscribed "Ohio State Board of Agriculture Premium," maker's mark "Blynn & Baldwin," 8 1/4" h. 303

Pitcher, Colonial Revival-style, domed foot, baluster-form body w/scroll handle topped w/a flat leaf, spout w/horizontal reeding, Chicago Silver Co., early 20th c., 8 3/4" h. 690

Pitcher, cov., coin, jug-form, baluster-shaped, the shaped rim beaded, domed cover w/cast swan finial, ear-shaped handle, on a beaded molded foot, monogrammed & dated in the center, Bigelow Bros. & Kennard, Boston, ca. 1860, 8 3/4" h. 518

Pitcher, jug-form, stepped round foot w/low stem, ewer-form body chased & embossed w/florals & foliage, plain central roundel, serpentine handle topped by a flat leaf, Gorham Mfg. Co., Providence, Rhode Island, third quarter 19th c., 7 5/8" h. 431

Pitcher, squat baluster-form on stepped domed foot, stamped w/a wide band of flat leaves around the lower section, scroll handle, scrolled rim, monogrammed, Dominick & Haff, retailed by Bailey, Banks & Biddle, early 20th c., 8 1/4" h. 633

Pitcher, squat baluster-form, the domed foot chased & embossed w/shells & seaweed, the body partially fluted w/overhanging girdle chased & embossed w/shells & dolphins on a stippled ground engraved w/cattails, foliate ear handle, rim rolled at spout & everted at sides w/half leaves, Tiffany & Co., New York, late 19th c., 10 3/4" h. 4,025

Pitcher, squat fluted form, the shaped rim & base w/molded scrolling, serpentine handle, monogrammed on one side, Smith Co., Denver, Colorado, ca. 1900, 5 3/4" h. 518

Pitcher, vasiform, the shaped molded rim on a beaded & banded neck w/engine-turned decoration, the handle w/cast stag's head thumbrest, on a domed foot, w/presentation & date inscribed on front, Gorham Mfg. Co., Providence, Rhode Island, third quarter 19th c., 7 5/8" h. 920

Pitcher, water, Japanese-style decoration, flared ringed base below the tall cylindrical body applied w/die-rolled bands, engraved w/aquatic plants & applied w/swimming fish, small rim spout, angled curved handle, marked & numbered, Tiffany & Co., New York, ca. 1880, 9 1/8" h... 9,000

Pitcher, water, coin, Classical-style, plain wide ovoid body w/a wide short cylindrical neck & high arched spout all w/molded borders, a capped double-scrolled handle, engraved w/a Gothic initial "B," marked by Hayden & Gregg, Charleston, South Carolina, ca. 1840, 8 1/4" h............ 2,587

Pitcher, water, baluster-form, chased overall w/scrolling blossoms on a stippled ground, centering an engraved monogram, A.E. Warner, Baltimore, 1874-89, 10" h............... 2,587

Pitcher, water, paneled baluster-form, chased decoration, monogrammed, Frank Smith, retailed by Bailey, Banks & Biddle Co., 10" h............................. 2,645

Pitcher, water, classical paneled baluster-form w/wide arched spout, angled handle & short pedestal w/rectangular foot, applied & engraved Colonial Revival scroll & floral designs, engraved monogram, Reed & Barton, early 20th c., 10 3/8" h. 863

Decorated Tiffany Water Pitcher

Pitcher, water, lobed baluster-form, a ropetwist footrim below the bulbous tapering body decorated w/overall undulating horizontal bands & set w/scroll-trimmed cartouches, long narrow spout over large cartouche, high arched ropetwist handle, Tiffany & Co., New York, late 19th c., 10 1/2" h. (ILLUS. on previous page) **2,530**

Kalo Shop Sterling Silver Pitcher

Pitcher, Arts & Crafts style, tapering ovoid body w/lobed ribs flanking a large central panel w/an applied monogram "B," short neck w/a wide arched spout & simple hollow C-form handle from the rim to the shoulder, stamped mark "Sterling - Hand Wrought - The Kalo Shop - Chicago - USA - 5 Pints," early 20th c., 8" d., 10 1/2" h. (ILLUS.) **2,860**

Pitcher, water, coin, tapering ovoid body on a ringed low foot, raised shoulder band below the wide cylindrical neck w/a wide, high arched spout & high C-scroll handle, the body chased w/foliate wreath centered w/an inscription dated 1846, Lincoln & Reed, Boston, 1838-48, 10 5/8" h. (dents) **1,035**

Pitcher, water, urn-form, engraved w/a monogram, mounted w/a leaf-capped scroll handle, Tiffany & Co., New York, ca. 1900, 12" h. **1,610**

Pitcher, water, bulbous baluster-form, ringed & floral-embossed foot below the body & neck embossed overall in the Kirk style w/flowers & ferns, wide rolled spout, floral-chased leafy C-scroll handle, monogrammed, Tiffany & Co., New York, ca. 1885, 12 1/4" h. **3,450**

Pitcher, ovoid body, the center chased w/a band of figures in a village scene, centered by two registers of foliage, the spout w/a beaded mask, mounted w/a leaf-capped scroll handle & on a flared foot, S. Kirk & Sons Co., early 20th c., 12 1/2" h. **3,450**

Ornate Kirk & Son Water Pitcher

Pitcher, water, wide ovoid form w/rounded shoulder to a wide short neck w/arched spout over a grotesque mask, high arched scrolled & beaded S-scroll handle, on a short pedestal w/domed foot, decorated overall w/repoussé & chased flowers, foliage & a band of scrolling grapevine on a matte ground, marked by S. Kirk & Son, Baltimore, ca. 1885, 13 1/4" h. (ILLUS.) **6,037**

Pitcher, water, coin, tankard-type, modeled as a tall slender slightly tapering tree trunk applied around the sides w/a wandering grapevine, high arched upright rim spout & long shaped branch handle, R. & W. Wilson, Philadelphia, ca. 1840, 14" h... **5,750**

Gorham Pitcher & Undertray

Pitcher & undertray, rounded rectangular baluster-form body chased w/masks, bands & swags of fruit, high arched spout over grotesque mask, ornate C-scroll handle, raised on four heavy paw feet, on a matching tray w/raised center platform & small bun feet, Gorham Mfg. Co., Providence, Rhode Island, code letters on base of each, ca. 1908, overall 12 1/4" h. (ILLUS.) **5,462**

One of Two Gorham Sterling Pitchers

Pitchers, footed baluster-form w/upright rounded spout & C-scroll handle, the body chased & embossed around the lower section w/dense floral sprays, a plain cartouche on one side, a monogrammed cartouche on the other side, the handle w/flat leaves at the top & base, Gorham Mfg. Co., Providence, Rhode Island, late 19th c., 7 3/4" h., pr. (ILLUS. of one).. **1,610**

Plate, plain round form w/a rolled rim, decorated w/repoussé clusters of grapes & engraved leaves, Wallace Silver Co., Connecticut, early 20th c., 10 1/2" d............. **230**

Plates, bread & butter, silver-gilt, round, the center of each engraved w/a monogram, the border pierced & chased w/paterae & swags, Durgin for Gorham Mfg. Co., 20th c., 6 1/4" d., set of 12 (gilt wear)..................... **747**

Plates, large round dished form w/overall hand-hammered surface & wide flanged rim, base engraved w/an initial, Shreve & Co., early 20th c., 10" d., set of 6.............. **1,150**

Platter, George III-style, round, engraved w/a trophy, the shaped border & body raised on scrolled foliate-capped feet, dated 1929, 20 1/4" d................................... **1,092**

Porringer, Art Nouveau style, ovoid hammered body w/reticulated foliate handle, early 20th c., 7 1/8" l., 1 3/4" h. **805**

Early American Silver Porringer

Porringer, coin, low rounded form w/a scroll-pierced tab handle w/monogram, by Henrick Boelen, New York City, mid-18th c., 7" l. (ILLUS.)................................ **1,035**

Porringer, coin, round deep bowl w/bomb sides & domed center, pierced keyhole handle, marked three times w/maker's mark, Elias Pelletreau, Southampton, New York, ca. 1760, 5 3/4" d..................... **5,175**

Porringer, coin, round w/pierced scrolling tab rim handle, Zachariah Brigden, Boston, Massachusetts, 1734-87, partial mark, 5 1/2" d. (repair)................................. **633**

Early Boston Porringer & Tankard

Porringer, coin, shallow rounded form w/ornate scroll-pierced tab handle w/monogram, handle stamped twice w/mark of Benjamin Burt, Boston, 18th c., repair to the rim at handle, minor dents, 5 1/4" d. (ILLUS. left) **1,265**

Porringer, ovoid bowl w/shaped & pierced handle w/engraved detailing, Tiffany & Co., 1902-07, overall 7 1/4" l......................... **403**

Porringer, shallow round bowl w/a scroll-pierced pointed rim tab handle, monogrammed, handle marked by Samuel Casey, South Kingsdon, Rhode Island, 1724-73, 5" d. (repairs)............................. **1,045**

Pot, cov., coin, tapering cylindrical form w/fluted rims & a scroll handle, cover w/a fruit finial, William Adams, 1830s-40s, 5 1/2" h. (monogram erased)......................... **259**

Fine Sterling Presentation Cup

Presentation cup, raised on a high domed & scalloped reticulated foot w/diapering, rocaille scrolls & roses, the ovoid body w/a gently ruffled rim, two curved horn handles set in stylized horn sockets, engraved on one side w/initials & dated 1899, Bigelow, Kennard & Co., 12" w. w/handles, 11 1/2" h. (ILLUS. on previous page) 3,105

Punch bowl, deep rounded bowl w/rolled & scalloped rim, raised on four cast grapevine feet, the body w/applied swags of grape clusters & leaves between satyrs heads, engraved monogram EAW, gilt interior, by George W. Shiebler & Co., New York, retailed by Irwin R. Brayton, ca. 1905, 14 1/2" d., 9 3/4" h. 5,750

Punch bowl, Japanese-style, deep footed bowl etched w/a scene of fish swimming among waterlilies & reeds below an embossed rim of churning waves, spot-hammered foot, Gorham Mfg. Co., Providence, Rhode Island, 1886, 13 1/4" d. 6,900

Rare Gorham Martelé Punch Bowl

Punch bowl, Martelé line, a shaped round wavy foot, the deep lobed body deeply repoussé & chased w/large dandelions & lilies, deeply scalloped everted rim, Gorham Mfg. Co., Providence, Rhode Island, 1898, 10 3/4" d. (ILLUS.) 25,300

Punch bowl & ladle, deep rounded bowl embossed & chased w/scrolling grapevine below an applied band of scrolling classical foliage, waved rim, beaded foot, the gilt interior w/engraved monogram, raised on a low round pedestal foot w/beaded edge, the ladle w/matching waved rim, the handle applied w/three-dimensional cast grapevine, engraved on reverse "1868 - S - 1893," both marked & numbered, Gorham Mfg. Co., Providence, Rhode Island, ca. 1893, bowl 13 1/2" d., 2 pcs. 6,600

Punch ladle, applied prunus blossoms finial on a vine-wrapped handle, gold-washed bowl, 20th c. 403

Punch ladle, coin, deep round bowl, long slender tapering handle w/rounded handle tip engraved w/a monogram, Joseph & Nathaniel Richardson, Philadelphia, 1785-91, 14 1/4" l. (dents in bowl) 633

Punch ladle, coin, elliptical bowl w/fiddle handle, engraved "James Johnson to Mary B. Dale, May 20, 1840," Davis, Palmer & Co., Boston, 12" l. (minor pitting) 230

Punch set: bowl & twelve punch cups; the bowl w/a wide domed foot chased w/a continuous floral band, the wide round body chased w/a continuous stylized chinoiserie landscape w/people & buildings, the footed cups w/matching designs on the sides of the bowls, Schofield Co., Baltimore, Maryland, early 20th c., bowl 14 5/8" d., the set 4,600

Simple 20th Century Punch Set

Punch set: punch bowl, 24 cups & round undertray; the bowl & cups w/deep plain gently flaring sides, on shallow round tray, each piece engraved w/the Vanderbilt coat of arms, Graff, Washbourne & Dunn, New York, retailed by Cartier, 20th c., bowl 14" d., undertray 22" d., the set (ILLUS.) 6,612

Salt dips, figural, a deep rounded urn-form bowl w/a wide rolled rim raised upon the tails of three upright dolphins resting on a tripartite platform & three paw feet, S. Kirk & Son, 1830-46, 3 1/2" h., pr. 1,035

Salt dips, figural, in English Regency style, modeled as an argonaut shell supported on the back of a dolphin on an oval wave-chased base, P.L. Krider, Philadelphia, ca. 1870, 3 5/8" l., pr. 2,012

Salt dips & spoons, open oyster shell-form, gold-washed bowl, Gorham Mfg. Co., Providence, Rhode Island, late 19th c., 4 7/8" l., pr. 1,495

Salver, George III-style, center engraved w/an armorial, shaped border applied w/intervals of scrolls, on four scroll feet, Howard and Co., New York, New York, ca. 1900, 22 1/2" l. 1,312

Sauceboat, coin, a punched beaded rim & leaf-capped flying multiple-scroll handle, pedestal foot w/beaded borders, engraved w/a contemporary monogram, Abraham Dubois, Philadelphia, ca. 1790, 6 3/4" l. 8,050

Sauceboats, coin, deep oval body w/a high & wide arched spout & beaded & entrelac rim band, an upright rounded leafy scroll handle, raised on four ram's head & hoofed leg supports, engraved w/a contemporary monogram & dated "June 1st 1859," marked "R & W," retailed by Bigelow Bros. & Kennard, Boston, ca. 1859, 7 1/2" l., pr. 2,300

Service plates, round w/bas-relief Italian Renaissance border designs, engraved foliate central monogram, Gorham Mfg. Co., Providence, Rhode Island, late 19th c., 10 3/4" d., set of 12 7,763

Serving bowl, rectangular w/lobed molded rim w/reeded scroll decoration, the reticulated sides w/molded floral swags & scallop shells within roundels, on four pad feet, Frank Herschede Company, Cincinnati, Ohio, 20th c., 11 1/2 x 14" 1,495

Serving dish, modeled as double grape leaves & bunches of grapes w/chased details, Watson Sterling, early 20th c., 10 5/8" l. 374

Serving spoon, coin, coffin-end handle, mark attributed to William Holmes, Jr., Boston, 1742-1825, 9 1/4" l. 55

Serving spoon, coin, bright-cut decoration, monogrammed, George Alexander & Peter Riker, New York, 1797-1800, 12" l. 805

Shakers, figural, realistically formed as seated pug dogs wearing collars, removable heads pierced on top, each engraved "M.O.R.," Dominick & Haff, New York, marked "D & H Sterling" & date lozenge for 1879, 2 3/4" h., pr. 4,887

Sherbet cups w/glass liners, each silvergilt bowl engraved w/cartouches & floral designs, Gorham Mfg. Co., Providence, Rhode Island, set of 10 977

Soup tureen, cov., coin, oval bomb form, the four paw-and-ball feet headed by acanthus, the everted rim applied w/dense band of flowers, leaves & scrolls, the two bracket handles cast & chased as grapevine capped by a rose, the domed cover w/an acanthus calyx surmounted by a floral ring handle, each side of the body engraved w/a coat-of-arms, crest & motto, the cover engraved w/crests, marked by Frederick Marquand, New York, New York, ca. 1830, overall 15 3/4" l. 12,650

Soup tureen, cov., oval, the reeded domed oval foot embossed & chased on the top w/flowers, the long rounded body & stepped, domed cover embossed & chased overall in the Kirk style w/flowers & leaves, the cover w/a reeded upright ring handle, gadrooned loop end handles on the body, monogrammed, Tiffany & Co., New York, ca. 1880, overall 13 3/4" l. 5,750

Soup tureen, cov., oval, the foot rim w/a die-stamped band, low pedestal supporting a plain squatty bulbous body w/die-stamped rim below the sloping domed cover w/a scroll-pierced & pointed handle w/turned & pointed finial, the long C-scroll end handles topped by figural infant bacchii, partly frosted finish, Wood & Hughes, New York, ca. 1865-70, overall 18 1/2" l. 5,462

Spoon, Arts & Crafts style, elongated tapering hand-hammered handle w/rounded end, wide pointed bowl, marked "Sterling Kalo H201," ca. 1910, 13 3/4" l. 316

Sterling Silver Spoon

Spoon, pierced bowl w/shell motif & decorated w/scrolls, marked on back of handle "Sterling," 4 1/2" l. (ILLUS.) 65

Stationery stand, the rectangular base mounted w/four graduated shaped rectangular dividers w/beaded rims, the front & rear dividers chased w/a pair of putti holding a wreath, w/beaded rims, engraved w/a monogram, on four scroll feet, Shiebler Co., ca. 1900, 8 3/4" l. 1,955

Sugar basket, coin, footed navette form, chased floral leaf decoration, swing handle, monogrammed, Ball, Black & Company, 1850s, 6 3/4" h., 6" l. 460

Sugar bowl, cov., coin, round ringed foot supporting a gently flaring hemispherical bowl w/molded rim & domed cover w/wide & low dished round handle, marked "IR" in square, Joseph Richardson Sr., Philadelphia, ca. 1748, 4 3/8" d. 20,700

Sugar bowl, cov., coin, squat baluster-form on a stepped round foot, wide band of engine-turning, one plain & one monogrammed cartouche, two serpentine handles, domed cover w/flower-form finial, Gorham Mfg. Co., Providence, Rhode Island, mid-19th c., 8" h. 173

Sugar bowl, cov., coin, baluster-form body w/applied foliate & star banding, on a square molded base, domed cover w/acorn finial, monogrammed, Thomas Fletcher & Sidney Gardner, Boston, 1808-25, 7" h. (minor dents) 345

Sugar bowl, cov., coin, a wide round ringed foot w/gadrooned rim band & applied scroll & foliate banding below the squatty bulbous body chased w/long acanthus leaves up the sides below the rolled foliate band rim, domed cover w/strawberry finial, C-scroll handles, monogrammed, Jonathan Stodder & Benjamin Frobisher, Boston, 1816-25, 7 3/4" h. (minor dents) 403

Sugar bowl, cov., baluster-form body w/applied rose banding & ram's head mounts on a square molded base, domed cover w/bud finial, keystone touch w/"DH," mid-19th c., 8 1/2" h. 316

Sterling Sugar Cube Holder

Sugar cube holder, low pierced ring-form
w/small ball feet & a thin swing handle,
engraved initials on the rim, marked "925
Fine - Sterling" & a bird emblem, 5 1/4" d.
(ILLUS. on previous page) **225**

Sugar urn, cov., coin, urn-form w/circular
foot on a square pedestal, beaded rims &
pierced gallery, the conical cover w/urn-
form finial, the body engraved w/a monogram, marked by Charles Moore & John
Ferguson, Philadelphia, ca. 1801-05,
11" h............ **3,680**

Sugar urn, cov., coin, urn-shaped body on
a flaring pedestal & square foot, a
stepped spire-form cover w/an urn finial,
row of chased beadwork above the body,
monogrammed, A.W. Robinson, Phila-
delphia, 1795-98, 10 3/4" h.................... **1,495**

Tablespoons, coin, oval pointed bowls &
long down-turned handles monogrammed "TSG" & numbered 1-6, mark
of Seril Dodge, Providence, Rhode
Island, ca. 1759-1802, 8 3/4" l., set of 6
(small tear in one bowl, minor dents) **690**

Tankard, cov., coin, footed baluster-form,
the round stepped foot w/a gadrooned
band, plain body, stepped & domed
hinged cover w/gadrooned rim band &
pierced shell-form thumbpiece above the
double scroll handle w/a heart-shaped
endpiece, engraved w/contemporary foliate monogram "BMD," marked three
times on base "JA" in script for Joseph
Anthony, Jr., Philadelphia, ca. 1785,
heavy weight, 9" h. **27,600**

Tankard, cov., coin, tapered cylindrical
body w/a hinged stepped & domed cover w/flame finial & scrolled thumbrest,
S-scroll handle w/terminal in the form of
a Queen Anne coin, body w/mid-19th c.
arms & initial, handle engraved w/ini-
tials, cover of later origin, George Han-
ners, Boston, ca. 1740, 8 3/4" h. **3,600**

Tankard, cov., coin, tapered cylindrical
form, the molded base band w/reeded
top, stepped domed cover w/flaming urn
finial, scroll thumbpiece, the handle applied w/a baluster & engraved w/"WEN" &
dated 1774, convex oval shield terminal
marked in center of base "R [pellet] FAIR-
CHILD" in a rectangle, Robert Fairchild,
Connecticut, ca. 1770, 9 3/8" h. **21,850**

Tankard, cov., coin, tapering cylindrical body
w/flaring ringed base, medial ring & flared
ringed rim, the stepped & domed hinged
cover w/an urn & flame finial, hollow
scrolled handle w/scrolled thumb-piece &
convex tip, monogrammed, a spout added
later & removed, some restoration, Benjamin Burt, Boston, 18th c., 9" h. (ILLUS.
on page 113 right with porringer) **7,475**

Tankard, cov., coin, tapering cylindrical
body w/ringed base & medial ring,
stepped & ringed domed hinged cover
w/scrolled thumbrest, C-scroll handle,
John Coney, Boston, ca. 1721, early
engraved initials & later script inscription dated 1854, 4 3/4" d., 8" h. (cover
of later origin) **9,200**

Early 18th Century Tankard

Tankard, cov., coin, tapering cylindrical
body w/ringed foot & medial band,
stepped domed hinged cover w/short
baluster finial, scroll handle w/a convex
shield terminal & scroll thumbrest, the
side engraved w/a later crest & name,
marks of William Cowell, Boston,
Massachusetts, ca. 1730, 7 1/2" h.
(ILLUS.)............ **7,475**

Tazza, a round shallow bowl w/a flaring
arching openwork rim, supported by a figural partly draped putto above a stepped
partly fluted flaring round base, Gorham
Mfg. Co., Providence, Rhode Island, dated 1871, 12 1/4" h.................... **2,300**

Tazza, wide shallow dished top w/a pierced-
work rim divided by floral designs & surrounding an etched bouquet in vases,
monogrammed in the center, raised on a
simple flaring round pedestal base,
Woodside Sterling Company, ca. 1910,
9" d., 4 1/2" h. **179**

Tazzas, a shallow flaring squared dish
w/rounded corners chased overall
w/flowers & ferns, raised on a high
domed base of four flaring scroll-em-
bossed legs, S. Kirk & Son,
Baltimore, ca. 1880-90, 7" w., pr. **1,725**

Tazzas, a shallow wide rounded dished top
w/the shaped border applied w/shells &
scrolls alternating w/paterae suspending
bellflowers, the center engraved w/a
monogram, raised on a slender tapering
standard & pierced flaring round foot, Tiffany & Co., New York, early 20th c.,
8 3/4" d., pr.................... **1,840**

Tazzas, a wide shallow bowl w/the wide
scalloped rim pierced w/scrolls & rose
branches, raised on a short pedestal
base w/the rim & flaring round foot cast &
pierced w/further scrolls & rose branches, Bailey, Banks & Biddle,
Philadelphia, ca. 1890, marked,
11 1/2" d., pr.................... **2,587**

Tazzas, the bowl w/chased & embossed rim & shaped edge, on a trumpet foot partially chased & embossed w/flowers on a stippled ground, S. Kirk & Son Co., early 20th c., 6 1/2" d., 3 1/4" h., pr. **633**

American Classical Tea Set

Tea & coffee service: cov. coffeepot, cov. teapot, cov. sugar bowl, creamer & waste bowl; coin, Classical style, each piece w/a gadrooned finial above a deep curved & decorated upright rim band over the rectangular lobed body on a pedestal above a stepped oval base on four ball feet, the die-stamped band on the shoulder of rural scenery, a single narrow band of anthemion leaves on the finial & at the upper & lower rims, William B. Heyer, New York City, first quarter 19th c., minor dents, coffeepot 11" h., the set (ILLUS.).... **3,565**

Tea & coffee service: cov. coffeepot, cov. teapot, cov. sugar bowl, creamer & waste bowl; each in squatty ovoid form, w/feet & applied rim decoration, scroll finials, engraved monogram inscription, Reed & Barton, 20th c., coffeepot 6 3/4" h., the set (minor denting)...................... **748**

Tea & coffee service: cov. coffeepot, cov. teapot, cov. sugar bowl, creamer & waste bowl; the urn-form coffeepot on four paw feet w/leaf joins, the cross-supports centering a paterae, the body w/dentilated & paterae shoulder, the hinged domed cover w/urn finial, the scroll handle w/ivory insulators, other pieces matching, each marked w/retailer's mark & mark of the Gorham Mfg. Co., Providence, Rhode Island, w/an oval mahogany tray w/paterae inlay & silver gallery w/bracket end handles, 1919, coffeepot 9 3/4" h., the set....... **3,680**

Tea & coffee service: cov. teapot, cov. coffeepot, cov. sugar bowl, creamer & waste bowl; each of paneled flattened baluster-form, handles w/ivory heat stops, monogrammed, Unger Brothers, early 20th c., coffeepot 5 1/2" h., the set **489**

Tea & coffee service: cov. teapot, cov. coffeepot, handled cov. sugar bowl, creamer & waste bowl; each of ovoid urn-form, angled handles, applied w/an oval monogrammed cartouche amid scrolling foliage, w/ovolo & stylized banded rims, Wallace Silversmiths, early 20th c., coffeepot 10 1/2" h., the set **1,955**

Tea & coffee service: cov. teapot, cov. coffeepot, kettle on lampstand, creamer, two-handled cov. sugar bowl, waste bowl & two-handled rectangular tray; Lord Robert patt., each piece of rectangular bomb form, the gadrooned rims w/foliate-capped shells at intervals, on four ball feet, engraved w/a monogram, International Silver Co., 20th c., tray 28" l., coffeepot 13 1/2" h., the set **5,462**

Tea & coffee service: cov. teapot, cov. coffeepot, tankard-style cov. hot milk pitcher, creamer, cov. sugar bowl, waste bowl & kettle on lampstand base; most pieces w/a squatty bulbous body, each repoussé & chased overall w/flowers & foliage on a textured ground, the finials in the form of blossoms, bases engraved "JK, April 27, 1905," marked by S. Kirk & Son Co., coffeepot 9 1/2" h., the set **9,775**

Tea & coffee set: cov. coffeepot, cov. teapot, creamer, cov. sugar bowl & waste bowl; Art Nouveau style, upright baluster-form bodies w/an undulating foot & a flaring rim w/wide sawtooth border, simple loop handle, the domed covers w/a cast flower finial, applied monograms, Tiffany & Co., New York, 1891-1902, coffeepot 12" h., the set **2,875**

Tea & coffee set: cov. coffeepot, cov. teapot, creamer & open sugar bowl; each of urn-form w/shaped embossed foliate rims, the pots w/waisted domed cover w/repoussé engraved swags w/urn finials, the bodies fluted w/repoussé engraved foliate swags & chased reeding on domed & embossed bases, monogrammed on the base, Shreve, Crump & Low, Boston, early 20th c., teapot 9 3/4" h., the set............................ **3,105**

Tea service: cov. teapot, cov. hot water urn on stand, creamer, sugar bowl missing cover, waste bowl; coin, all ovoid form on a domed stepped foot, beaded detailing, cover w/swan finial, the urn w/presentation inscription on one side, urn stand on four heavy paw feet w/scrolls & anthemion, monogrammed, Shreve, Stanwood & Co., 1860s, hot water urn 16" h., the set (burner missing)............................ **2,185**

Tea service: cov. teapot, cov. sugar bowl, creamer & waste bowl; coin, Classical-style, each shaped rectangular bomb form on a conforming base w/four leaf-capped paw feet, scroll handles, the teapot w/ivory insulators, the domed covers w/a star calyx & acorn finial, each engraved on one side "JAK," marked by Allcock & Allen, New York, ca. 1820, teapot 13" l., the set......................... **4,025**

Tea set: cov. teapot, cov. coffeepot, cov. handled sugar bowl & creamer; coin, each of oval form, the domed covers w/urn-form finials & borders of bright-cutting, the oval body w/a shield-shaped crest, the front depicting an eagle w/brood in a nest, the back w/a monogram w/floral, foliate & geometric bright-cut decoration, molded rim & base, angular reeded handles on sugar & creamer, angular ebonized wood handles on pots, Hugh Wishart, New York, New York, ca. 1784, coffeepot 8 1/2" h., the set (minor repair, dents) **3,738**

Tea set: cov. teapot, cov. sugar bowl & creamer; coin, Classical style, the oval teapot w/straight sides & concave rim, w/wood scroll handle & straight spout, the hinged domed cover w/a pineapple finial, the sugar & creamer each of urn-form on square pedestal foot, all w/beaded rims & bright-cut engraving on both sides w/floral garlands & a shield centering a monogram, teapot marked by Gerrit Schanck, New York, the creamer & sugar marked by John Schanck, New York, ca. 1795, teapot overall 12" l., the set **8,625**

Medallion Pattern Tea Set

Tea set: cov. teapot, cov. sugar bowl & helmet-form creamer; Medallion patt., the tapering ovoid bodies each applied w/a profile medallion & anthemion engraving, sugar w/ring handles, teapot & creamer w/angled handles, covers w/helmet-form finials, monogrammed, Ball, Black & Co., third quarter 19th c., teapot 6" h., the set (ILLUS.) **2,185**

Tea set: cov. teapot, creamer & cov. sugar bowl; Colonial Revival style, baluster-form bodies, domed covers w/reeded urn finials, molded rims gadrooned, on stepped round bases, Gorham Mfg. Co., Providence, Rhode Island, 1950, teapot 9" h., the set **690**

Tea set: cov. teapot, creamer, cov. sugar bowl & waste bowl; coin, footed tall pear-shaped bodies on the teapot, sugar & creamer, all pieces embossed & chased w/bands of scrolling ivy on a matted ground w/strapwork cartouches, beaded borders & urn finials, Albert Cole, New York, New York, ca. 1850-55, teapot 11 3/8" h., the set **3,450**

American Classical Tea Set

Tea set: cov. teapot, open sugar bowl & creamer; coin, each of Classical urn form decorated w/bands of pearls & herringbone design on the foot & shoulder, embossed acanthus leaves, the teapot w/animal head spout & scroll handle, the creamer w/a winged female figure on the scroll handle, the sugar w/applied female masks & laurel leaf handles, teapot & sugar marked, Anthony Rasch & Co., Philadelphia, 1820-30, teapot 9 3/8" h., the set (ILLUS.) **2,875**

Tea set: tete-a-tete-style w/a cov. teapot, cov. sugar bowl, creamer & cov. teakettle on stand; each w/a squat bulbous body w/engine-turned central band of Greek key, angular handles & knob finials, the stand w/a pointed reticulated lappet panel, on tall slender squared legs w/ivy leaf knees & scroll feet, monogrammed on both sides, Tiffany & Co., New York, ca. 1865-70, kettle 9 1/4" h., the set **2,185**

Tea set: cov. teapot, cov. sugar bowl & creamer; coin, Classical style, each piece w/a ringed pedestal foot supporting a bulbous lobed body below a stepped shoulder w/a scroll-cast band below a smaller leaf band, the domed covers w/leafy scrolls & a knob finial, ornate C-scroll handle, paneled swan's-neck spout on pot, John I. Monell & Charles M. Williams, New York City, ca. 1825, teapot 10 3/8" h., the set (very minor dents) **2,185**

Pierced Sterling Tea Strainer

Tea strainer, w/pierced handle & stylized floral pattern, mark of Frank M. Whiting Co. & "Sterling - 5005," 5 1/4" l. (ILLUS.) **125**

Sterling Silver Tea Strainer

Tea strainer, w/scalloped bowl decorated w/C-scrolls, 4 3/4" l. (ILLUS.) **125**

Wooden-handled Sterling Tea Strainer

Tea strainer, w/wooden handle, bowl decorated w/stylized C-scrolls & leaves, 6 3/4" l. (ILLUS.) 175

Tea tray, coin, oval, two-handled, molded rim & loop handles, the center engraved w/flowers & rococo scrolls, marked by Platt & Brother, New York, New York, 1825-34, 31 1/4" l. 4,600

Teakettle on lamp stand, the kettle w/a squat round body embellished w/an engraved band of Greek key, raised on a spreading foot similarly engraved, a serpentine spout w/flat leaf detail, domed cover w/Greek key border & corn finial, hinged handle w/ivory heat stops & ram's head terminals, w/a stand, possibly plated, w/scrolled arms & Greek key engraving, on rocaille feet, w/plated burner, Tiffany & Co., New York, 1854-70, kettle 9 1/2" h., the set 1,380

Teapot, cov., coin, Classical style, round stepped short pedestal foot below the bulbous squatty oblong body w/two stepped shoulder & cover bands of applied grape & leaf banding, the domed cover w/a basket of fruit finial, ornate C-scroll handle w/insulators & long swan's-neck spout, Henry Ball, Erastus Tompkins & William Black, New York, 1839-51, 10" h. 690

Teapot, cov., coin, bulbous ovoid body w/applied basket of fruit & flowers banding around the shoulder, raised on a flaring ringed pedestal base, figural serpent & fish-form handles & paneled serpent-form spout, domed cover w/a figural bird finial, marked "L. Allen," second quarter 19th c., 10 1/2" h. (minor dents) 978

Sterling Silver Top

Toy top, w/sections denoting card hands, faceted spinning surface, probably ebony, made by Gorham & marked "Sterling 50P," 2 1/2" d. (ILLUS.) 125

Tray, coin, oval w/gadrooned border enclosing an engraved design of flanking vases containing floral & foliate scrolls, on four scrolled feet, monogrammed, Gorham and Co., Providence, Rhode Island, 1848-65, 8 3/4 x 12" 374

Tray, coin, round w/beaded border enclosing an engraved scrolled foliate design, raised on three scrolled feet, monogrammed, Jones, Shreve, Brown & Co., Boston, 1854, 10" d. (slightly misshapen) 489

Tray, oval, the border engraved w/classical revival band & floral swags, Frank M. Whiting & Co., early 20th c., 15 5/8 x 22" 863

Tray, rectangular, the wide border & two handles applied w/urns of fruit alternating w/scrolling foliage, the center engraved w/a foliate monogram, Whiting Mfg. Company, ca. 1900, 33" l 5,175

Tray, round, the gently flared rim w/a raised twig & grapevine border, the center decorated w/an engine-cut design & a center cartouche w/monogram, A.G. Schultz & Co., retailed by Sylvan Bros., ca. 1913, 14" d. 1,232

Tray, round w/molded rim w/foliate & scroll designs, the sides w/embossed foliate decoration & castles on a matte background, the face w/engine-turned decoration surrounding an engraved roundel, monogrammed in the center, Loring Andrews Co., Cincinnati, Ohio, 20th c., 9" d 489

Tray, square w/rounded corners, the center engraved w/a border of rocaille decoration, the wide everted border applied w/foliage & scrolls, on three leaf-capped round feet, Tiffany & Co., New York, late 19th c., 11" w. 1,725

Tray, rectangular, shaped rim & chased floral decoration, Durgin, retailed by Bigelow, Kennard and Co., late 19th c., 12" l 489

Tray, square w/rounded corners, applied scroll border, engraved to center w/a monogram, early 20th c., 12 1/4" sq. 230

Tray, oval w/low dished edge & beaded rim, the center engraved w/a crest surrounded by a wide band of grotesque masks & foliage, beaded & turned squared end handles, Tiffany & Co., New York, overall 32 1/2" l 11,500

Tumbler, coin, slightly tapering cylindrical form w/ring bands at the rim & base, marked by E. & D. Kinsey, Cincinnati, Ohio, 1840-61, 3 1/2" h. 403

Tumbler, coin, barrel-form w/reeded banding, monogrammed, Asa Blanchard, Lexington, Kentucky, 1818-38, 3 1/8" h. (minor dents) 5,463

Large Tiffany Covered Tureen

Tureen, cov., oval, a stepped oval foot & short pedestal supporting the long squatty bulbous body w/slightly flared rim & large reeded square section end handles w/a beaded cube in the center & flat leaf terminals, the stepped domed cover w/a scroll-trimmed pierced heart-shaped handle on rayed leaves, monogrammed & dated, Tiffany & Co., New York, 1875-91, 8 1/2 x 15", 11 1/4" h. (ILLUS.) **5,175**

Tureen, cov., the oval body & domed cover chased overall w/blossoms on a stippled ground, mounted w/leaf-capped scroll handles, the base engraved w/a scrolling monogram, made & retailed by Bailey, Banks & Biddle, late 19th c., overall 13" l... **3,450**

Tureen, cover & liner, narrow oval form, domed cover & swelled base each embossed & chased overall w/a scene of a hound flushing game surrounded by flowers & fruit, finial in the figure of a large spread-winged bird perched on a rock, the liner w/hinged ring handles capped by lion masks, A.E. Warner, Baltimore, ca. 1845, 13" l., the set **2,300**

Urn-vase, cov., silver-gilt, swirl-ribbed domed pedestal foot supports the tall waisted ovoid body chased w/spiral lobes & swirled flowering stems, the domed swirl-ribbed cover w/flame finial, long double C-scroll leafy handles down the sides, engraved w/monograms & dates, Howard & Co., George III-style, New York, 1893, 20" h. **3,450**

Vase, Martelé line, the hammered bulbous body w/flared shaped & waved rim, the rim w/embossed leaves, the lobed body w/embossed daffodils, on a shaped domed foot w/embossed buds & leaves, w/embossed monogram, Gorham Mfg. Co., Providence, Rhode Island, ca. 1900, 8" h. **5,463**

Vase, the body vertically paneled w/foliate designs & scrolls & acanthus leaf decoration around the bottom, a molded, reeded rim above a repoussé frieze, a knopped stem above a repoussé foot w/molded bands, Gorham Mfg. Co., Providence, Rhode Island, early 20th c., 10 1/8" h. **978**

Vase, trumpet foot w/engraved band of lines & circles, tapered baluster-form body w/engraved laurel wreaths on each side,

one w/a monogram, everted rim w/engraved band similar to foot, J.E. Caldwell & Co., late 19th - early 20th c., 15 3/4" h. **748**

Small Sterling Bud Vase

Vase, bud-type, plain round foot below the slender swelled body chased w/cherubs & scrolls, 2 1/4" d., 6" h. (ILLUS.) **450**

Gorham Martelé Presentation Vase

Vase, Martelé line, three-handled presentation-type, a low serpentine flared & footed base below the wide swelled cylindrical lower body below the wide bulbous tapering upper half w/a tricorner rolled rim, large C-scroll handles from the shoulder to the lower base, worked w/ornate scrolling vines & grape leaves & clusters, engraved presentation & dated "1921," Britannia Standard, Gorham Manufacturing Co., Providence, Rhode Island, 9" h. (ILLUS.)................................... **9,200**

Vase, two-handled, cylindrical, the shoulder flat-chased w/Persian-style foliage on a stippled ground & suspended w/tassels & fringe, the narrow cylindrical neck mounted w/two arched & openwork foliate handles, Gorham Mfg. Co., Providence, Rhode Island, late 19th c., 9 1/2" h. **1,725**

Vase, baluster-form, on a spreading foot w/an openwork cornucopia & scroll rim, the flared neck w/a border of openwork cornucopiae, scrolls & acanthus leaves, marked by Dominick & Haff, New York, New York, ca. 1895, 11 1/4" h. **3,450**

Vase, hexagonal trumpet form w/matching domed foot, decorated w/acid-etched Colonial Revival decoration, Tiffany & Co., early 20th c., 11 1/2" h. 920

Vase, Martelé line, inverted baluster-form w/spot-hammered surface, the domed lobed base & body repoussé & chased w/berries & leaves, w/everted wavy & lobed rim, marked by the Gorham Mfg. Co., Providence, Rhode Island, ca. 1902, 14" h. 10,925

Vase, slightly flaring cylindrical form, chased & engraved at the shoulder w/shells & scrolling foliage, engraved w/a monogram, on a conforming circular foot, Tiffany & Co., New York, early 20th c., 14" h. 1,840

Vase, Art Nouveau style, small ringed foot supporting a compressed cushion-form lower body below the tall, slender waisted neck w/a widely flaring rim, long slender curved leaf handles from center body to underside of lower body, lower body w/scrolling chased tulips & leaves, the wide neck chased w/iris blossoms, Dominick & Haff, New York, ca. 1900, 15 1/2" h. 4,025

Vase, baluster-form w/a tall slightly waisted neck w/a widely rolled rim, the domed pedestal base w/leafy scroll feet, the lower bulbous body chased w/panels of scrolls & floral swags, the neck chased w/scroll-supported urns of flowers alternating w/panels w/applied lion masks & bearded faces, floral swags around the top of neck & scroll bands on the rolled rim, Gorham Mfg. Co., Providence, Rhode Island, special order, 1899, 17 1/2" h. 5,462

Vase, Art Nouveau style, trumpet-shaped, the base & lower body cast w/openwork calyx of Art Nouveau flowers & tendrils, plain flaring upper body w/small floral clusters around the rim, Whiting Mfg. Co., 1905, 19 1/4" h. 4,312

Vase, presentation-type, tall simple classic urn form, domed foot w/chased band supporting the tall body w/an applied girdle of oak branches around the shoulder, the short, wide cylindrical neck w/rolled, beaded rim flanked by high arched leafy scroll slender handles from rim to lower body, the body engraved w/a festoon of shamrock & badge of The Friendly Sons of St. Patrick on one side & presentation panel on the other, Reed & Barton, ca. 1910, 26" h. 6,325

Vases, 7" h., bud-type, Arts & Crafts style, flared rolled rim on cylindrical body tapering to a round disk base, hammered surface, impressed "Sterling Kalo 377G" on base, Chicago, early 20th c., pr. 1,840

Vegetable dish, cov., round, the border w/scrolls & foliage, Theodore B. Starr, New York, New York, early 20th c., 10 1/2" d. 431

Vegetable dish, open, oval w/beaded border, Tiffany & Co., New York, ca. 1907-38, 10" l. 201

Wine cooler, simple urn-form body w/an egg-and-dart rim band & twin upright folding rim handle rising from pairs of classical female heads, the body raised on four winged lion monopods w/paw feet, interior fixed cylindrical liner, the side engraved w/contemporary arms, Tiffany & Co., New York, ca. 1865, 13" h. 9,200

English & Others

The use of silver in England, both as a form of currency and also for decorative and utilitarian items, goes back to very early times. In the mid-1100s, in an effort to improve the realm's coinage, King Henry II brought in the Easterlings, coiners from eastern Germany; their silver coins were called "sterlings."

In 1300, King Edward I declared that wrought silver must be of the same standard as the coins of the realm. This marked the inception of the sterling standard in which 925 parts of silver per 1000 must be used; the remaining 75 parts per 1000 would be an added metal, usually copper, which had been found to be the most satisfactory alloy, giving greater strength to the silver without changing the lustrous color. Much fine work has been attributed to France, Germany and some of the Scandinavian countries, as well as other continental countries. It should be noted that much of this work was not marked either as to the maker, country or silver content. With study, however, it is possible to learn to identify pieces by their style. On the other hand, you will find that English works are very clearly marked with "hallmarks," which include a date-letter symbol indicating the year in which the item was made or assayed. Also included will be a town mark, indicating the location of the silversmith. A rampant lion mark denotes its English origin and usually there is also a mark with the initials of the maker. From the late 18th through the late 19th century an additional "monarch head" mark was also required.

Apostle spoon, the handle w/molded lamb, cross & winged cherub head w/a cast apostle terminal, engraved "St. Bartholomew" on the back, London, 1856, 9" l. $115

Coin Silver Ashtray

Ashtray, composed of three hammered Peruvian coins joined at base, w/tiny full-bodied llamas as feet, applied leaf forms for holding cigarettes, 2 x 4" (ILLUS.) 125

Basket, almond-shaped bowl w/a flanged upcurved rim w/reticulated band, on a reticulated footring, center arched swing handle, Peter & Ann Bateman, London, England, 1791-92, 14 3/4" l. (repair) 3,190

Basket, oval boat-shape w/wide flanged rim w/gadrooned rim & cast shells at ends, raised on a low oblong platform on ball feet, central swing handle, untraced maker, New Castle, England, 1812-13, 12 3/4" l. **1,100**

Oval Silver Basket

Basket, oval, flaring pierced basketweave sides, decorated w/garland swags & scrollwork, lion heads at sides w/rings in mouths form handles, indistinct hallmark, 2 1/2 x 3 1/8 x 5 1/2" (ILLUS.) **345**

Basket, oval w/deep rounded flaring delicately reticulated sides raised on an upright oval reticulated ring foot, pierced central swing handle, engraved coat-of-arms in bottom, Edward Aldridge (?), London, England, 1764-65, 15 1/2" l......... **4,180**

Basket, oval w/high lattice-pierced & galleried sides, pierced swing strap handle, Turin, Italy, 18th c., 7" l. **1,150**

Basket, square form w/each corner pierced & chased w/festoons & urns, the round center chased w/cherubs in a landscape, w/a foliate garland around the rim, Germany, ca. 1900, 14 1/2" l. **805**

Beaker, slightly tapering cylindrical form on a bulbous squat foot, chased & embossed w/stylized rocaille, the sides chased & embossed w/eagles on pediments bearing floral swags & sprays, w/two rococo cartouches centered by engraved crosshatching & fishscaling, Moscow, Russia, early 19th c., 6" h. **805**

Miniature Book with Silver Covers

Book, sterling silver covers decorated w/a scrolling leafy vine & blossom & titled "A Christmas Carol," complete paper contents, worn English hallmarks, dated 1904, 3/8 x 1 1/8 x 2 1/8" (ILLUS.) **165**

Bowl, broad body banded at the high waist w/an ovolo band, the rims applied w/gadrooned bands, St. Petersburg, Russia, 1841, 8 1/8" d. **575**

Bowl, footed, a stepped circular base issuing an openwork berry & foliate stem supporting a deep flaring inverted bell-form bowl, Georg Jensen Silversmithy, Denmark, Pattern No. 17A, 1925-32, 4" h.......... **690**

Bowl, low round footed form, a French coin set in the bottom, scroll handles, swag & ribbon decoration around the sides, engraved name & date on rim, France, 18th c., 5" d., 4" h.. **230**

Bowl, round, chased & repoussé w/scrolling flowers, thistles, grapes, foliage, C-scrolls & diaperwork on a matte ground, one cartouche engraved w/a crest & motto, the other side monogrammed & dated 1858, George IV period, George McHattie, Edinburgh, 1826-27, 10 3/4" d............. **2,185**

English Silver Bowl

Bowl, round, w/elaborate raised design of scrolls, flowers & leaves along flaring sides, marked "WC" & hallmarks for London, England, 4 3/4" d. (ILLUS.).................... **155**

Bowl, wide rounded body raised on a flared & pierced footring, the exterior w/a raised chrysanthemum decoration, scalloped rim w/molded edge, Chinese Export, Sing Fat maker, Canton, China, early 20th c., 6" d., 3" h. **345**

Bowl, footed, ribbed & fluted deep sides on a low foot, chased swag & ribbon border, engraved inscription under base, Hutton & Sons, Ltd., London, England, 1898-99, 9 1/4" d., 6 1/4" h.. **748**

Box, cov., in the form of a faux wood cigar box w/labels, Russia, late 19th c., 2 15/16 x 5 1/8", 1 5/8" h. **1,495**

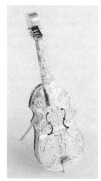

Silver Bass Fiddle Box

Box, cov., model of a bass fiddle, decorated w/cherubs & scrollwork, Europe, late 19th - early 20th c., 2 1/8 x 6 1/8" (ILLUS. on previous page) 795

Box, cov., oval, chased scene on the cover depicting a knight bowing to a group of ladies, engraved harbor scenes & floral decoration around the body, Holland, 19th c., 4 5/8 x 5 5/8", 2 1/2" h. 460

Box, cov., quatrefoil box w/sides & hinged cover flat-chased w/foliage on a stippled ground, the cover mounted w/five amethystine quartz cabochons, on four ball feet, Germany, ca. 1900, 4 3/4" l. 517

Small Round Silver Box

Box, cov., round w/flared base & rim, domed cover w/florette finial, Europe, late 19th - early 20th c., 1 1/2 x 1 1/2" (ILLUS.).. 125

Box, cov., wide bulbous ovoid body raised on low scroll-pierced feet, fitted w/a low domed cover, overall Rococo repoussé & cast designs including an engraved coat-of-arms & a Chinese man, John Langford & John Sebille, London, England, 1764-65, 5 1/4" h. 2,255

Sterling Silver Egg-shaped Box

Box, egg-shaped, two piece, Mexican sterling, 1 3/4 x 3 1/2" (ILLUS.) 79

Sterling Victorian Butter Dish

Butter dish, cov., w/metal insert, domed cover heavily engraved w/scrollwork & the initial "H," makers name & English hallmarks, late 19th c., 8 1/4" d., 5" h. (ILLUS.) 1,695

Cake basket, footed scalloped round shallow paneled dish w/applied scroll & floral rim, chased floral decoration, pierced swing handle, monogram & date under base, maker "C. & Co.," Sheffield, England, 1864-65, 13" d. 748

Cake basket, oval shape w/embossed leaf & bud rim, the openwork swing handle w/beaded S-scrolls, chased beaded band & chased spiral reeded decoration, on a reticulated oval base w/a twisted wire foot, marks of William Plummer, London, 1766, 13" l. 2,070

Silver Cart with Stork & Driver

Cart, figural two-wheeled cart w/a small figural boy driving, pulled by a large standing stork, worn hallmarks, Europe, late 19th c., 3" l., 2" h. (ILLUS.) 795

Caster, footed bulbous inverted pear-shaped lower body below a cylindrical neck fitted w/a tall domed & decoratively pierced cap, the body engraved w/a griffin, Samuel Wood, London, England, 1745-56, 7 3/4" h. (dents) 770

Caster, footed squatty bulbous inverted pear-shaped body w/a repoussé gadrooned design below a tapering cylindrical ringed neck engraved w/a "G," a fitted high domed ornately pierced cap w/a pointed finial, William Grundy, London, England, 1749-50, 9" h. (repair)................. 1,045

Casters, baluster urn-form, ribbed bands at neck, shoulder & base, Henry Chawner, London, 1791-92, 6 3/8" h., pr. 690

Caudle cup, miniature, of typical form, w/swirled, lobed lower body, mounted w/scroll handles, George I period, London, 1716, 2 3/4" l. over handles 460

Center bowl, cov., oval, the raised rim w/openwork design, gilt openwork insert, resting on an oval base w/similar decoration, Oporto, Portugal, 20th c., 7 5/8 x 11 3/8" 201

Center bowl, round w/lobed lower half, raised on a lobed round base, James Deakins & Sons, Sheffield, England, 1895-96, 10" d. 518

Centerpiece, oblong paneled navette form raised on a domed, paneled oblong foot, leafy scroll scalloped rim over gadrooned band, raised & chased side designs, figural child handle at each end, Germany, 19th c., 21 3/4" l., 12 1/4" h. 4,025

Centerpiece bowl, oval, the deep oval base applied w/scrolling vines & clusters below a lobed band, the deep bowl w/a flared rim & four pendent rings w/applied clusters around the rim, Georg Jensen Silversmithy, Copenhagen, Denmark, 1933-44, marked & numbered "296A," 14 3/8" l. 17,250

Russian Silver Chalice

Chalice, bell-form bowl w/engraved scrolls & oval reserves of religious figures, a Cyrillic inscription around the rim, a palmette-engraved baluster-form stem on a flaring domed foot further chased w/scrolls & figural panels, Russia, dated 1860 (ILLUS.) **1,650**

Chalice, tall cup form w/chased decoration, engraved inscription, .800 fine, Vienna, Austria, ca. 1897, 15 5/8" h. (slight dents) **1,035**

Cigar case, hinged four-finger style, presentation initials engraved on the lid & dated 1889, gold-washed interior, London, 1886, 3 1/8 x 5 1/4" **518**

Russian Embossed Cigarette Case

Cigarette case, rectangular, heavily embossed design of bears in woods, amethyst glass bead in clasp of lid, gold applied charm reading "From Momma 1-1-1917," hallmarked "84" & engraved "1914 Misha," Imperial-era Russia, 1/2 x 3 3/8 x 4 3/8" (ILLUS.) **395**

Edwardian English Coffee Server

Coffee server, cov., plain tapering cylindrical body w/closed rim spout, the cover w/a turned ivory finial, ivory C-form handle, maker's mark "SG," London, England, 1910-11, some dents, 8" h. (ILLUS.) **863**

Russian Coffee & Tea Set

Coffee & tea set: cov. coffeepot, cov. teapot, open sugar & creamer; each piece w/a fluted & tapering ovoid form, engraved oval wreath & vining border bands, ivory finials & heat stops, Moscow, Russia, late 19th c., coffeepot 7 1/2" h., the set (ILLUS.) **2,990**

Early English Silver Coffee Urn

Coffee urn, cov., the tall urn-form ribbed body w/a wide rim band w/a ribbed swag band around a wreath-form spigot hole, animal mask & ring side handles, tapering leaf-engraved shoulder to a flat rim fitted w/a domed leaf- and berry-engraved cover w/engraved pointed finial, raised on a waisted pedestal w/a gadroon band at the bottom & raised on a square plinth w/bun feet, London, England hallmarks, 1804-05 (ILLUS.) **3,025**

Coffeepot, cov., baluster-form, mounted w/a turned wood side handle, on three pad feet, Francois-Nicolas Rousseau, Paris, 1784, 7" h. **1,150**

Coffeepot, cov., footed tall tapering cylindrical form w/a stepped domed hinged cov-
er w/tall button finial, swan's-neck spout
& ornate C-scroll wooden handle, engraved w/a crest, George III period, Lon-
don, England, 1781, 9 1/2" h. **2,185**

Coffeepot, cov., low wide ringed foot on the
tall tapering cylindrical body w/a hinged
domed cover & turned pointed finial,
scroll-trimmed swan's-neck spout, S-
scroll wooden handle, engraved armorial
design w/a dog & "Perseverance," makers mark incomplete, London, England,
1744-45, 9 1/2" h. **2,640**

George II Coffeepot

Coffeepot, cov., of baluster-form on
spreading foot, serpentine spout & fruitwood handle, domed lid w/ovoid finial,
body engraved on both sides w/mono-
gram within foliate cartouches, George II
period, Richard Gurney & Co., London,
1754, 10 1/2" h. (ILLUS.) **1,840**

Coffeepot, cov., on four ball feet, oval trumpet foot, tapered oblong body, serpentine
spout, fruitwood loop handle, domed lid
w/oblong finial, George III period, Peter,
Ann & William Bateman, London, 1805,
12" l., 11 3/4" h. (engraving removal to
both sides) **1,035**

Coffeepot, cov., ovoid body raised on a flaring ringed round foot, the body repoussé
& chased w/scrolls, flowers & rocaille, the
ivory handle & scroll spout w/foliate joins,
the hinged domed cover w/similar decoration & surmounted by a baluster finial,
Lisbon, Portugal, 1770-1804, 11 3/4" h. **4,600**

Coffeepot, cov., presentation-type, pear-
shaped body on four scroll & shell feet,
the body chased & embossed w/flat
leaves around the lower portion & the
serpentine spout, reeded & leaf handle
w/ivory heat stops, the cover w/a flower-
form finial, engraved inscription dated
1853, Chinese Export, by Khecheong,
10 3/4" h. **3,105**

Coffeepot, cov., Rococo-style, pyriform, on
three paw feet headed by scrolls & cartouches, the swirled lobed body w/wood
scroll handle, the spout w/rocaille, shell &
floral join, the hinged high-domed cover
surmounted by a leaf & bud finial, Mons,
Belgium, 1762, 13 1/2" h. **9,775**

Coffeepot, cov., tall pyriform body cast
w/leafy scrolls continuing to a scrolled
spout & wooden handle, w/a domed cover, raised on a circular foot, George III
period, Francis Crump, London, En-
gland, 1769-70, 11 3/4" h. **1,093**

Coffeepot, cover & stand, the pot of a
lobed pear shape, on a domed foot
w/shaded edge, scroll handle w/ivory
heat stops, serpentine spout, domed
cover w/a flower finial, the stand raised
on four scroll legs mounted w/carved ivory flattened ball feet, w/an unmarked
burner, Holland, the pot 1876, the stand
1863, the pot 9 1/2" h., the set **633**

Ornate German Glass-lined Compote

Compotes, the raised oval flat-topped base
stamped w/a band of scrolls & shells supporting four legs composed of putto herm
flanked by husk swags supporting the
deep rounded reticulated bowl w/a design of winged putti, scrolls, swags & foliate baskets, a monogrammed cartouche
on two sides, clear glass liner, Germany,
.800 fine, late 19th c., 7 3/8" l., 6" h., pr.
(ILLUS. of one) **1,840**

Dutch Silver Cream Pitcher

Cow creamer, cov., figure of cow w/red glass eyes, handle formed by tail raised to brush off the fly applied to the cover, open mouth pours cream, Dutch, ca. 1900, 4" h., 5 1/2" l. (ILLUS. on previous page) **1,120**

Rare German Silver Cow Creamer

Cow creamer, cov., figure of cow w/red glass eyes, handle formed by tail raised to brush off the fly applied to the cover, open mouth pours cream, German, ca. 1900, , rare, 3 1/4" h., 4 1/2" l. (ILLUS.) **1,232**

Cow creamer, ornate flowers around lid w/fly perched on top, marks "R C" w/"M" in a shield, lion w/raised paw facing left, leopard's head, letter "e," English, ca. 1960, still being produced, expect to pay more for earlier versions, weight is 5.2 oz., 4 x 6" **500-700**

Creamer, bulbous base tapering to flared scalloped rim w/long pointed spout, raised on three hoof feet, ornate double C-scroll handle, the body w/Rococo repoussé floral decoration, John Harvey, London, England, 1750-51, 3 7/8" h. **385**

English Sterling Silver Creamer

Creamer, deep swelled plain boat-shape w/high, wide arched spout & reeded rim, simple arched strap handle, engraved under the rim w/a cartouche & monogram, Peter, Ann & William Bateman, London, ca. 1801, 4 7/8" h. (ILLUS.) **336**

Creamer, fluted helmet-form w/wide arched spout & beaded rim w/engraved band, high arched reeded handle, engraved overall w/foliates & scrolls, on an engraved round foot above a horizontally reeded octagonal plinth, monogrammed, Hester Bateman, London, 1789, 6 1/4" h. **489**

Early Russian Silver Creamer

Creamer, footed ovoid boat-form w/a lobed lower body below an applied floral shoulder band below the finely beaded rim w/wide arched spout, carved ivory C-form handle w/ear, gold-washed interior, Russia, 1829, 4 3/4" h. (ILLUS.) **374**

Creamer, w/rubbed marks for London, scroll handle, square base w/beaded rims, George III period, 1789, 7" h. **460**

Cup, circular base w/wide band of acorns on four leaf-capped claw feet fitted w/a flaring body & wide shoulder, separate collar w/a conforming acorn band, Central European, 5 3/4" h., 10 ozs. **345**

Demitasse coffee service: Art Deco style, the tall rectangular tapering pot chased & applied w/square strapwork bands & flat cover, long angled handle, ten matching short cup holders fitted w/cobalt blue porcelain liners & a rectangular tray w/curved ends w/rectangular hand hold; Austria, ca. 1930, tray 21 1/2" l., the set **2,185**

Demitasse set: cov. coffeepot, cov. sugar bowl & creamer; pear-form bodies w/chased Rococo shell & figural decoration, ivory heat stops, flower finials on covers, engraved inscription, Germany, late 19th c., pot 5 7/8" h., 3 pcs. **575**

Shell-form Sterling Silver Dish

Dish, shell-form, top ending in handle, decorated w/heavily chased floral and foliate body, made in Sheffield, England, dated 1889, 2 1/2 x 2 x 11" (ILLUS.) **616**

Dish cross, adjustable, w/shell-form tips on ends of cross-bars & raised on shell-form feet, a round burner in the center, William Plummer, London, England, 1767-68, 10 3/4" l. **2,200**

Sterling Egg Server with Egg Cups

Egg server, an oval tray w/a low pierced gallery edge & a tall central scrolling loop handle fitted w/scroll spoon brackets, pierced scroll feet, fitted w/a set of six footed egg cups w/pierced sides, English hallmarks, late 19th - early 20th c., 6 1/2 x 8 1/2", 9" h., the set (ILLUS.) **2,495**

Entree dishes, cov., rectangular w/cut corners, domed cover w/central oval ring handle, gadrooned border on base, engraved crests on cover & interior, John Schofield, England, 1798-99, 10 1/4" l., pr. **5,750**

Ewer, lobed spherical body, Paul Storr, England, 1831-32, 7 7/8" h. **575**

Ewer, Renaissance-style, the snail-form body w/flared spout & scrolled handle, raised on a repoussé oval foot, Austria, late 19th c., 11 1/2" h. **1,610**

Fish server, long flat blade curved & pointed along one side, pierced herringbone design, w/a Fiddle Thread & Shell patt. handle, Paul Storr, London, England, 1820-21, 11 3/4" l. **825**

Fish server, pointed oval silver blade w/scrolled edges & pierced interior surface, tapering rounded straight green horn handle, back engraved "Amicus - 1794," Samuel Godbehere, London, England, 1793-94, 11 3/8" l. (crack in horn handle) **303**

Russian Carte-de-Visite Picture Frame

Frame, for carte-de-visite picture, Art Nouveau style, hallmarked "84," Imperial-era Russia, 3 1/4 x 5 5/8" (ILLUS.) **295**

Gravy boat, deep boat-shaped bowl w/forked loop side handles w/grape cluster terminals, raised on a ribbed pedestal on attached oval undertray, Grape patt., No. 14, Georg Jensen Silversmithy, Copenhagen, Denmark, ca. 1930-32, 6 3/4" l., 4 1/2" h. **3,737**

George III Period Hot Water Kettle

Hot water kettle, cov., large bulbous ovoid body surmounted by a tall spire-form cover w/swelled top knop below a flame finial, looped shoulder handles w/large leaf terminals, a leaf-scrolled spigot w/arched T-form ivory handle, a waisted pedestal raised on a square w/a gadrooned border band above a pierced latticework apron & raised on four claw-and-ball feet, George III period, England, 18th c., overall 21" h. (ILLUS.) **2,300**

Hot water kettle on lampstand, the kettle w/an inverted pyriform body engraved w/scrolling floral leafage, continuing to a raffia-covered swing handle, raised on conforming stand w/leafage-cast cabriole legs w/aprons of openwork flowers & centering a fixed lamp, ending in shell feet, George II period, William Cripps, London, England, 1748-49, overall 14 1/4" h., 2 pcs. **1,610**

Hot water pitcher, cov., footed tall slender baluster-form body w/a domed hinged cover w/urn finial, pointed rim spout w/beaded decoration down the front, the lower half of the body w/repoussé swirled floral bands alternating w/ribbed bands, C-scroll wooden handle, Fuller White, London, England, 1747-48, 7 7/8" h. **1,650**

Silver Box-form Inkstand

Inkstand, rectangular low box on a scroll-trimmed base, the top cast in bold relief w/a band of Oriental figures, opens to three wells & a pen rest, Europe, late 19th - early 20th c., 3 1/2 x 5", 1 3/4" h. (ILLUS. on previous page) 295

Jardiniere, boat-shaped, w/floral swags & twining ivy, two plain scroll cartouches to either side, copper liner, French, .800 fine, early 20th c., 14" l., 8 1/2" w............... 1,380

Unique Turtle Shell & Silver Box

Jewelry box, cov., model of a turtle, the lid formed by an actual turtle shell, the base w/head & legs in silver, artist-signed, Europe, late 19th - early 20th c., 5 1/4 x 7 1/2", 3 1/4" h. (ILLUS.) 495

Mexican Silver Jewelry Box

Jewelry box, figural, in the shape of a dome-top trunk w/a hinged cover, marked "Clavel Sterling - 0.950," Mexico, 2 x 2 1/2" (ILLUS.) 395

Elaborate English Kettle on Stand

Kettle on stand, wide tapering ovoid body w/a high arched scroll handle & swan's-neck spout, decorated overall w/ornate repoussé scrolls & floral clusters surrounding a central cartouche, raised on a domed pierced scrolling base w/high scrolled legs ending in scrolled feet all centering a fuel burner, melon-form finial on cover, Edward, John & William Barnard, London, England, 1838-39, overall 16 1/4" h., 2 pcs. (ILLUS.) 2,415

Silver Cross-end Knife Rest

Knife rest, pierced cross-form ends joined by a slender bar, stamped number, Europe, late 19th - early 20th c., 3 1/4" l. (ILLUS.) 125

Ladle, ovoid bowl w/gold-washed interior, shaped stem & long carved ivory handle, Europe, 19th c., 15 1/2" l............................. 86

Ladle, ovoid bowl w/tapered back tipt stem, monogrammed, Dublin, Ireland, 1762, 13" l... 316

Heart-shaped Sterling Silver Mirror

Mirror, heart-shaped pierced frame ornately decorated w/birds, flowers, garlands & scrollwork, beveled mirror, purple velvet backing, 10 3/4 x 13 1/2" (ILLUS.) 2,495

Miniature Silver Crown

Model of a crown, miniature, pierced & engraved, marked w/a letter "M" under a crown & an indistinct animal mark, Europe, 1 1/2 x 2" (ILLUS.) **225**

Miniature Silver Slant-front Desk

Model of a desk, miniature, Rococo slant-front style, working drawers & fall-front, cabriole legs, indistinct hallmarks, Europe, late 19th - early 20th c., 2 1/8 x 2 1/4 x 3 1/8" (ILLUS.) **695**

Miniature Fireplace Grill with Fish

Model of a fireplace grill, miniature, a square rack w/a slender twisted handle, complete w/tiny fish, impressed dagger mark, Europe, late 19th - early 20th c., 3 1/2" l. (ILLUS.) **150**

Miniature Silver Floor Harp

Model of a harp, miniature, floor-model instrument fitted w/a tiny figure of an 18th c. man at the base & a small dog at the top, Europe, late 19th - early 20th c., 2 3/4" l., 4 1/4" h. (ILLUS.) **195**

Miniature Silver Wirework Settee

Model of a settee, miniature settee w/pierced wirework resembling wicker, unmarked, probably Europe, early 20th c., 2 1/2" l. (ILLUS.) **195**

Miniature Sewing Rocker in Silver

Model of a sewing rocker, back w/thin crestrail & lower rail, square seat, Europe, late 19th - early 20th c., 1 3/4" h. (ILLUS.).............. **150**

Miniature Silver Sleigh

Model of a sleigh, miniature open cutter, probably Europe, early 20th c., 1 7/8" l. (ILLUS.) **175**

Models of lady's shoes, each w/a small flaring heel & a bow on top, repoussé w/cherubs at various pursuits in landscapes, gilded interiors, Europe, late 19th c., 6 3/4" l., pr. (minor dents) **1,380**

Monteith, the domed circular foot chased w/sprays of blossoms, the circular bowl chased w/C-scrolls alternating w/sprays of foliage, the shaped border flat-chased w/a scroll rim, rubbed mark of maker, Birmingham, England, 1853, 6 1/2" d. **546**

Wang Hing Chinese Silver Mug

Mug, body applied w/lappet panels of bamboo & plum bushes alternating w/figures in gardens or landscapes, on a diaper-work ground, mounted w/a scrolling drag-on-form handle, Wang Hing, Chinese, late 19th c., wear to some high spots, 5 1/2" h, 12 ozs. (ILLUS.) 805

Mug, footed, gently flaring cylindrical body w/heavy ornate cast C-scroll handle, body w/chased floral design w/a monogram, E.J. & E.W. Barnard, London, England, 1839-40, 3 5/8" h. 468

Mug, footed ovoid body tapering gently to a flat rim, ornate double C-scroll handle, the body decorated w/Rococo repoussé florals & a monogram, John Swift, London, England, 1754-55, 4 3/4" h. (minor dents & repair) 660

Mug, footed, slightly ovoid body tapering to a flared rim, ornate double C-scroll handle, the body w/Rococo floral repoussé decoration, John Langlands, New Castle, England, 1759-60, 4" h. (restorations) 358

Mug, hunting-style, pyriform body repoussé w/a fox hunting scene, engraved w/a castle, fist & flag crest between leafy trees, w/scroll handle & on spreading circular foot, George III period, Newcastle, 1769, 5 1/2" h. 1,840

Silver Tabletop Music Stand

Music stand, table model, long S-scrolls supported by a swing-out back brace, European hallmarks, 8 3/4" w., 9 1/4" h. (ILLUS.) 200

Elaborate Dutch Neff

Neff (figural ship-form table centerpiece), realistically modeled as an early galleon under full sail w/sailors manning cannons & climbing rope, the removable deck opening to a plain hull, on four openwork wheels, Holland, w/English import marks for London, 1928, repairs, few losses, 14 1/2" h. (ILLUS.) 2,875

Nutmeg grater, straight-sided oval form, engraved decoration & monogram, "T.W." maker, Birmingham, England, 1799-1800, 1 3/4" l. 316

Pheasant-shaped Perfume Container

Perfume container, model of a pheasant, well-detailed, on an overall base w/a blue enamel band, removable head, Europe, late 19th - early 20th c., 5 7/8" l. (ILLUS.) 395

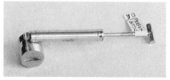

Miniature Fly Sprayer Perfume Sprayer

Perfume dispenser, model of a miniature fly sprayer, Europe, late 19th - early 20th c., 3" l. (ILLUS.) 45

Chair-form Silver Pincushion

Pincushion, miniature model of a side chair, Victorian style balloon-back w/a pierced scroll & floral design, cloth cushion seat, scrolled apron & cabriole front legs, worn hallmarks, probably Birmingham, England, early 20th c., 2" h. (ILLUS.) 175

Pig-shaped Silver Pincushion

Pincushion, model of a pig w/a cloth cushion in the top of the back, hallmarks for Birmingham, England, ca. 1905, 3 3/8" l. (ILLUS.) 395

Pitcher, cov., figural, circular base supporting the leafy head of a tall inverted turnip w/a hinged top & slender loop vine handle down the side, Koch & Bergfeld, Bremen, Germany, ca. 1890, retailed by Gotting, 17 1/2" h. 2,300

Pitcher, cov., footed baluster-form body on a domed foot w/vertical reeding, the body w/repoussé design of foliage, birds & putti around the lower section, the neck w/a band of fluting, short rim spout w/a putto, beaded serpentine handle, the domed cover w/vertical reeding, repoussé & vegetal finial, engraved name on base, .833 fine, Holland, late 19th c., 5 1/2" h. 259

Mexican Sterling Pitcher

Pitcher, fluted body flaring out to shoulder, flaring rim w/shallow spout, round stepped base, ring handle, marked "Sterling - 553," Mexican, 6" h. (ILLUS.) 185

Pitcher, tapered vasiform body, vertical reeding around body w/high spout, fluted round pedestal foot, cast S-scroll handle, Russia, 19th c., 8 1/2" h. 1,150

Pitcher, cov., baluster-form w/Huguenot-style cut-work details on cover & bowl, maker "L.G.," England, 1892-94, 9 1/2" h. 1,265

French Neoclassical Planter

Planter, Neoclassical design, oval form w/the sides chased & embossed w/husk swags on a pierced guilloché ground, a ribbon-tied undulating rim, two cast scroll rim handles, on pierced scroll & shell feet, w/fitted metal liner, France, late 18th - early 19th c., 14" l., 5 1/2" h. (ILLUS.) 1,725

Plates, round, w/a shaped border, engraved w/a mottoed crest below a coronet, w/a banded rim, maker's mark "M&K," Vienna, Austria, 1846, 10" d., set of 6 2,645

Ornate Indian Silver Punch Bowl

Punch bowl, deep wide bowl on a stepped & domed foot, the body of the bowl w/a detailed continuous East Indian tiger hunting scene w/a band of flat leaves around the bottom, the base w/another band w/hunting scenes above a narrow leafy band, w/silver removable liner, India, late 19th - early 20th c., 12 5/8" d., 10 1/2" h. (ILLUS.) 4,025

Punch bowl, deep wide ovoid bowl w/flared rim & round spreading foot, the bowl chased & embossed overall w/scenes of village revelry, gold-washed interior, Paul Storr, London, 1827, opposed by an engraved heraldic device, further marked by John Samuel Hunt, 1852, 12 1/8" d., 5 3/4" h. 8,050

Punch bowl, footed, circular form w/re-
poussé flower garlands around the sides,
later engraved monogram, raised on a
molded gadrooned foot, George IV period, William Eaton, London, 1825,
12 1/4" d.. 1,725

Punch bowl, the sides chased w/a wide
band of shells alternating w/acanthus
above a fluted lower body, on a conforming foot, Barnard, London, England,
1840, 10 1/4" d. 1,610

Punch ladle, deep round shell-form body,
long tapering handle w/rounded end engraved w/a lion's head, Thomas Chawn-
er, London, England, 1772-73, 13 1/2" l. 550

Punch ladle, the twisted handle knopped
w/molded foliates & acanthus leaves,
w/ivory end, the oval bowl reeded w/a
scalloped rim, rubbed marks, France,
.950 standard, second half 19th c.,
17 1/4" l. 173

Sake set: bowl & five sake cups; the
8 3/4" d., 4 3/4" h. bowl on a trumpet foot
w/hammered surface & w/curved optical
ribbing on the exterior, each 1 1/4" h. cup
on a low footring w/slightly flared rim, Japan, 20th c., the set 460

Salver, center engraved w/small ring of
dogwood blossoms within a large band of
rose blossoms, everted border cast
w/openwork oak leaves & acorns, Portu-
gal, late 19th c., 24" d. 1,840

Salver, in the Georgian style, the shaped
border applied w/a scroll rim, on three
leaf-capped scroll feet, London, England,
1904, 14" d. 1,150

Salver, round, footed, w/scrolled rim
w/shells, cast feet, the top finely engraved in the center w/a coat-of-arms for
"Edison," John Hutson, London, En-
gland, 1787-88, 18 1/2" d. 2,420

Sauce pan, slightly tapering cylindrical bowl
on a ringed, slightly flared foot, wide
rolled rim, cylindrical angled side handle
w/a turned wood grip, William Fleming,
London, England, 1716-17, bowl
3 5/8" d., handle 4 1/4" l. 1,155

Sauce tureen, boat-shaped on an oval
beaded foot, beaded edge & loop handles, engraved on one side w/heraldic
crest over husk swag w/coat-of-arms on
the other side, John Schofield, London,
England, 1784, 10 3/8" l., 5 3/4" h. 1,265

English Georgian Sauce Tureen

Sauce tureen, cov., deep oblong body engraved on one side w/a heraldic device,
w/applied rim cast as a stylized continuous hunting scene featuring stags &
hunting dogs, raised on four hairy paw
feet topped by rocaille shells flanked by
acanthus, two acanthus loop end handles centered by shells, domed cover w/a
band of vertical reeding & a finial formed
as entwined snakes on a leafy ground,
George III era, Jos. Craddock & William
Reid, London, 1819, 9" l. plus handles,
6 1/4" h. (ILLUS.)................................. 2,070

Sauceboat, boat-form w/a shaped molded
rim, two loop side handles, on a domed
round base attached to a circular underplate w/shaped edge, maker's mark "KK,"
Hungary, .800 standard, 20th c.,
7 3/4" d., 4" h. 460

Sauceboat, deep oblong boat-form w/high
arched spout, arched C-scroll handle,
raised on three small double-scroll legs,
beaded rim, Daniel Smith & Robert
Sharp, London, England, 1770-71,
8 1/2" l. (minor dents) 880

Sauceboat & underplate, oblong boat-
shape w/serpentine molded rim w/scroll
decoration, the body w/embossed rococo-style cartouches flanked by cattails,
a bunch of cattails below the cast ear
handle, the oval molded foot resting on
an underplate w/shaped rim & scroll
decoration, monogrammed, Europe,
probably Germany, 19th c., 8 7/8" l.,
6 1/4" h., 2 pcs. 1,265

Sauceboats, ovoid form w/scroll handle,
shell & hoof feet, A. Bros. Ltd., Birmingham, England, 1903-04, 6 1/2" l., pr. 316

Rare Server with Figure of Henry VIII

Serving spoon, figural handle, a detailed
full-figure handle w/King Henry VIII of
England, the figure above a blank cartouche over the English royal coat-of-
arms & scrolls bordering the wide shovel-form bowl, marked "800," probably
Europe, similar to one produced by the
Gorham Mfg. Co. around 1901, 9 1/4" l.
(ILLUS.)... 525

Silver Server with Cavalier Handle

Serving spoon, figural relief handle w/a standing cavalier blowing a horn, above pierced scrolls, chased scrolls in the large oval bowl, Europe, late 19th - early 20th c., 10 1/4" l. (ILLUS.) **550**

Server with Frederick the Great Figure

Serving spoon, figural relief handle w/a standing figure of Frederick the Great of Prussia, royal emblems at base of handle, chased scrolls in the wide shovel-form bowl, Europe, early 20th c., 11" l. (ILLUS.) **595**

Mary, Queen of Scots on Silver Server

Serving spoon, figural relief handle w/a standing figure of Mary, Queen of Scots, engraved initials in the wreath & swag-trimmed wide shovel-form bowl, back marked "800," Europe, early 20th c., 10 1/2" l. (ILLUS.) **645**

Silver Server with Napoleon Handle

Serving spoon, figural relief handle w/a standing figure of Napoleon I above his imperial emblem & his initial & swags in the large shovel-form bowl, Europe, early 20th c., 10 1/2" l. (ILLUS.) **550**

Large Server with Lady on Handle

Serving spoon, figural relief handle w/a standing lady in Victorian dress, above a section of pierced entwined branches, chased musical instruments & sheet music in the wide oblong handle, marked "800," Europe, early 20th c., 11 1/4" l. (ILLUS.) **595**

Ornate Pierced Serving Spoon

Serving spoon, the long oval bowl chased & pierced, a central figure of Moses & cherubs, a classical head below, the long flat handle w/pierced scrolls & masks & pierced griffins at the base, Europe, late 19th - early 20th c., 12" l. (ILLUS. on previous page) **750**

Sterling Silver Cat Shaker

Shaker, in the form of a cat sitting on its hind legs, screw closure in base, English hallmarks, early 20th c., 3" h. (ILLUS.)............... **195**

One of a Pair of Silver Shoe Buckles

Shoe buckles, rounded rectangular shape w/pierced decoration of stylized floral motifs, English, ca. 1790, 2 1/2 x 3", the pair (ILLUS. of one).. **112**

Bull-shaped Silver Skewer Set

Skewer set: full-figure model of a bull w/a slot in the back to hold the sword-shaped skewers, Europe, late 19th - early 20th c., 3 1/2" l., 2" h., the set (ILLUS.)...................... **260**

Snuff box, makers mark "F.B.," w/patent registration mark, formed as the head of a dog, the eyes set w/faceted red pastes, London, 1882, 1 3/4" l...................................... **288**

Snuff box, rectangular, hinged top engraved w/a courting couple, bottom engraved w/foliate pattern on stippled ground, gold-washed interior, Continental, possibly Dutch, 1 1/4" w., 2" l. **201**

Soup ladle, tapered handle w/engraved foliates, the terminal w/engraved crest within a cartouche, the reeded bowl w/repoussé beading, a chased eagle on the reverse, possibly Alexander Richards, Dublin, Ireland, 1766, 14 1/8" l.................. **1,093**

George III Soup Tureen

Soup tureen, cov., rectangular, the domed cover & body chased w/rose foliage & scrolls, centering a cartouche at each side w/one engraved w/an armorial, the cover mounted w/a rose branch-form handle, body w/acanthus & shell-capped handles, on four acanthus-capped scroll feet, Joseph Angel, George III period, England, 1817, cover & body bearing spurious Paul Storr maker's marks, the finial w/Joseph Angel maker's marks,15" l. (ILLUS.)............ **5,175**

Russian Silver Spoon

Spoon, engraving on handle & back of bowl in geometric design, marked "AP - 1893 - 84" next to a crest, Russian, 5 1/4" l. (ILLUS.).. **125**

Spoon, Onslow patt. stem & round scallop-form bowl, George III period, George Smith, London, 1779, 7" l.............................. **144**

Stuffing spoon, front tilt handle, engraved crest on reverse, maker "S.A.," London, 1769-70, 14 1/4" l. 345

Stuffing spoon, oblong bowl & long tapering handle w/rounded end w/a bright-cut oval, Hester Bateman, London, England, 1788-89, 12 3/8" l. 468

Sugar basket, navette form, swing handle, rim bands, monogrammed, R. & S. Hennel, England, 1818-19, 7" l. 345

Sugar bowl, cov., low-footed wide rounded body w/cylindrical sides & low domed cover, Rococo repoussé floral decoration, John Gibbons, London, England, 1722-23, 4" d., 3" h. 715

Sugar box, cov., squatty oval bomb form, on four splayed scroll feet, the fluted body engraved w/rocaille cartouches, the stepped hinged cover centered by an engraved eagle within a rocaille cartouche, mark w/the Cyrillic initials of Aleksei Vasil'ev Polozov, Moscow, Russia, 1764, 4 3/8" h. 2,760

Sugar caster, fluted tapered cylinder, the domed top w/pierced repoussé foliate decoration, knob finial, the rim beaded, the body w/repoussé acanthus leaves, on a molded shaped foot w/floral decoration, Henry Wilkinson & Co., Sheffield, England, 1851, 5 1/4" h. 201

Sugar shaker, spreading cylindrical form, London, England, ca. 1910, 5 1/2" h. 201

English Silver Sugar Spoon

Sugar spoon, long, trowel-shaped bowl, handle flaring out at end, both engraved w/scrolls, indistinct hallmarks, 3 5/8" l. (ILLUS.) 195

Russian Silver Sugar Spoon

Sugar spoon, scoop-shaped bowl, back engraved w/flowers, baluster-shape handle, Russian, 3 1/2" l. (ILLUS.) 245

Sweetmeat dishes, on a shaped rectangular slab base cast as water, the shell-form dish drawn by sea creatures, the reins held by two putti flanking a central standing putto on the stern poised as Neptune holding a trident-form fork, Odiot, Paris, late 19th - early 20th c., 5 1/2" l., 5" h., pr... 2,070

Tablespoon, oblong pointed bowl, long Fiddle Thread w/Shell patt. handle, Edinburgh, Scotland, 1829-30, 12" l. 138

Hester Bateman Silver Pieces

Tablespoon, rounded end back-tipt design, engraved monogram, Hester Bateman, London, England, 1785 (ILLUS. front) 316

Tankard, cov., baluster-form w/a low wide round foot, open scrollwork thumbpiece to the stepped, domed cover, double C-scroll handle w/heart-shaped terminal, engraved w/initials, mark of a London silversmith, dated 1776, 8 3/4" h. 3,900

Tankard, cov., ringed tapering cylindrical body w/a hinged flattened domed cover w/scrolled thumbrest, tapering S-scroll handle, Anthony Nelme, London, England, 1705-06, 8 1/2" h. (repairs) 4,840

Early English Sterling Tankard

Tankard, cov., slightly tapering cylindrical body w/a flaring ringed base, medial ring & rim band, hinged stepped domed cover w/volute thumbpiece, hollow scroll handle, front w/an engraved plain rococo cartouche, George I era, Thomas Tearle, London, 1725, 7 1/2" h. (ILLUS. on previous page) 3,220

Tankard, cov., stepped foot below the tapering cylindrical body w/bulbous lower section, engraved w/a central plain roundel flanked by geometrics & foliage sprays w/perching birds, geometric banding above & below, shaped ear handle, cover w/thumbpiece & flattened urn finial, Russia, makers mark "A.C.," 1894, 7 7/8" h. 863

Taper sticks, a squared domed & stepped foot supporting a slender double-knop standard below the slender ring-turned cylindrical candle socket, James Gould, London, England, 1723-24, 4 1/2" h., pr. ... 3,960

Tazza, figural, an allegory of Autumn, a child holding aloft a cornucopia, draped & seated on a plough w/a chain resting on sheaves of corn on a naturalistic ground, on a circular stepped base engraved w/a crowned cipher, a later glass dish, marked by Sazikov w/the Imperial Warrant, St. Petersburg, Russia, 1867, 28" h. 16,100

Tazza, ringed flaring round base w/gadrooned band between bands of palmettes, rising to a fluted knopped baluster stem, the circular dish chased w/elongated gadroons at intervals around the rim, marked by Assay Master Lourenco Ribeiro da Rocha, Bahia, Brazil, early 18th c., 13 1/4" d., 7" h. 8,050

Tea caddy, cov., oval cylindrical form w/low domed cover w/turned wood finial, decorated w/bright-cut florals w/swags & a lion head in a crown, possibly Samuel Woods, London, England, 1784-85, 5 1/4" h. 1,815

Tea caddy, cov., oval upright form w/stepped, domed cover w/urn finial, the sides engraved w/stylized florette & vine bands & a crest, Hester Bateman, London, England, 1789-90, 5 5/8" h. (ILLUS. on previous page back, w/tablespoon) 3,450

Tea caddy, cov., ovoid form, the body reeded on lower section, engraved on the front w/heraldic crest, the flush hinged cover w/carved ivory egg-shaped finial, Thomas Robins, London, England, 1794, 4 3/4" h. 1,495

Tea caddy, cylindrical w/large squatty bulbous cover, the body w/overall repoussé band of genre scenes within C-scrolls & foliate designs, Germany, early 20th c., 5" h.` 345

Tea & coffee service: cov. coffeepot, cov. teapot, creamer & cov. two-handled sugar; each of pear form, the flat-domed cover w/a foliate finial, engraved w/monogram, French, early 20th c., coffeepot 8 1/2" h., the set 1,150

Tea & coffee service: cov. teapot, cov. coffeepot, cov. kettle on lampstand, cov. creamer & cov. two-handled sugar bowl; each of partially reeded, rectangular section, Edwardian period, Birmingham, 1904, kettle on lampstand 12" h. 3,162

Tea & coffee service: cov. teapot, cov. coffeepot, open sugar bowl & creamer; Islamic-style, each of baluster-form on a rounded beaded flaring foot, the body chased & repoussé overall w/lobes & scrolls against a matted ground, one side w/vacant cartouche, the scroll handle w/ivory insulators & similar decoration, surmounted by a hinged domed cover w/a baluster finial, Robert Hennell III, London, England, 1870, coffeepot 11" h., the set 4,600

Tea service: cov. teapot, creamer & cov. two-handled sugar bowl; each of bomb rectangular form w/gadrooned rim, on four ball feet, rubbed marks for London, 1814, George III period, England, the set (solder repairs to teapot handle & creamer) 1,035

Tea service: cov. teapot, water jug, milk jug & cov. sugar bowl; "trompe l'oeil" style, each piece imitating the shape of an embroidered saddle bag cloth w/stylized scrolling foliage within a leaf border, the high domed caps joined to the bodies by link chains, the spouts w/stoppers joined by similar chains, each marked under the base "Made for Tiffany & Co.," engraved "D.G.C.," marked w/Cyrillic initials of Nikolai Vasil'evich Nemirov-Kolodkin, Moscow, Russia, 1896-1908, teapot 8 1/4" h., the set 6,325

English Silver Footed Tea Tray

Tea tray, circular on three ball & claw feet, shaped edge w/embossed flowerheads & applied shell & bead border, tray engraved w/scrolling leaves & flower-centered roundels, English, maker's mark "BG," 1921, 18 1/2" d. (ILLUS.) 1,840

Tea tray, oval w/pierced foliate scroll gallery, beaded rim & cut-out end handles, the field engraved w/bright-cut border, Diederik Willem Rethmeyer, Amsterdam, Holland, 1797, 26" l. 5,750

Teapot, cov., a bulbous ovoid body raised on a slender short pedestal & round foot, a short rolled neck w/a hinged domed cover w/pointed finial, the body ornately embossed w/flowers, fruits & rococo foliage framing a central oval reserve w/the monogram "C," scroll-decorated swan's-neck spout & decorative angled handle, mark of Walker and Hall, Sheffield, England, 1889-90, 9 1/4" h. 1,045

Teapot, cov., footed bulbous inverted pear-shaped body w/hinged dome cover w/berry finial, swan's-neck spout w/figural hawk head tip, arched & scrolling handle, the body w/Rococo repoussé scroll decoration, Samuel Courtauld, London, England, 1759-60, 6 3/8" h. (repair) 3,410

Teapot, cov., globular hexagonal form on a conforming rim foot, the sides cast & chased w/relief panels of Chinese scenes, the angular handle w/ivory insulators, the conforming cover surmounted by a Chinaman finial, John Lias, London, England, 1816, 5 1/2" h. 3,220

Teapot, cov., melon-shaped w/beaded openwork rim, the domed cover w/repoussé scrolls & urn finial, the body w/repoussé genre scenes within scrolls, upright cast handle w/embossed medallion heads, on a spreading circular base w/beaded edges, monogrammed, Holland, 19th c., .833 standard, 6 3/4" h. 460

English Victorian Sterling Teapot

Teapot, cov., Neoclassical-style, scalloped oval body engraved w/a plain foliate roundel on each side, a rim band w/a floral vine, a short serpentine spout, flat-topped ear handle, slightly domed hinged cover w/mushroom finial, Jas. Dixon & Sons, Sheffield, England, 1869, 6" h. (ILLUS.) 575

Teapot, cov., pear-shaped w/molded rim, the domed cover w/everted gadrooned rim & reeded bud finial, on a circular molded base w/repoussé gadrooned band, possibly Lewis Harmon or Lewis Herne, London, England, 1768, 10" h. 920

Teapot, cov., squatty bulbous form, faux bamboo finial, spout & handle, ivory heat stops, applied bas-relief prunus & bird decoration on the body, China Trade, China, 20th c., 5 1/2" h. 633

Teapot, cov., wide squatty bulbous body raised on four scrolled tab feet, the shoulder tapering to a flattened flanged neck w/hinged stepped, domed cover w/blossom finial, tapering swan's-neck spout, slender C-scroll handle, overall cast & repoussé floral decoration, maker's mark "GH," London, England, 1787-88, 6 3/8" h. 1,045

Teapot, cover & stand, octagonal form, the domed lid w/an engraved rim & wooden mushroom finial, the body w/bands of engraved foliates w/central cartouches, w/a similarly engraved & banded stand w/molded octagonal rim, on four reeded pedestal feet, Hester Bateman, London, 1788, 7" h. 4,888

Teapot & stand, maker's mark "W.F.," ovoid pot, partially reeded, straight spout, wooden ear handle, drop-in lid, monogrammed; the tray identically marked, on three ball feet, worn heraldic engraving to center (restorations), George III period, London, 1800, pot 9 1/2" l., 3 3/4" h. 489

English Silver Teaspoon

Teaspoon, trowel-shaped bowl pierced w/diamond-shaped holes along rim, bowl & handle decorated w/scrolls, leaves & shell motif, made by John Betteridge, England, ca. 1820, 3 1/4" l. (ILLUS.) 195

Toast rack, seven oval loops raised on a rectangular base frame w/small scroll & shell feet & an upright center handle, Hy. Wilkinson & Co., England, 1837, 6 1/2" l., 6 1/4" h. 345

Toast rack, small oblong dished tray on four small peg feet, arched toast loops around the top w/a central loop-topped handle, made to disassemble, unknown maker B.D., London, England, 1782-83, 5 3/4" l. 1,045

Torah shield, rectangular backplate w/shaped surmount (lacing applied crown) applied w/two columns at each side, each chased w/foliage, centering a pair of applied lions & a pair of shaped rectangular hinged doors, each w/Hebrew inscriptions, all above a long rectangular hinged door w/an open front, Russia, ca. 1890, 12" 2,300

English Sterling Silver Tray

Tray, footed shell-shaped tray w/elaborate scrollwork & engraved but indistinct initials, English, 9 1/2 x 16" (ILLUS.) 995

Oval Art Deco Silver Tray

Tray, long oval form decorated inside w/bands of leaftip & geometric Art Deco designs, probably Europe, early 20th c., 3 x 10 1/2" (ILLUS.) 85

Tray, oval, cast feet & open handles, the center engraved w/flowers & foliage w/a coat-of-arms, George Smith & Thomas Hayter, London, England, 1800-01, 25" l... **4,510**

Tray, rectangular, the shaped molded rim beaded, the face w/bands of engraved decoration, a central monogrammed oval, marked "Tizaine," France, mid-19th c., 11 1/8 x 13 3/4"................................... **546**

Tray, rectangular w/rounded ends, gadrooned handles & rim, engraved leafy scroll & crest decoration, marked "W.B." in rectangular cartouche, England, 1813-14, 23 7/8" l.................................. **2,300**

Fine Georgian Silver Tray

Tray, wide oblong form w/gadrooned border w/large cast shell devices at outer corners & smaller shells at the center sides, arched scroll- and shell-cast end handles, engraved in the center w/a large armorial crest, George III period, Thomas Robins, London, England, 1814-15, 30" l. (ILLUS.)...................... **9,200**

Vase, 8 1/4" h., reticulated silver, trumpet form on domed foot w/repoussé dragon, body pierced w/dragon & foliate panels, w/carved wooden stand, Chinese................. **259**

Vegetable dish, cov., elongated octagonal form w/molded rim & conforming flat-topped domed cover w/removable reeded scroll loop center handle, engraved on the side of the cover w/an armorial, George IV period, Robert Garrard, London, England, 1822-23, 12 1/2" l.............. **2,875**

Vegetable dish, cover & lampstand, the circular dish w/straight gadrooned rim & hinged bail handles on a lampstand w/three fluted cabriole legs ending in acanthus scrolls, mark of William Stroud, London, England, 1813, 11 3/4" h. **2,185**

Vegetable dishes, cov., shaped oblong form, the lobed body w/everted rim applied w/foliated scrolls, the conforming cover surmounted by a removable foliate ring-form handle, Robinson, Edkins & Aston, Birmingham, England, 1840, 13 1/2" l., pr. **3,680**

Vodka bucket, tapering circular form w/two bands of reeding & central foliate engraving, swing handle, Russian, mid-late 19th c., 6 1/2" h................................... **518**

Wash pitcher & bowl, tapering cylindrical tankard pitcher w/high arched spout & C-form hollow handle, footed wide rounded bowl w/flared rim, both w/overall hammered finish, G. Keller, Paris, France, ca. 1890, bowl 10" d., pitcher 13" h., pr. **4,600**

Wine bottle coasters, a turned wood base surrounded by low upright sides bright-cut engraved & pierced w/a lion crest centered by paterae alternating w/festoons, all centered by two scroll borders w/beaded rims, Hester Bateman, London, 1804, 5" d., pr. **1,560**

Wine coolers, urn-form, on four openwork foliate scroll feet under a cast circular rim w/anthemion & Bacchic panther heads, the fluted body w/two bracket handles entwined w/grapevine, the everted rim w/gadrooned border w/shells & foliage at intervals, engraved under the base w/inscribed marks, Pierre-Francois-Augustin Turquet, Paris, France, 1844-55, 10" h., pr.. **35,650**

Wine funnel, ribbed flower-form, marked "W.E.T.," Dublin, Ireland, 1820-30, 5 1/8" l. **403**

Sterling (Flatware)

Listed by item (individual pieces unless otherwise noted). All pieces are old and original.

Asparagus server

Olympian Asparagus Server

Olympian patt., Tiffany & Co., handle chased w/scene of Venus on her chariot w/putti riding dolphins trailing water leaves, the prongs w/chased fluting, engraved on reverse w/initials, 1878-91, 9 1/2" l. (ILLUS.) **$920**

Baby forks
Marie Antoinette patt., Dominick & Haff **20-25**

Berry forks
Empire patt., Whiting Mfg. Co....................... **20-30**
Violet patt., R. Wallace & Sons................... **35-45**

Berry spoons
Chrysanthemum patt., Wm. B. Durgin Co.,
9" 275-375
Colfax patt., Wm. B. Durgin Co., 8 3/4" 65-85
Dauphin patt., Wm. B. Durgin Co. 475-575
Egyptian patt., Whiting Mfg. Co. 250-350
Honeysuckle patt., Whiting Mfg. Co. 175-225
Ivory patt., Whiting Mfg. Co. 600-800
Jefferson patt., Gorham Mfg. Co. 65-85
Louis XIV patt., Towle Mfg. Co. 100-125
Louis XV patt., Whiting Mfg. Co. 85-95
Orange Blossom patt., Alvin Mfg. Co., 9" 275-375
Rustic patt., Towle Mfg. Co., gold-washed,
7 3/4" 65-95
Versailles patt., Gorham Mfg. Co., 8 3/4" 225-275

Bonbon spoons
Grande Baroque patt., R. Wallace & Sons... 32-40

Bouillon spoons
Bridal Rose patt., Alvin Mfg. Co. 35-45
Buttercup patt., Gorham Mfg. Co. 20-25
Etruscan patt., Gorham Mfg. Co. 18-25
Georgian patt., Towle Mfg. Co. 35-45
Lily patt., Whiting Mfg. Co. 40-55
Louis XIV patt., Towle Mfg. Co. 18-25
Madame Jumel patt., Gorham Mfg. Co. 15-20
Marguerite patt., Gorham Mfg. Co. 20-25
Mount Vernon patt., Lunt Silversmiths 15-20
Versailles patt., Gorham Mfg. Co. 35-45
Violet patt., R. Wallace & Sons 25-35

Butter serving knives (hollow handle)
Francis I patt., Reed & Barton 25-35
Jac Rose patt., Gorham Mfg. Co. 20-25
King Edward patt., Gorham Mfg. Co. 25-30
Lily of the Valley patt., Gorham Mfg. Co. 20-25
Mount Vernon patt., Lunt Silversmiths 20-25
Nocturne patt., Gorham Mfg. Co. 15-20
Pantheon patt., International Silver Co. 25-35
Rose (Baltimore) patt., The Steiff Co. 35-45

Butter spreaders (flat handle)
Cambridge patt., Gorham Mfg. Co. 15-20
English Shell patt., Lunt Silversmiths 12-14
Georgian patt., Towle Mfg. Co. 36
King Albert patt., Whiting Mfg. Co. 12-14
King Edward patt., Whiting Mfg. Co. 10
Kings patt., R. Wallace & Sons 20
Lily of the Valley patt., Gorham Mfg. Co. 12-14
Louis XV patt., Whiting Mfg. Co. 23
Madame Morris patt., Whiting Mfg. Co. 12-14
Majestic patt., Alvin Mfg. Co. 21
Manchester patt., Manchester Mfg. Co. 18
Mandarin patt., Whiting Mfg. Co. 12-14
Marie Antoinette patt., Dominick & Haff 25
Marlborough patt., Reed & Barton 16-18
Melrose patt., Gorham Mfg. Co. 18-22
Mount Vernon patt., Lunt Silversmiths 14-18
Nocturne patt., Gorham Mfg. Co. 12-14
Paul Revere patt., Towle Mfg. Co. 22
Plymouth patt., Gorham Mfg. Co. 12-15
Strasbourg patt., Gorham Mfg. Co. 22
Violet patt., Whiting Mfg. Co. 25
William & Mary patt., Lunt Silversmiths 12-14

Butter spreaders (hollow handle)
English Gadroon patt., Gorham Mfg. Co. 16-18
Melbourne patt., Oneida Silversmiths 12-14
Versailles patt., Gorham Mfg. Co. 18

Cake forks
Louis XIV patt., Towle Mfg. Co. 80

Cake knives
Louis XIV patt., Towle Mfg. Co. 75

Cake servers
Manchester patt., Manchester Mfg. Co. 31
Mandarin patt., Whiting Mfg. Co., silver
plate blade 34

Cheese scoops
Cambridge patt., Gorham Mfg. Co. 45
Kensington patt., Gorham Mfg. Co. 125
Strasbourg patt., Gorham Mfg. Co. 120

Cheese servers
Grande Baroque patt., R. Wallace & Sons .. 25-30

Chocolate muddlers
La Parisienne patt., Reed & Barton 135

Citrus spoons
Francis I patt., Reed & Barton 30-35
Hampton Court patt., Reed & Barton,
fluted 25-30
Labours of Cupid patt., Dominick & Haff 75

Cocktail forks
Audubon patt., Tiffany & Co. 50
Chantilly patt., Gorham Mfg. Co. 14-18
Grande Baroque patt., R. Wallace & Sons .. 25-30
Marlborough patt., Reed & Barton 16-20
Melrose patt., Gorham Mfg. Co. 20-25
Old Newbury patt., Towle Mfg. Co. 18-22
Paul Revere patt., Towle Mfg. Co. 16-20
Raleigh patt., Alvin Mfg. Co. 17
Rose Point patt., R. Wallace & Sons 15-18
Strasbourg patt., Gorham Mfg. Co. 18-22
Versailles patt., Gorham Mfg. Co. 22

Cold meat forks
Etruscan patt., Gorham Mfg. Co. 55
Florentine patt., Alvin Mfg. Co. 140
Francis I patt., Reed & Barton 55-65
French Antique patt., Reed & Barton,
pierced 64
Grande Baroque patt., R. Wallace & Sons .. 60-68
Hampton Court patt., Reed & Barton 55-60
Madame Jumel patt., Whiting Mfg. Co. 42-50
Manchester patt., Manchester Mfg. Co.,
small 31
Marlborough patt., Reed & Barton 64
Orange Blossom patt., Alvin Mfg. Co. 185

Cracker scoops, pierced
Chrysanthemum patt.,
Wm. B. Durgin Co. 750-950

Cream soup spoons
Camellia patt., Gorham Mfg. Co. 14-18
Damask Rose patt., Oneida Mfg. Co. 16-20
Francis I patt., Reed & Barton 30-35
Grande Baroque patt., Wallace & Sons 28-32
Lily of the Valley patt., Gorham Mfg. Co. 18-22
Marlborough patt., Reed & Barton 25-30
Nocturne patt., Gorham Mfg. Co. 12-16
Old French patt., Gorham Mfg. Co. 28-32

Cucumber servers
Fairfax patt., Wm. B. Durgin Co. 55
Lily patt., Whiting Mfg. Co. 375-425
Morning Glory patt., Alvin Mfg. Co. 85
Paris patt., Gorham Mfg. Co. 165

Demitasse spoons

Arabesque patt., Whiting Mfg. Co. 24
Blossom patt., Georg Jensen, 1904-08,
    3 3/8", set of 12 1,495
Francis I patt., Reed & Barton 22-25
Grande Baroque patt., Wallace & Sons 24
Hampton Court patt., Reed & Barton 18
Japanese patt., Tiffany & Co. 55
Lily patt., Whiting Mfg. Co. 25-30
Louis XIV patt., Towle Mfg. Co. 15
Louis XV patt., Whiting Mfg. Co. 12-16
Madame Jumel patt., Whiting Mfg. Co. 10-12
Marlborough patt., Reed & Barton 21

Dessert forks

Audubon patt., Tiffany & Co. 80
Chantilly patt., Gorham Mfg. Co., in original
    case, set of 12 350-375

Dessert spoons

Francis I patt., Reed & Barton 55-65
Frontenac patt., International Silver Co. 40-48
King Edward patt., Whiting Mfg. Co. 35-45
Louis XIV patt., Towle Mfg. Co. 52
Mignonette patt., Lunt Silversmiths 20
Old French patt., Gorham Mfg. Co. 36
Strawberry patt., Wm. B. Durgin Co. 40
Versailles patt., Gorham Mfg. Co. 55

Dinner forks

Angelo patt., Wood & Hughes 60
Bridal Rose patt., Alvin Mfg. Co. 38
Camellia patt., Gorham Mfg. Co. 20
Corinthian patt., Gorham Mfg. Co. 65
Damask Rose patt., Gorham Mfg. Co. 25
Etruscan patt., Gorham Mfg. Co. 38
Francis I patt., Reed & Barton 45-65
King Edward patt., Gorham Mfg. Co. 35
Kings patt., R. Wallace & Sons 48
Lily of the Valley patt., Whiting Mfg. Co. 60
Louis XIV patt., Towle Mfg. Co. 35
Louis XV patt., Whiting Mfg. Co. 25-35
Louis XV patt., Wood & Hughes 50
Madame Jumel patt., Gorham Mfg. Co. 32
Manchester patt., Manchester Mfg. Co. 24
Mandarin patt., Whiting Mfg. Co., silver
    plate blade 27
Marie Antoinette patt., Dominick & Haff 42
Marie Antoinette patt., Gorham Mfg. Co. 50
Melrose patt., Gorham Mfg. Co. 40-45
Old Colonial patt., Towle Mfg. Co. 42-48
Orange Blossom patt., Alvin Mfg. Co. 80
Paul Revere patt., Towle Mfg. Co. 45
Rose Point patt., R. Wallace & Sons 35
William & Mary patt., Lunt Silversmiths 20

Dinner knives

Buttercup patt., Gorham Mfg. Co. 49
Cambridge patt., Gorham Mfg. Co. 49
Damask Rose patt., Gorham Mfg. Co. 25
Etruscan patt., Gorham Mfg. Co. 36
Grand Duchess patt., Towle Mfg. Co. 34
Kings patt., R. Wallace & Sons 48
Louis XVI patt., Towle Mfg. Co. 38
Madame Jumel patt., Gorham Mfg. Co. 32
Majestic patt., Alvin Mfg. Co., silver plate
    blade 41
Marie Antoinette patt., Dominick & Haff 35
Old Colonial patt., Towle Mfg. Co. 32
Orange Blossom patt., Alvin Mfg. Co. 85
Rose Point patt., R. Wallace & Sons 35

Egg spoons

Japanese patt., Tiffany & Co., gold-washed
    bowl 75
Mayfair patt., Dominick & Haff 14

Fish forks

Old French patt., Gorham Mfg. Co. 55

Fish serving forks

Ivory patt., Whiting Mfg. Co. 475

Fish Serving sets (2-piece)

Luxembourg patt., Gorham Mfg. Co. 250
Undine patt., Wood & Hughes 495

Fruit knives

Grande Baroque patt., R. Wallace & Sons,
    hollow handle 41
Melrose patt., Gorham Mfg. Co. 28

Grapefruit spoons

Audubon patt., Tiffany & Co. 95

Gravy ladles

Angelo patt., Wood & Hughes 115
Cambridge patt., Gorham Mfg. Co. 42-48
Chantilly patt., Gorham Mfg. Co. 50-60
Chrysanthemum patt., Tiffany & Co. 395
Egyptian patt., Whiting Mfg. Co. 125
Francis I patt., Reed & Barton 60-70
Hampton Court patt., Reed & Barton 58
Italian patt., Tiffany & Co. 250
King Edward patt., Gorham Mfg. Co. 58
King Edward patt., Whiting Mfg. Co. 130
Louis XIV patt., Towle Mfg. Co. 48
Manchester patt., Manchester Mfg. Co. 31
Mount Vernon patt., Lunt Silversmiths 50
Nocturne patt., Gorham Mfg. Co. 55
Versailles patt., Gorham Mfg. Co. 145
Violet patt., R. Wallace & Sons 95

Gumbo spoons

Cambridge patt., Gorham Mfg. Co. 25-35
Manchester patt., Manchester Mfg. Co. 28
Mandarin patt., Whiting Mfg. Co. 24
Orange Blossom patt., Alvin Mfg. Co. 75-95

Ice cream forks

Louis XIV patt., Towle Mfg. Co. 40
Nocturne patt., Gorham Mfg. Co. 35
Violet patt., R. Wallace & Sons 45-65

Ice cream knives

Luxembourg patt., Gorham Mfg. Co. 225
Versailles patt., Gorham Mfg. Co. 250

Ice cream spoons

Lorraine patt., Alvin Mfg. Co. 35
Paul Revere patt., Towle Mfg. Co. 32
Peony patt., R. Wallace & Sons 38
Rose (Baltimore) patt., The Steiff Co. 28

Ice tongs

Florentine patt., Tiffany & Co. 450-550

Iced tea spoons

Buttercup patt., Gorham Mfg. Co. 33
Chantilly patt., Gorham Mfg. Co. 22
Hampton Court patt., Reed & Barton 26
Louis XIV patt., Towle Mfg. Co. 24
Marie Antoinette patt., Dominick & Haff 28
Nocturne patt., Gorham Mfg. Co. 25
Rose patt., R. Wallace & Sons 30
Virginian patt., Gorham Mfg. Co., set of 5 138

Jelly servers
Francis I patt., Reed & Barton.................... 30-35
Grande Baroque patt., R. Wallace & Sons... 30-35
Lily of the Valley patt., Gorham Mfg. Co..... 22-28

Lemon forks
Grande Baroque patt., R. Wallace & Sons........ 30
Hampton Court patt., Reed & Barton................. 25
King Edward patt., Gorham Mfg. Co.............. 18

Lettuce forks
Cottage patt., Gorham Mfg. Co......................... 55
Lily patt., Whiting Mfg. Co..................... 200-250
Renaissance patt., Dominick & Haff................ 175

Luncheon forks
Buttercup patt., Gorham Mfg. Co................... 15
Camellia patt., Whiting Mfg. Co.................... 18
Chantilly patt., Gorham Mfg. Co................... 18
Chrysanthemum patt., Wm. B. Durgin Co......... 95
Etruscan patt., Whiting Mfg. Co.................... 18
Francis I patt., Reed & Barton...................... 36
Hampton Court patt., Reed & Barton............... 30
King Edward patt., Whiting Mfg. Co............... 24
Lily of the Valley patt., Gorham Mfg. Co........... 26
Majestic patt., Alvin Mfg. Co........................ 28
Mandarin patt., Whiting Mfg. Co................... 24
Melrose patt., Gorham Mfg. Co..................... 28
Mignonette patt., Lunt Silversmiths 18
Nuremburg patt., Alvin Mfg. Co.................... 45
Old Colonial patt., Towle Mfg. Co................. 22
Orange Blossom patt., Alvin Mfg. Co............. 55
Plymouth patt., Whiting Mfg. Co................... 15
Rambler Rose patt., Reed & Barton 18
Rose Point patt., R. Wallace & Sons.............. 32
Strawberry patt., Wm. B. Durgin Co.............. 45
Versailles patt., Gorham Mfg. Co.................. 30
Violet patt., R. Wallace & Sons..................... 28
William & Mary patt., Lunt Silversmiths 18

Luncheon knives
Chantilly patt., Gorham Mfg. Co................... 18
Etruscan patt., Whiting Mfg. Co.................... 16
Francis I patt., Reed & Barton, silver plate
   blade 27
Frontenac patt., International Silver Co. 40
Grande Baroque patt., R. Wallace & Sons,
   silver plate blade....................................... 31
Kings patt., R. Wallace & Sons...................... 22
Lily of the Valley patt., Gorham Mfg. Co. 22
Majestic patt., Alvin Mfg. Co., silver plate
   blade 34
Mandarin patt., Whiting Mfg. Co., silver
   plate blade 23
Old Colonial patt., Towle Mfg. Co.................. 22
Parallel patt., Georg Jensen Silversmithy 65
Plymouth patt., Whiting Mfg. Co................... 12
Rambler Rose patt., Reed & Barton 15
William & Mary patt., Lunt Silversmiths 15

Meat forks
Jac Rose patt., Gorham Mfg. Co................... 55
Nocturne patt., Gorham Mfg. Co................... 65

Mustard ladles
Dauphin patt., Wm. B. Durgin Co.............. 150-200
Versailles patt., Gorham Mfg. Co.............. 125-150

Nut picks
Audubon patt., Tiffany & Co....................... 150
Broomcorn patt., Tiffany & Co...................... 65
Grecian patt., Gorham Mfg. Co..................... 45
Grecian patt., Whiting Mfg. Co..................... 28

Nut spoons
Lily patt., Whiting Mfg. Co., round............. 175-225

Olive forks
Marguerite patt., Wood & Hughes 23

Olive spoons
Fairfax patt., Wm. B. Durgin Co. 20-25

Oyster ladles
Fairfax patt., Wm. B. Durgin Co. 175
Japanese patt., Tiffany & Co., 1871-80,
   10 3/4"... 2000-2500

Pastry servers
Francis I patt., Reed & Barton, hollow han-
   dle 38
Hampton Court patt., Reed & Barton, hol-
   low handle 38
Louis XVI patt., Towle Mfg. Co...................... 85

Pickle forks
Cambridge patt., Gorham Mfg. Co. 30
Francis I patt., Reed & Barton 34
Grande Baroque patt., R. Wallace & Sons 27
Hampton Court patt., Reed & Barton............... 25
Lily of the Valley patt., Gorham Mfg. Co........... 24
Lily patt., Whiting Mfg. Co., long handle.......... 125
Louis XVI patt., Towle Mfg. Co...................... 30
Manchester patt., Manchester Mfg. Co............. 17

Pie knife,
Windham patt., Tiffany & Co., serrated 395

Punch ladles
Beacon patt., Manchester Silver Co. 150
Norfolk patt., Gorham Mfg. Co. 225

Salad forks
Broomcorn patt., Tiffany & Co...................... 115
Buttercup patt., Gorham Mfg. Co. 37
Camellia patt., Whiting Mfg. Co..................... 17
Chantilly patt., Gorham Mfg. Co. 25
Chrysanthemum patt., Tiffany & Co........ 115-150
Damask Rose patt., Gorham Mfg. Co. 30
Essex patt., Wm. B. Durgin Co....................... 18
Etruscan patt., Gorham Mfg. Co. 24
Fontana patt., Towle Mfg. Co. 30
Francis I patt., Reed & Barton 30-35
Grand Duchesse patt., Towle Mfg. Co. 30
Louis XIV patt., Towle Mfg. Co...................... 36
Louis XV patt., Whiting Mfg. Co..................... 40
Marie Antoinette patt., Dominick & Haff............ 32
Melbourne patt., Oneida Silversmiths 24
Pantheon patt., International Silver Co. 36
Richmond patt., Alvin Mfg. Co....................... 30
Rose (Baltimore) patt., The Stieff Co. 45-55
Rose Point patt., R. Wallace & Sons............... 34
Strawberry patt., Wm. B. Durgin Co................. 75
Violet patt., R. Wallace & Sons................ 35-45
Windham patt., Tiffany & Co. 65

Salad serving forks
Bridal Rose patt., Alvin Mfg. Co., 9"......... 275-325
Francis I patt., Reed & Barton 125-150
Melrose patt., Gorham Mfg. Co. 100-125

Salad serving sets (2-piece)
Cambridge patt., Gorham Mfg. Co. 200-275
Canterbury patt., Towle Mfg. Co............. 200-275
Francis I patt., Reed & Barton 250-325

Hampton Court patt., Reed & Barton,
fluted 175-225
Japanese patt., Tiffany & Co., gold-washed
bowls, 10" 2,500-3,000
Lily of the Valley patt., Gorham Mfg. Co. 175-225
Melrose patt., Gorham Mfg. Co. 200-250

Salad serving spoons
Bridal Rose patt., Alvin Mfg. Co. 275-325

Sauce ladles
Athenian patt., Whiting Mfg. Co. 35
Dresden patt., Whiting Mfg. Co. 65
Grande Baroque patt., R. Wallace & Sons... 35-40
Hampton Court patt., R. Wallace & Sons..... 30-35
King Edward patt., Gorham Mfg. Co. 25-30
Lily of the Valley patt., Gorham Mfg. Co. 25-30
Louis XIV patt., Towle Mfg. Co. 45
Louis XV patt., Whiting Mfg. Co. 35-40
Radiant patt., Whiting Mfg. Co. 45
Rose (Baltimore) patt., The Stieff Co. 55
Washington patt., R. Wallace & Sons 30
Winthrop patt., Tiffany & Co. 175

Serving fork
Versailles patt., Gorham Mfg. Co., 7 7/8" 225-275

Serving spoon
Bernadotte patt., Georg Jensen Silver-
smithy, medium 250-325

Soup ladle

Tomato Vine Pattern Soup Ladle

Tomato Vine patt., Tiffany & Co., the handle chased w/tomatoes, vines & leaves in
relief lapping over to the back, the oval
bowl w/a wide scalloped rim, 12 1/4" l.
(ILLUS.) 1,300-1,600

Soup ladles
Empire patt., Whiting Mfg. Co., large 395
Honeysuckle patt., Whiting Mfg. Co. 265
Rosette patt., Gorham Mfg. Co. 138

Soup spoon
Old Colonial patt., Towle Mfg. Co. 25-35

Soup spoons, oval
Buttercup patt., Gorham Mfg. Co. 25
Georgian patt., Towle Mfg. Co. 28
Ivy patt., Whiting Mfg. Co. 35
Louis V patt., Whiting Mfg. Co. 25
Louis XV patt., Wood & Hughes....................... 45
Manchester patt., Manchester Mfg. Co. 21
Marie Antoinette patt., Gorham Mfg. Co. 44
Old Colonial patt., Towle Mfg. Co. 28
Old French patt., Gorham Mfg. Co. 32
Rose patt., R. Wallace & Sons........................ 24
Strasbourg patt., Gorham Mfg. Co. 30
Violet patt., R. Wallace & Sons....................... 30

Steak carving forks
Mandarin patt., Whiting Mfg. Co. 30

Steak carving sets (2-piece)
Grande Baroque patt., R. Wallace & Sons 67

Strawberry fork
Louis XV patt., Whiting Mfg. Co. 25-30

Stuffing spoon
King George patt., Gorham Mfg. Co. 395

Sugar shells
Francis I patt., Reed & Barton 38
Hampton Court patt., Reed & Barton................ 26
Orange Blossom patt., Alvin Mfg. Co. 60

Sugar sifter
Virginia patt., Gorham Mfg. Co. 295

Sugar spoons
Canterbury patt., Towle Mfg. Co. 38
Dauphin patt., Wm. B. Durgin Co. 85
Egyptian patt., Whiting Mfg. Co. 45
Fontainebleau patt., Gorham Mfg. Co. 40
Francis I patt., Reed & Barton 35-45
Georgian patt., Towle Mfg. Co. 38
Grande Baroque patt., R. Wallace & Sons .. 30-40
Honeysuckle patt., Whiting Mfg. Co. 55
King Edward patt., Gorham Mfg. Co. 28
Les Cinq Fleurs patt., Reed & Barton.............. 26
Lion (Coeur de Lion) patt., Frank W. Smith
Co., gold-washed 127
Marlborough patt., Reed & Barton 30
Nocturne patt., Gorham Mfg. Co. 25
Pantheon patt., International Silver Co. 35
Rose (Baltimore) patt., The Stieff Co. 35
Rose Point patt., R. Wallace & Sons................ 20

Sugar tongs
Francis I patt., Reed & Barton 45-65
Lily patt., Whiting Mfg. Co., claw tips........... 85-115
Louis XIV patt., Towle Mfg. Co. 45
Louis XV patt., Whiting Mfg. Co. 38
Madame Jumel patt., Whiting Mfg. Co. 35
Medici patt., Gorham Mfg. Co. 150
Olympian patt., Tiffany & Co. 195

Table crumber

Lap-Over-Edge Table Crumber

Lap-Over-Edge patt., Tiffany & Co., the handle bright-cut engraved w/bamboo branches & spider web, the shaped blade w/chased designs, 1880-91, 12 3/4" l. (ILLUS.)................................. **1,000-1,400**

Tablespoons
Angelo patt., Wood & Hughes....................... **65-85**
Arabesque patt., Whiting Mfg. Co................. **65-85**
Buttercup patt., Gorham Mfg. Co.................. **50-65**
Chantilly patt., Gorham Mfg. Co.................. **50-65**
Francis I patt., Reed & Barton...................... **55-65**
Grande Baroque patt., R. Wallace & Sons, pierced.. **60-75**
Hampton Court patt., Reed & Barton............. **50-60**
Imperial Queen patt., Whiting Mfg. Co......... **60-75**
King Edward patt., Gorham Mfg. Co............. **45-55**
Kings patt., R. Wallace & Sons...................... **35-45**
Louis XV patt., Whiting Mfg. Co.................. **35-45**
Madame Jumel patt., Whiting Mfg. Co........ **35-45**
Madame Royale patt., Wm. B. Durgin.......... **50-58**
Manchester patt., Manchester Mfg. Co........ **25-35**
Marie Antoinette patt., Dominick & Haff...... **45-55**
Marlborough patt., Reed & Barton................. **48-55**
Maryland patt., Alvin Mfg. Co......................... **25-30**
Nocturne patt., Gorham Mfg. Co................... **45-55**
Old Colonial patt., Towle Mfg. Co................. **45-55**
Pantheon patt., International Silver Co.......... **45-55**
Raleigh patt., Alvin Mfg. Co............................ **30-40**
Strasbourg patt., Gorham Mfg. Co................ **50-65**
Versailles patt., Gorham Mfg. Co................. **55-70**

Tea strainers
Repoussé patt., Samuel Kirk & Sons......... **250-300**

Teaspoons
Buttercup patt., Gorham Mfg. Co.................. **14-18**
Cambridge patt., Gorham Mfg. Co............... **10-14**

Camellia patt., Gorham Mfg. Co................... **10-12**
Chrysanthemum patt., Tiffany & Co............ **60-70**
Damask Rose patt., Gorham Mfg. Co.......... **10-14**
Eloquence patt., Lunt Silversmiths **15-20**
English Gadroon patt., Gorham Mfg. Co..... **10-14**
English Shell patt., Lunt Silversmiths **10-12**
Etruscan patt., Gorham Mfg. Co................... **12-14**
Francis I patt., Reed & Barton **18-22**
Grande Baroque patt., R. Wallace & Sons .. **18-20**
King Edward patt., Whiting Mfg. Co............. **14-18**
King patt., Dominick & Haff **14-18**
Lily of the Valley patt., Whiting Mfg. Co..... **20-25**
Lily patt., Watson, Newell & Co..................... **18-22**
Lily patt., Whiting Mfg. Co. **20-25**
Louis XIV patt., Towle Mfg. Co..................... **12-15**
Louis XV patt., Whiting Mfg. Co. **10-13**
Lucerne patt., R. Wallace & Sons................. **14-16**
Madame Jumel patt., Whiting Mfg. Co......... **10-13**
Majestic patt., Alvin Mfg. Co......................... **15-18**
Manchester patt., Manchester Mfg. Co....... **10-12**
Marguerite patt., Gorham Mfg. Co............... **12-15**
Marie Antoinette patt., Dominick & Haff...... **10-14**
Marlborough patt., Reed & Barton **15-18**
Marquise patt., Tiffany & Co. **30-36**
Maryland patt., Alvin Mfg. Co. **12-14**
Mazarin patt., Dominick & Haff **12-16**
Melbourne patt., Oneida Silversmiths.......... **10-12**
Melrose patt., Gorham Mfg. Co. **14-18**
Michelangelo patt., Oneida Silversmiths...... **14-16**
Mignonette patt., Lunt Silversmiths **14-18**
Mount Vernon patt., Lunt Silversmiths......... **10-14**
Old Colonial patt., Towle Mfg. Co................ **12-15**
Old French patt., Gorham Mfg. Co. **15-18**
Pantheon patt., International Silver Co......... **14-16**
Plymouth patt., Gorham Mfg. Co.................. **10-12**
Poppy patt., Gorham Mfg. Co....................... **20-25**
Raleigh patt., Alvin Mfg. Co.......................... **10-12**
Rambler Rose patt., Reed & Barton............. **10-12**
Renaissance (Bearded Man) patt., Dominick & Haff... **26-32**
Rose Point patt., R. Wallace & Sons............ **14-16**
Tara patt., Reed & Barton **14-16**
Versailles patt., Gorham Mfg. Co................. **20-25**
Violet patt., R. Wallace & Sons..................... **16-20**
Violet patt., Whiting Mfg. Co......................... **20-25**
Wedgwood patt., International Silver Co. **12-14**

Tomato servers
Chrysanthemum patt., Wm. B. Durgin Co...... **275**
Francis I patt., Reed & Barton **75-85**
Hampton Court patt., Reed & Barton........... **55-65**
Louis XIV patt., Towle Mfg. Co.................. **100-125**
Nocturne patt., Gorham Mfg. Co......................... **85**
Sir Christopher patt., R. Wallace & Sons **85-95**

Vegetable spoon
Grape patt., Dominick & Haff............................. **150**

Sets
Acanthus patt., dinner service: twelve each tablespoons, luncheon spoons, tea-spoons, coffee spoons, demitasse spoons, dinner forks, luncheon forks, fish forks, pastry forks, fish knives, dinner knives & luncheon knives, four cold cut forks, two each vegetable serving spoons, jelly spoons & salt spoons, one each large serving spoon, gravy ladle, serrated serving spoon, sugar spoon, meat fork, large salad serving spoon, large salad serving fork, small salad serv-

ing spoon, small salad serving fork, cake knife, tomato server, pastry server, small serrated knife & pierced server; knives & serving pieces w/stainless steel blades, tines or bowls, designed by Johan Rohde in 1917, Georg Jensen Silversmithy, Copenhagen, Denmark, various dates, 168 pcs. **8,500-10,500**

Acorn patt., dinner service: six luncheon forks, six pastry forks, eight teaspoons & eight luncheon knives w/stainless steel blades; Georg Jensen Silversmithy, Copenhagen, Denmark, post-1945, 26 pcs. **1,400-1,650**

Acorn patt., dinner service: twelve each dinner knives, dinner forks, luncheon knives, luncheon forks, fish knives, fish forks, pastry forks, cocktail forks, soup spoons, tablespoons, dessert spoons, iced tea spoons, teaspoons, coffee spoons, demitasse spoons, grapefruit spoons, fruit knives, fruit forks, steak knives, butter spreaders & lobster picks, three each serving forks & serving spoons, one each sauce ladle, sardine server, bottle opener, letter opener, pickle fork, pie slice, fish slice & jam spoon; Georg Jensen Silversmithy, Copenhagen, Denmark, 1921 & after, 272 pcs. **16,500-20,500**

Arcadia Pattern Pieces

Arcadia patt., dinner service: twelve each dinner knives, dinner forks, dessert spoons, luncheon forks & salad forks, eleven teaspoons & eight luncheon knives; Georg Jensen Silversmithy, Copenhagen, Denmark, post-1945, 79 pcs. (ILLUS. of three) **3,500-4,500**

Back Tipt patt., dinner service: eight each dinner knives, dessert knives, dinner forks, luncheon forks, salad forks, butter

knives & soup spoons, ten teaspoons, two berry spoons & one each gravy ladle, lemon fork, cake server, cold meat fork, olive fork & seafood fork; Watson Company, Attleboro, Massachusetts, 74 pcs. **1,092**

Bernadotte patt., dinner service: twelve each tablespoons, luncheon spoons, ice cream spoons, coffee spoons, demitasse spoons, dinner forks, luncheon forks, salad forks, fish forks, fish knives, dinner knives, luncheon knives & butter knives, two each large servers, cold meat forks & fish servers, one each cake server, vegetable server, gravy ladle, meat fork, salad spoon, salad fork, cheese slice & cheese knife; some pieces w/stainless steel blades, tines or bowls, designed by Sigvard Bernadotte in 1930, Georg Jensen Silversmithy, Copenhagen, Denmark, post-1945, 170 pcs. **16,100**

Bittersweet Pattern Pieces

Bittersweet patt., dinner service: eight each dinner forks, salad forks, cake forks, tablespoons, soup spoons, teaspoons, dinner knives & butter spreaders; Georg Jensen Silversmithy, Copenhagen, Denmark, 64 pcs. (ILLUS. of three) **5,750**

Brocade patt., dinner service: eight each salad forks, luncheon knives, luncheon forks, butter knives, teaspoons & iced tea spoons, four dessert spoons & one each sugar shell & master butter server; International Silver Co., Meriden, Connecticut, 54 pcs. **633**

Castilian patt., dinner service: twenty-four dinner knives, eighteen teaspoons, twelve each luncheon knives, cheese knives, soup spoons, butter knives, bouillon spoons, dinner knives, luncheon forks, salad forks, cocktail forks, grapefruit spoons, iced tea spoons & dessert forks, three serving forks; engraved w/monogram "NAY," Tiffany & Co., New York, New York, 20th c., 195 pcs.............. **9,775**

Chateau Rose patt., dinner service: twelve each luncheon forks, soup spoons, salad forks, seafood forks, luncheon knives, teaspoons, 10 butter spreaders & a cake server; Alvin Corp., Providence, Rhode Island, ca. 1940, 83 pcs............................. **805**

Clinton patt., dinner service: thirty-six teaspoons, twenty-four cocktail forks, eighteen each dinner forks, luncheon forks, salad forks, bouillon spoons, soup spoons, demitasse spoons, dinner knives, luncheon knives & butter spreaders plus a two-piece carving set & eight serving pieces; Tiffany & Co., New York, New York, 232 pcs. **9,775**

Cluny patt., dinner service: thirty-six teaspoons, eighteen each dinner knives, luncheon knives, iced tea spoons, cocktail forks, salad forks, grapefruit spoons, dinner forks, butter spreaders, luncheon forks, soup spoons & dessert knives, twelve steak knives, seven tablespoons, six each sauce ladles, pairs of salad servers, dessert serving spoons, serving forks & fish knives, four each pie slices & pat slices, two cake combs & pair of ice tongs, basting spoon, crumb scoop & asparagus server; silver-gilt, some pieces monogrammed, Gorham Mfg. Co., Providence, Rhode Island, ca. 1890 & later, 297 pcs........................ **16,100**

Commonwealth patt., dinner service: eight each table forks, salad forks, cocktail forks, dessert forks, demitasse spoons, dessert spoons, grapefruit spoons, soup spoons, butter spreaders, 9 1/2" knives & 8 3/4" knives, twelve five o'clock spoons, ten teaspoons, two-piece salad serving set, two-piece fish serving set & one each cold meat fork, large serving spoon, cake saw, cake server, gravy ladle, sugar spoon, sugar tongs, butter serving knife, lemon fork, jelly knife, cheese knife, jelly spoon, ice tongs & roast carving fork & knife; hand-wrought, Porter Blanchard, Calabasas, California, 129 pcs.................. **8,050**

Devon patt., dinner service: twelve each dinner forks, salad forks, cake forks, seafood forks, soup spoons, teaspoons, grapefruit spoons, demitasse spoons, dinner knives & luncheon knives, sixteen butter spreaders & six fruit knives; Reed & Barton, Taunton, Massachusetts, 142 pcs.. **2,185**

Eloquence patt., dinner service: sixteen each salad forks, cocktail forks, iced beverage spoons, dessert spoons, cream soup spoons, luncheon knives, butter spreaders & steak knives, fifteen luncheon forks & teaspoons, thirteen demitasse spoons, twelve place spoons, three tablespoons, pierced tablespoons, butter serving knives & cake knives, two two-

piece salad serving sets, buffet spoons, buffet forks, gravy ladles, sauce ladles, bonbon spoons, sugar spoons, jelly servers, olive forks & sugar tongs, one cheese serving knife; Lunt Silversmiths, Greenfield, Massachusetts, 218 pcs......... **4,312**

English Gadroon patt., dinner service: ten each luncheon forks, salad forks, luncheon knives & butter spreaders, eight cocktail forks, twenty-three teaspoons, six demitasse spoons, two tablespoons, one each cream soup spoon, gravy ladle & cake server; Gorham Mfg. Co., Providence, Rhode Island, 92 pcs..................... **1,265**

Federal Cotillion patt., dinner service: twelve each luncheon forks, salad forks, ice cream forks, luncheon knives & butter spreaders, sixteen teaspoons, eight demitasse spoons, two-piece steak carving set, one berry spoon, salad serving fork, tablespoon, gravy ladle, pierced flat server, cold meat fork, bonbon spoon, sugar tongs, cream ladle, sugar spoon, jelly server, butter serving knife, lemon fork, olive fork, cake server & cheese server; Frank Smith Silver Co., Gardner, Massachusetts, 110 pcs............................ **2,300**

Francis I patt., dinner service: eight each dinner knives, dinner forks, soup spoons, teaspoons, butter knives, luncheon forks & seafood forks, plus one each sugar spoon, salad serving set, gravy ladle & two serving spoons; Reed & Barton, Taunton, Massachusetts, 1907, 62 pcs. **2,000-2,500**

Francis I Pattern Pieces

Francis I patt., dinner service: forty-two teaspoons, twenty-four each luncheon forks, salad forks, luncheon knives & butter spreaders (twelve w/silver blades), twenty bouillon spoons, twelve each dinner knives, soup spoons, demitasse spoons, coffee spoons, dinner forks, cocktail forks, ice cream forks, eight grapefruit spoons plus fourteen serving pieces, w/two wood cases; Reed & Barton, Taunton, Massachusetts, 20th c., 276 pcs. (ILLUS. of three) **9,000-10,000**

Heiress patt., dinner service: twelve cocktail forks, butter spreaders, iced beverage spoons, soup spoons & luncheon knives, eighteen salad forks, nineteen luncheon forks, twenty-four teaspoons, two serving spoons & cold meat forks & one gravy ladle, butter serving knife & sugar spoon; Oneida Silversmiths, Sherrill, New York, in fitted wooden case, 128 pcs. **900-1,000**

Imperial Chrysanthemum Pieces

Imperial Chrysanthemum patt., dinner service: twenty-four each table forks & dessert forks, twenty-one tablespoons, twelve each dessert spoons, teaspoons, fruit spoons, demitasse spoons, fish forks, cocktail forks, fish knives & butter knives, four condiment spoons & one each fish server, fish slice, serving fork, punch ladle & lobster server plus twenty-four table knives & twelve dessert knives & fruit knives w/stainless steel blades; the terminals chased w/flowerheads & leaves, also engraved w/a monogram, in fitted wooden case, 222 pcs. (ILLUS. of five) **6,500-8,000**

King Albert patt., dinner service: twelve each dinner knives, dinner forks, salad forks, ice cream forks, teaspoons, dessert spoons, cocktail forks & butter knives plus carving knife, meat fork, serving spoon, cheese knife, berry spoon & sugar castor spoon; Whiting Mfg. Co., Providence, Rhode Island, 102 pcs. **1,425**

King William patt., dinner service: eight each luncheon forks, salad forks, butter spreaders, dessert spoons, cream soup spoons & luncheon knives; monogrammed, Tiffany & Co., New York, New York, 1907-47, in fitted wooden case, 48 pcs. **978**

Kings patt., dinner service: twelve each dinner forks, dinner knives, butter spreaders & dessert spoons, 24 each teaspoons & salad forks plus seven serving pieces; engraved monogram, Towle Silversmiths, Newburyport, Massachusetts, ca. 1904, 103 pcs. **1,265**

Lap-Over-Edge Etched Pieces

Lap-Over-Edge Etched patt., dinner service: twenty-four each teaspoons & luncheon forks, twelve each dinner knives, luncheon knives, butter spreaders, dinner forks, dessert spoons & dessert knives, ten tablespoons, one sauce ladle & butter knife; etched w/plants, animals & fish, some identified on the back, engraved w/name "Scoville" in script on back, Tiffany & Co., New York, New York, ca. 1885, 132 pcs. (ILLUS. of four) **20,700**

Louis XIII Richelieu Pieces

Louis XIII Richelieu patt., dinner service: twelve each dinner knives, dinner forks, luncheon knives, luncheon forks, tablespoons, dessert spoons, lobster forks, teaspoons, fish knives, fish forks, demitasse spoons, three butter knives, two serving forks & one each soup ladle, sauce ladle, slice, cake knife & cheese knife; monogrammed, w/rattail bowls, trifid ends & cannon-handled knives w/stainless steel blades, Puiforcat, Paris, France, 20th c., in three fitted trays stamped w/maker's name, 144 pcs. (ILLUS. on previous page of three)............ **28,750**

Mansion House patt., dinner service: twelve each dinner knives, butter knives, dinner forks, luncheon forks, soup spoons & teaspoons plus thirteen serving pieces; Heirloom, Oneida Silversmiths, Sherrill, New York, 85 pcs.............. **600-700**

Old English Feather Edge patt., dinner service: twelve each dinner knives, dinner forks, salad forks, soup spoons, dessert spoons & teaspoons, together w/twelve cheese knives w/bone handles; Garrard & Co., Ltd., London, England, 1962-63, 84 pcs............................. **4,025**

Old English Pattern Pieces

Old English patt., dinner service: thirty-six each dinner knives & dinner forks, twenty-four each luncheon knives, luncheon forks & dessert spoons, twelve each fish knives, fish forks, dessert knives, dessert forks, tablespoons & teaspoons, four sauce ladles, pair of salad servers, pair of fish servers, one gravy spoon & four-piece carving set; in fitted oak cabinet w/five drawers & double doors, Francis Higgins, London, England, 1936, 229 pcs. (ILLUS. of three)................ **20,700**

Old French patt., dinner service: twelve each bread & butter plates, luncheon knives, dinner knives, fruit forks, luncheon forks, demitasse spoons, dessert forks, salad forks, iced tea spoons, egg spoons, citrus spoons, soup spoons, cream soup spoons, teaspoons & tablespoons, eleven each dinner forks & cocktail forks, ten butter knives & two master butter knives; in mahogany case, Gorham Mfg. Co., Providence, Rhode Island, ca. 1915, 220 pcs. **4,675**

Old Newbury patt., dinner service: eight each luncheon forks, dessert spoons & dinner knives, seven luncheon forks & cocktail forks, six butter spreaders & teaspoons & one each vegetable spoon, pastry server, cold meat fork & serving spoon; hand-wrought, Old Newbury Crafters, Newburyport, Massachusetts, 54 pcs.......................... **1,265**

Pine Tree patt., dinner service: twelve each dinner forks, salad forks, cocktail forks, butter spreaders, teaspoons, bouillon spoons & dinner knives, two tablespoons, two-piece salad serving set, one gravy ladle & cake server; in fitted case, International Silver Co., Meriden, Connecticut, 90 pcs............. **748**

Plymouth patt., dinner service: twelve each dinner forks, luncheon forks, salad forks w/gilt tines, cocktail forks, teaspoons, soup spoons, demitasse spoons w/gilt bowls, butter spreaders, dinner knives & luncheon knives, three tablespoons & one each cream ladle w/gilt bowl, olive spoon w/gilt bowl, pickle fork, butter serving knife, salad serving fork w/gilt tines & cake server; monogrammed "H.W.B.," Gorham Mfg. Co., Providence, Rhode Island, 129 pcs............. **920**

Repoussé patt., dinner service: eight each luncheon forks, salad forks, butter spreaders, teaspoons, coffee spoons & luncheon knives plus two serving spoons & ladles & one each serving fork, berry spoon, pickle fork, slice, sugar shell, butter knife, jelly slice & meat fork & knife; monogrammed, S. Kirk & Co., Baltimore, Maryland, 61 pcs................... **2,875**

Romance of the Sea patt., dinner service: eight each dinner knives, butter knives, soup spoons, salad forks, dinner forks & teaspoons; in fitted wooden case, R. Wallace & Sons Mfg. Co., Wallingford, Connecticut, 48 pcs. **1,035**

Rose patt., dinner service: eight each luncheon forks, salad forks, butter spreaders, bouillon spoons, demitasse spoons & luncheon knives, eleven small teaspoons, seven teaspoons, three tablespoons, two-piece steak carving set & one jelly server, sugar spoon, butter pick, lemon fork & gravy ladle; in fitted case, monogrammed "C," Steiff Co., Baltimore, Maryland, 76 pcs. **1,035**

Royal Danish patt., dinner service: twelve each luncheon forks, demitasse spoons, soup spoons & butter spreaders, ten tablespoons & dinner knives, nine dinner forks & teaspoons, eight cocktail forks & luncheon knives, seven salad forks, five dessert spoons, two large serving spoons & one salad serving fork, gravy ladle, large cold meat fork & pickle fork; International Silver Co., Meriden, Connecticut, 120 pcs............. **2,185**

Strasbourg patt., dinner service: eight each dinner knives, dinner forks, salad forks & butter knives, sixteen teaspoons, three serving spoons & one each ladle, berry spoon, slotted spoon & meat fork; gold-washed, in wooden cutlery box, Gorham Mfg. Co., Providence, Rhode Island, 55 pcs................................. **1,330**

Suffolk patt., dinner service: twelve each dinner forks, salad forks, cocktail forks, teaspoons, soup spoons, grapefruit spoons w/gilt bowls, demitasse spoons, butter spreaders & dinner knives w/silver plate blades plus one each large serving spoon, pastry server, lettuce fork & sugar spoon; monogrammed B, Alvin Corporation, Providence, Rhode Island, 112 pcs. **978**

Tapestry patt., dinner service: twelve each luncheon forks, dessert spoons, salad forks, luncheon knives, dessert knives, twenty-four teaspoons, plus nine serving pieces; Reed & Barton, Taunton, Massachusetts, ca. 1964, 93 pcs **1,380**

Versailles patt., dinner service: twelve each dinner knives, luncheon knives, bouillon spoons, teaspoons, dinner forks, luncheon forks & ice cream spoons, eleven each demitasse spoons & salad forks, eight butter knives, plus twelve serving pieces; Gorham Mfg. Co., Providence, Rhode Island, early 20th c., 126 pcs. **4,255**

Versailles Pattern Pieces

Versailles patt., dinner service: twelve each salad forks, dinner forks, teaspoons, soup spoons, dinner knives & butter spreaders, ten small teaspoons & eight seafood forks; monogrammed, Gorham Mfg. Co., Providence, Rhode Island, 1888, 90 pcs. (ILLUS. of three) **2,300**

Winchester patt., dinner service: twelve each dinner forks, salad forks, teaspoons, cream soup spoons, dinner knives & butter spreaders, two tablespoons & one cold meat fork; in fitted wooden case, Shreve & Co., San Francisco, California, 75 pcs **1,092**

Windsor patt., dinner service: eight each luncheon forks, teaspoons, demitasse spoons, luncheon knives, salad forks, soup spoons & butter spreaders, plus a meat fork & knife; monogrammed, Old Newbury Crafters, Inc., Newburyport, Massachusetts, retailed by Cartier, 58 pcs. (one handle separate from knife) **1,265**

Woodlily patt., dinner service: eight each luncheon forks, salad forks, butter spreaders, cream soup spoons & luncheon knives, sixteen teaspoons, two tablespoons & one gravy ladle & butter serving knife; in fitted wooden case, Frank Smith Silver Co., Gardner, Massachusetts, 60 pcs................ **1,150**

Silver Plate (Hollowware)

It appears that as early as 1801, experiments took place in England that proved that a current of electricity passing through a conducting liquid decomposed the ingredients of that liquid and caused their elements to be set free at the two immersed electric poles. This principle led to the inception of the electroplating industry. At first there seemed to be no direct use for the electroplating process, but between 1836 and 1838, the G.R. & H. Elkington firm of Birmingham, England, took out various patents for the process, and anyone interested in the method was required to go to Birmingham to study and pay a royalty and guarantee he would not deposit less than 1,000 ounces of silver per year. John Mead is thought to be the first person to utilize silver plating in the United States. Another early manufacturer of silver plated ware in this country was Rogers Bros. in Hartford, Connecticut. It was this firm that really entrenched the silver plating industry in the United States. Another early silver plating company was the Meriden Britannia Company, located in Meriden, Connecticut. The International Silver Company of Meriden was incorporated in 1898 and included a number of independent New England silversmiths. Originally, the manufacture of silver plated goods was located in New England and the northeastern states, mainly New York, Connecticut and Massachusetts. The use of the process spread to Maine, Maryland, New Jersey, Pennsylvania and Rhode Island, and by the late 19th century to Illinois, Ohio, Indiana and Wisconsin, and finally to California. Silver plated wares today can be found in different grades. The prime quality items are found in jewelry stores and jewelry departments in large department stores. There is, of course, an abundance of lower quality and lower priced wares which are available in discount stores, bargain basements and souvenir-type gift shops. It should be noted, however, that any piece with a reputable mark will be of the same quality whether retailed in a jewelry store or as an advertising premium. Antique silver plated wares are to be found in the same shapes and diversity as sterling silver pieces. Lovely tea sets, flatware, serving pieces, vases and other decorative wares are all available. Their style and beauty are the equal of sterling pieces, but the price is considerably lower. Keep in mind that the value of an early silver plated item depends on the condition of the plating, rarity of the form and collector demand. Worn or badly tarnished pieces may sell for very little. Replating is an option, but it can be expensive and may obliterate some of the detail and textured patina of an early piece.

Basket, round, w/swivel openwork decorated handle, repoussé grapevine decoration, made by Simpson, Hall, Miller & Co., 5 x 6" (ILLUS.) **195**
Basket, shaped body decorated w/a grapevine design, hinged swivel handle, on a pedestal base, ca. 1850, 12" d., 9 1/2" h....... **280**

Silver Plate Base or Holder

Base or holder, probably for decorative glass, top missing, circular stepped base is decorated w/applied figures of boy & begging dog & cylindrical shaft of holder w/flaring base, made by Aurora Silver Plate Co., style number 029, 3 1/4 x 5 1/4" (ILLUS.) **$295**

Pierced-design Basket

Basket, pierced base & swivel strap handle w/applied flower decoration, style number 1728, made by Meriden, 7 3/4 x 9 1/2 x 9 3/4" (ILLUS.) **245**

Swivel-handle Basket

Finely Woven Silver Plate Basket

Basket, wide shallow form composed of fine tightly woven silver wire w/blue glass beads around the rim & twisted wire loop handles, medallion in center bottom shows City Hall Square in Seattle, Washington, early 20th c., 6 1/4" d. plus handles (ILLUS.) **25**
Basket, footed, fluted form w/a gadrooned edge & twisted openwork bail handle, Pairpoint Quadruple Plate, signed, 9 1/4" w., 8" h. **83**

Silver Plate Engraved Baton Head

Baton head, round, engraved "Nancy Ruth Heverly - Center Point, Iowa - 1937" in diamond border, 2" d. (ILLUS.) **28**

Biscuit Warmer & Tray

Biscuit warmer & tray, cov., footed biscuit warmer has raised repeating design around top & bottom, narrow ribbed rims on lid & tray, lid w/decorated knob handle & tray w/decorative handles applied to raised rim, faint marks on bottom, 7 x 7 1/4 x 10 3/4" (ILLUS. on previous page) **400**

Scotsman Bookmark

Bookmark, shaft tapering to point, topped w/figure of Scotsman in tam & kilt, enamel detail, attached tassel, 3" l. (ILLUS.) **25**

Reed & Barton Footed Bowl

Bowl, deep oval shape w/scalloped rim & flat bottom on ball feet, sides decorated w/embossed flowers & figures of two girls, flowers embossed on ends to form handles, marked "708" on bottom, Reed & Barton, 3 1/2 x 4 x 6 3/4" (ILLUS.) **495**

Silver Plate Inscribed Bowl

Bowl, footed deep gently flared form inscribed "25 Years of Service - Northwest Orient Airlines," 6" w., 3 1/4" h. (ILLUS.) **42**

International Silver Bowl

Bowl, slightly squared form w/low flaring sides w/wide plain panels alternating w/scroll-stamped corner panels, International Silver Co., No. 1048, 6 1/2" w. (ILLUS.)... **25**

Art Nouveau-style Covered Box

Box, cov., Art Nouveau style, footed, decorated w/roses, marked on bottom "92 DL," possibly a hair receiver, 2 3/4 x 2 3/4 x 3 1/2" (ILLUS.)... **165**

Bud Vase with Chickens on Base

Bud vase, a fancy Victorian silver plate holder w/a round base topped by a figural rooster & hen, a small upright ring supports the slender deep amethyst blown glass trumpet-form vase w/enameled flowers, overall 6 1/4" h. (ILLUS.)................... **445**

Rare Bud Vase with Stork Base

Bud vase, base w/ringed tapering platform supporting a figural crane w/its head down standing in front of a leafy tree supporting a lily-form blown cranberry glass vase, indistinct marks on the base, 19th c., overall 13 1/2" h. (ILLUS.)...................... **1,295**

Rare Victorian Double Bud Vase

Bud vase, double-type, a domed base w/scroll tab feet, stamped w/ornate florals & issuing two ornate scrolling griffins, each holding a metal fitted w/a pale yellow blown glass vase w/a ruffled rim, base marked "H.L.& Co. - No. 4384," 19th c., 10 1/2" w., 9 3/4" h. (ILLUS.) **1,350**

Victorian Bud Vase with Girl on Base

Bud vase, figural base w/a round foot topped by a kneeling Victorian girl beside an upright stem w/long leaf brackets supporting the slender tapering shaded green to clear glass vase w/gilt enameling, base by Meriden, No. 66, overall 9 1/2" h. (ILLUS.)... **300**

Bud Vase with Unique Figural Base

Bud vase, ornate base w/small palmette feet on a rectangular platform supporting a pair of hippocampus issuing tall S-scroll supports ending in large flowerheads & holding a tall slender trumpet-form green glass vase w/gold band trim, base by Reed & Barton, No. 2230, 19th c., overall 11 3/4" h. (ILLUS.).. **695**

Bud Vase with Cherub Base

Bud vase, the base w/a round foot supporting a standing cherub in front of a pair of pierced flower & scroll uprights flanking a ring support for the clear trumpet-form blown glass vase, base w/Tufts mark & No. 1092, 19th c., overall 10 1/4" h. (ILLUS.).. **595**

Fancy Silver Plate Butter Dish

Butter dish, cov., spherical form w/ribbed dome top supported in circular ring raised on three cabriole paw-foot legs w/lion heads at top, front of top rolls back to reveal interior, marked "Trademark 1883 - Rogers Silver Co.," missing glass liner, 5 1/2" d., 4 1/2" h. (ILLUS. on previous page) 75

Cake stand, two-tiered, acanthus leaf & scroll details on the column, cast horse-heads at base, graduated scallop dished, 23" h. 633

Candelabra, a square stepped base & slender flaring squared column w/urn-form top socket inset w/two serpentine arms ending in urn-form sockets & centered by a third socket, marked "W.H. & S.B.," late 19th - early 20th c., pr. 605

Candelabra, five-branch, a central stem decorated w/pressed foliage design & scrollwork bands, supporting four scrolling arms each ending in a decorated socket & flanking a central socket, ca. 1895, 18" w., 19" h., pr. 252

Candelabra, five-light, each modeled as a young girl wearing a flowing robe & supporting a fluted torch issuing four additional scrolling candle arms w/foliate nozzle & bobêche, standing barefoot on a foliate molded capitol surmounting a square base w/fluted & shell molded frieze, a ram's mask in each corner above short hoof feet, 42 1/4" h., pr. 3,450

Candelabra, three-light, Art Nouveau style, a slender stem-form central shaft issuing from a bulbed openwork cluster of long leaves & supporting a blossom-form socket w/rolled edges, two further up-curved side arms w/matching candle sockets all above a slender lower standard issuing from a round pierced loop foot, Georges de Feure, France, ca. 1900, 13 3/8" h., pr. 5,640

Candelabra, three-light, Queen Anne-style, each w/a stepped, octagonal base continuing to a conforming stem & two scrolling candle arms w/faceted candle cup nozzles, 16 1/4", pr. 690

Silver Plate Candelabrum

Candelabra, three-light, the short central shaft cast w/blossoms & supporting a bulbous floral cast socket flanked by serpentine arms ending in matching sockets, round domed base w/wide cast blossom & scroll band, marked "Ballad Community," 9" w., 6 1/8" h., pr. (ILLUS. of one) 170

Candelabra, three-light, three-arm insert on pedestal base, egg-and-dart border designs, Reed & Barton, early 20th c., 13 7/16" h., pr. 230

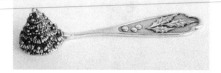

Christmas Tree Candle Snuffer

Candle snuffer, handle end decorated w/holly leaves & berries, snuffer is in the form of a decorated Christmas tree, 7 1/2" l. (ILLUS.) 45

Silver Plate Candleholder

Candleholders, a slightly domed round base w/a leaftip band centering an upright short leaf & bud issuing two upturned long slender arms ending in tulip-form sockets, marked "Her Majesty 1847 Rogers Bros. 009056 I.S.," 20th c., 10 7/8" w., 6 3/4" h., pr. (ILLUS. of one) 200

Candlestick, typical form, the stem w/engraved knops, the stepped circular base w/engraved bands, monogrammed, Europe, late 19th c., 8 3/4" h. 115

English Silver Plate Candlesticks

Candlesticks, a square molded base stamped w/a band of flowers & scrolls, the baluster-form stem w/four panels stamped w/flower sprigs, a shaped square floral knop above & below, a plain socket w/removable floral-stamped shaped square bobêche, England, 20th c., 12" h., pr. (ILLUS.) 403

Victorian Silver Plate Candlesticks

Candlesticks, square domed base, the shaft composed of two inverted bell-form sections centered by a knob, decorated overall w/panels of small rose sprigs, baluster-form socket w/wide rolled rim, Victorian, 12 3/8" h., pr. (ILLUS.) **195**

English Silver Plate Candlesticks

Candlesticks, squared scalloped wide foot below the tall ringed & baluster-turned standard & tall ringed & corseted socket w/a flattened rim, marked "Sheffield - E.P.N.S. - Made in England," early 20th c., 12 1/4" h., set of 4 (ILLUS. of part)........ **1,375**

Columnar Silver Plate Candlesticks

Candlesticks, weighted, stepped, reeded, circular bases & flaring capitals on simple shaft, 9 1/2" h., the pr. (ILLUS.) **65**

Silver Plate Card Basket

Card basket, stepped circular base holder in form of dolphin, which supports round tray w/engraved floral decoration & scalloped rim, handle w/applied openwork floral decoration, 7 x 9 3/4" (ILLUS.) **450-850**

Card holder, a pedestal-based compote form w/full-figural parakeets around the standard, scrolled handles mounted on sides of rim, applied leaves on the sides, good original plating, Webster & Son, New York **375**

Silver Plate Card Tray

Card tray, four-lobed squared-shape tray decorated w/engraved flowers & insects, attached to round base by three legs & two applied leaf & flower supports, maker's name indistinct, 5 7/8 x 6 1/4" (ILLUS.)............. **175**

Footed Card Tray

Card tray, in the shape of an Oriental fan w/handle, decorated w/engraved shapes of lily pads & assorted flora, on three turtle-shaped feet, marked "3518," 8 x 10" (ILLUS.) 365

Fluted-rim Card Tray

Card tray, rectangular, footed, w/fluted rim and tray embossed w/design of oak leaves & acorns, w/applied bird perched atop two-pronged side handle curving over center of tray, marked on bottom "Jan. 31, 1893 - 1430," Pairpoint, 5 3/4 x 6 x 7" (ILLUS.) 395

Pierced-side Card Tray

Card tray, rectangular, tray depicts sailing ship & a deer on the shore, pierced sides & skirt, floral- & scroll-decorated feet, handles w/openwork design of cherubs trying to rein in bumblebees amid sunflowers, style number 1082, 4 x 5 1/4 x 8" (ILLUS.) 395

Tufts Footed Card Tray

Card tray, ring border tray w/three applied figures of bonneted girls holding tray and forming trays feet, surface decorated w/Kate Greenaway-style design of courting couple in leaf garland border & "MP" in heart shape below, J.W. Tufts, Boston (ILLUS.)... 895

Center piece, figural, in the form of a Victorian highwheel ordinary bicycle w/a wire frame around the back holding five clear glass Inverted Thumbprint patt. shot-sized glasses, a dinner bell on the handle bars & fitted w/a figural male bisque uniformed rider, ca. 1890s, the set 303

Chafing dish, cov., Arts & Crafts style, round low cylindrical sides above the deep rounded bottom & a long tapering square riveted ebony side handle, the low domed cover w/an angular loop handle, raised on a frame w/four flat buttress-style legs w/block feet & joined by slender cross braces centered by a ring to hold the cylindrical handled burner, cover marked "Als ik Kan," Gustav Stickley, from Stickley's Craftsman restaurant in New York, all parts marked "THE CRAFTSMAN - INTERNATIONAL SILVER CO.," 17" l., 10 1/2" h. 2,970

Unusual Lobster-footed Chafing Dish

Chafing dish, cover & burner, the slightly flaring deep cylindrical dish w/a straight turned wood side handle raised on a tripod base w/figural upright lobsters forming the legs & joined by cross braces centered by the burner, a domed cover w/a turned wood knob, impressed "San Benort," lamp impressed "Lagco" within a laurel wreath, American, early 20th c., wear to high spots, overall 10" h. (ILLUS. on previous page)... **287**

Chafing dish, cover & stand, the cartouche-form dish w/gadrooned borders, raised on a stand w/cabriole legs, George III-style, England, early 20th c., 16" l., the set.. **258**

Cheese Ball Holder

Cheese ball holder, wide footed base decorated w/scrollwork curves up to flat circular holder w/three inward-curving prongs to hold cheese, applied handle w/scrollwork, made by Wilcox, style number 42, dated June 2, 1891, 4 1/2 x 6 3/4 x 10" (ILLUS.) **525**

Silver Plate Child's Cup

Child's cup, w/handle, slightly bulbous form embossed w/scene of little boy in hat playing a lute in wooded landscape w/rabbits & trees, made by Queen City Silver Co., Cincinnati, Ohio, 2 1/4 x 2 3/4 x 3 1/2" (ILLUS.) **85**

Old Silver Plate Cigar Holder

Cigar holder, barrel-shaped w/ruffled rim, embossed floral band around the base, engraved w/a smoking cigar, Wilcox Silver mark on base, 2 3/4" d., 3" h. (ILLUS.).. **25**

Girl Figure with Clock

Clock, figural, in form of bonneted girl holding folds of cloak open, w/clock set in folds on one side, 2 1/2 x 7 x 7" (ILLUS.)...... **795**

Wilcox Cocktail Pitcher

Cocktail pitcher, cov., domed base & body decorated w/embossed scrollwork, flowers & leaves, short spout, decorated handle, style number N59, Wilcox, in the Paisley design, 12 1/2" h. (ILLUS.) **225**

Art Deco Silver Plate Cocktail Set

Cocktail set: cocktail shaker, six glasses & serving tray; Art Deco style, the shaker w/a tall ovoid body w/cylindrical neck fitted w/a mushroom domed cover, short angled shoulder spout & long angled handle, each conical cup on a flared foot, all pieces decorated w/an applied anchor & rope design, impressed maker's mark, retailed by Bernard Rice & Sons, ca. 1930, tray 2 3/4 x 9 1/2", shaker 13 1/4" h., the set (ILLUS.) **575**

Cocktail set: shaker & twelve matching stemmed cocktails; the footed swelled cylindrical shaker w/a hammered finish tapering to a fitted cover, short angled rim spout & angled loop handle, matching conical cocktails w/tall slender stems & round feet, marked "Homan plate on nickel silver W.M. Mounts. Made in U.S.A.," & patent number, wines by the Meriden Silver Plate Co., early 20th c., the set **77**

Cocktail shaker, lighthouse-form, Meriden Silver Plate, International Silver Co., 20th c. **1,840**

Covered Coffee Container with Spoon

Coffee container, cov., rolled foot, hand-hammered & pierced decoration above pierced letters spelling "COFFEE," blue glass liner, spoon attaches to holder, 3 7/8 x 5 1/2" (ILLUS.) **35**

Coffee service: cov. coffeepot, cov. sugar, creamer & tray; Art Deco style of geometric form w/green Bakelite handles, ca. 1930, coffeepot 8 1/2" h., the set **2,185**

Plated Coffeepot, Creamer & Sugar

Coffee service: cov. coffeepot, creamer & open sugar; Classical-style w/hammered surfaces decorated w/shields & garlands, stylized geometric handles, marked on bottom "Sheffield - made in USA" & other marks, style number 0618 on each, coffeepot 10" h., the set (ILLUS.) **245**

Coffee urn, cov., baluster-form body w/applied vintage detail & engine-turned bands, Reed & Barton, late 19th c., 17" h. **230**

Coffee urn, cov., tall ovoid urn-form body tapering to a short flared rim w/domed cover, long loop side handles, slender base w/loop-handled spigot above high scroll-cast legs supporting the burner, cast vintage details & engraved Neoclassical designs w/a relief-cast Minerva head medallion on the back, marked "Rogers, Smith & Co., New Haven, Conn.," late 19th - early 20th c., 17 3/4" h. **385**

Coffee urn & warmer, cov., the tall ovoid lobed body w/a tall waisted neck w/flaring ruffled rim & inset domed cover, arched scroll handles from the rim to the shoulder, ornate spigot on the lower body, detailed cast leaf & flower design, raised on a matching scroll-trimmed base w/small burner raised on S-scroll legs, Reed & Barton, late 19th - early 20th c., overall 17" h., the set **275**

Floral-decorated Coffeepot

Coffeepot, cov., domed ringed base raised on applied leaf-style feet, lower pot w/engraved flowers, upper part, spout & handle w/raised flowers & leaves, pierced finial on flat lid, style number 2902, Simpson, Hall, Miller & Co., 11" h. (ILLUS. on previous page) **245**

Reed & Barton Footed Coffeepot

Coffeepot, cov., on outward curving legs decorated w/flower & leaves, bottom of pot decorated w/stylized birds, flowers & leaves, hinged domed lid w/knob handle, decorative thumbpiece on pot handle, style number 2962, Reed & Barton, 5 1/2 x 9 x 13 1/4" (ILLUS.) **225**

Coffeepot with Stand & Warmer

Coffeepot, stand & warmer, cov., on domed rectangular stand w/warmer, decorated w/grape clusters, scrolls, flowers & leaves, 14 3/4" h., the set (ILLUS.) **425**

Apollo Silver Co. Collar Button Box

Collar button box, cov., round, footed, embossed decoration, lid decorated w/figure of prancing devil and "Where is my collar button?," Apollo Silver Co., 2 1/4 x 2 3/4" (ILLUS.) **185**

Plated Collar and Cuff Box

Collar & cuff box, cov., square, applied openwork fern, scrollwork & shield design on sides and extending to feet, top engraved "Collars and Cuffs," 6 3/4" (ILLUS.) **900**

Late Victorian Decorated Compote

Compote, a wide round domed foot & short pedestal supporting a deep bowl w/a wide & deeply rolled & flared rim stamped w/ornate scrolls, swags & blossoms, Wilcox Silver mark, No. 819, last quarter 19th c., 9 1/2" d., 5 3/4"h. (ILLUS.) **125**

Plated Compote with Squirrel

Compote, deep rounded bowl w/figure of squirrel sitting on a branch eating an acorn applied to rim, on a slender pedestal w/domed foot, marked "Sheffield USA," 6" d., 9" h. (ILLUS.) **325**

American Silver Compote

Compote, engraved line decoration & initials of newlyweds & dated 1869, shaped rim & base on short foot, handles decorated w/lions' heads, marked on bottom "Rogers Smith & Co., New Haven, Conn. No. 1299," 9 x 13 1/2", 6" h. (ILLUS.)........ **2,950**

Camel Condiment Holder

Condiment holder, base holding form of a camel standing at a well, harness has ring holders at each side of camel, hallmarked but other marks indistinct, 4 x 4 1/4 x 4 3/4" (ILLUS.) **350**

Basket-form Condiment Holder

Condiment holder, in the form of a woven basket containing three egg-shaped holders for salt & pepper shakers & mustard cup, w/spread-winged baby bird perched on rim, English, indistinct maker's mark on bottom, 5 1/2" h. (ILLUS.) **1,295**

Victorian Silver Plate Cracker Jar

Cracker jar, cov., squatty bulbous body on tiny scroll feet, fitted low domed cover w/disk finial, twisted bail handle, engraved on the front w/"Crackers" enclosed by leafy flower sprigs, Rockford Silver Plate Co., No. 401, 6 1/4" d. (ILLUS.) **165**
Creamer & cov. sugar bowl, each w/shoulders embossed w/stylized flowers, the bodies etched w/floral swags, each w/the Pairpoint mark, 3" h., pr. **165**

Victorian Silver Plate Set

Creamer, cov. sugar & spooner, each w/a tapering cylindrical body bright-cut w/stylized flowers & leafy sprigs, flared mouth & angular handles, Meriden Britannia Co., No. 1800, ca. 1890, the set (ILLUS.).. **75**

Silver Plate Creamer & Sugar

Creamer & open sugar, slightly tapering lobed oval Classical shape w/overall hammered finish, delicate scroll handles, each 5 1/4" wide, 3 1/2" h., pr. (ILLUS.).......... **42**

Silver Plate Handled Cup

Cup, cylinder shape on flared base, repeating panels w/stylized floral design around rim & base, made by Rockford Silver Co., style number 288, 3 x 4 x 4 1/4" (ILLUS.) **45**

Silver Plate Ewer-form Cup

Cup, ewer form w/handle, bulbous lower part on rolled base & engraved "Florence 88," slightly flaring top third w/embossed birds & floral design, made by Meriden, style number 151, 2 1/2 x 3 1/2" (ILLUS.) **35**

Abstract Design Dish

Dish, abstract shape decorated w/molded flowers, bee & cicada, style number 524M, Simpson, Hall, Miller & Co., 4 1/2 x 6 1/4 x 7 1/2" (ILLUS.)........................ **325**

Oval Dish with Stamped Grapes

Dish, long shallow oval form w/boldly stamped clusters of grapes & leaves, Homan Silverplate Co., No. 1685T, patented in 1903, 6 3/4 x 11" (ILLUS.) **295**

Dish, long shallow oval form w/the wide border stamped w/an ornate grapevine design, indistinct mark, late 19th - early 20th c., 8 x 12 1/4" (ILLUS., top next page)........... **195**

Silver Plate Egg Cup

Egg cup, figural egg form, two-part, divided at center & engraved w/flowers, a figural chick & wishbone at the sides, chick head finial (ILLUS.) **179**

Pretty Dish with Grapevine Design

Egg server, comprising six egg cups w/reticulated bands, on banded circular feet, & a stand w/shaped rim, the central handle above twisted wire decoration, on four ball feet, England, late 19th - early 20th c., the set **230**

Silver Plate Four-lily Epergne

Epergne, four-lily, w/circular ringed base holding four removable metal trumpets, one rising straight up from center, others slanting out at angle at intervals, 11 1/2 x 11 1/2" (ILLUS.) **45**

Silver Plate Epergne

Epergne, in the form of a palm tree w/sinuous trunk and six palm fronds, w/a fox running at the circular, ringed base, topped w/a cranberry glass trumpet-shaped flower, 6 1/2" h. (ILLUS.) **1,495**

Fancy Miniature Silver Plate Frame

Frame, table model, miniature, ornately stamped rococo scrolls around the sides w/roses at the top corners, Gorham mark & number 350, late 19th - early 20th c., 3 3/4 x 5" (ILLUS.) **95**

Reed & Barton Goblet

Goblet, round stepped ringed base w/baluster-shape stem, decorated w/stylized flowers, scrolls & fans, style number 4702, Reed & Barton, 7" h. (ILLUS. on previous page) **65**

Hair receiver, cov., round, the cover w/an Art Nouveau design of repoussé florals, marked by the Pairpoint Mfg. Co., No. 7403, quadruple plate, 3 1/4" h. **77**

Art Nouveau Hairbrush

Hairbrush, Art Nouveau style, decorated at one end w/the head & shoulders of a woman in profile w/long flowing hair, heavily embossed w/floral & whiplash design, 1 3/4 x 2 1/4 x 7 1/4" (ILLUS.) **21**

Victorian Silver Plate Hairbrush

Hairbrush, tapering oval head decorated w/repoussé flowers & plants, swirl pattern on handle, Victorian, 3" w., 10" l. (ILLUS.) **18**

Hairbrush & Hand Mirror Set

Hairbrush & hand mirror set, Art Nouveau beveled design of roses & garlands, mirror measures 9 3/4" l., the set (ILLUS.) **125**

Old Silver Plate Hip Flask

Hip flask, flattened rectangular form w/rounded corners & hinged domed cap on spout, overall hammered finish w/engraved center shield, late 19th - early 20th c., 3 3/4 x 6" (ILLUS.) **65**

English Hot Water Kettle on Stand

Hot water kettle on stand, the squatty bulbous melon-lobed kettle w/high arched reeded swing handle & swan's-neck spout tilting in an ornate shell- and scroll-cast four-footed stand, w/burner, England, late 19th c., 14 1/2" h. (ILLUS.) **460**

Hot water urn, cov., urn-form body flanked by loop handles & fitted w/a warmer below, overall decoration of grapevines, American-made, ca. 1885, 10" d., 15" h. **280**

Hot water urn, cov., urn-form body flanked by two lion mask handles, raised on elongated shells, beadwork legs ending in claw feet, shaped cover, fitted on a round base w/warmer, American-made, ca. 1880, overall 17" h. **420**

Silver Plate Humidor

Humidor, cov., rectangular w/sides & lid decorated w/flowers & leaves, ball feet, lid topped w/applied spread-winged eagle on branch, made by Reed & Barton, style number 85, 4 3/4 x 5 3/4 x 6" (ILLUS.) **450**

Ice water set: cov. pitcher, goblet, footed bowl & tray; decorated w/scenes of people drawing water at a well, Reed & Barton, ca. 1880, pitcher 14 3/4" h., the set 403

Silver Plate Inkstand

Inkstand, oblong beaded-rim base holds square glass ink bottle w/silver lid & collar beside cat standing on hind legs, 2 1/4 x 3 1/2 x 4 1/2" (ILLUS.) 295

Silver Plate Devil Head Inkwell

Inkwell, cov., figural grinning devil head w/top of head hinged, resting on two legs & tip of goatee, w/glass insert, 2 1/2 x 3", 2 3/4" h. (ILLUS.) 110

Art Nouveau Jewelry Box

Jewelry box, cov., Art Nouveau style, decorated w/embossed decoration of maiden w/flowing hair standing next to a large rose, velvet lining, marked "Mermod and Jackson Jewelry Co. - Derby Silver Co. - 3464," 3 x 6 1/2 x 7" (ILLUS.) 595

Singing Bird Knife Rest

Knife rest, in the form of a singing bird perched on ball end of knife rest attached to scroll support that sits on round base w/floral detail, 2 x 2 3/4", 5" l. (ILLUS.) 235

Squirrel Knife Rest

Knife rest, rod supported at two ends by figures of squirrels holding acorns, bottom marked "Reed & Barton," style number 90, 1 3/4 x 1 7/8", 4 1/4" l. (ILLUS.) 245

Lion Knife Rest

Knife rest, rope twist shaft between two similar upright shafts, each held by rampant lion, stepped base embossed w/flowers, 2 x 2 3/8", 4" l. (ILLUS.) 275

Oaken Bucket Match Holder & Striker

Match holder, in the form of old oaken
bucket w/two branch handles on sides,
sitting on raised base ribbed for striking
matches, 4" l. (ILLUS.) **325**

Match Holder & Striker with Dog

Match holder & striker, in the form of a
hunting dog standing next to slightly flaring cylindrical holder w/openwork crown-
like top rim, made in Boston, style num-
ber 2692, 2 5/8 x 2 3/4 x 3" (ILLUS.) **295**
Meat dome, oval high domed shape w/top
loop handle, monogrammed "R," 18" l. **172**
Mirror plateau, tapered cylindrical sides
raised on three large scroll feet w/maiden
head knees, the rolled rim w/embossed
grape decoration, the base w/beading,
probably England, late 19th c., 17 1/4" d.,
4 1/2" h. **575**

Miniature Silver Plate Stirrup

Model of stirrup, miniature, brass w/plating,
marked "Eglentine," 1 1/4 w., 1 1/4" h.
(ILLUS.) **25**

Cockatoo Napkin Ring

Napkin ring, domed stepped circular base
holds cockatoo perched on stylized
branch, ring sits atop tail, marked "738,"
4" h. (ILLUS.) **595**

Bud Vase/Napkin Ring

Napkin ring, Egyptian Revival style, ring
engraved w/floral decoration and applied
busts of Egyptian-style women on either
side, their arms elongated to form feet of
napkin ring, a trumpet form bud base
mounted on top of ring, 5 5/8" h. (ILLUS.) **495**

Elaborate Horse & Cart Napkin Ring

Napkin ring, in the form of a two-wheeled cart pulled by a prancing horse, ring sits atop cart & is engraved w/leaves & flowers, marked "Meriden," style number 213, 1 3/4 x 2 1/2 x 3 1/4" (ILLUS.) **750**

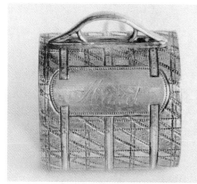

Valise Napkin Ring

Napkin ring, in the form of a valise complete w/strap handle and "Maud" engraved in rounded rectangular space on front, 1 3/4 x 2 x 2 1/4" (ILLUS.) **225**

Floral Motif Napkin Ring

Gnome Napkin Ring

Napkin ring, ring supported on either side on backs of two bearded gnomes w/splayed legs, 1 1/8 x 2 1/2 x 3 1/4" (ILLUS.) **65**

Cherub Napkin Ring

Napkin ring, round stepped base holds cherub w/head turned away shyly holding ring engraved "Father," made by Tufts, Boston, style number 1546, 2 1/2 x 3 x 3 3/4" (ILLUS.) **995**

Square Napkin Ring

Napkin ring, square shape, decorated w/applied cherub & stylized leaves, edges pierced w/scroll decoration, marked "RS & Co.," style 333, 1 7/8 x 2 7/8 x 3 1/2" (ILLUS. on previous page) **445**

Square Embossed Napkin Ring

Napkin ring, square, sides decorated with embossed birds & foliage, corners in form of knobbed pillars, 1 3/4" square, 2" h. (ILLUS.) **75**

Lion Napkin Ring

Napkin ring, stepped base holds reclining lion figure, ring rests on lion's back and is engraved with "HEP" and floral motifs, 1 1/4 x 2 1/4 x 2 1/2" (ILLUS.) **475**

Triangular Napkin Ring

Napkin ring, triangular shape on claw-and-ball feet, w/pierced floral rims and crossed wishbones forming a border around engraved leaf frond decoration & "Best Wishes," made by Meriden, style number 630, 1 7/8 x 2 3/8 x 3" (ILLUS.) **175**

Triangular Bee Napkin Ring

Napkin ring, triangular, w/simulated hammered surface decorated w/embossed bee, unadorned edges, 1 3/4 x 2" (ILLUS.) **125**

Oriental Motif Napkin Ring

Napkin ring, w/knob feet & applied fan decoration engraved w/Oriental motifs & "Mother," marked indistinctly, 2 x 2 x 2 3/4" (ILLUS.) **90**

Elaborate Napkin Ring Holder

Napkin ring holder, in the form of a chariot w/head of woman on front, pierced wheels & edge trim in stylized floral motif, handle curves over holder & ends in form of curving feather, also holds small butter plate, pepper cellar & salt dish, marked "Racine Silver Plate Co.," 4 3/4 x 7", 7" h. (ILLUS. on previous page) **1,450**

Nut Dish with Squirrel

Nut dish, oval bowl in the form of sectioned petals creating scalloped rim, on triangular-shaped feet decorated w/flowers, applied figure of squirrel sits on branch curving over inside of bowl, marked on bottom w/indistinct style number, 6 1/2 x 8" (ILLUS.) **225**

Nut or Candy Dish

Nut or candy dish, oval petal design, style number 839, Pairpoint, 5 x 8 3/4" (ILLUS.) **32**

Leprechaun Paperweight

Paperweight, round domed base decorated in stylized oak leaves, acorns & flowers holds mushroom on which hatted leprechaun sits, marked "Reed & Barton," 3" h. (ILLUS.) **250**

Silver Plate Pipe Holder

Pipe holder, holder sits on flaring rimmed base decorated w/applied leaves & flowers, two flowers applied to edge of holder to keep pipe in place, marked "Warranted," indistinct style number, 2 1/2 x 2 1/2 x 3 1/2" (ILLUS.) **295**

Pitcher, character-type w/grotesque face, Reed & Barton, late 19th c., 6 3/4" h. **86**

Pitcher, chased acorn branch design below an acorn leaf border, lobed foot w/acorn leaf design, grotesque face under spout, American-made, ca. 1855, 11 1/2" h. **489**

Pitcher & bowl set, Art Nouveau style, the baluster-form pitcher w/a tall neck & upright pointed spout, a looped high whiplash handle & spreading round foot, chased w/two female profile busts, tulips & whiplash designs, the bowl w/a wide flaring rim chased w/tulips & whiplash leaves, both impressed "Anezin Hnos & Cia," Europe, early 20th c., bowl 18" d., pitcher 18 1/2" h. **287**

Pitchers, water, bulbous form, engraved w/foliage & flowerheads, cast w/a ruffled C-scroll spout & leaf-capped C-scroll handle, the domed cover w/a swirled knop, Toronto Silver Plate Co., Canada, 10 1/2" h., pr. **373**

Platter, oval, the shaped rim gadrooned , w/an engraved crest & coat-of-arms, probably England, late 19th - early 20th c., 12 3/4 x 17 1/2" **144**

Platter, round w/shaped rim embossed w/foliate & scroll designs w/devil's head medallions, central foliate designs surrounding an engraved coat-of-arms, on three embossed foliate feet, Ellis-Barker, Birmingham, England, late 19th c. **690**

Punch set: bowl on fitted stand & six goblets; each decorated w/flowers, Meriden Britannia Co., ca. 1880, bowl & stand 16" h., the set **690**

Ring Bowl with Bird

Ring bowl, undecorated bowl sits on branch, bird w/spread wings & holding ring in its beak perches on branch applied to side of bowl, 4 x 4 x 4 1/2" (ILLUS.) **350**

Heart-shaped Ring Box

Ring box, cov., in the form of a heart-shaped lock, decorated w/a key & engraved on top "Love laughs at locks," pierced sides, 1 x 3 1/4 x 4 1/2" (ILLUS.) **175**

Footed Safety Pin Holder

Safety pin holder, cov., rectangular, footed, decorated on top w/leaf garland design, engraved shape of safety pin & "Baby's Friend," raised scrollwork decoration on sides, 3/4 x 1 5/8 x 3 1/4" (ILLUS.) **125**

Victorian Salt Cellar with Sphinx

Salt cellar, a round dish perched atop three small figural sphinx feet, late 19th c., 3" d., 1 1/2" h. (ILLUS.) **40**

Silver Plate Salt Cellar

Salt cellar, in the form of a dolphin carrying a shell on its back, rimmed base w/design depicting ocean waves, handle in the form of a ribbed leaf, 2 x 2 3/4 x 4 1/2" (ILLUS.) **275**

Silver Plate Dolphin & Shell Salt Cellar

Salt cellar, in the form of a stylized dolphin carrying a shell on its tail, rimmed base, 2 1/2 x 3 x 4" (ILLUS.) **275**

Silver Plate Salt Dispenser

Salt dispenser, footed urn form, engraved "Salt" on front, w/special spring-loaded plunger for dispensing salt through bottom, marked "Rasnik Co.," 3 1/2" h. (ILLUS.) **49**

Modern Egg-shaped Shakers

Salt & pepper shakers, egg-shaped, rubber stoppers in base, 20th c., 3" h., pr. (ILLUS.) **10**

Sauceboats, oval foot w/gadrooned bands supporting the oval boat-shaped bowl w/high, wide arched spout & high looped handle, decorated in the late Georgian taste w/overall repoussé flowers & shellwork, Tiffany & Co., New York, late 19th c., 7 3/4" l., pr. **748**

Serving dish, cov., double, a rectangular two-section dish w/a flanged rim w/gadrooned borders & shells & foliage, raised on curved paw feet, turned faux ivory end handles, removable wells w/domed rectangular covers, crown mark w/"C.S.C." & stars, late 19th - early 20th c., 12 1/2 x 20 1/2", 7 1/4" h. **248**

Serving dish, cov., flat-bottomed oval base w/wide flanged rim, flat-topped domed cover w/angled loop handles, hand-hammered surface, by Meriden, No. 2210, late 19th - early 20th c., 8 1/2 x 11" (ILLUS., below) **75**

Sewing Accessories Holder

Sewing accessories holder, in the form of a giant thimble balanced on scissors & needles that sit on round stepped base, made by Tufts, Boston, style number 2603, 9" h. (ILLUS.) **350**

Serving Dish with Hammered Decor

Aluminum

Art Deco style cast-aluminum ashtray with a stylized Airedale on rim, 5 1/8" long, $65.

Courtesy of John Kruesel, Rochester, Minn.

Table crumber set with tray and scraper decorated with roses, by Everlast, $27-35.

Courtesy of Dannie Woodard, Weatherford, Texas

Unique Art Deco aluminum punch bowl, underplate and ladle with a modern geometric decoration, by Laird, $405-475.

Courtesy of Dannie Woodard, Weatherford, Texas

Left: Large 12"-tall aluminum vase with zinnia decoration, by Wendell August, $275-300.

Above: Small fish-shaped aluminum dish with old circular Everlast mark, $25-40.

Right: Aluminum wastebasket in the embossed Apple pattern, by Everlast, $75.

Courtesy of Dannie Woodard, Weatherford, Texas.

Aluminum

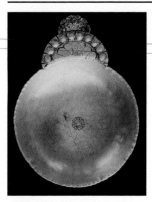

Left: Unique round nut dish with punched design and tab handle, by Florence Kimbell, $30-40.

Courtesy of
Dannie Woodard,
Weatherford, Texas

Oval upright aluminum pitcher with artist-signed floral design, Canterbury Arts, $75.

Courtesy of Dannie Woodard,
Weatherford, Texas

Rare all-aluminum patio cart with hammered intaglio leaf decoration, complete with all serving pieces, $650.

Courtesy of Dannie Woodard, Weatherford, Texas

Cast-aluminum turtle-shaped corkscrew with worn paint, 4 1/4" long, $95.

Courtesy of R. and K.
Townsend, Rochester, Minn.

Left: Aluminum silent butler with embossed Fern & Berry pattern, by Canterbury Arts, $27-35.

Right: Ovoid silent butler with scalloped rim and lily and leaf design on cover, by Everlast, $25.

Courtesy of
Dannie Woodard,
Weatherford, Texas

Brass

Above: Very early brass book-shaped box with engraved Biblical scenes, the interior divided into two sections, Europe, ca. 1750, 2 1/2 x 4 3/4", $1,500.

Left: Late Victorian cast-brass easel-form picture frame in the form of the Masonic emblem, patent-dated in 1899, 7 x 9 5/8", $145.

Photos courtesy of John Kruesel, Rochester, Minn.

Right: Pair of stamped brass candleholders marked on the bottom "Gorham Giftware L17," 3 3/4" high, $40.

Courtesy of Jim and Dorothy Bernatz, Rochester, Minn.

Unique Victorian cast-brass hanging paper clamp in the form of a mallard duck head with original paint and glass eyes, 5" long, $125.

Courtesy of John Kruesel, Rochester, Minn.

Left: Ornate late Victorian cast-brass mirror featuring a cherub on each side, goldtone finish, 8 x 12 1/4", $165.

Courtesy of John Kruesel, Rochester, Minn.

Oval stamped-brass late Victorian frame with scroll ends, 6 1/4 x 10 1/4", $65.

Courtesy of John Kruesel, Rochester, Minn.

Bronze

*Cast-bronze model of Airedale,
4" long, $90.*

Courtesy of John Kruesel,
Rochester, Minn.

*Art Nouveau style cast-
bronze dish with the fig-
ure of a nude woman
standing in billowing
surf, marked on the
back "EXTRA,"
5 x 7", $300.*
Courtesy of R. and K.
Townsend, Rochester,
Minn.

*Cast-bronze elephant-shaped
paperweight advertising Milk Bone
dog biscuits, 5" long, $250.*
Courtesy of R. and K. Townsend,
Rochester, Minn.

Chrome

Compote with chrome nude lady stem supporting an amber glass dish, Farber Brothers mark, 5 1/2 x 7 1/2", $125-150.

Courtesy of Judy and George Swan, Dubuque, Iowa

Candlesticks with clear glass sockets in pierced chrome bases, Krome Kraft by Farber Brothers, 4 3/4" high, pair $80-90.

Courtesy of Judy and George Swan, Dubuque, Iowa

Ice bucket in dark emerald green glass within a chrome frame, Farber Brothers, 6" high, $75-100.

Courtesy of Judy and George Swan, Dubuque, Iowa

Above: Bulbous green glass and chrome salt and pepper shakers, Farber Brothers, 3 1/2" high, pair $20-25.

Left: Chrome and glass cocktail glass with purple glass bowl, by Farber Brothers, 5 3/8" high, $25-30.

Courtesy of Judy and George Swan, Dubuque, Iowa

Copper

Hand-made copper funnel with spring-loaded brass thumb control, marked "Patent Allowed," 5 1/2 x 7 3/4", 8" long, $85.

Courtesy of Jim and Dorothy Bernatz, Rochester, Minn.

Late 19th-early 20th century copper coffeepot with white metal handle, spout and shoulder band, indistinct mark, 10" high, $45.

Courtesy of John Kruesel, Rochester, Minn.

Iron

Cast-iron bottle opener in the form of a parrot on a perch, original paint, 5" high, $95.
Courtesy of R. and K. Townsend, Rochester, Minn.

Cast-iron hanging paper clamp in the form of a laughing black man, numbered on the back "5247," ca. 1900, 4" high, $125.
Courtesy of Mark Moran, Rochester, Minn.

Unique cast-iron wall-hanging fraternal order emblem for the Modern Woodmen of America, with original paint, late 19th-early 20th century 7 3/4 x 12 1/4", $400.
Courtesy of Mom's Antique Mall, Oronoco, Minn.

Cast-iron sad iron trivet marked by the Cleveland Foundry Company, old black paint, 4 1/2 x 6", $25.
Courtesy of Mark Moran, Rochester, Minn.

Below: Cast-iron rooster-shaped windmill weight with original worn paint, ca. 1900, 17 x 18", on a later stand, $2,400.
Courtesy of Jim and Dorothy Bernatz, Rochester, Minn.

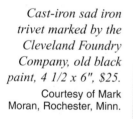

Cast-iron sad iron trivet marked by the Enterprise Mfg. Co. with a script "E" in the center, 4 1/2 x 6 1/8", $25.
Courtesy of Mark Moran, Rochester, Minn.

Cast-iron toy surrey with fringe on top, complete and with original paint, marked "Stanley Toys," 11 3/4" long, $295.
Courtesy of R. and K. Townsend, Rochester, Minn.

Lead

Small cast-lead statue of a nude
boy checking the bottom of his foot,
4 3/4" high, $35.
Courtesy of R. and K. Townsend,
Rochester, Minn.

Silver

*Left: Lovely English sterling silver egg
cup stand with tall scroll-pierced center
handle and scroll feet, complete with
six pierced egg cups, late 19th-early
20th century, overall 9" tall, $2,495.*
Courtesy of Mark Moran, Rochester, Minn.

*Miniature silver stork pulling a cart
driven by a small boy, worn marks,
Europe, late 19th-early 20th century,
3" long, $795.*
Courtesy of Mark Moran, Rochester, Minn.

*Miniature model of a bull,
serves as a holder for dessert
skewers, Europe, late 19th-early
20th century, 3 1/2" long, $260.*
Courtesy of Mark Moran,
Rochester, Minn.

Silver

From left: Mary, Queen of Scots is featured on the handle of this ornate silver serving spoon, the bowl engraved with the original owner's initials, stamped "800," Europe, late 19th-early 20th century, 10 1/2" long, $645. Large silver serving spoon featuring figure of Napoleon Bonaparte on the handle above an imperial eagle and Napoleon's monogram in the bowl, Europe, late 19th-early 20th century, 10 1/2" long, $550. Large silver serving spoon with a figure of Henry VIII of England forming the handle, stamped "800," Europe, early 20th century, 9 1/4" long, $525. Large silver serving spoon with a figure of Frederick the Great, King of Prussia, forming the handle, Europe, late 19th-early 20th century, 11" long, $595. Large silver serving spoon with a figural handle of a standing Victorian woman holding a rose, musical instruments and sheet music in the bowl, stamped "800," Europe, late 19-early 20th century, 11 1/4" long, $595.

Courtesy of Mark Moran, Rochester, Minn.

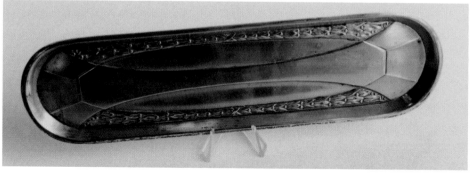

Oval silver tray with a stylized Art Deco design, marked,
Europe, ca. 1930s, 3 x 10 1/2", $85.

Courtesy of R. and K. Townsend, Rochester, Minn.

Silver

Unique silver jewelry box in the shape of a tortoise with a real shell lid, artist-signed, Europe, late 19th-early 20th century, 5 1/4 x 7 1/2", $495.

Courtesy of Mark Moran, Rochester, Minn.

Sterling silver figural pig pincushion, Birmingham, England, ca. 1905, 3 3/8" long, $395.

Courtesy of Mark Moran, Rochester, Minn.

Miniature silver crown topped by a cross and featuring engraved decoration, Europe, late 19th-early 20th century, 2" high, $225.

Courtesy of R. and K. Townsend, Rochester, Minn.

Silver inkstand with an embossed Oriental scene on top, opens to two wells and a pen rest, Europe, late 19th-early 20th century, 3 1/2 x 5", $295.

Courtesy of Mark Moran, Rochester, Minn.

Figural silver pheasant made as a perfume container with a removable head, trimmed with blue enamel, Europe, 5 7/8" long, $395.

Courtesy of Mark Moran, Rochester, Minn.

Miniature book with floral-decorated sterling silver covers, Dickens' "A Christmas Carol," worn English hallmarks dated 1904, 1 1/8 x 2 1/8", $165.

Courtesy of Mark Moran, Rochester, Minn.

Silver Plate

Right: Victorian bud vase with a fancy silver plate holder featuring a standing crane beside a palm tree supporting a shaded cranberry glass vase, overall 13 1/2" high, $1,295.
Courtesy of R. and K. Townsend, Rochester, Minn.

Late Victorian silver plate tobacco humidor with three crossed pipes on the cover and an applied band of flowers and scrolls around the base, mark of E.G. Webster & Son, No. 431, 5 1/4" diameter, 4 5/8" high, $85.
Courtesy of John Kruesel, Rochester, Minn.

Long oval silver plate serving dish with grape clusters and leaves in bold relief, Homan Silverplate Co., patented Dec. 22, 1903, 6 3/4 x 11", $295.
Courtesy of R. and K. Townsend, Rochester, Minn.

Victorian silver plate compote with a wide rolled rim ornately stamped with blossoms and swags, Wilcox Silver Plate Co., No. 819, 9 1/2" diameter, 5 3/4" high, $125.
Courtesy of Mark Moran, Rochester, Minn.

Late Victorian silver plate bulbous cracker jar with engraved flowers and leaves around the word "Crackers," Rockford Silverplate Co., style number 401, 6 1/4" diameter, 6" high plus handle, $165.
Courtesy of John Kruesel, Rochester, Minn.

Silver Plate

Left: Victorian double bud vase in an ornate domed silver plate base with scrolling griffins supporting blown pale yellowish glass vases, overall 9 3/4" high, $1,350.
Courtesy of R. and K. Townsend, Rochester, Minn.

Miniature silver plate picture frame featuring ornate stamped rococo scrolls, marked with a Gorham mark, ca. 1900, 3 3/4 x 5", $95.
Courtesy of John Kruesel, Rochester, Minn.

Victorian three-piece silver plate tea set with a spoon holder, covered sugar and creamer, Meriden Silver Plate Co., No. 1800, the set $75.
Courtesy of John Kruesel, Rochester, Minn.

Right: Simple two-light candleholder in silver plate marked on the base "Her Majesty - 1847 - Rogers Bros - 009056 - I.S.," 10 7/8" wide, 6 3/4" high, 20th century, per pair $200.
Courtesy of Jim and Dorothy Bernatz, Rochester, Minn.

Left: Silver plate candelabrum with embossed bands of roses and scrolls, Ballad Community, early 20th century, 9" wide, 6 1/8" high, per pair $170.
Courtesy of Jim and Dorothy Bernatz, Rochester, Minn.

Spelter

Fancy Art Nouveau spelter jewelry box
featuring a reclining putto among scrolls
and flowers on the cover, scrolling vines and
flowers around the side, gold finish, lined
with fabric, early 20th century,
4 1/2 x 6 1/4", 4 1/4" high, $275.
Courtesy of R. and K. Townsend, Rochester, Minn.

Unusual spelter three-handle
souvenir cup with the embossed
date "October 3, 1899," figural
dragon handles, 5" wide, 4" high,
$150.
Courtesy of R. and K. Townsend,
Rochester, Minn.

Figural spelter book end
featuring a laughing musketeer, marked on the back
"Artbronz - Copyright KB.
W.," broken sword and surface cracks, 8 1/2" high,
per pair $60.
Courtesy of Mark Moran,
Rochester, Minn.

Above: Little spelter
box featuring a
seated dog drinking
from a wine flask on
the cover, painted
gold surface, early
20th century, 3 1/2"
high, $95.
Courtesy of Mom's Antique
Mall, Oronoco, Minn.

Right: Art Nouveau
style spelter jewelry
box with a cherub and
flowers on the cover,
gold finish, marked on
base "NB Rogers SP Co. -
5," ca. 1910, 3 x 4 1/2",
2 3/4" high, $50.
Courtesy of Mark Moran,
Rochester, Minn.

Steel

Small cylindrical steel box with a tiny figural Scottie dog handle and Scottie feet, original pale green paint, No. 3442, 3 1/2" wide, 4 1/4" high, $175.

Courtesy of R. and K. Townsend, Rochester, Minn.

Tin and Tole

Early punched-tin Paul Revere-style candle lantern, early 19th century, 5 1/2" diameter, 16 1/2" high, $500.

Courtesy of John Kruesel, Rochester, Minn.

Stamped tole spice canister set in rectangular basket tray, original worn japanned surface, tray 5 3/8 x 8", late 19th-early 20th century, the set $95.

Courtesy of Mom's Antiques Mall, Oronoco, Minn.

Early tin flour scoop with soldered construction, 9 1/2" long, $15.

Courtesy of Mark Moran, Rochester, Minn.

Left: Commemorative tin canteen with inset copper medallions on each side referring to the 26th Grand Annual Encampment of the Grand Army of the Republic, Washington, D.C., 1892, 4 3/8 x 5", $260.

Courtesy of John Kruesel, Rochester, Minn.

Left: Graduated set of tin pitcher-form measures with the seal of the State of Minnesota Railroad and Warehouse Commission, tallest 6 5/8" high, the set $125.

Photos courtesy of John Kruesel, Rochester, Minn.

Metal Medley

Late 19th century cast-iron match holder in the form of a woman's high-top boot, original worn paint, 5 1/2" high, $75.
Courtesy of Mom's Antique Mall, Oronoco, Minn.

Delicate stamped-brass Victorian frame with an openwork flowering vine design, 5 x 8 1/4", $58.
Courtesy of John Kruesel, Rochester, Minn.

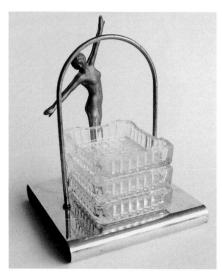

Art Deco style chrome ashtray stand with three clear glass ashtrays in front of a cast, gold-painted figure of a nude woman, 5" square, 6 3/4" high, the set $85.
Courtesy of R. and K. Townsend, Rochester, Minn.

Right: Hammered aluminum wastebasket featuring over-all floral bouquet decoration, signed in the pattern "CC Pflantz," by Canterbury Arts, $195.

Courtesy of Dannie Woodard, Weatherford, Texas

Left: Simple covered silver plate serving dish with an overall hammered finish, Meriden Silver Plate Co., No. 2210, 8 1/4 x 11", $75.
Courtesy of R. and K. Townsend, Rochester, Minn.

Metal Medley

Cast-iron woodpecker-shaped doorknocker with original worn paint, 2 1/2 x 3 3/4", $165.

Courtesy of Mom's Antique Mall, Oronoco, Minn.

Simple Modernist design silver plate bowl by International Silver, 20th century, 6 1/2" wide, $25.

Courtesy of R. and K. Townsend, Rochester, Minn.

Cast-iron book end with an Airedale and Scottie standing among tree roots, dull copper finish, 4 1/2 x 5 1/4", the pair $130.

Courtesy of John Kruesel, Rochester, Minn.

Left: Victorian silver plate bud vase holder featuring a kneeling girl at the base below long leaves supporting a shaded green to clear glass bud vase with gold decoration, the base marked by the Meriden Silver Plate Co., overall 9 1/2" high, $300.

Courtesy of R. and K. Townsend, Rochester, Minn.

Right: Dark green glass server with a chrome collar and hinged cover, 10" high, $125-150.

Courtesy of Judy and George Swan, Dubuque, Iowa

Cast-iron toy ice wagon and horse with original paint, early 20th century, 8 1/4" long, $395.

Courtesy of R. and K. Townsend, Rochester, Minn.

Metal Medley

Standing Airedale cast-iron doorstop with traces of original paint, 8 5/8" long, 8" high, $300.

Courtesy of
John Kruesel,
Rochester, Minn.

Spelter bank in the form of a John Deere tractor, copper finish, third edition from the Deere Credit Union series, 6" long, 3 1/4" high, $60.

Courtesy of Jim and Dorothy Bernatz,
Rochester, Minn.

Green opaline glass bud vase supported in a fancy silver plate holder featuring a pair of hippocampus at the base, the holder marked by Reed & Barton, No. 2230, ca. 1875-90, overall 11 3/4" high, $695.

Courtesy of R. and K.
Townsend, Rochester, Minn.

Above: Unique Victorian silver plate vase holder featuring figures of a rooster and hen, holding an early amethyst enamel-decorated bud vase, overall 6 1/4" high, $445.

Right: Miniature silver Victorian-style side chair with a pierced back and a pincushion seat, probably Birmingham, England, early 20th century, 2" high, $175.

Photos courtesy of R. and K.
Townsend, Rochester, Minn.

Ornate pierced and scroll-trimmed large serving spoon with a scene of Moses in the center of the bowl and dragons flanking the base of the handle, Europe, late 19th-early 20th century, 12" long, $750.

Courtesy of Mark Moran,
Rochester, Minn.

Silver Plate Sewing Box

Sewing box, in the form of a suitcase w/mesh strap handle, opens from either side, each heavily decorated w/raised scroll & floral designs, 1 3/8 x 2 1/2", 4" l. (ILLUS.) **95**

Shaving Mirror & Holder

Shaving mirror & holder, lid unfolds to become mirror attached to flared cylindrical holder base w/engraved decoration for soap & shaving brush, marked "Patented Jan. 18, 1910," size closed 3 1/2 x 6 1/4 x 6 3/4" (ILLUS.) **165**

Trumpet-form Shot Cup

Shot cup, trumpet form engraved "AD" on flared base w/leaf pattern, marked "CGH & Co.," 3" h. (ILLUS.) **35**

Owl Smoking Accessory

Smoking accessory, consisting of figure of owl on branch attached to three hollow tree stumps w/removable inserts for holding cigarettes, matches & ashes, 5 x 7 x 7 1/2" (ILLUS.) **750**

Four-prong Plated Spool Holder

Spool holder, rounded triangular footed base w/raised rim ornately decorated, center holds four knobbed prongs for spools, Meriden, No. 2110, 2 1/8 x 5" (ILLUS.) **145**

Silver Plate Spoon Holder

Spoon holder, narrow oblong shape w/pierced leafy scroll sections at each end, upright angled strap handles, 1 3/4 x 8", 3" h. (ILLUS.) **35**

Silver Plate Stamp Box

Stamp box, cov., rectangular, embossed "U.S. Mail" on top, w/floral design border and sides, 5/8 x 1 3/4 x 2" (ILLUS.) **125**

Cufflink Box

Stud box, cov., round, footed, decorated w/applied flowers, silver stud on lid, marked on bottom "W.B. Mfg. Co. - No. 2503," 2 1/4 x 3" (ILLUS.) **145**

Rectangular Stud or Cufflink Box

Stud/cufflink box, cov., rectangular, sides decorated w/scrollwork, top engraved "Here's Your," w/small doorknob-style handle in lower right corner, short ball feet, made by Homan Mfg. Co., 1 1/4 x 2 x 2 3/8" (ILLUS.) **145**

Round Stud or Cufflink Box

Stud/cufflink box, cov., round, lid impressed "Oh Joy Here It Is," short ball feet, maker's mark indistinct, 2 1/4 x 2 3/4" (ILLUS.) **145**

Basketweave Stud Box

Stud/cufflink box, cov., round, sides w/basketweave design, applied silver stud on lid, marked "Superior Silver Co - 120," 2 x 2 1/2" (ILLUS.) **145**

Ornate Silver Plate Sugar & Liner

Sugar bowl, cover & liner, ornate silver plate stand w/open sides below a land-scape-stamped rim band w/squared side handles over scrolled panels alternating w/leaf-stamped scalloped panels above the scroll-trimmed short pedestal on a round flared foot, fitted w/a blue Inverted Thumbprint patt. blown glass insert fitted w/a domed silver plate cover w/fanned fini-al, late 19th c., 5" d., 8 3/4" h. (ILLUS. on previous page)... **395**

Decorative Basket with Glass Liner

Sweetmeat basket, flaring reticulated body w/long narrow ovals decorated w/hat-form bosses w/ribbon & basket trim, twisted rope bands around the base & reeded rim, arched swing bail handle, co-balt blue glass liner, probably Europe, late 19th - early 20th c., resilvered, 6 1/2" d., 7 1/8" h. (ILLUS.) **175**

Victorian Syrup Pitcher

Syrup pitcher, cov., flared base, body w/engraved scrollwork, tapering at top, flared rim, tapering cylindrical lid topped w/head of woman, thumbpiece on handle also head of woman, marked "Manning Bowman & Co. - 767," w/patent dates of 1865 & 1873, 8" h. (ILLUS.)........................... **495**

American Silver Plate Syrup Pitcher

Syrup pitcher, cov., footed bulbous ovoid body decorated w/large repoussé blos-soms & leaves & tapering to a plain flared neck w/ruffled rim & hinged flower-em-bossed cover w/knob finial, angled han-dle, Wilcox Silver Plating Co., late 19th c., 4" d., 4 1/2" h. (ILLUS.) **95**

Tantalus, marked "Grinsell's Patent," for three decanters, rectangular tray on four bun feet, handle w/circular rod supports w/plain ball knops, inverted thistle-cut glass decanters w/quadripartite place neck collars & circular prism-cut stop-pers, w/three associated bottle labels, two sterling, one plated, late 19th c. (crack to one decanter) **374**

Tantalus set, a silver plate rectangular tray on four bun feet, the handle w/circular rod supports w/plain ball knops, holds three glass decanters w/inverted thistle-cut de-signs & quadripartite plated neck collars & circular prism-cut stoppers, w/three as-sociated bottle labels, marked "Grinsell's Patent," England, late 19th c., the set........... **489**

Tea & coffee service: cov. coffeepot, cov. teapot, cov. sugar bowl, creamer & relat-ed tray; each piece of a simple, Classical, tall urn-form w/domed cover & button fin-ial, swan's-neck spout & high angled handles, oblong tray w/cast loop end handles, American-made, 20th c., cof-feepot 10 5/8" h., the set **220**

Tea & coffee service: cov. teapot, cov. cof-feepot, creamer, cov. sugar bowl & tray; Art Deco style, each of faceted globular form w/angular handles, the tray w/ten curved sides & rounded handles, de-signed by Maurice Dufrene, Christofle, France, ca. 1925, tray 10" l., the set **2,300**

Tea & coffee service: cov. teapot, cov. coffeepot, creamer, handled cov. sugar
bowl, waste bowl & oval tray; each piece
of flaring chamfered rectangular section
w/pendent bellflowers at each corner, the
shaped tray w/cut-out handles at each
end, engraved w/a monogram, Gorham
Mfg. Co., Providence, Rhode Island, 20th
c., tray 23" l., the set 345

Tea & coffee service: 18" h. cov. hot water
urn w/double handles, cov. 10" h. coffeepot, cov. 11" h. teapot, 8 1/2" h. cov. sugar bowl & 6" h. creamer; all w/acanthus
leaf legs, the bodies etched w/meadow
flowers, leaves & grasses, the urn w/a
spout & ivory handle marked "Patent Jan.
1869," Meriden Britannia Company, the
set 688

Silver Plate Tea & Coffee Set

Tea & coffee set: cov. teapot, cov. coffeepot, cov. hot water kettle, milk pitcher,
cov. sugar, creamer, waste bowl & tray; a
Classical form paneled body w/etched
floral design, tray w/double handles, Barbour Silver Co., patt. #5314, ca. 1895
(ILLUS.) 952

Tea & coffee set: cov. teapot, cov. coffeepot, kettle on stand, open sugar & creamer w/a similar pair of sugar tongs; each
w/a tapering ovoid body, ivory kettle handle, horn heat stops & wooden finials,
G.&S., London, England, 19th c., the set 288

Tea set: cov. teapot, cov. coffeepot, open
sugar & creamer w/large similar oval tray;
each piece w/a bulbous ovoid body
raised on a short pedestal base, coffeepot & creamer w/tall trumpet necks, each
piece w/high upright loop handles, ornately engraved rococo designs, marked
"J.B. & S. - EP - H.W.," probably
English, ca. 1855, the set 1,100

Tea set: cov. teapot, cov. sugar bowl,
creamer & spooner; each w/a tall bulbous
body tapering to a flared & cupped rim,
each raised on four tall outswept animal
leg feet, ornate angular handles, the
body w/a band of decorative engraving,
pointed cover w/handled urn-form finials,
marked "Quadruple Plate - Wilcox Silver
Co.," ca. 1875-80, teapot 12" h., the set
(plating worn) 138

Tea tray, rectangular, repoussé border,
w/end handles, 19th c., overall 31 3/4" l. 345

Tea tray, scalloped molded rim w/reticulat-
ed sides, the interior engraved w/foliate &
scroll designs, Germany, 19th c.,
18 3/4 x 23" 230

Teakettle on stand, squat bulbous body
w/beaded rim & flower finial on the cover,
an upright scroll handle, a plain body, the
stand w/cast foliate swags & four scroll
legs w/shell feet, Shreve, Stanwood &
Co., Boston, 1860-69, 11" h., the set 288

Attractive Silver Plate Teapot

Teapot, cov., round foot below the wide
squatty bulbous body tapering to a short
flared neck w/a domed hinged cover,
leafy scroll-trimmed spout & C-scroll handle, marked on bottom "Silver on Copper
[crown] S [shield]," probably England,
late 19th - early 20th c., 8" h. (ILLUS.) 100

Tennis Motif Toast Rack

Toast rack, w/seven pairs of crossed tennis
rackets attached to rectangular open
footed base to hold toast, ring handle at
top, 3 1/2 x 5 1/4", 5 1/4" h. (ILLUS.) 295

English Silver Plated Toast Rack

Toast rack, golf motif, a rectangular tray base w/scalloped edge mounted w/five pairs of crossed golf clubs to form the rack, a ring handle at the top, on small feet, resilvered, England, late 19th - early 20th c., 3 1/2 x 5 1/4", 5 1/4" h. (ILLUS. on previous page) **295**

Victorian Silver Plate Humidor

Tobacco humidor, wide round foot below the wide squatty ringed body w/an applied band of flowers & scrolls, low domed cover fitted w/three long figural crossed pipes, Webster & Sons mark, No. 431, late 19th - early 20th c., 5 1/4" d., 4 5/8" h. (ILLUS.)............ **85**

Hissing Cat Toothpick Holder

Toothpick holder, figural, form of a hissing cat w/raised tail stands next to cylinder-shaped holder decorated w/landscapes & flowers, marked on bottom "Tufts - 3411," 2 x 2 1/4 x 2 3/4" (ILLUS.) **350**

Bulldog Toothpick Holder

Toothpick holder, figural, growling bulldog sits next to holder w/fluted flaring rim, bottom marked "Derby Silverplate Co., - 2306," 2 1/8 x 2 3/4 x 3 1/2" (ILLUS.)............ **295**

Souvenir Toothpick Holder

Toothpick holder, figural, in the form of a cherub on pierced floral base, carrying an egg-shaped holder w/pierced floral-decorated edge, front of holder engraved "Souvenir of Spokane, Wash.," 2 1/8 x 3 1/2" (ILLUS.) **175**

Figural Dolphin Toothpick Holder

Toothpick holder, figural, modeled as a dolphin standing on its tail w/its mouth wide open, scrolled wave base, late 19th c., 2 1/2" h. (ILLUS. on previous page) **235**

Monkey Toothpick Holder

Toothpick holder, figural, round stepped base holds figure of monkey holding staff & carrying on its back a basket w/basketweave decoration & rope twist rim, Meriden, 3 1/3" h. (ILLUS.) **550**

Umbrella Toothpick Holder

Toothpick holder, figure of boy sitting atop turtle & holding reins in one hand & umbrella in the other, the umbrella covered w/holes to insert toothpicks, 4 1/2" h. (ILLUS.) **995**

Toothpick Holder on Fluted Base

Toothpick holder, in form of bag w/drawstring top sitting on fluted base that also holds form of rat gnawing on bag, bag engraved "This is the rat that ate the malt," Pairpoint, style 3708, 3" h. (ILLUS.) **175**

Billy Goat Toothpick Holder

Toothpick holder, in the form of a billy goat next to a large sack w/flared rim, Meriden, 2 1/4 x 2 3/4 x 3" (ILLUS.) **375**

Sheaf of Wheat Toothpick Holder

Toothpick holder, in the form of a hollowed sheaf of wheat, beside which stands a hatted boy holding scythe, 3 1/2" h. (ILLUS.) 345

Porcupine Toothpick Holder

Toothpick holder, in the form of a porcupine w/holes in body for toothpicks, which look like quills when inserted, on octagonal base, marked on bottom "Meriden," 3 1/4" l. (ILLUS.) 195

Rabbit Toothpick Holder

Toothpick holder, in the form of a rabbit crouching under foliage next to stump, which holds toothpicks, marked on bottom "Simpson, Hall Miller & Co. - 33," 2 1/8 x 2 1/2 x 2 3/4" (ILLUS.) 375

Peek A Boo Toothpick Holder

Toothpick holder, leaf-shape base holds cherub peeking around side of bellflower, which holds toothpicks, w/fluted flaring rim & engraved on side "Peek A Boo," 2 1/8 x 2 1/4 x 2 1/2" (ILLUS.) 225

Hen & Barrel Toothpick Holder

Toothpick holder, rectangular base holds figure of hen peeking around bulbous wooden open barrel, bottom marked "Aurora - 332," 2 x 2 1/4 x 3" (ILLUS.) 325

Pan-Pacific Expo Tray

Tray, commemorating the 1915 Pan-Pacific Expo in San Francisco, raised rim embossed "San Francisco - 1915" & center embossed w/image of North & South America and ships sailing through Panama Canal, 1/2" deep, 5" d. (ILLUS.) 55

Tray, oval, handled, a gallery rim w/end handles & pierce work, geometric designs on the top, on four compressed ball feet, silver over copper, mark of Ellis-Barker Silver Companies, late 19th - early 20th c., 14 1/2 x 22" 358

Tray, oval, the wide dished border band cast w/a continuous scene of village people & landscapes, the oval interior engraved w/a rusticated design, International Silver Co., late 19th c., 13" l. 230

Tray, oval w/an applied grapevine border w/etched scrolling floral & foliate designs in the center, loop end handles & short scrolling feet, American-made, late 19th - early 20th c., 17 1/2 x 26 1/2" 280

Tray, rectangular, mirrored interior, chamfered corners & a pierced gallery, on four pierced scroll feet, early 20th c., 24" l. 977

Tray, rectangular w/rounded corners, pierced scroll & floral design in center w/monogrammed cartouche, end handles, Wilcox Silver Plate Company, 20th c., 9 x 20" 132

Tray, round w/scalloped scrolling foliate slightly raised rim, centering a round center heavily engraved w/floral & foliate designs, raised on four scrolling feet, ca. 1900, 7 1/4" d., 1 3/4" h. 224

Tureen, cov., classical urn-form body w/loop end handles, raised on a pedestal base, domed cover w/finial, Gorham Mfg. Co., dated 1910, 8 x 14 1/2", 11" h. 420

Tureens, cov., in the late Georgian taste, oval footed base w/gadrooned bands below the wide squatty bulbous oval lobed base w/reeded loop end handles, the domed, stepped cover decorated overall w/repoussé flowers & shellwork, Tiffany & Co., New York, late 19th c., overall 13" l., pr. 1,725

Vase, large compressed bottle-form, chased overall w/large rose blossoms & foliage, w/gadrooned rim, engraved w/monogram, ca. 1900, 10" d. (wear to high spots) 345

Vase, Arts & Crafts style, bulbous form, hand-hammered surface, rim decorated w/four riveted mounts, Derby Silver Co., Derby, Connecticut, 11" d., 7" h. 316

Vase, Art Nouveau style, a bottle-form vessel w/an ornately molded naturalistic decoration including waves in the background w/molded carp & aquatic flowers & two full-figure mermaids wrapped around the neck & base, a lobster, snail & more flowers, France, ca. 1900, 23" h. (some losses) 1,725

Ornate Silver Plate Vase Holder

Vase holder, cylindrical, the sides composed of narrow pierced scroll bands & wide scroll & blossom-embossed bands, Wilcox company mark, No. 3377, missing glass liner, late 19th c., 2 3/4" d., 4 5/8" h. (ILLUS.) 33

Vegetable dish, cov., deep round form w/a gadrooned rim & cover, the cover w/a central rosette surmounted by a cast silver & wood bud finial, the upright S-scroll handles w/wood grips, probably England, late 19th - early 20th c., 8 3/4" d. 259

Vegetable dish, cov., urn-form body w/double handles, repoussé & chased floral & C-scroll decoration, marked by L & WS, 16" l., 9" h. 275

Vegetable dish, cov., oblong w/scalloped, domed sides & rope edging on the base, ornate domed cover, electroplating on copper, early 20th c., 12" l. 28

Warming tureen, cov., round w/a domed cover, beaded detail, engraved decoration & crest, inner 1-quart bowl, 19th c., 9" d., 12" h. 316

Wine coasters, after a Regency design, oval, each cast & pierced w/bacchanalian scenes & applied w/a cast grapevine rim, center w/engine-turned decoration, early 20th c., 10 1/4" l., pr. 920

One of Two Fine English Wine Coolers

Wine coolers, classical ovoid body on a short lobed stem w/a stepped round foot, a wide short everted rim, ornate ram's head shoulder handles, the body w/a central foliate & scroll engraving around a roundel, engraved Greek key bands around the shoulder & bottom, Mappin & Co., England, late 19th c., 12 1/4" h., pr. (ILLUS. of one) 2,760

Silver Plate (Flatware)
Arbutus (Wm. Rogers & Sons) - 1908

Detail of Arbutus Pattern Flatware

Arcadian (Rogers Bros. 1847) - 1884

Arbutus Butter Pick

Butter pick (ILLUS.) **$30**

Detail of Arcadian Pattern Flatware

Arbutus Pie Fork

Pie fork (ILLUS.) **18**

Arcadian Berry Spoon

Berry spoon (ILLUS.) **45**

Arbutus Salad Fork

Salad fork (ILLUS.) **25**

Arcadian Sugar Shell

Sugar shell (ILLUS.) **20**

Arcadian Sugar Tongs

Sugar tongs (ILLUS.) 35

Assyrian Head (Rogers Bros. 1847) - 1886

Detail of Assyrian Head Pattern

Assyrian Head Nut Cracker

Nut cracker (ILLUS.) 125

Assyrian Head Pickle & Sugar Tongs

Pickle tongs (ILLUS. left) 75
Sugar tongs (ILLUS. right) 65

Assyrian Head Teaspoon

Teaspoon (ILLUS.) 24

Berkshire (Rogers Bros. 1847) - 1895

Detail of Berkshire Pattern Flatware

Berkshire Chipped Beef Fork

Berkshire Sugar Tongs

Berwick a.k.a. Diana (Wm. Rogers) - 1904

Berkshire Gravy Ladle

Detail of Berwick Pattern Flatware

Berkshire Ice Cream Spoon

Berwick Cake Server

Berwick Ice Cream Fork

Ice cream fork (ILLUS.) **40**

Berwick Salad Fork

Salad fork (ILLUS.) **30**

Carnation (W.R. Keystone) - 1908

Detail of Carnation Pattern Flatware

Carnation Berry Spoon

Berry spoon (ILLUS.) **48**

Carnation Iced Tea Spoons

Iced tea spoon (ILLUS.) **35**

Carnation Strawberry Fork

Strawberry fork (ILLUS.) **38**

Carnation Sugar Shell

Sugar shell (ILLUS.) **20**

Charter Oak (Rogers 1847) - 1906

Baby spoon, bent-handled **35**
Butter spreader, individual **20**
Fruit spoons, gold-washed bowl, set of 6 .... **110**
Orange knife, hollow-handled **20**
Sugar spoon **20**
Tomato server **158**

Charter Oak Cake Slice

Cake slice (ILLUS.) **225**

Charter Oak Food Pusher

Food pusher (ILLUS.) **40**

Detail of Charter Oak Pattern Flatware

Charter Oak Berry Spoon

Berry spoon (ILLUS.) **65**

Charter Oak Ice Cream Fork

Ice cream fork (ILLUS.) **125**

Charter Oak Ice Cream Knife

Ice cream knife (ILLUS.) **85**

Columbia Butter Fork

Butter fork (ILLUS.) **45**

Charter Oak Tomato Server

Tomato server (ILLUS.) **175**

Columbia (Rogers Bros. 1847) - 1893

Columbia Cake Server

Cake server (ILLUS.) **55**

Detail of Columbia Pattern Flatware

Columbia Punch Ladle

Punch ladle (ILLUS.) **225**

Columbia Salad Fork

Salad fork (ILLUS.)... **65**

Columbia Tomato Server

Tomato server (ILLUS.) **65**

Floral (R. Wallace 1835) - 1902

Detail of Floral Pattern Flatware

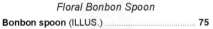

Floral Bonbon Spoon

Bonbon spoon (ILLUS.) **75**

Floral Cake Server

Cake server (ILLUS.).. **55**

Floral Individual Cake Fork

Cake serving fork, individual (ILLUS.) **55**

Floral Food Pusher

Food pusher (ILLUS.).. 55

Floral Sugar Tongs

Sugar tongs (ILLUS.)... 65

Grape (Rogers)
Berry spoon 55
Butter knife, master 40
Childs fork 30
Cream soup spoon 35
Demitasse spoon 30
Dinner knife, hollow-handled............................... 45
Iced tea spoon 40
Meat fork 45
Salad fork 50
Sugar shell 35
Tablespoon, large 30
Teaspoon 15

Grenoble a.k.a. Gloria (Wm. A. Rogers) 1906

Detail of Grenoble Pattern Flatware

Grenoble Fruit Spoon

Fruit spoon (ILLUS.)... 20

Grenoble Ice Cream Fork

Ice cream fork (ILLUS.)... 40

Grenoble Ice Cream Spoons

Ice cream spoon (ILLUS.) 37

Grenoble (Rogers)
Butter knife, master size... 8
Butter spreader, individual..................................... 9
Cold meat fork 33
Dinner fork 15
Dinner knife 15
Gravy ladle 40
Iced tea spoon 12
Mustard ladle 75
Pastry fork 35
Pie server 50

Salad fork 45
Soup spoon, oval bowl 22
Sugar spoon 22
Teaspoon 8

Grosvenor (Oneida Community) - 1927

Detail of Grosvenor Pattern Flatware

Grosvenor Bonbon Spoon

Bonbon spoon (ILLUS.) 55

Grosvenor Cheese Server

Cheese server (ILLUS.) 65

Grosvenor Salad Fork

Salad fork (ILLUS.) 20

Hanover (Rogers)

Bouillon spoon 7
Butter knife, individual 10
Dinner fork 10
Dinner knife 12
Olive spoon 30
Salad fork 30
Soup ladle 85

Holly (E.H.H. Smith) - 1904

Detail of Holly Pattern Flatware

Holly Berry Spoon

Berry spoon (ILLUS.) 150

Holly Individual Butter

Butter, individual (ILLUS.) **45**

Holly Crumber

Crumber (ILLUS.) **195**

Holly Salad Fork

Salad fork (ILLUS.) **175**

Holly Sugar Shell

Sugar shell (ILLUS.) **85**

Holly Tomato Server

Tomato server (ILLUS.) **375**

Japanese (Holmes Booth & Hayden) -1879

Detail of Japanese Pattern Flatware

Japanese Berry Fork

Berry fork (ILLUS.) **32**

La Concorde (Wm. A. Rogers) - 1910

Japanese Gravy Ladle
Gravy ladle (ILLUS.) **40**

Detail of La Concorde Pattern

Japanese Oyster Fork
Oyster fork (ILLUS.).. **25**

La Concorde Cocktail Forks
Cocktail fork (ILLUS.) **24**

Japanese Seafood Fork
Seafood fork (ILLUS.)... **25**

La Concorde Grapefruit Spoon
Grapefruit spoon (ILLUS.) **25**

La Concorde Teaspoons

La Vigne (Rogers Bros. 1881) - 1908

Detail of La Vigne Pattern Flatware

La Vigne Cream Ladle

La Vigne Pie Fork

La Vigne Sugar Tongs

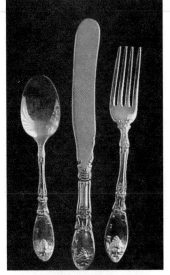

La Vigne 3-piece Youth Set

Youth set: spoon, $15; knife, $25; fork, $20;
the set (ILLUS.) 60

Moselle (1847 Rogers)
Beef fork 165
Berry spoon 165
Berry spoon, gold-washed bowl 125
Butter knife, twist handle 33
Cold meat fork 50
Gravy ladle 55
Jelly spoon 95
Luncheon knife, hollow-handled 26
Meat fork, 7 1/2" l. 58
Pickle fork, long handle 112
Soup spoon, oval bowl 38
Teaspoons, set of 12 200-250

Moselle (American Silver Co.) - 1906

Detail of Moselle Pattern Flatware

Baby spoon, curved handle 60
Berry spoon 165

Moselle Cake Serving Fork

Cake serving fork, individual (ILLUS.) 195
Casserole spoon 150

Moselle Cheese Scoop

Cheese scoop (ILLUS.) 200
Cold meat fork 50
Demitasse spoon 25

Moselle Ice Cream Fork

Ice cream fork (ILLUS.) 250
Jelly spoon 95

Moselle Lettuce Fork

Lettuce fork (ILLUS.) 275
Oyster ladle 350
Punch ladle 750
Soup spoon, oval bowl.. 25

Moselle Sugar Shell

Sugar shell (ILLUS.) 65
Sugar spoon 55
Tablespoon 30
Teaspoon 20

Moselle Tomato Server

Tomato server (ILLUS.) 350

Mystic (Rogers & Bros.) - 1903

Detail of Mystic Pattern Flatware

Mystic Berry Spoon

Berry spoon (ILLUS.) 45

Newport (1847 Rogers Bros.) - 1879

Mystic Cold Meat Fork

Cold meat fork (ILLUS.) **25**

Mystic Fruit Spoon

Fruit spoon (ILLUS.) **20**

Mystic Soup Ladle

Soup ladle (ILLUS.) **85**

Detail of Newport Pattern Flatware

Newport Butter Serving Knife

Butter serving knife, master (ILLUS.) **25**

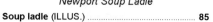

Newport Cocktail Fork

Cocktail fork (ILLUS.) **42**

Newport Soup Ladle

Soup ladle (ILLUS.) **85**

Newport Nut Pick

Nut pick (ILLUS.) **20**

Newport Sugar Shell

Sugar shell (ILLUS.) **20**

Newport Pie Fork

Pie fork (ILLUS.) **40**

Newport Sugar Tongs

Sugar tongs (ILLUS.) **45**

Newport Youth Knife

Youth knife (ILLUS.) **65**

Old Colony (Rogers Bros. 1847) - 1911

Detail of Old Colony Pattern Flatware

Old Colony Berry Spoon

Berry spoon, small (ILLUS.) **35**

Old Colony Cake Serving Fork

Cake serving fork, individual (ILLUS.) **45**

Old Colony Carving Set

Carving set: red meat carving knife, red meat carving honer, red meat carving fork; the set (ILLUS. right to left) **195**

Old Colony Meat Fork

Cold meat fork (ILLUS.) **20**

Old Colony Dinner Fork

Dinner fork, hollow handled (ILLUS.)................ **32**

Old Colony Tablespoon

Tablespoon (ILLUS.).. **24**

Orange Blossom (Rogers Bros.)
Butter spreader, individual **9**
Butter spreader, master.. **15**
Fruit spoons, set of 6 .... **45**
Ice Cream fork **23**

Raphael (Rogers & Hamilton) - 1896

Detail of Raphael Pattern Flatware

Raphael Berry Spoon

Berry spoon (ILLUS.).. **75**

Raphael Individual Butter

Butter, individual (ILLUS.).................................... **25**

Raphael Citrus Fruit Spoon

Citrus fruit spoon (ILLUS.) **35**

Raphael Ice Cream Fork

Ice cream fork (ILLUS.) 45

Raphael Seafood Fork

Seafood cocktail fork (ILLUS.) 38

Raphael Sugar Shell

Sugar shell (ILLUS.) 35

Vintage (Rogers Bros. 1847) - 1904

Detail of Vintage Pattern Flatware

Vintage Cake Serving Fork

Vintage Ice Cream Fork

Ice cream fork (ILLUS.) 125

Vintage Ice Cream Spoon

Ice cream spoon (ILLUS.) 95
Ice spoon 150
Iced tea spoon 75
Jelly knife 75

Vintage Jelly Trowel

Jelly trowel (ILLUS.) 125
Meat fork 43
Olive fork 55
Olive spoon, open bowl..................................... 44
Pastry fork 55

Vintage Pickle Fork

Pickle fork (ILLUS.) 75
Pie server 125

Vintage Salad Fork

Salad fork (ILLUS.) 75

Vintage Salad Serving Fork

Salad serving fork (ILLUS.)................................. 85

Vintage Salad Serving Spoon

Salad serving spoon (ILLUS.) 125
Seafood fork 16
Soup spoon 11
Sugar spoon 20
Sugar tongs 85
Tablespoon 16
Teaspoon 8

Vintage Tomato Server
Tomato server (ILLUS.) 225
Youth set, 3 pcs. (w/original box) 57

Windsor (Wallace & Son)

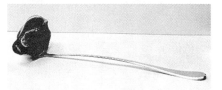

Punch Ladle by Wallace
Punch ladle, 15" l. (ILLUS.) 45

Yale I (Wm. Rogers) - 1894

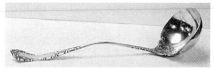

Large Silver Plate Ladle
Ladle, curved handle decorated w/flowers &
scrollwork, 12 1/2" l. (ILLUS.) **78**

Spelter

Spelter is the generic name for items made of zinc. Beginning in the 19th century zinc was often alloyed with lead and later aluminum to produce decorative objects. Novelty items and statuary could be cast and given a bronze or other finish to resemble much more expensive pieces. Similar alloys are also referred to as white metal.

Devil Ashtray
Ashtray, in the form of a spread-winged
devil w/goatee, horns & bat ears,
1 3/4 x 5 x 5" (ILLUS.) **$175**

Nodding-head Figure Ashtray
Ashtray, spelter & tin, base w/nodding-
head figure of black boy standing smoking a cigar, original worn paint, made in
Austria, 3 x 4 x 4 1/2" (ILLUS.) **295**

Spelter Baby Shoe Bank

Bank, model of a baby shoe, copper finish, 2 x 5", 2 3/4" h. (ILLUS.) **14**

John Deere Tractor Bank

Bank, model of a John Deere tractor, issued by the Deere Credit Union, third edition, copper finish, 6" l., 3 1/4" h. (ILLUS.) **60**

Spelter "Despair" Book End

Book ends, bronzed finish, rounded arch upright, relief cast w/allegorical figure of "Despair," weighted base, 5 1/2 x 6 1/4", pr. (ILLUS. of one) **69**

Spelter Elephant Book End

Book ends, copper finish, model of trumpeting tusked elephant on weighted round base, 5 x 6", 5 1/2" h., pr. (ILLUS. of one) **69**

Musketeer Spelter Book End

Book ends, figure of a standing musketeer laughing & holding a broken sword, bronzed patina, marked "Artbronz - Copyright KB.W.," cracked surfaces, 8 1/2" h., pr. (ILLUS. of one) **60**

Horse Head Book End

Book ends, image of turned horse head w/flaring nostrils & open mouth, on stepped base, gold finish, 4 1/2 x 4 1/2 x 6", pr. (ILLUS. of one on previous page) **95**

Sulgrave Manor Book End

Book ends, in image of Sulgrave Manor, North Hamptonshire, George Washington's family home in England, base forms lawn, marked "JB 22386," 2 x 4 x 5", each (ILLUS. of one) **75**

Frankart Scottie Book End

Book ends, model of a Scottie dog on a rectangular base w/backplate, bronzed finish, marked "Frankart Inc. Patent Applied for," 5 1/2" l., 3 3/4" h., pr. (ILLUS. of one) **125**

Souvenir Calendar Holder

Calendar holder, souvenir in the form of a galleon in full sail attached to a shield embossed w/ "The Wrigley Building - Chicago" and image of the building, which holds complete paper date cards for calendar, 1 3/4 x 2 3/8 x 4" (ILLUS.) **95**

Spelter Coffin Plate

Coffin plate, cartouche decorated w/engraved "At Rest," w/embossed flowers & leaves forming partial border, marked on back "CC Co. - 58," 4 x 8 1/2" (ILLUS.) **10**

Early Engraved Coffin Plate

Coffin plate, flat rectangular form w/scroll border, engraved "Our Loved One," 2 x 3 5/8" (ILLUS.) **15**

Handled Commemorative Cup

Cup, three-handled, each handle in the form of a winged dragon, embossed on the side "October 3rd. 1899," silvered finish, 5" w., 4" h. (ILLUS.) **150**

Spelter Art Deco Holder with Woman

Dish holder, figural, a seated stylized Art Deco nude woman w/a dished tray in her lap & her arms outstretched, on a rectangular base, dark finish, 6" h. (ILLUS.) **145**

Figurine of Man Riding Elephant

Figurine, black man riding tusked elephant, w/original paint, 1 x 2 1/4 x 2 5/8" (ILLUS.) **295**

Figurine of Hippo Swallowing Man

Figurine, hippo swallowing human, bottom half of which protrudes from hippo's mouth, w/applied swirls of water plants, original paint, 1 1/2 x 2 x 2 5/8" (ILLUS.) **395**

Figural Incense Burner

Incense burner, in the form of a Moor in cloak & turban sitting next to a lidded, handled woven basket w/holes in lid for incense, original paint in black, brown, red, blue & white, 3 1/4 x 4 1/8 x 5 1/2" (ILLUS.) **395**

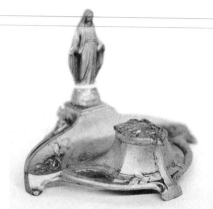

Spelter Inkstand with Virgin Mary

Inkstand, footed oblong dish w/raised cov., inkwell & pen trough cast w/roses below a raised standing figure of the Virgin Mary, gold finish, 4 1/2 x 5", 4" h. (ILLUS.) **79**

Spelter Eiffel Tower Inkstand

Inkstand, image of Eiffel Tower rises from center, flanked by two circular wells w/star-like designs on lids, pen rest in front, style number 2170, French, 3 x 4 x 6 1/2" (ILLUS.) **185**

Souvenir Inkstand

Inkstand, souvenir of Valley Forge, Pennsylvania, w/image of Washington's headquarters & "Washington Memorial Chapel" embossed on lid & base, pen rest in front, gold finish, 1 1/4 x 4 x 5 (ILLUS.) **95**

Silver-finish Eiffel Tower Inkstand

Inkstand, square lidded inkwell in front of image of Eiffel Tower on stepped base, w/pen rest between the two parts, marked LL 10 on bottom, silver finish, 4 x 4 1/8 x 5 1/2" (ILLUS.) **135**

Inkwell with Seated Dog on Cover

Inkwell, cov., the hinged top w/a seated small spaniel-like dog drinking from a wine flask, atop a columnar base w/dolphins at each corner, worn gilt finish, 3 1/2" h. (ILLUS.) **95**

Camel Inkwell

Inkwell, in the form of a reclining camel, polychrome decoration, hinged top lifts off camel's saddle, camel hump holds ink, 6" l. (ILLUS.) **395**

Whippet Inkwell

Inkwell, in the form of the head of a whippet, w/glass eyes, head forms lid, neck is well for ink, 3 1/2 x 3 3/4 x 5 1/2" (ILLUS.) **295**

Monkey Inkwell

Inkwell, seated monkey holds a square-shaped bowl for ink, 2 x 3 1/2 x 3 1/2" (ILLUS.) **85**

Owl Inkwell

Inkwell, square wooden base holds figure of owl standing w/mouse clutched in its talons, hinged head covers well for ink, 6 1/2" h. (ILLUS. on previous page) **135**

Cupid & Flowers on Jewelry Box

Jewelry box, cov., Art Nouveau style, flared undulating scroll & flower base, the flat cover w/a full-figure reclining Cupid holding an arrow, gold painted finish, lined in fabric, early 20th c., 4 1/4 x 6 1/4", 4 1/2" h. (ILLUS.) **275**

Spelter Art Nouveau Jewelry Box

Jewelry box, cov., footed oval form boldly cast w/Art Nouveau-style roses, gold finish, lined in pink fabric, early 20th c., 4 x 6", 4 1/2" h. (ILLUS.) **75**

Jewelry box with Cupid on Cover

Jewelry box, cov., rectangular casket-form w/serpentine sides, the cover cast in relief w/a cupid & flowers, the base w/serpentine sides w/scrolls & peg feet, worn gold finish, marked on bottom "NB Rogers SP Co - 5," 3 x 4 1/2", 2 3/4" h. (ILLUS.) **50**

Spelter Heart-shaped Jewelry Box

Jewelry box, cov., stylized heart shape, the hinged cover trimmed w/scrolls around a central shield, further scrolls around base, worn silver finish, early 20th c., 3 x 3 3/8" (ILLUS.) **45**

Jewelry & Perfume Holder

Jewelry & perfume holder, oblong fabric-covered base w/pierced brass feet holds figure of girl holding a flower in one hand & a basket meant to hold jewelry in the other, flanked by two glass perfume bottles w/cut-glass stoppers that fit into indentations in base, 3 x 5 1/2 x 6 1/2" (ILLUS.) **595**

Advertising Letter Opener

Letter opener, copper finish, handle in the figure of a nude woman w/arm raised behind head advertising the Minneapolis Auditorium, an image of which appears in circle on blade, marked "patent pending," 8 1/2" l. (ILLUS.) **65**

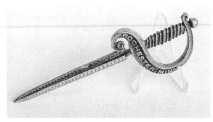

Souvenir Cutlass Letter Opener

Letter opener, in the shape of a cutlass, souvenir of "Rochester, Minn.," which appears in raised letters on curved hilt, 6 1/3" l. (ILLUS.) **88**

Cotton Bale Match Holder & Striker

Match holder & striker, hollowed-out cotton bale w/two figures of black boys leaning against it, one sitting next to a watermelon, the other standing & peeking around the corner, marked on front of bale "Cotton," 2 1/4 x 2 1/4 x 2 1/2" (ILLUS.) **225**

Mexican Border Service Medal

Medal, commemorative, "Mexican Border Service" & "1916" embossed in banner border, in commemoration of raid, probably by Pancho Villa, 1 1/2 x 1 3/4" (ILLUS.) **35**

Spelter Dog with Three Faces

Model of a dog, seated animal w/the head having three different faces, marked on base w/patent number 123112, 5 1/4" h. (ILLUS.) **195**

Gold-painted Spelter Pheasant

Models of pheasants, standing bird w/long tail, gold finish, 15" l., 6 1/2" h., pr. (ILLUS. of one) **35**

Spelter Basket-shaped Music Box

Music box, model of small woven wicker basket w/swing handle, enclosing music box works & lined w/red velvet, 2 1/2 x 2 3/4", 2" h. (ILLUS.) **12**

Paperweight, figural advertising-type, standing bearded gnome smoking a pipe & holding a toolbox, marked on front of the square base "Bill Drite with Insulite," "Bill Drite" also on the sides of base, copper finish, 2 1/2" sq., 4" h. (ILLUS.) **85**

Typewriter Paperweight

Paperweight, commemorative, in the shape of a typewriter, marked at top "Underwood" and on reverse "Golden Jubilee Dinner, to Matthew S. Eglar, April 28, 1939," 1 3/8 x 2 3/4 x 2 3/4" (ILLUS.) **75**

Advertising Paperweight

Paperweight, rectangular base w/"Upper Mississippi Towing Corporation" on side of base, topped w/image of towboat "Harriet Ann" in choppy water decoration, 5 1/2" l. (ILLUS.) **95**

Husky Dog Advertising Paperweight

Paperweight, copper finish, rectangular base holds figure of Husky dog standing w/head turned to side, side of base reads "Western Oil & Fuel Company" (which sold Husky Gas), 2 3/8 x 4 x 4 1/4" (ILLUS.) **295**

Bear Advertising Paperweight

Paperweight, rounded rectangular base holds figure of a bear, w/"Chicago, Milwaukee & St. Paul RY. - to Puget Sound - electrified" on side of base, 4 5/8" l. (ILLUS.) **195**

Caricature Pencil Sharpener

Pencil sharpener, caricature of a black man's face, traces of original red & white paint, 1/2 x 1 1/8 x 1 1/2" (ILLUS.) **145**

Bill Drite Figural Paperweight

Black Uncle Sam Pencil Sharpener

Pencil sharpener, caricature of black man
  wearing Uncle Sam-type top hat & bow
  tie, original black, red, white & blue paint,
  made in Occupied Japan, 1/2 x 1 1/8 x 2"
  (ILLUS.) **165**

Pistol Pencil Sharpener

Pencil sharpener, in the form of a pistol
  w/hinged tin top & original green paint,
  made in Germany, 1/2 x 1 3/4 x 2 5/8"
  (ILLUS.) **75**

Pistol Pencil Sharpener with Eraser

Pencil sharpener, in the form of a pistol,
  w/original paint & removable eraser
  where gun's magazine would go, made in
  Germany, 3/8 x 1 1/4 x 1 3/4" (ILLUS.) **50**

Bottle-shaped Pencil Sharpener

Pencil sharpener, in the shape of a Coca-
  Cola bottle, w/original red paint, 1 3/4" h.
  (ILLUS.) **85**

Flower Grip Pencil Sharpener

Pencil sharpener, w/stylized openwork
  flower grip, 1/2 x 1 1/2" (ILLUS.) **45**

Spelter Shoe Pincushion

Pincushion, model of woman's high-heeled
  shoe, copper finish w/ornate cast scroll &
  lattice decoration, fabric lining, marked
  on base "JB - 1248," 7 3/4" l., 3 1/2" h.
  (ILLUS.) **59**

Art Deco Ring Holder

Ring holder, Art Deco style, in the form of a two-dimensional elephant balancing on painted ball, all on triangular stepped base, elephant trunk holds rings, 3 1/4" h. (ILLUS.)` **95**

Greyhound Bus Salt & Pepper Shakers

Salt & pepper shakers, model of Grey-hound bus, original rubber wheels, silver paint w/blue trim & cork stoppers, Japan, 2 3/4" l., pr. (ILLUS.) **79**

Spelter Souvenir Shakers

Salt & pepper shakers, square tapering form, cast w/scenes & souvenir markings for Ft. Snelling, Minnesota, scroll trim, early 20th c., 2 3/8" h., pr. (ILLUS.) **20**

Spelter Sewing Case

Sewing case, rectangular, w/hinged lid, top w/rectangular miniature framed photo of the Mohawk Trail set in oval garland & bow border, 2 x 2 1/2" (ILLUS.) **75**

Advertising Snuff Scoop

Snuff scoop, advertising "Weyman's Copenhagen Snuff," bowl holds one ounce, long, curved applied handle, 10 1/2" l. (ILLUS.) **145**

Souvenir Thermometer

Thermometer, in the form of a dog standing in rustic doghouse, w/original paint in red, green, blue, yellow & white, souvenir of Lake Benton, Minnesota, 4 3/8" h. (ILLUS.) **225**

Frog & Snail Toothpick Holder

Toothpick holder, figural, in the shape of a frog pulling a snail shell w/a bee on the end, marked w/style number "3462," 2 x 2 1/2 x 4 1/2" (ILLUS.) **295**

Spelter Toy Stock Truck

Toy, stock truck w/worn original red paint, rubber wheels, marked on bottom "Hubley Kiddie Toy - Lancaster, Pa." & on inside of cab top w/"2," 6 5/8" l. (ILLUS.) **85**

Footed Spelter Vase

Vase, bulbous form tapering at neck & slightly flaring outward at lip, on three short feet, decorated w/figure of girl feeding carrots to rabbits, marked "Germany," 6 1/4" h. (ILLUS.) **195**

Figural Spelter Vase Holder

Vase holder, figural, weighted figure of a nude young girl bending backward w/arms outstretched to hold the missing vase, black finish, 8" h. (ILLUS.) **200**

Steel

Although small amounts of steel have been made since the Iron Age, the modern steel industry was not developed until the mid-19th century, when Englishman Henry Bessemer created the Bessemer process for refining iron. American ironmaker William Kelly independently developed a similar process about the same time. The new method of steel production was based on the discovery of the British metallurgist Robert Mushet. In 1857, Mushet found that when you added an alloy of iron, carbon and manganese called spiegeleisen during the refining of iron, it helped remove oxygen and control the carbon content of the steel. The Bessemer method was the main form of steel production in Britain and the United States until the early 20th century and made them leaders in the industrialized world. Eventually a more efficient method of refining steel, the open-hearth method, replaced the Bessemer method. Today, even more modern and efficient methods are used in Japanese and European steel mills, causing serious setbacks for outdated American plants. Since the late 19th century, steel has been a major material in the building of modern American society - everything from railroads to household appliances and automobiles to tablewares. Below, we list a small selection of early decorative objects made from this durable and versatile alloy. Collectors of sterling silver and silver plate flatware should be aware that "stainless steel" for knife blades did not come into common use until the late 1920s. Before that time true steel was used, and it could rust if not carefully dried and polished.

Unusual Box with Scotties

Box, cov., cylindrical, w/three small figural Scottie dog feet & a standing Scottie finial on the cover, original worn pale green paint, marked on base w/number 3442, ca. 1930s, 3 1/2" d., 4 1/4" h. (ILLUS. on previous page) $175

Can opener, Sieger, 5 1/2" 15

Steel Wick-trimming Snuffer

Candle snuffer, wick-trimming scissors w/old blackened surface & raised lip to catch wick trimmings, 6" l. (ILLUS.) 45

Egg beater, "Ladd Beater July 7, 1908 Oct. 18, 1921," 11 1/2" 25

Stainless Steel Kraut Chopper

Kraut chopper, stainless, w/cast-iron handle, two blades, made by Acme & marked "patent pending," 1 3/8 x 5 1/4 x 5 1/2" (ILLUS.) 12

Advertising Letter Opener

Letter opener, w/brass handle embossed "Weber & Judd Co. - Pharmacists - Rochester Minn.," 7 1/4" l. (ILLUS.) 35

Mixer, stainless steel, "Japan Bicor Battery Power," 9" 15

Christmas Chocolate Mold Sheet

Mold, chocolate, sheet w/Christmas shape molds, sheet measures 10 3/4 x 16 3/4" (ILLUS.) 295

Pot scraper, advertising-type, marked "Case Tractors" 95

Steel Key-wind Toy Truck

Toy, cast, key-wind, pickup truck w/original box, made in U.S. Zone Germany, marked on bottom "Varianto Lasto 3042" & "patents applied for," Schuco, 1 1/2 x 1 3/4", 4 1/4" l. (ILLUS.) 250

Cast-steel Schuco Limousine with Box

Toy, cast, key-wind, red limousine w/original box, marked "Varianto-Limo 3041" & "Made in U.S. Zone Germany," Schuco, 1 1/2 x 1 1/2", 4 1/4" l. (ILLUS.) 250

Heinz Toy Delivery Truck

Toy, stamped, Heinz delivery truck w/original worn paint, primarily white, green & red, rubber wheels, decorated w/Heinz pickle logo in center of circle that reads "Pure Food Products" around border & "57 Varieties" inside, signs on side of truck read "Baked Beans - Bottled Vinegars & Rice Flakes," top of cab has NRA eagle symbol in red, white & blue, marked on bottom "Metalcrafts Corporation - St. Louis," 4 x 5 1/2", 12" l. (ILLUS. on previous page)..... **795**

Steel Pan American World Toy Plane

Toy airplane, friction, in the style of Pan American World plane, wings detach, painted red, green & tan, made in Japan, 11 1/2" l. (ILLUS.) **395**

Douglas Seven Seas Toy Airplane

Toy airplane, friction (when wheels are spun, the propellers revolve), in style of Douglas Seven Seas plane, red, white & blue, made in Japan, 17 1/4" l. (ILLUS.) **275**

Toy Airplane with Plastic Propellers

Toy airplane, in the style of Pan American plane, w/plastic propellers & retractable wheels, blue & white, marked "Made in Western Germany," 11 1/4" l. (ILLUS.) **195**

Steel Toy Hansom Cab

Toy hansom cab, figure of horse pulling blue hansom cab w/driver perched at rear, painted image of a man in bowler hat inside, possibly German, 12 3/4" l. (ILLUS.)....... **450**

Tin & Tole

Tin is a soft silvery-white metal with a low melting point. It is imported into the United States from the major tin producing countries, including Malaysia, Indonesia, Bolivia, Thailand, the former Soviet Union, China and Brazil. The first American tinsmiths took up residence in Berlin, Connecticut, in 1738. Prior to this time, tin was scarce and expensive. Tinplate (sheet iron rolled very thin and coated with layers of molten tin) was not produced in the U.S. until tin was discovered near Goshen, Connecticut, in 1829. Early peddlers traveled the rural areas, first on foot and later using brightly painted green and yellow carts that opened up to display their wares. It is reported that they covered areas from Canada to New Orleans and to the Lake Erie and Detroit region. The early wares carried by the peddlers were plain, undecorated utilitarian wares such as basins, candle molds and sconces, pitchers, pails, coffeepots, cream whippers, cookie cutters, graters and other such items. Tole wares appeared in England at Pontypool, near the Welsh border, around 1720. In the 1760s the colorfully decorated ware made its way to France, where it was an immediate success. Some tole had a "japanned" background. "Japanning" refers to painting the surface with asphaltum, which is a transparent black substance with a tar base. A good deal of the American tole ware had the dark brown or black background, but some work from Maine had a bright blue background, while other areas might use a cream or mustard yellow ground. Some pieces from Pennsylvania have a red or orange background. The designs on American tole were primarily stylized floral or fruit decoration in brilliant shades of red, green, blue, yellow and white. These decorated wares include document boxes, coffeepots, canisters and tea caddies, bread trays, apple and serving trays, candle sconces, jardinieres and many other decorative or utilitarian items. Today, collectors prize the country appeal of early plain and punched tin wares and brightly colored tole wares. Since there has been a great collector interest in these wares for over seventy years, there are numerous quality reproductions on the market, so careful study is necessary to select the best early examples.

Apple corer, T-handle, handmade, 5" **$15**
Apple corer, tin & wood, "Boye Pat No. 1206403 Made in USA" **15**

Football Arena Advertising Ashtray

Ashtray, tin, in the form of a football arena w/printed details of field surrounded by bleachers full of fans, advertising Chesterfield cigarettes, "They Satisfy" in red letters in center, 5 3/8 x 6 1/4" (ILLUS.) 65

Tin Armored Car Still Bank

Bank, still, tin, in the form of an armored car in red, black & silver-grey, w/plastic wheels, windup alarm sounds when back door is opened, made in Japan, 4 x 4 1/2", 9 3/4" l. (ILLUS.) 145

Barn candle lantern, punched tin & glass, a pierced pyramidal cap w/large ring strap handle above a tin framework enclosing panes of glass, one side a door & each side fitted w/wire guards, candle socket inside, 19th c., 11 1/2" h. plus handle (some resoldering on wire guards) 110

Barn lantern, pierced tin & blown glass, a metal frame w/the top pierced w/a star & diamond design, the base separates from the removable oil font, mid-19th c., 14 3/4" h. (very minor dents) **1,955**

Painted Tin & Glass Barn Lantern

Barn lantern, tin & glass, triangular, two glass panels, one hinged, in a painted tin frame w/angled top & arched heat vent w/a wire bail handle w/wooden grip, hanging loops on the back, interior fitted w/a glass kerosene lamp & chimney, painted brown w/black trim, mid-19th c., no reflector, one hanging loop missing, corrosion & paint wear, 19" h. (ILLUS.) **345**

Bicycle lantern, miniature, painted tin, a cylindrical dark brown japanned tin case w/a pointed vented top & wire loops at the back, fitted on the front w/revolving red & green interior lenses, late 19th - early 20th c., 4 3/4" h....................................... **165**

Biscuit cutter, tin, egg-shaped handle above small round biscuit cutter marked "Egg Baking Powder"................................. **275**

Biscuit cutter, tin, Jenny Wren advertising on strap handle **15**

Biscuit cutter, tin, Rumford advertising, 3 1/2" **15**

Toleware Box

Box, cov., tole, painted & polychrome-decorated, lion head handle on domed lid appears to be original, Pennsylvania, first quarter 19th c., 6 x 7 1/2 x 10" (ILLUS.) ... **1,080**

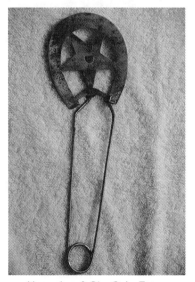

Horseshoe & Star Cake Turner

Cake turner, tin, horseshoe-shaped w/star marked "M.C.W. Cake Turner, Pat. Apr. 2. 07," wire handle flips it (ILLUS. on previous page) **115**

Can opener & jar opener combination tool, tin, "Distributed By C.S. Ripley & Co Cleveland, Ohio," 8 1/4" **25**

Tole Hanging Candle Box

Candle box, tole, cylindrical body w/two tabs for hanging, old red & yellow grained paint w/red, white, yellow & black floral decoration, 14 3/8" l. (ILLUS.) **908**

Candle lantern, pierced tin Paul Revere-type, cylindrical w/hinged door & conical top w/ring strap handle, pierced designs w/the initials "N.A." in the door, 13 1/2" h. plus handle (some battering & repair) **303**

Two Old Candle Lanterns

Candle lantern, punched tin Paul Revere-style, cylindrical w/curved hinged door & conical top w/vent holes & a ring strap handle, pierced overall w/a star & diamond design & the punched inscription "P.O. More, Bellfontaine, O.," rusted finish, 13 1/4" h. plus handle (ILLUS. right) **633**

Paul Revere-type Tin Lantern

Candle lantern, punched-tin Paul Revere-style, cylindrical w/a pierced design of circles & quarter arcs, a hinged door on the side, a tall conical cap w/pierced design & vent holes, large strap ring handle at top, 19th c. (ILLUS.) **110**

Candle lantern, punched-tin Paul Revere-style, cylindrical w/pierced design circles & rays on the hinged door, overall piercing around the sides, a tall conical cap w/pierced design & vent holes, large strap ring handle at top, 19th c. (light pitting overall, a small hole) **275**

Candle lantern, tin & glass, a pyramidal tin cap pierced w/a star & rayed arch design below the large ring strap handle, tin frame & base enclosing glass sides w/one forming the door opening to a candle socket, marked Parker's Patent 1855, Proctorsville, Vt., 7 1/2" h. plus handle **358**

Candle lantern, tin & glass, a small cylindrical tin font base supporting a large round clear blown glass globe w/a cylindrical cap & conical pierced top w/ring strap handle, traces of old dark japanning w/light rust, 10" h. plus handle (candle socket replaces font) **385**

Early Patented Candle Lantern

Candle lantern, tin & glass, a tin framework w/glass sides & door w/wire protectors, pyramidal top pierced w/stars & circles, large strap ring handle, stamped "Parker's Patent - 1855 - Proctersville, VT," mid-19th c., 15 3/4" h. (ILLUS.) **523**

Candle lantern, tin & glass, hexagonal, tall upright form w/six vertical glass panels each w/vertical wire guards & two forming the door, tall crimped conical vented cap w/ring handle, single candle socket inside, New England, early 19th c., 15 1/2" h. (minor corrosion, electrified) **805**

Candle lantern, tin & glass, upright square dark tin framework w/four glass sides, one forming a hinged door w/cross-form wire guard, flat top w/cylindrical capped vent cover w/shaped wire swing bail handle, old glass, some soldered repair, 13 1/2" h. plus handle (ILLUS. left w/Paul Revere-style) **358**

Candle lantern, tin, hanging-type, eight-sided tapered glass globe w/a tin font, base & top, mushroom top w/ring handle, top & base w/star & diamond-shaped piercings, 10" h. plus ring handle (brass burner appears to be old replacement) **330**

Pierced Tin Paul Revere Lantern

Candle lantern, tin, Paul Revere-style, cylindrical w/hinged door & conical top
w/large ring handle, pierced overall
w/starburst & other designs, old black
paint, 19th c., overall 16 1/2" h. (ILLUS.)...... **500**

Early Tin Candle Mold

Candle mold, tin, eight-tube, rectangular
top & base plates, original worn black
paint, 19th c., 3 1/2 x 6", 10 1/2" h.
(ILLUS.)... **160**

Tin Candle Mold

Candle mold, tin, four-tube, on rectangular
foot, base handle missing, base
2 1/4 x 5 1/2, 11" h. (ILLUS.) **129**

Tin Candle Sconce

Candle sconces, tin, round, crimped reflectors & crimped-edge pans, reflectors
w/concentric crimped circles & small center mirrors, minor resoldering, 8 3/4" h.,
pr. (ILLUS. of one)...................................... **2,310**

Tin Miniature Suitcase Container

Candy container, tin, miniature model of
suitcase in gold decorated w/red & pink
Teenie Weenie comic characters, 1922,
near mint, 1 1/4 x 3 1/2 x 5" (ILLUS.)............ **295**
Canister set, tole, rectangular low-sided tray
w/overhead strap handle holding eight covered cylindrical canisters, original worn japanned surface, tray 5 3/8 x 8", 4 1/2" h.,
the set (ILLUS., top next page)............................ **95**

G.A.R. Souvenir Canteen

Old Tole Canister Set

Canteen, tin, souvenir-type for the G.A.R.,
large inset copper medallion in the side
w/picture of the U.S. Capitol & inscribed
"Souvenir - Twenty-sixth Grand Annual -
Encampment - Washington, D.C. - 1892,"
reverse medallion reads "We Drank From
the Same Canteen - 1861-65," 4 3/8 x 5"
(ILLUS. on previous page) **260**
Chandelier, tin, six-light, a round flat band
fitted w/six candle cups w/drip trays suspended from three chains of linked metal
rods joined to a small top disk, 19th c.,
26" h. (wear) **1,725**
Chocolate grater, tin, "Edgar Pat Nov. 10,
1890," 8 1/2" **300**

Parker Co. Coffee Mill

Coffee mill, wall canister-type, cylindrical
black tin canister & lid, eagle decal, iron
grinding body embossed "The Chas.
Parker Co., Meriden, Conn.," attached
metal glass holder below, also marked
"Eagle No. 044" & "Pat. Applied For"
(ILLUS.) **275**

Victorian Coal Hod

Coal hod, cov., tole, Oriental decoration including Japanese woman & crane, flow-
ers, etc., original black paint & faint decoration, domed lid w/embossed ray tole
designs and ring handle, side handles
are attached to Minerva heads, short
cast-iron feet w/animal faces, complete
w/lift-out insert, Victorian, 20" h. (ILLUS.) **220**
Coffee measure, tin, small cup w/flat han-
dle advertising ice cream **14**

Lightning No. 23 Coffee Mill

Tole Coffeepot & Document Boxes

Coffee mill, wall canister-type, cylindrical tin canister, green & white litho-printed "Lightning No. 23 Coffee Mill, Belmont Hardware Co.," angled mounting bracket, tin receiving cup hangs below (ILLUS., on previous page) **325**

Coffeepot, cov., tin, flaring cylindrical foot below the flaring cylindrical lower body & tapering cylindrical upper body, punched overall w/fine wrigglework including an urn of tulips & other flowers on each side & four bands of entwining lines, domed cover w/brass finial, angled swan's-neck spout, strap handle w/grip, first half 19th c., 11 1/4" h. (dents & resolder) **1,595**

Coffeepot, cov., tole, tapering sides w/gooseneck spout, strap handle, domed cover, worn dark japanning w/a white circle on each side w/strong folk-style yellow, red & green flowers including tulips, yellow stylized foliage border around short flaring base, 10 1/4" h. (ILLUS. above, left) **1,210**

Combination tool, tin, flat apple corer w/apple peeler & grater at end, 8 1/2" l............ **20**

Combination tool, tin, funnel-shaped, can be used as funnel, apple corer, cookie cutter, pie crimper or grater for corn or horseradish, patented in 1868 (beware of reproductions) **175**

Cookie cutter, eagle, scalloped-edge tail & wings, 6" h. (very light rust) **165**

Tin Elephant Cookie Cutter

Cookie cutter, elephant, w/strap handle, 4 5/8" l. (ILLUS.) **55**

Gingerbread Girl Cookie Cutter

Cookie cutter, heavy tin, gingerbread girl, no signature (ILLUS.) **20-30**

Tin Gingerbread Woman Cookie Cutter

Cookie cutter, heavy tin, gingerbread woman, large, edges & corners turned in, no signature (ILLUS.) **20-30**

Cookie cutter, tin, a large heart w/a backplate pierced w/two holes, applied back handle, 8 1/4" l. **50**

Cattoline Shortening Cookie Cutter

Cookie cutter, tin, advertising type, Cattoline Shortening, w/fold-down handle, given by companies in the early 1900s (ILLUS.) **25-35**

Amish Horse & Buggy Cookie Cutter

Cookie cutter, tin, Amish horse & buggy, by Eugene Valasek, Canton, Ohio (ILLUS.) ... **20-25**

Large Tin Cookie Cutter

Cookie cutter, tin, bakery-type, w/outline of man in flat-top hat, large oval handle, 7 5/8" l. (ILLUS.) **220**

Beelzebub Cookie Cutter

Cookie cutter, tin, Beelzebub, replica of an antique cutter, made to look old (ILLUS.) .. **10-20**

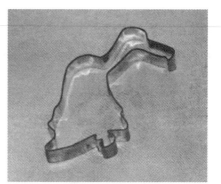

Buzzard Cookie Cutter

Cookie cutter, tin, buzzard, by Little Fox Factory, Bucyrus, Ohio (ILLUS.) **5**

Crinkled Circle Cookie Cutter

Cookie cutter, tin, circle, crinkled edges, early 1900s (ILLUS.) **25-35**

Circle Cookie Cutter

Cookie cutter, tin, circle, used for several purposes such as apple corer, funnel, do-nut cutter or cookie cutter, early 1900s (ILLUS.) **50-75**

Cookie cutter, tin, early handmade heart in hand design, 3 x 4" **350**

Cookie cutter, tin, early handmade horse w/rider, spot-soldered, 5 x 6 1/2" **275**

Cookie cutter, tin, early handmade pig, spot-soldered, 3 x 4" **45**

Cookie cutter, tin, figure of soldier on horseback wearing plumed helmet, 9" l., 10" h. (some rust & a loose seam) **935**

Gingerbread Boy Cookie Cutter

Cookie cutter, tin, gingerbread boy, w/handles, signed E. Valasek, 1979, Canton, Ohio (ILLUS.) **15-20**

Signed Gingerbread Girl Cookie Cutter

Cookie cutter, tin, gingerbread girl, w/handles, signed by Gene Valasek, 1980, Canton, Ohio (ILLUS.) **15-20**

Gingerbread Man Cookie Cutter

Cookie cutter, tin, gingerbread man, flat back, signed by B. Cukla, Hammer Song, Boonsboro, Maryland (ILLUS.) **10-15**

Tin Fish Cookie Cutter

Cookie cutter, tin, model of fish, flat backplate w/large vent hole, 3 x 4" (ILLUS.) **14**

Tin Bear Cookie Cutter

Cookie cutter, tin, model of standing bear, flat backplate, 2 3/4 x 3 3/4" (ILLUS.) **14**

Tin Walking Bear Cookie Cutter

Cookie cutter, tin, model of walking bear w/flat backplate & vent holes, 2 1/4 x 3 1/4" (ILLUS.) **17**

Bird Cookie Cutter

Cookie cutter, tin, outline of bird, narrow (ILLUS.) **10-20**

Waving Gingerbread Boy Cookie Cutter

Cookie cutter, tin, outline of gingerbread boy waving, by Little Fox Factory, Bucyrus, Ohio (ILLUS.) **5**

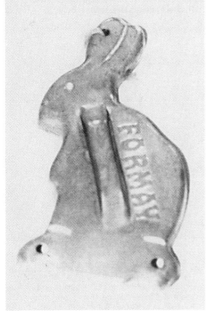

Rabbit Cookie Cutter

Cookie cutter, tin, rabbit, standard self handle, sold on West Coast, Formay, Swift & Co., 3 x 8 1/8" (ILLUS.) **25-50**

Cookie cutter, tin, spread-winged eagle w/the head facing to one side, scallop-tipped tail, on a flat rectangular back w/pierced hole, 19th c., 6" h. (very light rust) **165**

Cookie cutter, tin, stylized design of a running rabbit, w/backplate pierced w/two holes, applied back handle, 7 1/4" l. **50**

Cookie cutter, tin, stylized figure representing Santa Claus, w/a rectangular backplate w/hole, marked Cake Art Germany, 4 1/2 x 11 1/2" (soldered seam loose) **138**

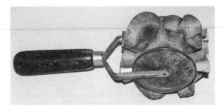

Roller-type Cookie Cutter

Cookie cutter, tin & wood, roller cutter w/six designs, 9" (ILLUS.) **65**

Cookie or cake cutter, tin, handmade bulbous short squatty heart design w/back cut close to design, 3 1/2" w., 3" h. **45**

Cookie or cake cutter, tin, handmade elephant form, no handle **175**

Corn cutter, tin, marked Corn Cutter Pat. Applied For Nesco **65**

Creamer, cov., tole, cylindrical body tapering from base, short spout, strap handle, worn japanning w/yellow lines & red & green rose-like flowers, 4 1/4" h. (ILLUS. top right, w/other various toleware on page 221) **330**

Miniature Cutters & Container

Cutters, miniature, eleven various tin designs in cov. 3 1/2" d. round tin container, the set (ILLUS.) **95**

Document box, cov., tole, miniature, rectangular w/hinged domed lid w/wire bail, good japanned ground w/yellow lines & a white front band w/red & green flowers, first half 19th c., 2 1/4 x 4 1/8", 2 7/8" h. (minor edge wear, hasp incomplete) **165**

Document box, cov., tole, rectangular, dark japanning w/bright green foliage & red flowers & berries on front, yellow scrollwork & stripes on domed lid w/tin hasp & wire bail handle, 5 5/8 x 6 1/2 x 9 3/8" (ILLUS. on page 213 right with coffeepot & other document box) **440**

Document box, tole, cov., rectangular, dark japanning w/white swags on front & sides & strong full-petaled red & yellow flowers & green leaves, yellow designs on domed lid w/brass bail handle, oval escutcheons, tin hasp, 3 5/8 x 4 3/4 x 8 1/4" (ILLUS. middle with coffeepot & other document box on page 213) **440**

Unpainted "Minerva" Doll Head

Doll head, tin, unpainted except teeth, inset glass eyes, marked on front "Minerva, " marked on back "Germany - 7," 6 1/4" h. (ILLUS.) **75**

Tin "Minerva" Doll Head

Doll head, tin, young girl w/center-parted hair, glass eyes, marked "Minerva" on front & "Germany" on back, original worn pink & tan paint, 3 3/4" h. (ILLUS.) **95**

Egg beater, tin, base marked "Made In United States of America A&J," top marked "Full Vision Beater Set," 7 1/2" **40**

Egg beater, tin, Betty Taplin model w/red plastic cup, 6 oz., 6" l. **50**

Egg beater w/syllabub, tin, lightly stamped "The Wonder Cream Whip & Egg Beater Absolutely Unequalled" **75**

Egg Baking Powder Egg Separator

Egg separator, tin, advertising "Egg Baking Powder" (ILLUS.) **150**

Egg separator, tin, advertising, marked "Use Puritan Fadeless Dyes - None Better" **25**

Tin Owl Egg Timer

Egg timer, stamped, three-minute egg timer, glass vial attached to the form of an owl perched on a stump w/a clock design on its chest & "Three Minute Egg Timer" embossed at the bottom, 6 1/2" h. (ILLUS.).......... **145**

Early Tin Flame Minder

Flame minder, tin, a flat-topped disk w/the narrow sides pierced w/diamond-shaped opening's, the top stamped "Flame Minder [crown] Kitchen King," used to control heat intensity on a wood-burning kitchen range, 6 1/4" d., 1" h. (ILLUS.) **10**

Old Tin Flour Scoop

Flour scoop, tin, deep rounded shovel end w/tubular handle, soldered construction, 9 1/2" l. (ILLUS.) 15

Flour sifter, tin, divided w/lids on both ends, marked "Bromwells Multiple" 28

Flour sifter, tin & wood, "Duplex Sifter 5 cup, Pat. Nov. 1917 & 1922, Mfg. by Ull-rich Tinware Co." 30

Flour sifter/scoop, tin w/half round wire mesh scoop & removable screwed-on long handle, marked "Pillsbury's Flour Universal Scoop with Flour Attachment"...... 110

Fluid lantern, blown glass & tin, a short cylindrical tin font w/brass collar below the squatty onion-form clear glass globe topped by a cylindrical top w/pointed cap & large ring handle, the top w/star & diamond pierced designs, old pitted finish, mid-19th c., 10" h. plus handle 440

Food mold, tin, deep heart-shaped form w/the flat top pierced w/stylized leafy stems & small blossoms, small strap handle at the top, on three small feet, 4 1/2" l., 3 1/8" h. (small old soldered repair) 385

Funnel, tin, advertising, marked "Forbes Quality Coffee," 3" 50

Funnel cake pourer, tin, handmade, long handle w/funnel attached to end 35

Tin Headlamp

Headlamp, tin, rectangular, w/punched holes around base, large round glass pane, nickel-plated burner, flattened dome chimney, for traction engine (trolley or tram), burned kerosene, ca. 1900, 24" h. (ILLUS.) 1,200

Jar lid reformer, tin, unmarked, 7 1/2" 20

Jar opener, tin, "Perfect, Pat Pending," 7 1/4" 15

Jar opener, tin, "The Turney Mfg. Co. Detroit, Mich Pat Oct 31, 1905" 30

Jar opener & jar lifter combination tool, tin, Hotong, 10" 25

Juicer, tin w/wall mount, "Dazey Churn & Mfg Co, St. Louis, MO" 40

Lunch pail, tin, rectangular, no tray 65

Pressed-tin Match Holder

Match holder, pressed tin, backplate w/scalloped border shows image of building in circle below banner w/"Carnegie Library - Newton, Kansas," square holder for matches attached to front w/"Matches" embossed on it, decorative leaf borders at corners of both pieces, 3 1/4 x 5" (ILLUS.)...... 125

Tin Mammy Match Holder

Match holder, tin, hanging-type, backplate w/stamped image of a black Mammy against hammered background, leaning on two match containers w/hammered finish centered by striker section, overall gold paint, 4 3/4 x 5 1/2" (ILLUS.).................... 49

Tin Owl Match Holder

Match holder, tin, hanging-type, stylized owl backplate w/pierced eyes, two half-round ridged match holders, black paint, 3 1/2 x 4 5/8" (ILLUS.) 29

Measures, tin, pitcher-type, slightly tapering cylindrical body w/tapering flaring rim band, wide strap handle, each bearing the seal of the State of Minnesota Railroad and Warehouse Commission, tallest 6 5/8" h., graduated set of 3 (ILLUS. below) 125

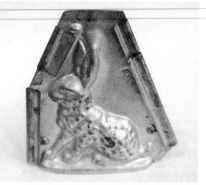

Tin Sitting Rabbit Chocolate Mold

Mold, chocolate, in the form of a sitting rabbit, 1 1/4 x 5 x 5 1/2" (ILLUS.) 95

Mold, tin w/tube in center, marked "Silvers Pudding Mold Brooklyn, NY," 5" h., 3 1/2" d. base 50

Muffin pan, tin, 12-cup size, plain 12

Muffin pan, tin, six-cup size w/three different designs 35

Mug, tole, very slightly tapering cylinder shape w/rolled rim at base & strap handle, w/original floral decoration in red, yellow & brown on a ground of very worn brown japanning, 5 3/4" h. (ILLUS. right with sugar bowl on page 221) 385

Soccer Player Chocolate Mold

Mold, chocolate, boy soccer player w/crossed arms & w/foot resting on ball, 1 1/2 x 3 1/2", 7" h. (ILLUS.) 45

Rare Early Nautical Lantern

Graduated Set of Tin Measures.

Nautical lantern, tin & glass, a clear glass hexagonal fixed globe in the Beaded Double Bulls-eye patt. fitted w/a cylindrical pierced tin top w/conical cap & ring strap handle, a pierced short cylindrical font base, mid-19th c., corrosion, restoration, 12" h. (ILLUS. on previous page) **2,300**

Tin Minstrel Noise Maker

Noise maker, tin, drumhead-like piece w/handle, decorated w/figures of dancing black minstrels within decorative border, original paint in reds, blues & yellows & original printed design, noise is produced when ball at end of shaft fastened to handle is swung against it, made in Germany, 6 1/2" l. (ILLUS.) **245**

Nutmeg grater, japanned tin, paper label reading "The Rapid Nutmeg Grater," 6" **250**

Nutmeg grater, tin, coffin-style, 5" **15**

Nutmeg grater, tin, cylindrical pocket-type, hinged lid folds down to reveal grater, 1" d., 2 1/2" h. (traces of japanning) **110**

Rare Carsley Nutmeg Grater

Nutmeg grater, tin, marked "H. Carsley, Patented Nov. 20, 1855, Lynn, Mass," rare (ILLUS.) **975**

Nutmeg grater, tin, "MTE Co.," 4 1/4" **75**

Nutmeg grater, tin, "The Boye Nutmeg Grater Pat Apl'd For," 6" **85**

Triangular Nutmeg Grater with Plunger

Nutmeg grater, tin, triangular w/wood plunger, stamped "Patented Oct. 13th 1857," remnants of blue japanning (ILLUS.) **550**

Tin Oil Lamp

Oil lamp, tin, w/lidded opening on top, strap handle & straight spout where wick end comes out, 1 3/4 x 2", 5 1/2" l. (ILLUS.) **85**

Pastry mixer, tin, "Lambert Patent 486255" **20**

Tin Alarm Clock Pencil Sharpener

Pencil sharpener, plated tin, in the form of an alarm clock w/printed dial, made in Germany, 1/2 x 1 1/8 x 1 3/4" (ILLUS. on previous page) 65

Tin Radio-shaped Pencil Sharpener

Pencil sharpener, tin, model of a table radio, w/peeling paint, made in Germany, 1/2 x 1 1/8 x 1 3/8" (ILLUS.) 55
Pie lifter, tin, flat plate w/green handle, two flat metal arms above plate 55
Pie pan, tin, impressed "Crusty Pie" w/sun rays extending from center, 9 1/2" d 15
Rolling pin, tin w/wood handles, unmarked 300
Scoop, tin, flour scoop w/advertising for Neyhart Hardware Co., Williamsport, Pennsylvania 20
Sifter, tin, child's version, marked "Hunter-toy-Sifter; Pat. May 16.71 - Apr. 7.74 Buy A Large One," approximately 2" h 350
Signal lantern, tin & glass, a short cylindrical base w/font & tall pierced cylindrical top w/conical cap & large loop handle, fitted w/a blown cranberry glass globe engraved "C.R.R.," first half 19th c., 12 1/2" h. plus handle (replaced brass font w/burner) 1,100
Skater's lantern, tin & glass, a cobalt blue glass pear-shaped globe fitted w/a pierced tin domed cap w/wire bail handle, on a tin burner ring on a domed tin font base, late 19th - early 20th c., 6 3/4" h. 275

Skater's lantern, tin & glass, round base w/burner & round pierced domed vented top w/wire bail handle, clear glass globe, marked "Dietz Sport," 7 3/4" h. 193
Skimmer, tin, 5 3/4" d. bowl w/punched six-pointed star, w/handle 13" l. 65
Spatula, tin w/steel handle, heart cut-out in tin base, Rumford advertising, 11 1/2" 50
Spoon, tin w/steel handle, advertising, marked "Kitchen Bouquet Inc." on handle along w/measurements for 1/2 teaspoon, 1 teaspoon & 1/2 tablespoon, 11 1/2" l. 20
Spoon, tin w/wood handle, one side of spoon has rolled edge w/jagged teeth, patented in 1901, no markings 65
Spoon rest, tin, advertising, marked "The Big Store - McCammon Investment Co. Props." 65

Tole Sugar Bowl & Mug

Sugar bowl, cov., tin, tapered body w/slightly flaring base, w/original floral decoration in red, yellow & green on a very worn dark ground, 3 3/4" h. (ILLUS. w/mug) 385
Sugar container, cov., tole, cylindrical, tapering to short base, worn japanned ground w/large red fruit & green leaf design, lid w/finial, red & yellow leaves on bare tin, 3 1/2 x 4" (ILLUS. bottom left, w/other various toleware) 550
Tea caddy, cov., tole, cylindrical, red ground w/pinkish white band at top, w/red, yellow & green flowers, 4 1/8" h. (ILLUS. top left, below, w/other various toleware) 495
Tea caddy, tole, cylinder body, cone-shape neck, dark japanned ground w/design of a red ball shape w/copper-colored feathering, 6 3/4" h. (ILLUS. second from right, below w/other various toleware) 358

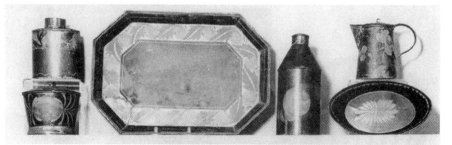

Various Toleware Pieces

Tea strainer, tin, advertising-type, marked "Royal Crest Dairy" **25**
Tinder box, cov., tin, low cylindrical form w/the top half lifting off, flat top centered by a candle socket, finger ring on base half, interior damper lid w/flint & over-sized striker, 19th c., 4" d. **413**

Tin Windup Minstrel Dancers

Toy, windup, tin, in black, white, red & blue paint, rectangular base holds two dancing black men in minstrel outfits, made in U.S.A., 3 x 5 1/2", 8" h. (ILLUS.) **795**

Tin Windup Walking Robot Toy

Toy, windup, tin, walking robot, eyes light up & clear plastic chest shows spinning gears, marked "KO Made in Japan," 11" h. (ILLUS.) **465**

Tin Frog Toy Clicker

Toy clicker, tin, stamped model of frog w/original green, yellow & red paint, marked "Life of the Party Products," 2 x 3" (ILLUS.) **13**
Travelers lantern, tole & glass, square scalloped frame, collapsible w/mica panels, brown japanning w/yellow stenciling & label "Minors Patent, Jan 24th 1865," 5 1/8" h. (minor wear) **385**
Tray, tole, long, octagonal, japanned ground w/white band w/red & green fruit & leaves, yellow rim strip, center has faint red crystallization, 8 1/2 x 12 3/8" (ILLUS. second from left, w/other various toleware on previous page) **330**
Tray, tole, oval, dark japanned ground w/yellow wavy line & red & yellow center design, 6 7/8" l. (ILLUS. bottom right, w/other various toleware on previous page) **1,760**

Beehive Pattern Whale Oil Lantern

Whale oil lantern, glass & tin, a clear mold-blown Beehive patt. glass globe fitted w/a pierced cylindrical top w/conical cap & ring strap handle, pierced cylindrical font base w/flared round foot, mid-19th c., paint loss, minor corrosion, 12 1/2" h. (ILLUS.) **1,035**
Whale oil lantern, tin & glass, a round tin base w/flared foot supporting the clear blown glass pear-shaped globe, cylindrical cap w/conical top w/pierced designs & large ring handle, removable font w/whale oil burner, worn original brown japanning, probably New England Glass Co., first half 19th c., 11" h. plus handle **358**

Brass tongs each w/a lighthouse-form handle, on a matching stand w/lighthouse & rock-form base, stamped on the bottom w/the Rostand trademark, Rostand Mfg. Co., Milford, Connecticut, early 20th c., andirons, 29 3/4" h., the set $7,050.

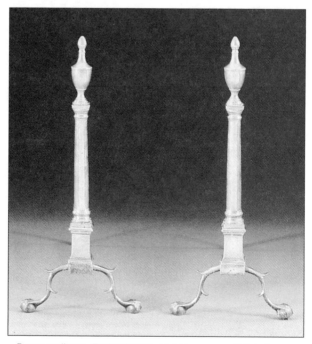

Brass andirons, Federal style, an acorn on urn finial above a tapering columnar shaft over a box plinth, on spurred cabriole front legs w/ball-and-claw feet, American, ca. 1800-10, 25 1/2" h., pr. $2,115.

Copper bowl, Arts & Crafts style, deep rounded & tapering sides w/a rolled rim, decorated w/chased & repoussé waves highlighted w/silver beads of spray & a silver rim, rich patina, impressed mark of Arthur J. Stone, ca. 1901-12, 5 3/4" d., 2 3/4" h., **$6,300.-6,400.**

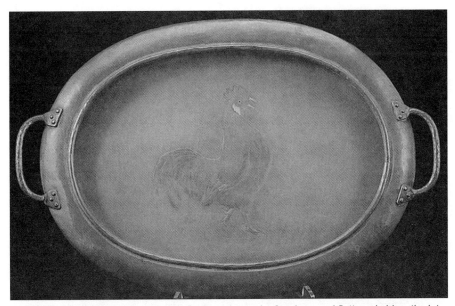

Copper tray, hand-hammered, Arts & Crafts style, oval w/low incurved flattened sides, the interior w/a tooled & painted picture of a rooster covered in glass, arched riveted end handles, original light brown patina, leather signed "G.M. Lee," copper w/windmill mark of Dirk Van Erp, 1912, 16 x 24", **$2,000.-2,500.**

*Copper box, cov., Arts & Crafts style, hand-hammered, a rectangular slightly domed cover widely overhanging the rectangular box, signed "H. Dixon - San Francisco - 1920," **$900.-1,000.***

*Copper vase, patinated ribbed widely flaring oval form w/a scalloped rim, raised on a small oblong foot, dark brown & green patina, inscribed "M. Zimmermann maker - 1463-1915 B" & artist's cipher, Marie Zimmermann, 1915, scratches, 11 1/2" w., 6 7/8" h., **$4,300.-4,400.***

Copper dresser tray, Arts & Crafts style, hand-hammered, long rectangular form w/a dished center, the wide flat rim embossed w/an intertwined linear design at the ends, patina cleaned, incised Jarvie mark, early 20th c., 6 x 12",
$2,800.-3,000.

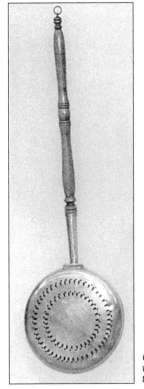

*Copper teakettle, cov., dovetailed construction, flat-bottomed bulbous form w/wide rounded shoulder centering a low-domed fitted cover, angled swan's-neck spout, high arched strap swing handle stamped "I. Roberts Phila.," Israel Roberts, Philadelphia, early 19th c., **$1,800.***

*Copper chestnut roaster, cov., bed warmer-form, round pan w/pierced cover engraved w/tulip designs, a long ring- and baluster-turned wood handle, dents in base, 36" l., **$358.***

Copper measure, haystack-form, wide flared base below the sharply tapering conical dovetailed body w/a narrow neck & flared rim w/spout, hollow C-form handle, stamped "Gallon," England, 19th c., 12" h., **$250.-300.**

Copper jug, hand-hammered, dovetailed construction, flat-bottomed gently flaring cylindrical form w/wide rounded shoulder centered by a small tapering cylindrical neck, arched strap shoulder handle, 9 1/2" h., **$550.**

Copper vase, hand-hammered, Arts & Crafts style, gently swelling cylindrical form w/bulbed top & closed rim, excellent original patina, closed box mark of Dirk Van Erp, San Francisco, early 20th c., 6" d., 10" h., **$5,500.**

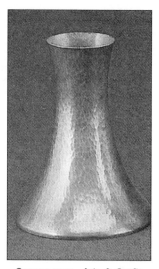

Copper vase, Arts & Crafts style, hand-hammered, tall corseted shape w/a wide base, fine original dark patina, closed box mark of Dirk Van Erp, early 20th c., 7" d., 9 1/2" h., **$1,870.**

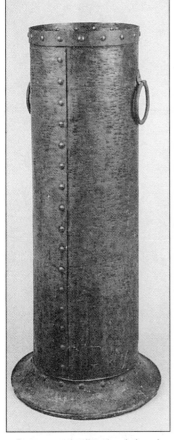

Copper umbrella stand, hand-hammered, Arts & Crafts style, flaring round foot riveted to the tall cylindrical riveted body w/a riveted rim band, two loose swing handles at sides, dark patina, America, early 20th c., some wear & discoloration, 11" d., 26 1/2" h., $288.

Copper vase, Arts & Crafts style, hand-hammered, urn-form w/a round disk foot below the urn-form body w/a very tall waisted neck w/flared rim, long slender S-scroll handles issuing from the bottom & ending at the rim, impressed mark of L. & J.G. Stickley, No. F15, early 20th c., 10" d., 18" h., $4,400.

Copper weathervane, molded & gilded model of a steeplechase horse, molded in two parts, the horse w/hole-eyes, notched mouth, windswept, stamped & serrated mane & tail, leaping w/forelegs tucked under & rear legs extended over a stamped sheet metal fence on a vertical rod support, A.L. Jewell, Waltham, Massachusetts, mid-19th c., on modern base, 37" l., 34" h., $94,600.

Copper weathervane, copper & iron, molded copper figure of the Statue of Liberty wearing a radiating crown & holding a torch in an extended hand, on a rectangular platform, the arrow below w/a corrugated copper tail, mounted on iron directionals & two copper spheres, no stand, several dents, minor loss on tail, American, ca. 1886, 56 1/2" h., **$23,500.**

Copper weathervane, molded copper model of a steam-driven locomotive & tender car, overall verdigris patina, mounted on a hollow copper rod, no stand, American, late 19th c., minor dents, 75" l., 29 1/2" h., **$237.**

*Left to right: gilt-copper weathervane, running horse with a flattened body, no stand, couple of small dents, American, late 19th c., 26 1/4" l., 16" h., $2,468; gilded tin model of an eagle perched on a rockery weighted base and holding a scales in its beak, maker's tag for MR. Frond Co., Camden, New Jersey, late 19th c., imperfections, 32 3/4" w., 19 1/4" h., **$1,800;** gilt-copper weathervane, running horse, full-bodied animal with copper head and hollow body, no stand, American, late 19th c., gilt wear, minor dent, 41 1/2" l., 21" h., **$4,113.***

Copper dish, ten-sided tray-form "Dinanderie," dish, Art Deco style, patinated copper w/inlaid silver geometric designs, stamped "3960 - Jean Dunand," France, ca. 1925, 14 1/4" w., **$8,813.**

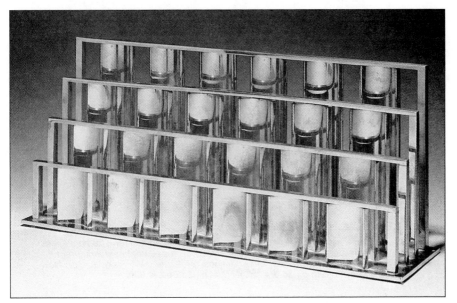

Chromed bronze letter rack, Art Deco style, four tiers of rectangular upright frames fitted w/curved sheet dividers, attributed to Jacques-Emile Ruhlmann, France, ca. 1925, 19 5/8" l., 8 1/4" h., **$11,750.**

Cast-iron aquarium, the shell- and foliate-decorated octagonal tank frame w/glass sides centering a rockery-form fountain, raised on a pedestal cast w/figural herons on a molded round base, imperfections, probably J.W. Fiske & Co., New York, last quarter 19th c., 36 3/4" w., 47 3/4" h., **$3,500.-4,000.**

Left to right: cast-iron watch hutch, an upright scroll-cast frame with a round opening resting on a base cast with further leafy scrolling surrounding a spread-winged eagle, traces of black paint, light rust, 19th c., 10 1/4" h., **$80. - $100.;** cast-iron card tray, a standing figure of a blackamoor holding a shallow basket-form tray, atop a stepped rectangular base, base with advertising for The Hoefinchoff & Lane Foundry Co., Cincinnati, Ohio, 1875-1903, old black, gold, silver and red paint, 9" h., **$550.-600.**

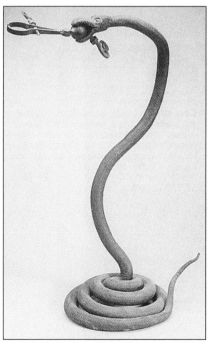

Cast-iron hitching post, figural, a standing black boy wearing a hat, scarf, vest & long pants, his right arm extended w/a closed fist, the left hand in his pocket, last half 19th c., repaired, 24 1/2" h., **$800.-1,000.**

Iron holder, hand-wrought, figural, a tall upright snake w/a coiled lower body, holding in its open mouth a ball joint w/caliper-form clamp, 19th c., 20 1/4" h., **$2,500.-3,000.**

Cast-iron umbrella stand, figural, a standing sailor holding a coiling rope support & resting atop crossed oars, anchor & various other nautical items, oblong low shallow drip pan base w/acanthus leaf cast border, removable pan, marked "1927 Marcy Foundry Co.," repainted, 27 1/2"h., **$2,750.-3,000.**

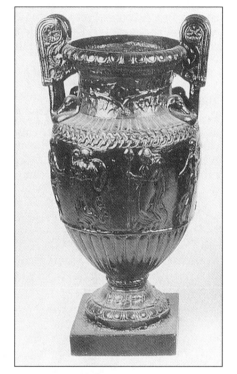

Cast-iron urns, classical-style, the large ovoid body w/a narrow angled shoulder to a wide cylindrical neck w/swelled rim, high arched scroll- and blossom-cast handles from rim to shoulder, the body cast in high-relief w/a continuous band of classical figures, the neck cast w/vines, the ribbed lower body resting on a short domed pedestal w/a square foot, early 20th c., repainted, 32" h., pr., **$2,100.-2,300.**

Cast-iron mirror, table model, the oval mirror swiveling on a frame cast w/flags beneath a crown, oak
leaves & acorns, set on two suits of armor raised on
a base pierced w/a military trophy & shield form feet,
cold-painted, mid-19th c., 19 3/4" h., **$747.**

Cast-iron fireplace insert, a bowfront flat base w/a
small raised lip, scalloped side panels w/relief-cast
fans & faces, biscuit corners on the top w/circular &
oval fans, original seamed brass finials, signed
"Wyer & Noble," early 19th c., originally had feet,
back plate cracked, base 22 3/4" w., 28" h., **$330.**

Iron utensil rack, hand-wrought, a flattened bar w/double scrolls at each end, an upright center flat bar w/pairs of small scrolls below the large forked curled-under top scrolls, 28" l., 14 1/2" h., $1,980.

Cast-iron stove plate, rectangular form, the top w/two arched reserves separated w/spiral columns, one side w/a man on horseback, the other w/an urn of vining flowers, embossed wording "Shfarwell Furnace in Oly - Dieter Weiker," Friedensburg, Bucks County, Pennsylvania, 19 x 22", $605.

Far left and right, iron hand-wrought andirons, modeled as upright coiled serpents, the head with an open mouth and projecting tongue, S-form body ending in a coiled tail, bolted to a log support, found in New York state, surface rust, 19th c., 19 3/4" h., pair, $5,463; back row left, hand-wrought iron trivet, model of a coiled snake, incised underside, on three short scroll legs, found in Pennsylvania, minor surface corrosion, 19th c., 4 3/4 x 10 1/2", 3 1/4" h., $978; back row center, hand-wrought iron calipers, the handle in the form of a coiled snake continuing to a shaft with four bifurcating riveted arms, with stand, possibly Boston Foundry, late 18th c., surface corrosion, 12 3/4" w., 17" h., $2,875; back row right, hand-wrought iron door handle, modeled as a snake, the head with an open mouth and teeth, curving body and coiled tail, with stand, late 19th - early 20th c., surface corrosion, 12 1/4" l., 3 1/2" h., $1,150; front row left, hand-wrought iron miniature andirons, knife blade-style, polyhedron finial on shaft, arched legs to penny feet, American, late 18th - early 19th c., worn black paint, 4" w., 6 3/4" h., pair, $58; front row, right, hand-wrought iron miniature andirons, gilded forward looped finial on a simple square shaft above curved front legs with penny feet, American, early 19th c., 3 1/2" w., 5" h., pair, **$460.**

Left to right: cast-iron hitching post modeled as a dog's head with a large ring in the mouth, traces of black paint, with stand, American, 19th c., minor surface rust, 11" w., 12" h., $4,025; sand-cast iron gate latch, model of a duck's head, the head forming the articulated handle, possibly California, late 19th c., with stand, weathered surface, 3 3/4 x 7", 3 1/2" h., $230; cast-iron hitching post modeled as a diminutive horse head, long and small rings in the mouth, traces of black paint, Rochester, New York, ca. 1850, on stand, 4 1/2" w., 9 7/8" h., $1,840; cast-iron hitching post modeled as a small horse head hinged on a post cap so it nods, traces of black paint, patented in 1889 by W.H. Vaughn, Quincy, Illinois, no stand, losses, 7" w., 5" h., $316; cast-iron hitching post top, model of a large horse head with loop and ring in the nose, old weathered surface, American, 19th c., with stand, 4 1/4 x 9 1/2", 11 1/2" h., $633.

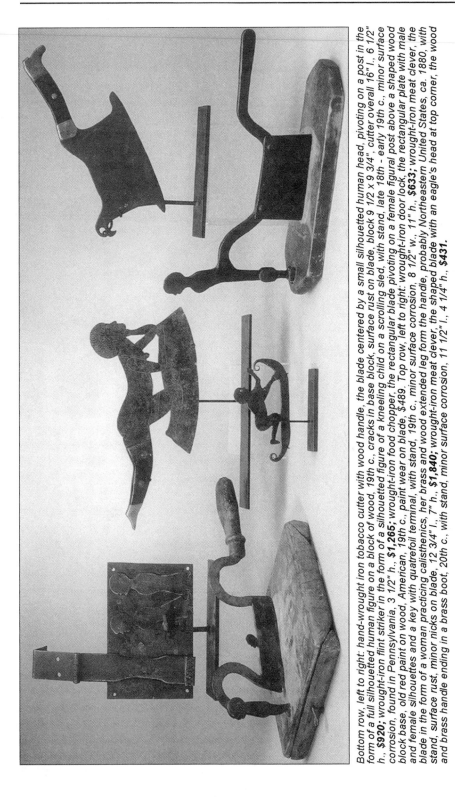

Bottom row, left to right: hand-wrought iron tobacco cutter with wood handle, the blade centered by a small silhouetted human head, pivoting on a post in the form of a full silhouetted human figure on a block of wood, 19th c., cracks in base block, surface rust on blade, block 9 1/2 x 9 3/4" cutter overall 16" l., 6 1/2" h., $920; wrought-iron flint striker in the form of a silhouetted figure of a kneeling child on a scrolling sled, with stand, late 18th - early 19th c., minor surface corrosion, found in Pennsylvania, 3 1/2" h., $1,265; wrought-iron food chopper, the rectangular blade pivoting on a female figural post above a shaped wood block base, old red paint on wood, American, 19th c., paint wear on blade, $489. Top row, left to right: wrought-iron door lock, the rectangular plate with male and female silhouettes and a key with quatrefoil terminal, with stand, 19th c., minor surface corrosion, 8 1/2" w., 11" h., $633; wrought-iron meat clever, the blade in the form of a woman practicing calisthenics, her brass and wood extended leg form the handle, probably Northeastern United States, ca. 1880, with stand, surface rust, minor nicks on blade, 12 3/4" l., 7" h., $1,840; wrought-iron meat clever, the shaped blade with an eagle's head at top corner, the wood and brass handle ending in a brass boot, 20th c., with stand, minor surface corrosion, 11 1/2" l., 4 1/4" h., $431.

*Cast-iron gate weight, modeled as a full sun face, loop handle at top, Massachusetts, late 18th c., w/stand, 9" d., **$10,925.***

*Top row, left to right: cast-iron model of a cat head, large stylized head with long whiskers, mounting holes in ears and nose, patinated, late 19th c., with stand, 8 x 8", **$1,495;** wrought-iron model of a standing horse, silhouetted sheet on a rectangular stand, old pitted surface, possibly New York state, 19th c., 9 1/2" l., 8 3/4" h., **$978;** cast-iron architectural fragment, large slightly curved plaque cast in bold relief with a lion head, old weathered surface, American, late 19th c., with stand, 1 x 11", 15" h., **$1,725.** Front row, left to right: cast-iron model of a spread-winged eagle perched on a rockwork base, old black paint with white spots, American, late 19th c., 5 1/2 x 11", 3 1/2" h., **$242;** cast-iron doorstop in the form of a fat seated bear, open legs, painted brown, American, late 19th - early 20th c., 2 1/2 x 5 1/4", 4 1/2" h., **$1,150.***

*Cast-iron water trough, rectangular, a high arched back splash plate w/the maker's name along the base & a small cast lion mask spout over a grilled overflow drain in the base, the main drain stopped w/a iron plug, the whole set on a bracket base, J.W. Fiske & Co., New York, New York, late 19th c., 24 x 35 1/2", 38" h., **$1,293.***

Far left and right: cast-iron andirons in the form of an African-American man standing with hands on bent knees, early paint with white shirt, red pants, black skin and painted facial features, paint imperfections, minor corrosions, ca. 1870, 12 1/2 x 16 1/2", 19 1/2" h., pair, $1,380. Center: cast-iron hitching post finial in the form of a stylized head of an African-American man holding a ring and chain in his mouth, 19th c., later stand, 5 1/2 x 6", 9 1/2" h., $2,300.

Left to right: cast-iron windmill weight in the form of a seated squirrel, light brown paint, on original base, attributed to Elgin Wind Power & Pump Co., Elgin, Illinois, early 20th c., new black metal stand, 13 1/2 x 17 1/4", $3,220; painted sheet iron stand, a large standing chicken, weathered putty-colored paint and faintly stenciled word "DINNERS," American, 23 1/2 x 28 3/4", $805.

Cast-iron hitching post finial, a stylized head of Napoleon cast in the full round, detailed hair & facial features,
fringed epaulets on shoulders, a ring on one side of
shoulder, on a cylindrical attachment base, American,
19th c., 8" h., **$4,465.**

Cast-iron wall plaques, half-round model of a fruit-filled
cornucopia, the horn painted bright red w/yellow trim,
the fruits in red, green & black, American, early 20th c.,
15" l., pr. **$225.**

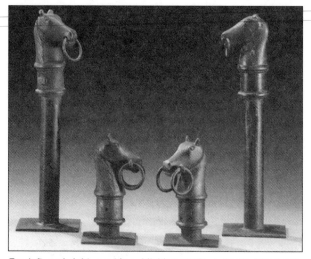

Far left and right: cast-iron hitching posts, a horse head with articulated ears, mane, eyes and nostrils, cast in the full round, pierced mouth with iron ring above a cylindrical post, on a later square base, American, 19th c., 20 1/2" h., pair, **$621;** *cast-iron small hitching posts, a horse head with articulated ears, eyes, mane and nostrils cast in the full round, mouth pierced and holding a bar with a ring at each end, on a cylindrical base, on a modern foot, American, 19th c., overall 9 1/2" h., pair,* **$1,058.**

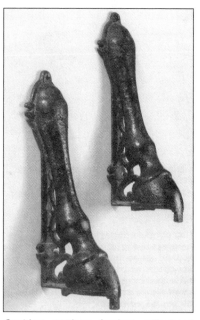

Cast-iron hitching post finial, modeled as a human hand w/closed fingers above a ruffled cuff, cast in the full round, a chain attached from side to side, on a modern base, American, late 19th c., overall 9 1/4" h., **$3,760.**

Cast-iron carriage fenders, articulated horse hoof & ankle cast in the full round & backed by an L-shaped bracket & scrollwork, marked on sides w/maker's name & address, painted black, William Adams & Co., Philadelphia, late 19th c., 6x10", 25" h., pr. **$2,585.**

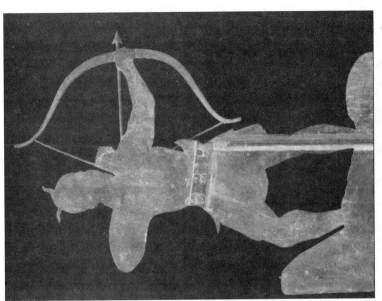

Sheet copper & zinc weathervane, silhouetted figure of a Native American w/a zinc left arm drawing a bow & arrow, traces of yellow paint, attributed to A.L. Jewell, Waltham, Massachusetts, mid-19th c., 16 1/2" w., 26" h., **$11,750.**

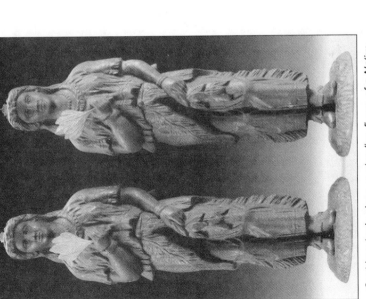

Cast-iron trade signs, a standing figure of a Native American princess cast in the full round, articulated hair, facial features, fringed clothing & shoes, applied green-painted hair ornament & tobacco leaf held in right hand, on a rocky base, remnants of brown paint, American, late 19th c., 7 1/2 x 7 1/2", 25" h., pr. **$11,163.**

*Cast-iron gate, rectangular openwork form centering a War of 1812 cap surrounded by military trophies including crossed rifles, swords, bugle & shot bag marked "U.S.," & acorn leaves, flanked on each side by crossed darts & above & below by a band of circles, the top set w/stars flanked by spear points, repainted in green, red, black & white, American, late 19th c., 77" l., 45 1/4" h., **$5,875.**

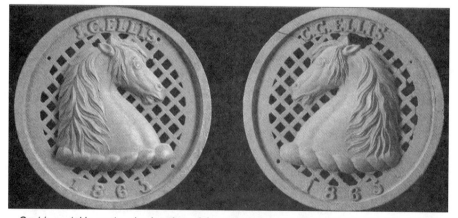

*Cast-iron stable vents, circular pierced form centering a relief-molded profile horse head above a torso on lattice ground enclosed by a roundel, one cast w/"C.G. Ellis - 1865," the other "J.C. Ellis - 1865," probably J.W. Fiske & Co., New York, New York, ca. 1865, 18" d., pr. **$1,998.**

*Left to right: cast-iron hitching post in the form of a tall tree trunk with molded bark, cast in the round with stubby branches and a meandering berried vine above a grassy base, trunk painted brown, vine and grass painted green, American, 19th c., 35 3/4" h., **$353;** cast-iron hitching post with an open trefoil finial above a flattened flaring shaft pierced with quatrefoil and round openings, painted brown, American, late 19th c., modern base, 10" w., 39" h., **$705;** cast-iron hitching post with a realistic horse head finial with detailed curly mane, ears, eyes, nostrils and mouth with ring above a lobed capital flanked by rings, over a fluted column with lion heads and scrolls at the base, painted brown, modern square foot, American, late 19th c., 35 1/2" h., **$2,233;** cast-iron hitching post with a realistic horse head finial with finely cast details above a lobed capital over a tall fluted column footed by lion heads and scrolls above a faceted base, modern metal foot, American, late 19th c., 8 1/2 x 9", 48 3/4" h., **$2,115;** cast-iron hitching post with a stylized horse head finial with pronounced ears and delineated mane above a side ring and fluted column, new square, painted black, American, late 19th c., 27 1/2" h., **$705;** cast-iron hitching post with a ring finial above a tapering neck over a tall spiral-cast column with a stylized leaf base band and plinth, new square foot, painted yellow, American, late 19th c., 11 3/4 x 12", 49" h., **$1,058.***

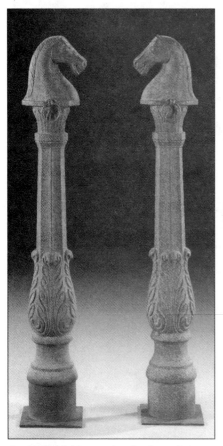

Left to right: cast-iron hitching posts, the top formed by a looped swan's head with a feathered and imbricated neck, above a slender three-part ribbed shaft, painted black, modern base, American, 19th c., 52 1/2" h., pair, **$2,115;** cast-iron hitching posts with the finial cast as eagle's head with detailed crown, eyes and beak above a feathered neck over a baluster-form shaft with scrolled decorations above a ball and plinth base, traces of black paint, modern foot, American, mid-19th c., 46 1/2" h., pair, **$4,465.**

Cast-iron hitching posts, the top w/a horse head cast in the round w/a detailed mane, eyes, nostrils & mouth above a ring & oval leaf-cast capital above the faceted column w/acanthus leaves around the bottom on a waisted cylindrical base, modern foot, attributed to J.W. Fiske & Co., New York, New York, late 19th c., 48" h., pr. **$4,465.**

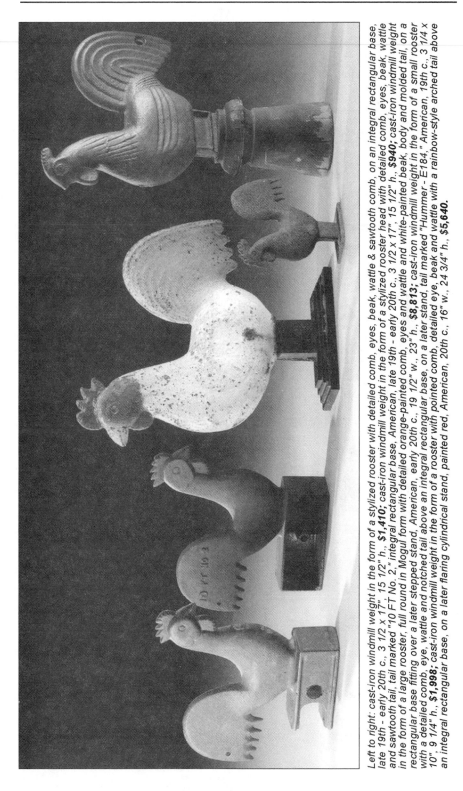

Left to right: cast-iron windmill weight in the form of a stylized rooster with detailed comb, eyes, beak, wattle & sawtooth comb, on an integral rectangular base, late 19th - early 20th c., 3 1/2 x 17", 15 1/2" h., **$1,410;** cast-iron windmill weight in the form of a stylized rooster head with detailed comb, eyes, beak, wattle and sawtooth tail, tail marked "10 FT No. 2," integral rectangular base, American, late 19th - early 20th c., 3 1/2 x 17", 15 1/2" h., **$940;** cast-iron windmill weight in the form of a large rooster, full round in Mogul form with detailed orange-painted comb, eyes and wattle and white-painted beak, body and molded tail, on a rectangular base fitting over a later stepped stand, American, early 20th c., 19 1/2" w., 23" h., **$8,813;** cast-iron windmill weight in the form of a small rooster with a detailed comb, eye, wattle and notched tail above an integral rectangular base, on a later stand, tail marked "Hummer - E184," American, 19th c., 3 1/4 x 10", 9 1/4" h., **$1,998;** cast-iron windmill weight in the form of a rooster with pointed comb, detailed eye, beak and wattle with a rainbow-style arched tail above an integral rectangular base, on a later flaring cylindrical stand, painted red, American, 20th c., 16" w., 24 3/4" h., **$5,640.**

Left to right: pewter bowl, shallow wide form with flanged rim, Thomas Danforth III, Philadelphia, 1807-13, minor wear and scratches, 11 5/8" d., **$380-
400;** pewter teapot in a tall tapering "lighthouse" shape with flared base and
domed cover, swan's-neck spout and C-scroll handle, Freeman Porter, Westbrook, Maine, 1835-60, finial wafer missing, minor cover dents, 10 3/4" h.,
$250-300; pewter charger, round with wide flanged rim, eagle touch of Sam-
uel Pierce, Greenfield, Massachusetts, 1807-31, minor wear and pitting, 11
1/4" d., **$350-400.**

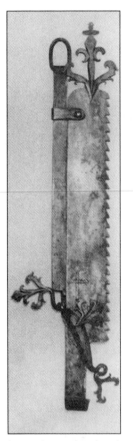

Pewter figures of Westerners, standing man wearing a top
hat, frock coat & kneebreeches, raised on a waisted rectangular pedestal base w/scroll-cast trim, overall polychrome decoration, China, late 18th - early 19th c.,
imperfections, 7 1/2" h., pr. **$3,000.-3,200.**

Iron trammel, hand-
wrought, scalloped &
scrolled finials on top,
side bar & catch,
engraved detail w/a
cross & "1809," adjusts
from 43" to 60", **$495.**

Tole tea canisters, cov., cylindrical form w/rounded shoulder & short cylindrical neck, dark green ground decorated in gilt w/Chinese characters, applied label reading "Parnall & Sons Ltd. Manufacturer - Complete Shop Fitters for all Trades - Narrow Wine St. Bristol," England, 19th c., now mounted as lamps, pr. **$1,610.**

Tin w/silver gilt model of a rooster, ornate stylized bird w/scalloped comb & wattle, separate wing feathers & ornate arching tail feather, on slender legs perched on a carved wood rockwork base, Europe, probably 19th c., gilt wear, minor losses, 24 1/2" l., 29" h., **$1,100.-1,500.**

Tole document box, cov., rectangular w/a gently domed hinged cover w/wire loop handle, the front decorated w/two birds & leafy branches of fruit, the sides w/a band of leaves in orange, green, yellow & white on a black ground, attributed to Mercy North, Flycreek, New York, late 18th - early 19th c., wear, 6 1/2 x 9 5/8", 7 1/4" h., **$1,150.**

Tole urn, Classical style, the tall body raised on a slender pedestal w/a flared round foot, fitted w/a tall slender pointed cover w/acorn finial, high wide arched loop side handles, decorated w/floral sprays & birds w/scalloped floral & repeating gilt leaf borders, weighted base, paint loss, one lower handle detached, probably France, 19th c., one of a pair **$600.-1,000.**

Tin coffeepot, cov., the angled ovoid body decorated on each side w/wrigglework flowers in two-handled pots & four spiral-twisted punchwork lower bands, the hinged domed cover w/a turned finial, angled gooseneck spout, strap handle w/grip impressed "J. Ketterer" for John B. Ketterer, Pennsylvania, mid-19th c., 11 1/2" h., **$3,300.**

Left to right: tall cylindrical tole mug with a strap handle, original dark brown japanning with a white rim band with floral decoration in red, green and yellow, good color, 19th c., some wear, 4 1/2" h., $675-775; tole deed box, deep rectangular sides with hinged flat cover with ring bail handle, worn original brown japanning with white band and stylized floral bands in red, green and yellow, with hasp, good color, 19th c., 8 1/8" h., $600-700.

Left to right: tole document box, deep rectangular form with hinged gently arched cover with loop bail handle, decorated with flowers and fruit in red, yellow and green on a black ground, wear, small dents, early 19th c., 4 3/4 x 10", 6 1/2" h., $403; tole coffeepot, tall tapering cylindrical form with gooseneck spout and strap handle, hinged domed cover with scrolled finial, decorated with fruit and leaves in a diamond formation in shades of orange, yellow and green on a black ground, wear, small hole, first half 19th c., 10 1/4" h., $863.

*Left to right: tole coffeepot with a tall tapering cylindrical body with flared foot, the domed cover with a small finial, angled long spout, C-form handle with hand grip, original black ground decorated with yellow birds, red pomegranates and yellow stylized leaves, lid unattached, minor paint loss, repair to finial, 19th c., 10 1/2" h., **$1,100-1,400;** tole deed box, deep rectangular sides with hinged domed cover with wire loop handle, old red japanned ground decorated with red, yellow and green fruit and foliage and yellow stylized leaf borders, 19th c., minor scratches, 5 1/8 x 9 1/2", 6 1/2" h., **$5,500-6,000.***

*Left to right: tall tole coffeepot with a flared foot below the gently tapering body, angled gooseneck spout, strap handle with grip, domed cover with small finial, old polychrome floral decoration with bands on dark brown ground, in white, green, yellow and red with some touch-up, early 19th c., 10 1/2" h., $523; tall tole cylindrical mug with strap handle, original floral decoration in red and yellow on a worn dark ground, early 19th c., 5 3/4" h., **$245.***

Tole canister, cov., cylindrical w/hinged flat cover w/wire loop handle, red japanned ground, decorated around the top & cover w/red cherries & green leaves on a white band, yellow stylized leaves & swag borders, leaf decoration on top of cover, minor scratches, 19th c., 6 1/2" d., 6" h., **$400.-600.**

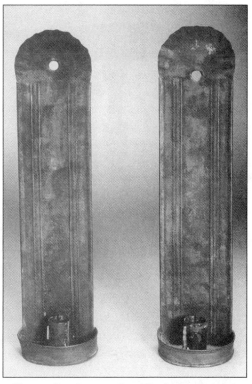

Tin candle sconces, the tall ribbed backplate w/rounded & crimped top w/hanging hole, half-round base compartment w/candle socket, minor corrosion, vestiges of black paint, 19th c., 3" w., 13 1/2" h., pr. **$650.-750.**

Tin coffeepot, cov., a flared foot below a flared cylindrical lower body & a tall tapering cylindrical upper body w/ringed bands up the sides, lower domed small cover w/replaced opalescent glass knob, long angled spout, large strap handle w/grip at shoulder, 19th c., 11" h., **$350.-450.**

Tole tray, rectangular w/rounded corners, angled edges w/end hand holes, the center decorated w/a garden landscape w/classical ruins & figures, Europe, early 19th c., paint loss, 30" l., **$2,000.-2,200.**

Tole tray, rectangular w/rounded corners & wide flanged rim w/pierced end handles, the center decorated w/a scene of the Annunciation in color, stylized flowers around border, on a dark ground, losses, wear, Europe, 19th c., 24" l., **$400.-800.**

Tin cheese sieve, deep cylindrical form w/a ring of holes around
the top above three continuous
bands of tiny holes around the
body, vertical loop strap rim handles, raised on three ring feet, 4
1/2" d., 4 1/4" h., **$125.-150.**

Tin coffeepot, cov., flared round
foot below short ringed lower
body & tapering ringed upper
body w/a small opening w/fitted
low domed cover, reinforced strap
handle, angled upright spout, 19th
c., 11" h., **$300.-400.**

Tole chestnut urns, cov., deep
rounded oblong body raised on a
square slender pedestal on a
stepped rectangular base, S-scroll
shoulder handles & a waisted flaring
neck supporting a high domed &
stepped cover w/a paneled &
pointed gilt finial, decorated overall
w/painted foliage in gold & sienna on
a black ground, Europe, 19th c., 5 x
9 1/2", 12" h., pr. **$2,300.-2,500.**

Tole figures of a man and woman,
each in traditional peasant dress &
carrying a cylindrical kindling basket on their back, polychrome decoration, stepped round base,
Switzerland, 19th c., 14" h., pr.
$2,500.-3,500.

Left to right: tall tole coffeepot with tapering cylindrical body with flared base, hinged domed cover, large strap handle with grip, angled spout, dark brown japanning decorated with colorful florals in red, green, brown, blue and yellow, wear, old paint touch-up, repairs, 19th c., 10 1/2" h., **$495;** *tole deed box, deep rectangular sides with hinged domed cover with small wire bail handle, dark brown japanned ground decorated with a band of colored scallops around the cover edge and further scallops around the sides, leafy sprigs on front below a white band painted with colorful florals in yellow, red, green and black, painter's mark on band, bottom seams loose, minor wear, 19th c., 8 3/4" l.,* **$850-950;** *tall slightly tapering cylindrical tole coffeepot with flared foot, domed hinged cover, strap handle, angled spout, black ground decorated with colorful florals in red, green, yellow and white, crusty surface with some touch-up repair, interior and bottom rust, some battering, 19th c., 9 1/2" h.,* **$900-1,000.**

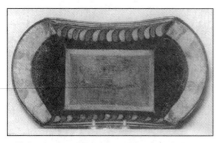

Tole tray, rectangular w/rounded flared ends, incurved sides, japanned ground w/yellow stripe & red & green daubing, white edge on ends w/red & green fruit decoration, some wear, 8 x 14", **$385.**

Tin nutmeg grater, triangular w/wood plunger, stamped "Patented Oct. 13th 1857," remnants of blue japanning, **$550.**

Tin nutmeg grater, marked "H. Carsley, Patented Nov. 20, 1855, Lynn, Mass," rare, **$975.**

*Left to right: tole deed box, deep rectangular sides with low domed hinged cover with wire bail, hasp at front, original dark brown japanning decorated with stylized florals in red, yellow, white and faded green, minor wear, 19th c., 10" l., **$950-1,000;** tall cylindrical tole mug, strap rim handle, worn original dark brown japanning with a large single stylized blossom on the front in red, yellow and white, 5 3/4" h., **$975-1,200.***

*Tole deed box, cov., rectangular w/domed top w/applied wire bail handle, scrolled strap on front, the base decorated w/red, yellow & green painted floral decoration on a black ground w/yellow trim, Pennsylvania, 19th c., 4 x 8 1/4", 4 1/2" h., **$1,998.***

Tinned sheet metal & iron wire chandelier, 12-light, the wire stem headed by a hanging hook above four serpentine arms each ending in a four-leaf green-painted candle socket over four projecting wires w/ball termini above eight serpentine arms each ending in a similar yellow-painted candle socket, probably French, 19th c., 17 1/2" d., 15 1/2" h., $3,290.

Tole tray, rectangular w/rounded corners & cut-out end handles, the rim in black & gold bronze bands, the center painted w/a walking tiger framed by a border of stencilled flowers & leaves in red, green & gold on a black ground, American, 19th c., 15 3/4 x 22", $3,290.

Tole coffeepot, cov., domed & hinged top above a flaring cylindrical body w/applied strap handle & arched spout, on a flaring round base, black ground painted w/red & green fruit & leaves & yellow trim, Pennsylvania, 19th c., 10 1/2" h., $4,465.

Coin silver waste bowl, footed deep bulbous bowl tapering to a flaring crimped rim, the body w/a continuous Chinese landscape scene w/people, trees, flowers, etc., J.E. Caldwell & Co., Philadelphia, mid-19th c., 4 5/8" h., $550.-650.

Sterling tankard, cov., flaring ringed foot below the tapering cylindrical ringed body w/a hinged stepped & domed cover w/pineapple finial, corkscrew thumbpiece, C-form handle, engraved initials "JLH" in oval & under swag on the front, marked under rim "REVERE" in rectangle, Paul Revere, Boston, ca. 1765, 10" h., $8,000.-10,000.

Sterling punch set, footed bowl w/reticulated rim, 12 handled cups & a ladle w/reticulated handle end; the deep bowl w/a widely flaring base, monogrammed on the side of bowl & cups, Dominick & Haff, early 20th c., retailed by Smith Patterson & Co., bowl 11 3/4" d., 8 7/8" h., the set $2,600.-3,600.

American coin pitcher, wide ovoid body tapering to a cylindrical neck w/a wide, high arched spout, angled leaf-cast handle, the sides chased w/naturalistic floral sprigs, handle w/bearded face at the corner, Ball, Black & Co., mid-19th c., 11" h., $1,000.-1,500.

Coin silver porringer, round shallow bowl w/pierced "keyhole" handle, handle engraved "DFS," base engraved "Dorothy Farnham Smith 1753-1801," marked twice "T. Edwards" in rectangle, Thomas Edwards, Boston, ca. 1740, 5 1/2" d., **$2,000.-2,500.**

Coin cann, footed baluster-form w/ornate S-scroll handle, engraved on bottom "FG to RG," marked under rim "J. Coburn" in rectangle, John Coburn, Boston, ca. 1775, 5 3/8" h., **$2,000.-2,500.**

American sterling bowl, round deep center w/a wide flanged rim hand-decorated w/an ornate repoussé floral border in the Chrysanthemum patt., footed base, marked "Hand Decorated S. Kirk & Son Sterling 179A," late 19th - early 20th c., 11" d., **$700.-800.**

Sterling punch bowl, of bombé circular form, the hammered surface w/frosted finish, the han-
dles formed as realistic horse heads, a bit below each, the sides applied in full-relief
w/bunches of grapes & overlapping vines stemming from a tendril which encircles the short
pedestal, stepped & molded foot, gilt interior, Dominick & Haff, New York, New York, retailed
by Theodore B. Starr, 1882, overall length 21 3/4", $32,200.

Sterling tea and coffee service, cov. teapot, cov. coffeepot, cov. sugar bowl, creamer, waste
bowl & kettle on lampstand; each in Classical Revival style of hexagonal vase form on ped-
estal bases, applied swags of flowers, beaded borders, matching elongated octagonal tray
w/incurved sides, Redlich, New York, New York, ca. 1925, kettle on stand overall 13" h., the
set $7,475.

Sterling soup tureen, cover, platter and ladle, Wave Edge patt., squatty lobed bombé form w/heavy loop handles, marked, Tiffany & Co., New York, New York, ca. 1885-95, tureen overall 17 1/2" l., the set **$23,000.**

Left to right: coin silver salver, circular shallow dish with molded rim on a tall capstan foot with molded base, the center of the top engraved with contemporary initials, the back engraved with scratch weight, marked three times, Johannis Nys, Philadelphia, ca. 1715-20, 5 1/16" d., 2 1/4" h., $60,250; coin silver porringer, round bombe body with slightly domed center, the handle pierced with geometric designs and engraved with contemporary initials, the side of the body engraved with a succession of later owners' initials, Johannis Nys, Philadelphia, ca. 1715-20, 5 1/8" d., $9,200.

Coin silver tankard, cov., plain slightly tapered cylindrical form w/molded rim & base band, flat domed cover w/shaped peak, lobate scroll thumbpiece, the hinge decorated w/wriggle-work, the scroll handle engraved w/early initials, shield terminal, John Coney, Boston, ca. 1690-1700, 6 1/4" h., $32,200.

Coin silver tankard, cov., tapered cylindrical form engraved w/arms in rococo cartouche above a molded girdle, stepped domed cover w/urn finial, scroll handle engraved w/early initials, the lower handle terminal applied w/a grotesque mask, marked on the body, William Simpkins, Boston, ca. 1750-60, 8 1/2" h., **$6,325.**

American sterling urn, cov., tall elongated classical form w/ringed upper body below the flared rim w/a ringed domed cover w/pointed finial, double-C-scroll long handles, raised on a knobbed pedestal & ringed, domed foot, heraldic crest engraved on each side, Durgin Silver Co., ca. 1900, 18 1/2" h., **$1,200.-1,400.**

Coin silver tea service, cov. teapot, cov. sugar urn & creamer; each of classical form, the teapot oval w/beaded border at foot & rim & the hinged cover w/urn finial, straight spout wooden loop handle, the creamer & sugar of vase form on a square base, each engraved w/a monogram within a mantle, teapot 12 3/4" l., John Vernon, New York, New York, ca. 1792, the set $8,365.

Sterling tea and coffee service, cov. teapot, cov. coffeepot, creamer, cov. sugar bowl, waste bowl & kettle on lampstand; the upper parts of the fluted bodies cast w/roses & foliage on matted grounds, framed by scrollwork, flower basket finials, marked on bases w/presentation inscription, Whiting Mfg. Co., New York, New York, retailed by H. Murh's Sons, ca. 1905, kettle on stand overall 13" h., the set $6,900.

Sterling tea and coffee service, cov. teapot, cov. coffeepot, cov. sugar bowl, creamer, waste bowl & kettle on lampstand; Aesthetic Movement style, each of tapered square form w/cast floral finials & branch form ear handles w/shaped ivory heat stopper, each body w/overall embossed decoration of different flowers, on textured grounds, supported by four peg feet, w/inscriptions on the bottoms, Gorham Mfg. Co., Providence, Rhode Island, 1880-81, kettle overall 12 1/2" h., the set **$12,650.**

Sterling compote, open, Martelé type w/fairy design, the wide shallow bowl w/shaped rim hammered w/chased fairies & poppies, on a slender flaring pedestal chased w/poppies & leaves, signed & dated on the base, Clemens Friedell, Pasadena, California, 1914, 10 1/2" d., 6 3/4" h., **$9,775.**

Coin silver tea and coffee set, cov. teapot, cov. coffeepot, cov. sugar bowl & creamer; coin, classical design w/oblong bulbous lobed body on a stepped oval base, domed cover w/sheaf of wheat finial, applied fruit & foliate banding, paneled serpent-form spouts on pots & C-scroll handles, William B. North & Co., New York, New York, 1822-29, minor dents, repairs to coffeepot base, coffeepot 10" h., the set $3,300.-3,500.

Silver tea and coffee service, cov. teapot; cov. coffeepot, creamer, waste bowl, sugar tongs, tea caddy missing cover & kettle on lampstand; each rounded & lobed body embossed w/iris, chrysanthemum, bamboo & cherry blossoms, openwork iris finials, in a fitted wood case, by Arthur & Bond, Yokohama, Japan, the oval tray w/a pebbled surface, the rim embossed w/chrysanthemums, by Samurai Shokar, Yokohama, Japan, early 20th c., the set $10,925.

*Center: large English silver plated lazy susan, early 20th century, rectangular, the central covered soup tureen with domed lid with chased decoration and cast finial, the rim and base gadrooned, surrounded by four covered serving dishes, the domed lids with engraved decoration, with gadrooned rims, all on the rectangular lazy susan with gadrooned rim and four celluloid handles, length to handles 23 1/4", **$1,955.** Far left and right: silver plate candelabra, three-light, of typical form, the central waisted sconce with cast flame finial, above a floral-embossed drip tray, two reeded scroll arms support a candle socket, the floral knopped stem above a stepped square base with embossed floral bands and shaped rims, England, early 20th c., 17 1/2" h., pair, **$230.***

Left to right: silver urn, classical form, the body with beaded and foliate bands above floral festoons, the tall pagoda-form cover with cast and engraved bud finials, the cover with bands of foliate and beaded decoration, loop handles with molded acanthus terminals, on a slender pedestal with circular base with similar decoration, gilt interior, John Schofield, London, England, 1784, 16 1/2" h., $2,415; silver tureen, classical urn form, the domed cover with urn finial, the molded rim with beaded band, engraved decoration on the loop handles, the long oval base with a beaded band, on a short oval pedestal base, engraved crests on cover and coats-of-arms on the body, John Schofield, London, England, 1785, 8 1/2 x 17 1/2", 12 1/2" h., $5,750.

*Left to right: silver bowl, a blossom petal-form body with a shaped rim, the sides chased and embossed with panels of flowers, birds and carp on a textured ground, a plain roundel on one side, scrolling serpentine handles, on a flaring round foot, China, Kaishu script marks, late 19th c., 13" l., **$805**; silver teapot, squatty spherical body with domed cover with dragon finial, the sides chased and embossed overall with a continuous battle scene, one side engraved with a mottoed crest within a shield, serpentine spout ending in a dragon's head, serpentine dragon-form handle, short stepped ovoid foot, Wang Hing, Canton/Hong Kong, China, late 19th - early 20th c., 6"h., **$690;** silver cup, deep rounded bowl with embossed floral and prunus panels and a central shield cartouche, molded rim and cast dragon-form handles, knopped stem and domed foot with embossed leaves, Hoaching, Canton, China, second half 19th c., 8 1/2" h., **$2,415.***

*Far left and right: silver candlesticks with hexagonal shafts and wide base, the tapered candle socket with removable bobeche, the shafts applied with dragons, panels engraved with presentation inscription dated 1934, weighted foot with applied dragons, marked "Y.C.Co.," China, 8 1/4" h., pair, **$1,380.** Second from left and right: silver bowls, deep rounded forms on plain foot-rings, embossed around the sides with prunus branches on a textured ground, presentation inscriptions around the footrings, Wang Hing, Hong Kong, China, also with a third bowl (not illustrated) with lobed reticulated sides embossed and engraved with dragon and cloud reserves, supported by three cast dragon feet, with a blown cranberry glass insert, Wan Nam & Co., Hong Kong, late 19th - early 20th c., 5 1/2" d., the group of three, **$1,380.** Center: silver compote, wide shallow flaring bowl with a scalloped reticulated edge engraved with prunus blossoms, raised on three-part stem formed as three flowering trees, offset by small applied cranes, on a squat, lobed pear-form base engraved with scrolling florals and a shaped rim applied with similar scrolls, Wang Hing, Canton/Hong Kong, China, late 19th - early 20th c., 7" h., **$1,093.***

English silver fish slice, half-round dished blade bright-cut w/florals & scrolls, twist-carved long ivory handle, Atkin Brothers, Sheffield, 1891, 13 7/8" l., $350.-450.

Silver cake basket, rectangular dished form w/steep lobed sides & leaf-cast end-to-end swing handle, raised on a rectangular foot, handle & rim w/engraved armorial crest, Philip Rundell, London, 1821-22, 14" l., $1,725.-1,825.

Silver teapot and coffeepot, cov., each of lobed form on four scroll feet, leaf-clad scroll spout & handle w/ivory insulators, the hinged cover w/acorn finial, the coffeepot w/two engraved crests,   each marked, Paul Storr, London, England, 1836-1837, teapot 10 3/4" l., coffeepot, 8 1/2" h., pr. $4,780.

Silver tea and coffee set, cov. teapot, cov. coffeepot, cov. kettle on stand, cov. sugar bowl & creamer, each of squatty bulbous melon-lobed form w/cast mythological sea figures on the necks & shoulders, Germany, 800 fine, late 19th c., the set **$7,000.-7,200.**

Silver tea urn, cov., classical form, the tall tapering body w/an undulating bead-trimmed shoulder w/upturned scroll handles, flaring tall neck w/domed cover & urn finial, a spigot w/carved ivory handle on the lower front above the beaded-ring pedestal & squared undulating base raised on four small paw feet, Charles Wright or Chas. Woodward, London, 1775-76, minor dents, 20 1/2" h., **$2,500.-3,000.**

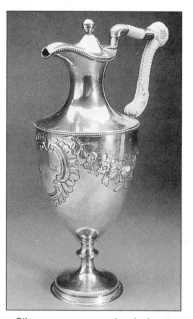

Silver ewer, cov., classical urn-form w/a tall flaring neck w/long spout & hinged domed cover w/knob finial, raised on a ringed pedestal base w/domed & beaded round foot, the angled handle of carved ivory, chased floral & scroll decoration around the body, Abraham Peterson & Peter Podie, England, ca. 1783, dents, 12 3/8" h., **$1,100.-1.300.**

GLOSSARY OF SELECTED METALWARES TERMS

Acanthus - A type of decoration taken from the acanthus leaf.

Alloy - A combination of two or more metals, usually achieved in a molten state.

Applied - Parts such as handles, finials and spouts are sometimes made separately and applied to the body of a piece by soldering.

Assay - The qualitative or quantitative analysis of a substance, especially an ore.

Base metal - An alloy or metal of low value applied with a plating, as in silver plating.

Beading - A decoration, usually used for borders, composed of small continuous half spheres.

Bell metal - An alloy of tin and copper used to make bells.

Bleeding - Description of a piece of Sheffield Plate ware in which the copper base is exposed.

Bobeche - The flat saucer-like ring on candlesticks that catches the wax drippings from the candles.

Bright-cut - A type of decorative edging cut into silver to form facets.

Britannia standard - The higher standard for silver required in England from March 1697 to June 1720. It consists of 958 parts of silver per 1,000 or 11 oz. dwt. per 12 oz., an increase of 8 dwt. pure silver per pound over sterling standard.

Buffing - Removal of the outer layer of metal with an abrasive rotating wheel in order to polish the article to a high finish.

Burnishing - Light polishing to increase the luster, entails the use of a hard, smooth, curved tool.

Carat - Measurement of the weight and purity of gold, meaning the twenty-fourth part of weight of the whole (pure gold is 24 carats).

Cartouche - The enclosure for inscriptions, initials or ornamental designs, often very intricate.

Casting - The pouring of molten metal into a frame containing casting sand.

Chasing - The technique of modeling the metal's surface by use of a punch and hammer.

Coin - Used to indicate 900/1,000 parts of silver and 100/1,000 parts of copper, the standard used for coinage in the early 1800s.

Date-letter - Letter stamped on silver indicating the year the article was made or assayed. This system was required by the Assay Office in London; it was not used in America until the 19th century, and then not consistently.

Diaper - Decoration consisting of a continuous diamond-shaped pattern.

Die - A metal stamp struck by a hammer to impress a maker's mark.

Dramweight (Dwt.) - see Troy weight

Embossing - Forming raised designs on the surface by hammering on the reverse.

Engraving - The technique of cutting designs into metals with a scorper or graver, removing metal in the process.

Escutcheon - A shield-shaped form surrounding heraldic devices and coats-of-arms; also the area surrounding a keyhole.

Finial - An ornamental terminating part, such as on a lid.

Flange - A projecting rim or edge of an item.

Flat chasing - A low-relief surface decoration.

Flatware - A term generally referring to knives, forks, spoons and serving pieces, also plates and other flat table items.

Fluted - Decorated with ornamental parallel, vertical, half-round grooves.

Forging - The technique of shaping metal by heating and then hammering.

Gadrooning - An ornamental band embellished with fluting, reeding, beading or other continuous pattern.

Gilding - The process originally entailing coating the surface of metal with gold and mercury, then heating the piece to evaporate the mercury (more recently accomplished by electrolysis). Parcel gilding is partial gilding, achieved by covering parts not to be gilded with a resistant substance.

Goldsmith - An artisan capable of making articles of gold or silver.

Guilloché - An ornamental border formed of two or more bands interlaced in such a way as to repeat a design.

Hallmark - A mark used in England to stamp gold and silver articles that met established standards of purity.

Hollow handle - A handle made in two sections and soldered together.

Hollowware - Serving pieces such as bowls, pitchers, goblets and the like.

Japanning - A black enamel or asphaltum finish of a type originally used in the Orient as a background for painted decoration.

Maker's mark - The identifying mark or device used by an individual artisan.

Matte finish - Roughened texture or dull finish obtained by chasing or dotting punches struck closely together.

Oxidizing - The technique of darkening certain areas of silver to emphasize the design, accomplished by the application of a sulfur compound.

Parcel gilt - see Gilding

Patera - A stylized petaled design in either an oval or circular form.

Pennyweight - see Troy weight

Pierced work - A decorative method in which the metal is cut away to form a design.

Pricked work - A decoration formed by needlepoint engraving.

Rattail - A means of reinforcement or decoration in which two pieces of silver are joined by a spiny ridge, particularly the join between the bowl and handle of a spoon.

Reeding - A convex decorative ornament having parallel strips resembling thin reeds (the opposite of fluting).

Repoussé - A decorative relief device accomplished by hammering from the reverse side, frequently further enhanced by surface chasing of detail.

Reticulated -Pierced designs or patterns that have a netted appearance.

Rococo - Characterized by elaborate profuse designs intended to produce a delicate effect. (The word is derived from the French rocailles and coquilles—"rocks" and "shells.")

Scorper - A small chisel used for engraving.

Serrated - Having notched, tooth-like projections.

Strapwork - An applied decoration consisting of interlaced bands and scrollwork or pierced scroll and ribbon patterns, often enclosing floral motifs and other devices.

Touch mark - An impressed maker's mark.

Troy weight - Standard weight system in English-speaking countries for gold, silver and precious stones (5,760 grains or 12 oz. to Troy pound).

Vermeil - French gold-plating technique from the mid-1700s that was banned early in the 19th century because of the danger from the mercury used. Vermeil today is produced by electrolysis.

BIBLIOGRAPHY

ALUMINUM

Woodard, Dannie A. and Billie J. *Hammered Aluminum Hand Wrought Collectibles.* Weatherford, Texas: Aluminum Collector's Books, 1983.

Woodard, Dannie A., *Hammered Aluminum Hand Wrought Collectibles, Book Two.* Weatherford, Texas: Aluminum Collector's Books, 1993.

BRASS, COPPER & BRONZE

Burks, Jean M. *Birmingham Brass Candlesticks.* Charlottesville, Virginia: University Press of Virginia, 1986.

Gentle, Rupert and Rachael Feild. *Domestic Metalwork, 1840-1820.* Woodbridge, Suffolk, England: Antique Collectors' Club Ltd., 1994.

_____. *English Domestic Brass, 1680-1810 and the History of Its Origins.* New York, New York: E.P. Dutton & Co., 1975.

Kauffman, Henry J. *American Copper and Brass.* Camden, New Jersey: Thomas Nelson & Sons, 1968.

McConnell, Kevin. *Heintz Art Metal Silver-on-Bronze Wares.* Westchester, Pennsylvania: Schiffer Publishing, Ltd., 1990.

CHROME

Kilbride, Richard J. *Art Deco Chrome - The Chase Era.* Stamford, Connecticut: Jo-D Books, 1988.

Sferrazza, Julie. *Farber Brothers Krome Kraft, A Guide For Collectors.* Marietta, Ohio: Antique Publications, 1988.

IRON & OTHERS

Mitchell, James R. *Antique Metalware.* New York, New York: Universe Books, undated.

Revi, Albert Christian, Editor. *Spinning Wheel's Collectible Iron, Tin, Copper & Brass.* Hanover, Pennsylvania: Everybody's Press, Inc., 1974.

Southworth, Susan and Michael. *Ornamental Ironwork, An Illustrated Guide to Its Design, History, & Use in American Architecture.* Boston, Massachusetts: David R. Godine, 1978.

PEWTER

Cotterell, Howard Herschel, Adolphe Riff and Robert M. Vetter. *National Types of Old Pewter.* Princeton, New Jersey: The Pyne Press, 1972.

Ebert, Katherine. *Collecting American Pewter.* New York, New York: Charles Scribner's Sons, 1973.

Laughlin, Ledlie Irwin. *Pewter in America, Its Makers and Their Marks, Volumes I & II.* Barre, Massachusetts: Barre Publishers, 1969.

_____. *Pewter in America, Its Makers and Their Marks, Volume III.* Barre, Massachusetts: Barre Publishers, 1971.

Montgomery, Charles F. *A History of American Pewter.* New York, New York: E.P. Dutton, 1978.

Moore, N. Hudson. *Old Pewter, Brass, Copper, and Sheffield Plate.* Rutland, Vermont: Charles E. Tuttle Company, 1972; original edition by Frederick A. Stokes Company, New York, 1905.

Nadolski, Dieter. *Old Household Pewterware.* New York, New York: Holmes & Meier Publishers, Inc., 1987.

Scott, Jack L. *Pewter Wares from Sheffield.* Baltimore, Maryland: Antiquary Press, 1980.

SILVER - STERLING & COIN

Belden, Louise Conway. *Marks of American Silversmiths in The Ineson-Bissell Collection.* Charlottesville, Virginia: The University Press of Virginia, for The Henry Francis du Pont Winterthur Museum, 1980.

Bentley, Jane, Editor. *Early American Silver and Its Makers.* New York, New York: Mayflower Books, Inc., 1979.

Carpenter, Charles H. with Mary Grace Carpenter. *Tiffany Silver.* New York, New York: Dodd, Mead & Co., 1978.

_____. *Gorham Silver, 1831-1981.* New York, New York: Dodd, Mead & Co., 1982.

de Castres, Elizabeth. *Collecting Silver.* London, England: Bishopsgate Press, Ltd., 1986.

Ensko, Stephen G.C. *American Silversmiths and Their Marks - The Definitive (1948) Edition.* New York, New York: Dover Publications, Inc., 1983.

Fales, Martha Gandy. *Early American Silver.* New York, New York: Funk & Wagnalls, 1970.

Fennimore, Donald L. *The Knopf Collectors' Guides to American Antiques - Silver & Pewter.* New York, New York: Alfred A. Knopf, Inc., 1984.

Green, Robert Alan. *Marks of American Silversmiths Revised (1650-1900).* Key West, Florida: self-published, 1984.

Hood, Graham. *American Silver.* New York, New York: Praeger Publishers, 1973.

Kovel, Ralph and Terry. *Kovel's American Silver Marks, 1650 to the Present.* New York, New York: Crown Publishers, 1989.

McClinton, Katharine Morrison. *Collecting American 19th Century Silver.* New York, New York: Charles Scribner's Sons, 1968.

Rainwater, Dorothy T. *Encyclopedia of American Silver Manufacturers, 3rd Edition.* West Chester, Pennsylvania: Schiffer Publishing, Ltd., 1988.

_____. *Sterling Silver Holloware - Gorham Manufacturing Co., 1888 - Gorham Martelé - Unger Brothers, 1904 - American Historical Catalog Collection.* Princeton, New Jersey: The Pyne Press, 1973.

Poole, T.R. *Identifying Antique British Silver.* North Pomfret, Vermont: David & Charles, Inc., 1988.

Turner, Noel D. *American Silver Flatware, 1837-1910.* Cranberry, New Jersey: A.S. Barnes and Co., Inc., 1972.

Ward, Barbara McLean & Gerald W.R. Ward, Editors. *Silver in American Life - Selections from the Mabel Brady Garvan and Other Collections at Yale University.* Boston, Massachusetts: David R. Godine, Publisher, 1979.

Wyler, Seymour B. *The Book of Silver - English, American, Foreign.* New York, New York: Crown Publishers, 1937, Twenty-fifth Printing, April 1972.

SILVER PLATE

Davis, Fredna Harris and Kenneth K. Deibel. *Silver Plated Flatware Patterns, 2nd Edition.* Dallas, Texas: Bluebonnet Press, 1981.

Hagan, Tere. *Silverplated Flatware, An Identification and Value Guide, Revised Fourth Edition.* Paducah, Kentucky: Collectors Books, 1981.

Rainwater, Dorothy T. and H. Ivan. *American Silverplate.* West Chester, Pennsylvania: Schiffer Publishing, Ltd., 1988.

Snell, Doris. *American Silverplated Flatware Patterns, A Pattern Identification and Reference Guide.* Des Moines, Iowa: Wallace-Homestead Book Co., 1980.

The Meriden Britannia Silver-Plate Treasury - The Complete Catalog of 1886-7, with 3,200 Illustrations, by The Meriden Britannia Co. New York, New York: Dover Publications, 1982.

Victorian Silverplated Holloware - Rogers Brothers Mfg. Co., 1857 - Meriden Britannia Co., 1867 - Derby Silver Co., 1883 - American Historical Catalog Collection. Princeton, New Jersey: The Pyne Press, 1972.

APPENDIX

GUIDELINES TO MARKINGS ON COMMON METALWARES

Until the arrival of the Industrial Revolution and the mass-production of metalwares in the late 19th century, most quality hand-crafted metal objects carried only simple stamped markings — if they were marked at all. With mass-production it became important for manufacturers to have their products recognized by the buying public; as a result, stamped and incised marks became commonplace on everything from humble pots and pans to exquisite silver centerpieces.

The following guidelines should prove helpful in recognizing typical markings found on antique and collectible metalwares.

ALUMINUM

Because the mass-production of aluminum didn't begin until the early 20th century, most items will be clearly marked. Shown above are the marks of the three major makers of hammered and stamped aluminum products of the 1930s-1950s era.

Heintz Art Metal Shop Mark

BRASS, COPPER AND BRONZE

Very early examples of hand-crafted brass, copper and bronze were seldom marked by the maker. English and European pieces before the 19th century are more likely to be marked than American-made pieces; and because American makers were copying English and foreign styles, it can be very difficult to determine where an unmarked piece was made. By the early 20th century more mass-produced kitchenware pieces were being marked, and there was a revival of hand-craftsmanship during the Arts and Craft Movement. Arts and Crafts artisans such as Dirk Van Erp and the Roycrofters often stamped logos or special markings on their best wares. One marking to become familiar with is that of the Heintz Art Metal Shop of Buffalo, New York. It produced a wide range of decorative bronze items featuring sterling silver inlay beginning in 1915. Its logo, shown on the previous page, is a diamond surrounding the initials "HAMS." This logo is sometimes found in conjunction with additional wording or patent information.

CHROME

Chrome plating became widespread in the 1920s and 1930s when it began to supersede silver-plated and nickel-plated wares; therefore, most pieces are clearly marked. The two major producers of chrome wares were Chase and the Farber Brothers with their "Krome Kraft" line. These firms' marks are shown above.

John Danforth's lion mark
ca. 1773-93

Ashbil Griswold's eagle mark
ca. 1807-15

R. GLEASON

Roswell Gleason's name
stamp, ca. 1821-71

PEWTER

Pewter has been one of the most popular and commonly used metalwares for hundreds of years in the Orient as well as Europe, England and America. As far back as the 15th century, there have been strict controls on its production in Europe and England, where years of training as an apprentice were required before one became a "master" and could apply one's own "touch mark" to pieces. In early times, only very simple symbols such as a crown, rose or lion were used to denote quality because most people were illiterate and any wording would have been meaningless. By the 18th century, however, most English and American pewterers were also including their names or initials as part of their personalized touch mark. Prior to the American Revolutionary War, American pewterers used symbols similar to their English counterparts; after the Revolution most such symbols were replaced with our patriotic eagle. By the first quarter of the 19th century, the final period of true pewter production, often just the maker's name and city were stamped on pieces. Most early pewter marks were stamped in intaglio, which means the background is recessed with the symbol or letters raised in relief.

On the previous page we show copies of three typical American pewter marks of the late 18th and early 19th centuries. Remember, pieces stamped "Genuine Pewter" will date from the Colonial Revival era of the 1920s, when antique pewter was widely copied.

SILVER

British Silver

Sterling silver produced in the British Isles, especially in England, is undoubtedly one of the

**Leopard's head
(London mark)**

Date letter

**Lion passant
(England)**

Monarch's head

easiest types of antique metalware to identify and date. This is because the English require that each piece of sterling silver be carefully assayed and marked with a series of simple markings call hallmarks.

The use of hallmarks in England began in the late 15th century. Pieces of sterling produced in London were required to be stamped with a small leopard's head mark (a symbol for London) and a date letter indicating the year of production. By the mid-16th century, another marking was added, the lion passant (a side view of a walking lion). The lion passant became the symbol for sterling silver produced in England, while in later years a thistle mark was used to indicate silver made in Scotland and a harp was used on silver produced in Ireland. Over the centuries, silver assaying offices were opened in the English cities of York, Sheffield, Birmingham, Chester and Exeter. Each city was assigned a town symbol to use in place of the leopard's head used on London-made products. The English have been very strict about upholding the sterling silver standard (925/1000 pure silver), and every piece of English sterling silver will carry the markings described above as well as the initials of the individual maker.

For collectors of antique English silver, the date letter is especially of interest, and there are reference books that illustrate these series of letters used since the 15th century. The letters appear in a recurring cycle running from A to Z (but omitting the letter J), and each letter represents a new year in the chronological series. For each complete series of date letters, the style or form of the letters was changed. For example, you will find Gothic letters in one series and Roman-style letters in another; one series will be in all caps while the next will be all lower case.

Finally, another hallmark was added to this series during the period from 1784 to 1890. This was a duty mark represented by the use of the profile bust of the reigning monarch's head. Any silver made during Queen Victoria's reign from 1837 to 1890, for instance, will include a mark showing her profile.

An example of a typical series of English hallmarks is illustrated above. It represents a piece of sterling silver assayed in London in the year 1876-77. No maker's mark is included with this series although most pieces will also include such a marking.

English Sheffield Plate

A series of marks used by Sheffield plater J. Rodgers & Sons, ca. 1822

As explained in the text, Sheffield plating was an early process of layering copper with a thin layer of pure silver to produce a cheaper version of sterling silver objects.

Although the process was developed in the 1740s, it wasn't until the 1780s that many English Sheffield platers were allowed to mark their products. The English government did not want these markings confused with the hallmarks used on pure sterling silver. Illustrated here is a series of marks used by Sheffield plater J. Rodgers around 1822. Note that there is no lion passant mark or city mark as found on sterling hallmarks, and the individual letters are not date letters.

Remember, in the late 19th and early 20th centuries many American and English silver plating companies would include the phrase "Sheffield Silver" or "Sheffield Plate" in their markings. These pieces were not produced using the early Sheffield process because neither the words "Sheffield Plate" nor "Sheffield Silver" ever appeared on the early Sheffield plate pieces.

American Silver

Early American silver is not as easy to identify and date as old English silver because our silversmiths were not allowed to use the English system of hallmarks. American colonial makers could only mark their wares with a name or initials. Because these tiny markings are often badly worn, it can be difficult to attribute surviving pieces to a specific maker.

American silver was not held to the same standard of purity as English wares, so it is generally referred to as "coin" silver, approximately 900/1000 parts pure silver. The term "coin" derives from the fact that in Colonial America the wealthy sometimes had their silver coinage melted down and made into a useful and decorative silver object.

During the early 19th century, some American silver makers did attempt to mislead the buying public by using a series of "pseudo-hallmarks" somewhat resembling the true English hallmarks. Sometimes a series of these marks was used in conjunction with the stamped maker's name. Pseudo-hallmarks often included an eagle, a letter, a man's head, a star, or an anchor. Today we have no way of determining if these markings had any real significance, but it is generally believed they were marketing gimmicks used to confuse the general public. A typical stamped maker's mark is illustrated here as well as a series of typical American pseudo-hallmarks from the early 19th century.

In addition to a maker's name and perhaps pseudo-hallmarks, some American silversmiths in the early decades of the 19th century would stamp their pieces with the words "Coin" or "Pure Coin" to indicate the pieces' quality. Some pieces of coin silver will also carry the stamped name of the retailer rather than the actual maker of the piece.

Name stamp of J. Lukey,
Pittsburgh, Penn., ca. 1830-40

Typical American Pseudo-hallmarks

Around 1860, the American government adopted the use of the English sterling silver standard. American pieces made after that era will include the word "Sterling" with the maker's mark. It is important to remember that English sterling silver was never marked with the work "Sterling."

Illustrated here are three typical American sterling silver markings used by notable Victorian silver manufacturers.

**R. Wallace & Sons,
Wallingford, Connecticut**

**Whiting Mfg. Co.,
Providence, Rhode Island**

**Gorham Company,
Providence, Rhode Island**

American Silver Plate

Very soon after the electroplating process for silver was developed in the 1840s, American manufacturers began to mass-produce plated wares, especially table flatware. By the mid-19th century, large quantities of silver plated flatware and tablewares were available to the American buying public and most of it was clearly marked with a trademark. Illustrated here are three typical silver plate markings from the late 19th century. Note that each includes the term "Quadruple" or "Quadruple Plate." This refers to pieces that carried the heaviest plating of silver; slightly lesser wares might be marked "Triple Plate." "Quadruple Plate" does not mean that a piece was dunked four times in the plating solution as some sources have stated; the term was simply a marketing tool used by manufacturers to indicate quality pieces.

**Barbour Silver Co.,
Hartford, Connecticut**

**Wm. A. Rogers, Ltd.,
New York, New York**

**Wilcox Silver Plate Co.,
Meridan, Connecticut**

Some other markings that you may encounter on American silver plated pieces are a series of stamped numbers or the initials "EPNS" or "EPBM." The numbers have nothing to do with the date of the piece but were simply factory style numbers. The Initials "EPNS" stand for "electroplated nickel silver," while "EPBM" stand for "electro-plated Britannia metal."

GOLD AND SILVER PLATE.

WHITE METAL.   NICKEL SILVER.

No. 1927. PLAIN TEA SET—OVAL.

Style.	Set of Six Pieces.	Coffee.	Tea, Six Half Pints.	Water, Five Half Pints.	Sugar.	Cream, Gold Lined.	Slop, Gold Lined.
Plain,	$54.00 (BACKBONE).	$12.50	$10.50	$9.25	$6.75	$8.00	$7.00
Chased,	62.00 (BACK).	14.50	12.50	11.00	7.50	8.75	7.75

No. 56—26 inch Chased WAITER, $50.00 (BACON).   Patent Plate Glass Protector, $7.50 extra (BAD).
No. 1927 KETTLE, Plain, Nine Half Pints, $24.00 (BAG).   Chased, $26.00 (BAIL).

No. 1927 URN.
Twelve Half Pints.
Plain,   .   . $31.00 (BAIT).
Chased,   .   .   34.00 (BAKE).

No. 1927 BUTTER DISH.
With Patent Crystal Drainer.
Plain,   .   . $8.25 (BALL).
Chased,   .   .   9.00 (BAND).

No. 1927 SPOON HOLDER.
Gold Lined.
Plain,   .   . $6.75 (BALD).
Chased,   .   .   7.50 (BALE).

No. 1927 SYRUP CUP.
With Plate.
Plain,   .   . $7.00 (BANE).
Chased,   .   .   7.75 (BANG).

(322)

A typical page of Victorian silver plate wares
as shown in the 1886-87 catalog of
The Meriden Britannia Silver-Plate Treasury.
Courtesy of Dover Publications, New York, New York.

European Silver

Unfortunately for American collectors, the European countries did not use an easy-to-follow system of marking their silver. Each country or kingdom seemed to have its own version, and deciphering these today can be difficult. Sometimes only a city stamp, emblem, or a maker's name or initials were used on early silver from regions of France, Germany or Northern Europe. The only overall reference book that offers assistance in identifying such markings is *The Book of Old Silver, English, American, Foreign* by Seymour B. Wyler (Crown Publishers, 1972).